4 lines in title

1st of / vg. author was
a Director of
Public Assistance for Commonwealth of Kentucky (only 3 Commonwealths in the U.S.)- He uncovered Garrison's attribution
of the Republican party to "Moral
agitation."

THE SLAVERY CONTROVERSY

The University of North Carolina Press, Chapel Hill, N. C.; The Baker and Taylor Company, New York; Oxford University Press, London; Maruzen-Kabushiki-Kaisha, Tokyo; Edward Evans & Sons, Ltd., Shanghai; Dekker en Nordemann's Wetenschappelijke Boekhandel, Amsterdam.

THE SLAVERY CONTROVERSY
1831-1860

By

ARTHUR YOUNG LLOYD, Ph.D.

CHAPEL HILL
THE UNIVERSITY OF NORTH CAROLINA PRESS
1939

PRINTED IN THE UNITED STATES OF AMERICA BY THE SEEMAN PRINTERY,
DURHAM, N. C.; BOUND BY L. H. JENKINS, INC., RICHMOND, VIRGINIA

TO

MY MOTHER

MABEL YOUNG LLOYD

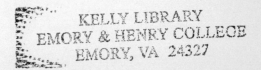

PREFACE

IT IS HOPED that this study may throw new light upon the slavery controversy as a part of the sectional struggle preceding the War Between the States. Earlier writers have assumed that the aggressive slavocracy endeavored to extend the institution of slavery, but was frustrated in its efforts by the abolitionist crusade. On the contrary the Southern people early deprecated slavery as an evil and protested its increase. Physical environment determined that the Southern colonies should become agricultural while those of New England developed commercially and industrially. Slave labor was found to be profitable only in the former section. Sectional interests and the struggle for the political balance of power led to an attack upon slavery during the Missouri controversy in 1819. Despite this the South did not defend slavery during the following decade, but on the contrary showed great interest in the emancipation and colonization societies which found their greatest support in the Slave States. Indeed it was not until the abolition attack came in 1831 that the South undertook a systematic justification.

Anti-slavery sentiment in the North may be grouped into three classes: the philosophical group, led by Channing and Wayland, that condemned slavery as a moral evil; the political or free-soil school of thought, later led by Lincoln, that sought to restrict the limits of slavery and to use political means to gain its ends by establishing a sectional group to control the Union; and, finally, the radical abolitionists, led by Garrison, Weld, Bourne, Foster, and others, that demanded the immediate abolition of slavery without compensation or any plan of adjustment and denounced the South in harsh terms.

As the Southern people defended their institutions against the charges of the radicals, they evolved a new philosophy which proclaimed slavery to be a "positive good" rather than the previously accepted view that the system was a "necessary evil." A phase of this movement is evident in the historical and scriptural justification of the institution. Economically slavery was justified on the premise that white labor was not feasible under the semitropical conditions necessary for the production of Southern staples. Even more important in consolidating Southern opinion was the effect abolition might have upon race relations. This led to the justification of slavery as a social necessity. The spokesmen of the South contended that only through slavery could two such different races live together peacefully. This problem of race relations, which the abolitionists failed to recognize, was expressed in the statement that "the negro question lies far deeper than the slavery question."

This study would not be complete without a concluding chapter dealing with the political significance of the abolitionist attack, pointing out the constant struggle between industrial and agricultural systems for political power and control of the Federal Government which characterized the period. The slavery controversy was in a larger sense part of the political struggle which paved the way for the election of a president in 1860 on a sectional platform, and the consequent organization of the Southern Confederacy.

The controversial literature of the period largely furnished the materials for this study. Hundreds of books and pamphlets provided the anti-slavery charges and the pro-slavery arguments. In addition to this type of material, the records of Congress, the reports of various anti-slavery societies, numerous newspapers and periodicals, and the writings and speeches of both Northern and Southern leaders provided excellent sources. The limitations of this volume prohibit the listing of all sources of material; therefore the bibliography must be selective rather than comprehensive.

This study would have been published earlier except for the fact that the author has been on leave of absence from academic duties during the past three years, serving as director of public assistance of the Commonwealth of Kentucky. Without the help of Mrs. Harriet Chappell Owsley, Nashville, Tennessee, and Miss Isabel Howell of the Vanderbilt University Library in editing the manuscript and bibliography, it is doubtful that this work could have been published even at this time. The author is deeply grateful to Dr. Frank L. Owsley, professor of history, Vanderbilt University, for his advice and constant encouragement, and is appreciative of the many suggestions concerning the manuscript made by Dr. W. C. Binkley, Professor Irby R. Hudson, and others at Vanderbilt University. The courtesies granted the author by Mr. W. T. Couch and his assistants of The University of North Carolina Press are appreciated. To his colleagues at Morehead State Teachers College, and friends in other colleges and universities who have read various parts of the manuscript, the author expresses his gratitude. The stenographic services of Miss Eunice Franklin have been valuable.

The author alone assumes responsibility for the conclusions expressed and for any shortcomings which this study may have.

A. Y. LLOYD

March 17, 1939
Frankfort, Kentucky

CONTENTS

[xi]

THE SLAVERY CONTROVERSY

CHAPTER I

PERIOD PRIOR TO 1831

WITH the appearance of the *Liberator* on January 1, 1831, William Lloyd Garrison began his violent attack upon the slaveholders of the South.[1] The abolition propaganda which followed had its foundation upon an emotional appeal concerning the conditions of the enslaved Negroes laboring under the plantation system of the Southern States. By 1831, Negro slavery had been practiced in that section for over two hundred years. In the month of August, 1619, a Dutch man-of-war had slowly sailed up the James River until it reached the small Virginia colony at Jamestown. There the Dutch trader sold twenty Negroes to the planters and Negro slavery was introduced into the English-American colonies.[2] Probably none of these planters, eager for the additional labor required to clear the forests, to plant crops, and to aid them in wresting a livelihood from the New World, realized that he was introducing an economic and social system which would later form the basic foundation of Southern agriculture and society. Neither could he look into the future and predict that this same system of slavery would be used by the Garrisonian abolitionists as the moral basis of their condemnation of Southern institutions more than two hundred years later. Between the introduction of Negro slaves in 1619 and the launching of the "New Abolitionists" movement in 1831, many changes occurred which must be accorded their proper places in history. In order to have a

[1] See discussion in Wendell Phillips Garrison, and Frances Jackson Garrison (hereafter cited as Garrisons), *William Lloyd Garrison*, I, 224-25.

[2] J. W. Keifer, *Slavery and Four Years of War*, I, 10-11; Lyon Gardiner Tyler, *England and America, 1580-1652*, p. 81.

general knowledge of the situation in 1831, and to view the causes of the rise of sectionalism and the resulting controversies that led to the struggle between an industrial North and an agrarian South, it is well to select certain pertinent historical facts and weave them into a summary of the events and conditions occurring prior to the abolition crusade.

The fact that the original colonies were able to achieve their independence and organize under a new government of united states must not be allowed to imply that these colonies were really united in every sense of the term. Even before the Revolution, certain essential differences found among these colonies classified them into groups. Although connected by a common mother country, these early English colonies were to a great extent alien to each other in racial inheritances, religious beliefs, economic interests, social organization, and political affinities. These early differences were destined to become more clearly defined as other diversities transformed the colonies into two great geographic, economic, and political sections.[3]

The early settlers of the East were descended from that class of English who were Puritan in their religion and Roundhead in their politics.[4] The Dutch settled largely in New York and New Jersey. The Quakers of England and Wales, under the leadership of William Penn, were the first settlers in Pennsylvania, although by 1700 the population of that colony was at least half non-English and included Germans, Swedes, Dutch, French, Danes, and Finns. As the colonies gradually developed from straggling frontiers into rich and powerful communities before the American Revolution, the population was rapidly increased by immigration, much of it from non-English sources. The most numerous of these newcomers were the German Protestants, who, upon being driven from their fatherland by religious persecution,

---

[3] Charles M. Andrews, *Colonial Self-Government, 1652-1689, passim.*
[4] William Chauncey Fowler, *The Sectional Controversy*, p. 7.

settled mainly in Pennsylvania, one hundred thousand establishing themselves in that colony between 1700 and 1775.[5] A group of French Huguenots, driven from France after 1763 by the persecution of Louis XIV, settled mainly in the Carolinas, thereby making a contribution to the characteristics of that section.[6] Religious persecution also caused a large number of Scotch-Irish Presbyterians to leave Ireland and pour into America through the ports of Philadelphia and Charleston; many of these later migrated to the frontier that became the states of Kentucky and Tennessee. It seems quite probable that the natural racial antagonisms, combined with religious differences between the Quakers, Puritans, and Congregationalists of the East and the Episcopalians and Presbyterians of the South, aided in the alienation of the two sections and the endowment of each with certain distinctive characteristics.[7]

In addition to these sectional diversities it is necessary to take into consideration the effect of a new geographical environment. Although the ethical influences and the political experiences of the colonists were predominantly English, the new physical environment in which they were transplanted created characteristics that may be called distinctly American. This same physical environment also aided the growth of sectional differences. Just as the great expanse of the Atlantic Ocean that lay between the English colonies and their mother country became a determining factor, which, despite their sentiments of loyalty, changed them from Englishmen to Americans, so did the varied character of the coast line, the coastal plains, and the mountainous ranges from Maine to

[5] William H. Wannamaker, "The German Element in the Settlement of the South," *South Atlantic Quarterly*, IX (April, 1910), 144; William E. Dodd, *The Cotton Kingdom*, p. 23.

[6] Fowler, *op. cit.*, p. 7; also "The Black Race in North America," *Southern Literary Messenger*, XXI (November, 1855), 664.

[7] Fowler, *op. cit.*, pp. 7-8; also Augustin Cochin, *The Results of Slavery* (translated by Mary L. Booth), pp. 7-14.

Florida develop in Virginia and New England "types of men distinctly their own, with occupations, manners, dialect, interests and outlook upon life different from those of Englishmen"[8] and different from each other. The great coastal plain that stretched from a narrow belt of lowland in northern New England to a fertile plain about two hundred miles in width in the Carolinas presented a wide divergence in soil, climate, and configuration.[9]

In New England, the settlers found a soil largely glacial in origin varying from boulder clay, fairly fertile but extremely difficult to cultivate, to a strip of practically useless sandy land, in the southeastern part. Short summers and long, severe winters restricted the growing season for agricultural products and combined with the relatively small area of suitable land effectually to prevent that section from ever becoming a great agricultural region.[10] However, when it was found that the scanty soil on the rocky hills provided but a meagre subsistence, the thrifty Yankee turned to various trades for a livelihood.[11] The combination of good harbors and heavy forests affording an excellent supply of timber along the coast not only invited shipbuilding but enabled the settlers to build better and cheaper vessels on New England's rocky shores than could be produced anywhere in Europe.[12] Encouraged by the mercantilistic policy of Great Britain as expressed in the Navigation Acts, the shipbuilding industry soon became of great importance in the New World.[13] Not only did these New England ships carry most of the trade of the colonies, but they gradually extended their range to all parts of the world. Through the use of these

[8] Thomas Jefferson Wertenbaker, *The First Americans, 1607-1690*, p. 2.
[9] *Ibid.*, p. 10.   [10] *Ibid.*, p. 11.
[11] William B. Weeden, *Economic and Social History of New England, 1620-1789*, I, 293-310.
[12] Oliver Perry Chitwood, *A History of Colonial America*, pp. 460-61, estimates that ships could be produced in New England costing from one-fifth to one-half less per ton than in the British Isles.   [13] Wertenbaker, *op. cit.*, p. 11.

swift sailing schooners another great industry pushed its way
into prominence. The development of the cod and mackerel
fisheries provided New England with a needed staple for
foreign trade and with the growing importance of whale
fishing resulted in an industry of great economic significance
to that section.[14]

The long winters of New England encouraged a system
of home-manufacturing—the production of many essential
articles in the way of household furniture and clothing, the
preparation of furs, the manufacture of flax into linen, and
dyeing and finishing. Gradually the home industries were expanded and mills for weaving, casting furnaces for the utilization of iron ores, rolling and slitting mills to produce nails
and iron rods, paper mills, as well as those producing naval
supplies were set up, often in violation of the English mercantile policies.[15] Not least among Yankee industries was that
of distillation of rum. Both Massachusetts and Connecticut
became important in this industry though Rhode Island soon
surpassed them both in the proportion produced. Local lum-
bermen and fishermen demanded "a strong stimulant to
ameliorate their heavy diet of pork and Indian corn,"[16] and
rum soon became an important item of trade.

As a matter of fact it had for some time been an important
factor in the West Indies trade. Cargoes of fish, lumber,
horses, provisions, and some British manufactured goods had
been exchanged with these islands for sugar, molasses and
rum. But it was soon found that the molasses could be transferred to New England and made into rum cheaper than the
liquor could be obtained in the West Indies.[17] This, then,
formed the basis for the famous "triangular trade" from
New England to Africa to the West Indies. After trying
unsuccessfully to exchange dry goods for Negro slaves on

[14] Weeden, *op. cit.*, Vol. II, *passim.*
[15] *Ibid.*, pp. 492-501; also Wertenbaker, *op. cit.*, pp. 49-86.
[16] Weeden, *op. cit.*, II, 501.   [17] *Ibid.*, pp. 501-2.

the coast of Africa, the Yankee traders were glad to turn to rum when they found that no other article of merchandise could be compared with it for large profits on the African coast. Exchanging the rum for slaves who tremendously overcrowded the space previously occupied by the rum, the New England traders returned to the West Indies where part of the slaves were bartered for a sufficient amount of molasses to make another cargo of rum. The surplus slaves, which represented the enormous profit of the venture, were usually disposed of along the southern coasts as the vessels returned to New England to resume the triangular voyage.[18] Governor Hopkins stated that for thirty years prior to 1764 the colony of Rhode Island alone had annually sent eighteen vessels carrying 1,800 hogsheads of rum to Africa. This commerce of rum and slaves annually yielded about $200,000 for remittance from Rhode Island to Great Britain. Though the demand was great, many losses were incurred in early voyages due to the uncertainty of securing captives on the coasts. Therefore, with characteristic Yankee efficiency, as the trade increased a thorough system was established. Slave-pens were built and into these the savages were herded ready for the ships so that the regularity of the traffic would reduce former losses.[19]

Not only did the inhabitants of New England become a commercial, industrial, and seagoing people,[20] but their economic interests gave rise to a difference in social organization. In that section, the failure of an agricultural and the rise of a commercial system led, along with religious factors, to the clustering of all habitations in small hamlets and the centering of economic and political interests as well as social life around the town.[21] This was, of course, in marked contrast

<hr/>

[18] *Ibid.*, pp. 458-68; E. B. Greene, *Provincial America, 1690-1740*, p. 286.

[19] See Weeden, *op. cit.*, II, 459, for above figures concerning Rhode Island and pp. 460-62 for other descriptions of this trade.

[20] Chitwood, *op. cit.*, pp. 433-93.

[21] Wertenbaker, *op. cit.*, pp. 49-86, describes the New England town.

to the growth of the plantation system in the South—the more scattered population in the agricultural communities and the larger political divisions in the form of counties. In both sections class distinctions were recognized. In the South the large landholders were at the apex while the slaves constituted the lower stratum. In New England, class distinctions prevented inferiors from occupying certain positions in churches, public inns, and other public places, and from wearing certain types of clothing and other distinguishing marks of high rank.[22]

In the group of settlements known as the "middle colonies," the coastal plain was wider, the land more fertile, the rivers more suitable for inland commerce, though with fewer good harbors than along the rocky shores of New England. The soil, being more adaptable to agriculture, produced a variety of grains and provided pastures for cattle and sheep. As a result, the people were not forced to depend on the sea for a living and this group of colonies tended to remain for many years agricultural rather than commercial.[23]

In the Southern colonies, the much wider coastal plain and greater fertility of soil, together with the long, hot summers which permitted an extended growing season, made it inevitable that this section would become one devoted to extensive agriculture. Timber for shipbuilding abounded, as it did in New England, but the Southern colonists did not build a great many ships; nor did they sail the seas in trade as did their northern neighbors, though they had harbors adapted for this purpose. And despite the fact that the soil was suitable for the raising of the grains so successfully cultivated in the middle colonies, the Southerners did not grow them to any extent. Rather did they turn to the production of a staple crop for which they found their soil and long growing season admirably suited and which they discovered would

[22] *Ibid.*, Chaps. II-III.   [23] *Ibid.*, p. 12.

yield them immense profits in the world market. For the purpose of getting this crop to market, the South was fortunately provided with a number of deep, connecting rivers and creeks which furnished the planters an easy means of shipping their product and also facilitated the settlement of the colony further inland.[24] The utilization of this staple crop and its resulting profitable exchange with the Old World enabled them to secure many of the comforts and luxuries which prevented the rapid lowering of standards that ordinarily fell to the lot of settlers in a wilderness.[25] As the soil of Virginia was peculiarly suited to the production of tobacco, the settlers in this colony cultivated it almost to the exclusion of all other agricultural products. The Virginia planter found that he could secure six times the profit from tobacco that he could from any other product,[26] and at one time at least it was grown in the very streets of Jamestown. By 1627 the exports of tobacco reached a half a million pounds a year.[27]

With the possibility of great profit in the production of this staple, the greatest need of the tobacco colonies became that of securing sufficient cheap labor, for although tobacco did not require skilled labor it did require almost constant attention the year around. With the abundance of free land it was practically an impossibility to acquire adequate free laborers. Though the mother country had a large number of unemployed these either lacked the funds to migrate to America, or if they did so they preferred to take up land of their own rather than to work for wages. Because of the lack of money among the English laborers a system of indenture came into existence under which the planters paid the immigrant's passage and the latter bound himself out to work until the cost was paid.[28] Usually four or five years of work would

---

[24] *Ibid.*, p. 13. Also see U. B. Phillips, *Life and Labor in the Old South.*
[25] Avery Craven, *Edmund Ruffin, Southerner: A Study in Secession*, p. 49.
[26] Wertenbaker, *op. cit.*, p. 22.
[27] *Ibid.*   [28] *Ibid.*, p. 24.

be sufficient to pay off his debt, and at the end of this time he became a freeman and often a landholder himself. Under this system, between 1635 and 1705 some 100,000 to 140,-000 indentured servants came to Virginia alone.[29]

Although Negro slaves were first brought into the colony in 1619,[30] the number of blacks was negligible for a hundred years.[31] This slow growth of the Negro population in the Southern colonies is attributable to several causes. Probably of greatest importance was the fact that the slave trade was monopolized by the Spanish, Dutch, and Portuguese, who during most of this time, under the operation of the English Navigation Laws, were not permitted to trade with the colonies. Too, the Southerners were somewhat hesitant about bringing in large numbers of uncivilized blacks to reside among them as long as the red savages remained a constant menace in the interior. Yet it was inevitable that the handicap of insufficient labor supply would lead to the importation of cheap labor both as the demand for tobacco increased and as the number of freeholders recruited from the ranks of indentured servants gradually acquired the potential acreage.

In contrast to the centering of the economic and social interests in small towns in New England, the Southern colonies tended toward the establishment of large plantations. The staple crops of Virginia and the Carolinas were tobacco, rice and indigo. All of these crops required fertile soil; and tobacco cultivation quickly exhausted the most fertile. This, in turn, led to the necessity of constantly clearing new ground, and as a rule the planter acquired not only sufficient land for present cultivation, but also for tillage in the future. Later as slavery became more prevalent large plantations were needed to keep the slaves employed the year around. Also, slave labor was likely to be extremely inefficient unless supervised by a white overseer. Since white labor was very

[29] *Ibid.*, p. 25.
[30] See above, p. 3.   [31] Wertenbaker, *op. cit.*, p. 23.

scarce, the overseer could demand a high wage for his services and this the planter could afford to pay only when he had a large number of slaves to be supervised.[32] It is a natural conclusion that the combination of fertile soil, mild climate, long growing season, and adequate transportation facilities—the physical endowment of the South—made of the South an agricultural section. The desire to produce great staples in demand in Europe created the problem of acquiring sufficient cheap labor which the system of indenture did not solve. The introduction of Negro slaves came as one possible solution to this labor problem; and the slaves in turn, combined with the nature of the crops, created the plantation rather than the small farm system in the South. And all of these factors aided in creating a type of colony entirely different from that found in New England and resulted in the development of sectional interests that were certain to conflict.

Since the climate in the Southern colonies was well suited to the Africans and enervating to the whites, slaves could be so profitably used in the production of tobacco, indigo, and rice that within a relatively short time the owner would be reimbursed for the original cost. This fact, coupled with the inability to secure free laborers, caused the institution of slavery to spread slowly but surely over the South, even in localities where it had been previously prohibited.[33] It is interesting to note that the majority of the slaves sold in the Southern colonies were imported by merchants and traders of New England, who "amassed . . . vast sums of . . . rapidly acquired and ill-gotten wealth" from the slave trade.[34] As the institution of slavery spread, the growing number of blacks created a feeling of alarm in the Southern colonies. This was expressed in various protests and petitions from Virginia, North Carolina, and Georgia for the prohibition of the

[32] Chitwood, op. cit., p. 448.
[33] James Ford Rhodes, History of the United States, I, 4-5.
[34] Hilary A. Herbert, The Abolition Crusade and Its Consequences, p. 37.

slave trade.[35] In 1761, the Virginia Assembly, in an attempt
to pass a prohibitory act, imposed a high duty on imported
slaves.[36] The opposition of the Southerners to the importation of slaves during this period may be attributed to the
fear of a possible servile insurrection, the evil influence of
newly imported savages upon acclimated Negroes, and the
menace of diseases being brought into the colonies.[37] However, due to the enormous profits which the traders of both
the mother country and New England derived from the slave
trade, to the mercantile policy of Great Britain which fostered
such a course, and to the fact that "the King of England was
interested in the profits of the iniquitous trade," the prohibitory measures of the colonies were vetoed and their protests were in vain.[38] This view is borne out by an Englishman writing about slavery in America in 1824. He stated
that "in their behalf it may be urged, that, even while they
were colonies, they strove continually, to prevent the introduction of slaves, by our people; that they petitioned our
government against the trade; and passed laws half of a century before we did for the abolition of it."[39]

During the pre-Revolutionary period, the New England
group of colonies, being commercial rather than agricultural,
found that slaves could not be used profitably in industry or
fishing, while the high mortality of the blacks transferred
from the tropics to the cold winters of the North Atlantic
made them a potential source of great loss.[40] The fact that
slavery never gained much foothold there seems to have
been based on purely economic reasons, for the institution was
given a trial without moral objections. The Puritan colonists

[35] *Ibid.*, p. 38. In the colony of Georgia, the trustees had forbidden slavery in
the beginning of the settlement. See E. Merton Coulter, *A Short History of
Georgia*, p. 55.

[36] Rhodes, *op. cit.*, I, 735.

[37] William S. Jenkins, *Pro-Slavery Thought in the Old South*, pp. 29-30.

[38] Herbert, *op. cit.*, p. 38; Rhodes, *op. cit.*, I, 8.

[39] "A Summary View of America," *Blackwood's Magazine* (London), XVI
(December, 1824), 641.   [40] Weeden, *op. cit.*, II, 450-63.

freely received and used Indian slaves at an early date. Even Cotton Mather, in the use of his black servant, showed as "little regard for the rights of man as the Boston merchant or Narragansett planter."[41] It is indeed fortunate for the moral development of the abolitionist descendants of these Puritan fathers that in the New England section "the climate was too harsh, the social system too simple, to engender a good economic employment of black labor."[42] Whatever the cause of the decline of slavery in the New England colonies, whether it was due to climate, to the character of their products, to the influx of European immigration which supplied a more eligible type of laborer and one more suitable to industrial needs, or to a combination of causes, it is true that these colonies early began to take steps toward gradual emancipation.[43]

Though at a later date the abolitionists professed that this abolition of slavery in the industrial colonies was dictated by the high principle of desiring to better the condition of the African, it appears that "when we reflect on the number of those people who found their way to the Southern colonies without having attained the liberty which was promised them,"[44] the chief operation of the Yankee traders in abolishing slavery "was to transfer Northern slaves to Southern markets."[45] Certainly the South viewed with apprehension the work of the New Englanders in bringing slaves into the South. As early as 1736, Colonel William Byrd, receiver-general of Virginia, lamented the fact that so much rum and so many Negroes were brought into Virginia by Yankee dealers. In a letter to a Georgia friend concerning the ex-

---

[41] *Ibid.*, p. 450.   [42] *Ibid.*, p. 451.

[43] The first law against slavery was enacted in Rhode Island on May 18, 1652. This prevented slaves from being held in bondage after more than ten years. *Niles Weekly Register*, XLI (1831-1832), 88.

[44] "The Black Race in North America," *Southern Literary Messenger*, XXI (November, 1855), 642.   [45] Herbert, *op. cit.*, p. 52.

clusion of both from that state, he wrote: "tho' with Respect to Rum, the Saints of New England I fear will find out some trick to evade your Act of Parliament. They have a great dexterity at palliating a perjury so well as to leave no taste of it in the mouth, nor can any people like them slip through a penal statute. . . . They import so many Negros hither. . . . I am sensible of many bad consequences of multiplying these Ethiopians amongst us."[46]

During the Revolutionary period, with its emphasis upon human rights, many of the Southern leaders regretted the existence of the institution of slavery and looked with hopeful eyes to its possible eradication in the future. The application of the natural rights philosophy to slavery was made by Thomas Jefferson in the form of an indictment against the King of England for encouraging slavery and the slave trade.[47] George Washington, although a slaveholder, wrote that it was among his "first wishes to see some plan adopted by which Slavery, in this country, may be abolished by law."[48] Patrick Henry criticized slavery as being "inconsistent with the Bible, and destructive to Liberty," while still a fourth Virginian, John Randolph, gave his support to the cause of emancipation by freeing all of his slaves after his death by will.[49] The ideals of liberty and equality fostered by the Revolutionary spirit turned the attention of some to the inconsistency of advocating the natural rights of man and not freeing the Negroes. This view probably led to the

[46] A. B. Hart, Source-Book of American History, pp. 119-21.

[47] "He has waged cruel war against human nature itself, violating its most sacred rights of life and liberty in the persons of a distant people who never offended him, captivating and carrying them into slavery in another hemisphere, or to incur miserable death in their transportation thither." A. A. Lipscomb and A. E. Bergh (editors), The Writings of Thomas Jefferson, I, 34.

[48] Letter to John F. Mercer of Maryland, Sept. 9, 1786, George Livermore, An Historical Research Respecting the Opinions of the Founders of the Republic on Negroes as Slaves, as Citizens, and as Soldiers, p. 59.

[49] J. S. C. Abbott, South and North, pp. 105, 106.

formation of an American anti-slavery society at Philadelphia, April 14, 1775.[50]

However, not all of the sentiment during this period was of the anti-slavery type. As early as 1751, George Whitefield, one of the early apostles of Methodism in Georgia, in a letter to Mr. B—— stated: "As for the lawfulness of keeping slaves, I have no doubt, since I hear of some that were bought with Abraham's money, and some that were born in his house." Although not approving the slave trade, he did not mind purchasing slaves "in order to make their lives comfortable, and lay a foundation for breeding up their posterity in the nurture and admonition of the Lord."[51] One contemporary author used economic necessity as a basis for slavery, arguing that the Negro was by nature better suited for the production of staple commodities in the hot climates and that the country was showing progress as a result of slave labor.[52]

Considering the South as a whole during this period, it may be concluded that slavery was on the decline. Certainly the institution was not held in as high regard in the South at the time of the Revolution as it had been a hundred years earlier. Only twice in the history of the South was slavery considered as a "positive good." In the tobacco colonies during the last half of the seventeenth century, governmental restrictions and glutted markets forced the planters to substitute Negro slaves for the more expensive indentured servants and brought about a reorganization of the plantation system in order to provide for division of labor. This resulted in the simplification of tasks to suit the inferior workers and to

[50] M. Janney, *A History of the Religious Society of Friends, from its Rise to the Year 1828*, places the date a year earlier.

[51] March 22, 1751, in *A Select Collection of Letters of the Late Reverend George Whitefield* . . . (London, 1772), II, 404. Hereafter cited as Whitefield, *Letters*.

[52] Bernard Romans, *A Concise Natural History of East and West Florida*, pp. 103-10.

secure the economies of large-scale production. Also in the rice swamps of the Carolinas and Georgia, the blacks thrived under a climate that caused the whites to sicken and die. It was during this time that slavery seemed to be a good solution to the problem of securing cheap labor, making ignorant Africans profitable and, at the same time, solving the race problem involved.[53] During the last part of the eighteenth century slavery was declining in favor among the Southern people and, as will be seen, it was not until after the abolitionist attack that the institution became a "positive good" again.

For the most part the slaveholders, about the time of the Revolution, considered slavery, from a moral and religious viewpoint, as an evil and as such sincerely desired to be rid of it. Webster described their attitude when he asserted that all of the eminent Southern leaders felt that slavery was "an evil, a blight, a scourge, and a curse," nor were there any "terms of reprobation of slavery so vehement in the North at that day as in the South."[54] The system of slavery—so interwoven in the very foundation of the social and economic structure of the Southern States—with its large increase in the number of Negroes in the region, caused the white people to be alarmed at the menace of the race question. "The indefinable dread of a slave insurrection—an insurrection incited by negroes from the West Indies—haunted the minds of the whites" and was the controlling motive be-

---

[53] Craven, op. cit., pp. 120-21. See also "The Black Race in North America," Southern Literary Messenger, XXI (November, 1855), 641.

[54] In speech of March 7, 1850, Works of Daniel Webster, V, 334. An excellent compilation of early Southern anti-slavery sentiment can be found in Daniel R. Goodloe, The Southern Platform: or, Manual of Southern Sentiment on the Subject of Slavery. As an abolitionist Goodloe collected the anti-slavery views of Southern leaders and states in his preface that "their testimony is almost unanimous against the institution." Also compare some contemporary Southern opinions given in Charles S. Sydnor, Slavery in Mississippi, pp. 231, 239-42; R. B. Flanders, Plantation Slavery in Georgia, p. 282. The latter gives some contemporary opinions in Georgia.

hind the opposition to the slave trade from 1791 to 1807.[55]
The insurrection in Santo Domingo in 1791 "aroused the
people of the State [North Carolina] to a realization of the
potential danger of a large negro population" and resulted in
1794 in a fine of 100 pounds for importing slaves.[56] Governor Winthrop Sargent of the Mississippi Territory, in a
circular letter to the slaveholders, dated November 16, 1800,
commented upon the recent "intended insurrection" in Virginia and demanded the "best endeavours to produce perfect
submission to the statutes for the Regulation of Slaves."[57] In
1803, Governor William C. C. Claiborne of Mississippi
lamented to James Madison that he feared "this Territory
must soon be overrun, by the *abandoned of that unfortunate
race.*"[58]

Although the Southerners seemed to agree that some
solution of the problem was necessary, they were by no means
unanimous in their opinions as to the best way in which emancipation could be achieved. Many of the leaders advocated
and urged various means of gradual emancipation, but always
with a provision for the removal of the free Negroes. As
early as 1776, Thomas Jefferson prepared a comprehensive
plan to provide for colonization.[59] The General Assembly of
Virginia passed resolutions favoring colonization in 1800,
1802, and 1805.[60] Again, in December, 1816, the Virginia
General Assembly passed a resolution which advocated the
elimination of the evil of free Negroes by colonizing all free
blacks and subsequently manumitted slaves that were willing
to go to Liberia.[61] As a result of this resolution the American

---

[55] Rosser Howard Taylor, *Slaveholding in North Carolina: An Economic View*, p. 27.   [56] *Ibid.*, p. 25.

[57] *Mississippi Territorial Archives, 1798-1803*, pp. 311-12.

[58] *Ibid.*, p. 374. Italics in *Archives*.

[59] "Africa in America," *Southern Literary Messenger*, XXII (January, 1856), 2.

[60] *Ibid.*; see also Goodloe, *op. cit.*, pp. 29-37.

[61] "Africa in America," *Southern Literary Messenger*, XXII (January, 1856), 3-4; Herbert, *op. cit.*, pp. 44-45.

Colonization Society was formed in 1817.[62] The membership of this organization included many great statesmen and philanthropists from both the North and the South. At various times the organization was headed by such men as Monroe, Madison, and Marshall, while Henry Clay was "one of the eloquent advocates of the scheme" for remedying one of the greatest evils of emancipation.[63]

Because they would be most vitally affected by the creation of a potential race menace in the event of emancipation, the colonization idea found its greatest support among the people of the South. The plan was early endorsed by some of the Southern States. Georgia, following Virginia in 1817, was supported by Maryland and Tennessee in 1818, while Vermont, the first northern state to support the movement, did not do so until 1819.[64] The Mississippi Colonization Society, though not founded until 1831, was one of the strongest. After five successful years as an auxiliary of the American Colonization Society the Mississippi group withdrew from the larger organization and formed a separate African colony for Mississippi emigrants.[65] That the restoration of the Negroes to their African homes met with considerable response in the South is evident in the fact that out of the fifty-seven societies auxiliary to the Colonization Society in 1826, forty-four were in the slaveholding states.[66] At this same time, "of the 143 emancipation societies in the United States, 103 were

[62] For official account of this organization see the *Annual Reports of the American Colonization Society, with the minutes of the meeting and of the board of directors,* 1st-91st, 93rd (1818-1910).

[63] Herbert, *op. cit.,* p. 45. See also Stephen B. Weeks, "Anti-Slavery Sentiment in the South," *Publications of the Southern History Association,* II (April, 1898), 87-130, for an excellent account.

[64] Herbert, *op. cit.,* p. 45; also see Asa Earl Martin, "Anti-Slavery Societies in Tennessee," *Tennessee Historical Magazine,* I (1915), 261.

[65] Sydnor, *op. cit.,* pp. 203, 214. This colony established by Mississippi was not very successful since Southern opinion by this time was changing very rapidly as a result of the attack of the abolitionists, and the colonization society was not receiving as much support as it had earlier.

[66] John Bach McMaster, *History of the United States,* V, 213.

in the South."[67] The following year Benjamin Lundy, in his *Genius of Universal Emancipation*, estimated that there were approximately one hundred and thirty anti-slavery societies in the United States with a total membership of 6,625; of these, one hundred and six societies and 5,150 of the members were in the slaveholding states.[68] The fact that the four abolition newspapers founded between 1819 and 1828 were published in the South seems to prove the greater interest in the latter section.[69] A writer in one of these abolition papers in 1820 stated that "it appears to be the general opinion of citizens of the United States, from Maine to Georgia, that slavery is wrong—that it is a national evil; and that, to avert the visitation of retributive justice, something is necessary to be done; but what that something is, seems to be a subject of much discussion among the people." He adds that though there are "many who acknowledge slavery to be a moral evil, and that it is criminal," the question "what shall we do with them?" always arises.[70] From these facts it may at least be concluded that the question of slavery was openly discussed in the South with a view to ascertaining the best means of abolishing the evil without endangering the social and economic system of the Southern States.

Just as the institution of slavery was declining, new inven-

[67] Herbert, *op. cit.*, p. 54, quotes Judge Temple's *Covenanter, Cavalier, and Puritan*, p. 208.

[68] Weeks, "Anti-Slavery Sentiment in the South," *Publications of the Southern History Association*, II (April, 1898), 88-89.

[69] *The Emancipator*, founded in Tennessee in 1820; *The Genius of Universal Emancipation*, founded in Tennessee in 1821; *The Abolition Intelligencer*, founded in Kentucky in 1822; and *The Liberalist*, founded in Louisiana in 1828.

[70] *The Emancipator*, of April 30, 1820, reprints article by "Modern Listner" from *East Tennessee Patriot*. See reprint by B. H. Murphy, Nashville, 1932. This writer adds that even those condemning slavery say that "It will not do to liberate them in their ignorant and savage state; that it would be better to continue them in a state of perpetual bondage, than to free them, unless they were to be immediately colonized in their own country; for if they were to continue among us, we should become, in a few ages, an entire mixed race by marriages, and by illicit connexions; besides the humiliating circumstance of their coming to an equality with ourselves, which no person of spirit can anticipate, but with abhorrence."

tions in the form of the cotton gin and improved spinners
within a few years lifted cotton from an almost unknown
export to one of great importance, of which even the increased production could hardly keep pace with the rapidly
growing world demand. Cotton was indigenous to America
and the soil and climate of the Southern States were well
adapted to its growth,[71] yet during the early colonial period
it never attained the importance of rice, indigo, or tobacco.
Cotton had been grown in Virginia as early as 1628, but for
over a century the amount produced was very limited and
was used only in the colony itself.[72] In 1748 seven bags of
the cotton fibre were exported from Charleston, South Carolina; by 1770 the quantity shipped from all ports had increased to only ten bags.[73] The greatest obstacle to the production of cotton during this time was the excessive labor required to separate the cotton fibre from its seed, and as a
result the cultivation of the crop was limited to sections where
very cheap labor could be obtained.[74] The bulk of the crop
consisted of the short-fibred variety and the separation of one
pound of cotton from the seed was an average day's work for
a slave.[75] Eli Whitney, a Northern visitor in Georgia, over-
came this difficulty by inventing in 1793 a gin[76] for the separation of the cotton fibre by machinery.

One author in describing the effect of various inventions
upon cotton culture concluded that "through the ingenuity of
. . . Richard Arkwright,[77] James Hargreaves, and Eli
Whitney—the earliest of their inventions dating from about

[71] Keifer, op. cit., I, 30.

[72] "The Black Race in North America," Southern Literary Messenger, XXI
(November, 1855), 670.   [73] Ibid.

[74] Rhodes, op. cit., I, 25; John Elliott Cairnes, The Slave Power: Its Character,
Career, and Probable Designs! p. 106.   [75] Rhodes, op. cit., I, 25.

[76] Phillips, op. cit., pp. 95-96; Cairnes, op. cit., p. 107; "The Black Race in
North America," Southern Literary Messenger, XXI (November, 1855), 670.

[77] Arkwright obtained a patent for the spinning frame in 1761. "1779.—Mule
spinning invented by Hargrave [Hargreaves], or rather perfected by Crompton."
DeBow's Review, IV (December, 1847), 546.

1760—the weaving of cotton had a century later become one of the leading and most vital industries in the world" and the Southern States enjoyed through soil, climate, and "an industrial system believed to be essential to its successful production" what was thought to be "an unshakable monopoly of an indispensable staple."[78]

As modern inventions facilitated the production and manufacture of cotton, the growth of this industry from an insignificant position to one of great economic importance can be easily ascertained from actual statistics. Following the invention of the cotton gin, the growth of the cotton industry was comparatively steady from 9,000 bales in 1791 to 1,038,000 bales in 1831.[79] In 1806 Great Britain imported more cotton from Brazil and the East and West Indies than she did from the United States. But between 1810 and 1820 the United States passed the other countries in the amount of cotton exported to Great Britain.[80] And beween 1791 and 1860 the production of cotton increased more than a thousandfold.[81]

Thus the inventive genius of man, the opening of a vast territory of rich lands favorable to cotton culture,[82] and the increased world-wide demand for cotton products all checked the decline of the institution of slavery and combined "to weave that network of cotton which formed an indissoluble cord, binding the black, who was threatened to be cast off, to

[78] C. F. Adams, *Trans-Atlantic Historical Solidarity*, p. 88; see also Rhodes, *op. cit.*, I, 26; Richard Hildreth, *History of the United States*, IV, 545; Webster, *op. cit.*, V, 338.

[79] Weeks, "Anti-Slavery Sentiment in the South," *Publications of the Southern History Association*, II (April, 1898), 89: 1791—9,000 bales; 1801—211,000; 1811—269,000; 1821—1,038,000; 1841—1,635,000.

[80] Cotton shipped to England:

1810—From U. S.	246,759 p'kgs.	From others	314,414 p'kgs.		
1820— " "	302,395 "	" "	268,256 "		
1830— " "	618,527 "	" "	252,960 "		
1840— " "	1,237,500 "	" "	202,100 "		
			(including Egypt)		

In 1806, only 124,939 packages were shipped to England. *DeBow's Review*, III (May, 1847), 439.

[81] Rhodes, *op. cit.*, I, 26.   [82] The Louisiana Purchase, 1803.

human progress,"[83] and incidentally binding the economic interests of the Southern section to agriculture. This was a golden age in the development of the South. The need for cheap labor in the interior was great, and the belief that slaves were essential to cotton production, together with the promise of large profits from the new, fertile soil, caused a migration westward of both whites and blacks; and the system of slavery increased in proportion as cotton cultivation spread over new areas.[84]

Yet, even with the increased profits resulting from exploiting the soil with slave labor, reports of the men who lived and visited in the South in those days offer little evidence to show that the attitude of the Southern people changed radically in regard to the system of slavery. A Virginia slaveholder in speaking of slavery to Olmsted stated his desire for some satisfactory plan to relieve Southern slaveholders of the evil but expressed his doubt that any better system could be devised whereby the great benefits enjoyed by the African would be increased.[85] Basil Hall, who travelled in this country in 1827 and 1828, believed that the slaveholders were "a class of men who are really entitled to a large share of our indulgence"; that no men were more ready than most of the American planters to grant "that slavery is an evil in itself and eminently an evil in its consequences," but that to do away with it seemed "so completely beyond the reach of any human exertions" that he considered the abolition of slavery as the "most profitless of all possible subjects of discussion."[86]

Due to the large number of slaves and their rapid natural

---

[83] T. P. Kettell, "The Future of the South," *DeBow's Review*, X (February, 1851), 132.   [84] Craven, *op. cit.*, p. 122.

[85] F. L. Olmsted, *Journey in the Seaboard Slave States*, I, 48. Hereafter cited as *Seaboard Slave States*. Slavery was on the wane according to the report of the Comptroller of South Carolina which showed a decrease in that state of 33,856 slaves between 1824-1826. *Niles Weekly Register*, XLI (October 22, 1831), 145.

[86] Rhodes, *op. cit.*, I, 366.

increase, colonization was not practical as a method of removing the evil of free blacks through emancipation.[87] Nevertheless, colonization societies were strongly supported by the
Southern people until 1831. After that date the movement
for colonization declined as a result of both the change in
Southern opinion and the opposition of the abolitionists to
the American Colonization Society. Experience proved that
when the slaves were gradually emancipated the freed Negroes stirred up great discontent among the slaves, while the
blacks themselves gained but little and were in many instances
"great losers by emancipation."[88] It was pointed out that
though laws could make them free, "laws cannot change their
colour" and the freed slaves, though relatively insignificant in
proportion to the total population, made up a high percentage
of the paupers and inmates of the prisons.[89]

An Englishman, viewing the conditions in the United
States, wrote in 1824 that he questioned the feasibility of any
form of emancipation and added that "sudden emancipation
of the whole, at once is impossible; and if it could be done"
the policy would be the "height of madness" while "amalgamation—(by marriage)—never will take place."[90] As late as
1828, Gerard C. Brandon, governor of Mississippi, stated
that "Slavery is an evil at best," and asserted that it handicapped the Southern States.[91] S. S. Prentiss, a citizen of the
same state, wrote in 1831 that freeing the slaves would not
be of any advantage to them, while colonization was "impossible on account of their number." While looking upon the
institution as an evil he was convinced that it was "too deep-
rooted to be eradicated" and that the real "sin of the business

[87] The same general idea is expressed in *Blackwood's Magazine*, XVI (1824),
642.
[88] *African Repository*, I (May, 1825), 91.
[89] *Ibid.*, pp. 91-92.
[90] *Blackwood's Magazine*, XVI (1824), 642.
[91] Ruth B. Hawes, "Slavery in Mississippi," *Sewanee Review*, XXI (April,
1913), 227.

lies at the door of those who first introduced slavery into this country."[92]

It is evident that as late as 1831 the Southern people, in spite of the extension and profitableness of the institution, still regarded slavery as an evil, though a necessary one since they thought it was the best means by which the two races could live together peacefully. During the last years of this period, they accepted it as such, nor was there any vigorous defense except that which was occasionally created by agitation. Prior to the radical abolition attack, Northern leaders such as Dr. William E. Channing viewed the problem more nearly from a national than from a sectional aspect. Channing, though later a leader of the philosophical abolitionists, wrote to Daniel Webster in 1828 and pointed out the necessity for cautious exertions to aid the South in abolishing the evil of slavery. In this he stated that the Northern people should assure the South that "we consider slavery as your calamity, not your crime, and we will share with you the burden of putting an end to it." He continued by asserting that unless they did sympathize with the South and offer to share the "toil and expense of abolishing slavery" in a friendly way, the matter would be made far worse "by rousing sectional pride and passion for its support," a condition which would divide the country and "shake the foundations of government."[93]

The question of slavery and the attendant evils of emancipation presented a serious problem to the Southern people and no one realized more than they that it was one which required careful and thoughtful consideration in order to obtain a wise solution. Perhaps the social phase of the problem could have been worked out had the "Christianity of the South . . . been left to its own time and mode" of accom-

[92] *Ibid.*, p. 228.
[93] Channing to Webster, May 14, 1828, in Webster, *op. cit.*, V, 366-67. Herbert, *op. cit.*, p. 48, notes that Webster did not give this letter out until 1851.

plishing it and "without external force but the force of kindly, respectful consideration and forebearing Christian fellowship."[94] Had there not been powerful and dominating economic and political interests involved which prevented the North from supporting the South in a friendly effort to achieve emancipation, in such a way as to benefit the slaves and at the same time provide for a solution of the race question, in all probability the South would have abolished the institution of slavery in a peaceful way.

In surveying the social and economic influences affecting slavery prior to 1831 the historian is constantly impressed with the importance of antagonistic sectional differences. These fundamental diversities between the two sections, New England and the South, are also reflected in the various political controversies of the period. The dark shadow of the slavery issue was often cast over the sectional struggles, not necessarily as the sole cause but largely as a part of other fundamental differences. At still other times the slavery agitation was but the moral issue which cloaked a partially hidden but nevertheless important economic or political motive. In order to understand fully the abolitionist attack of 1831, the political intrigues of the period which touched the slavery issue must be considered.

As has already been pointed out, the emphasis upon natural rights during the Revolutionary period was conducive to proposed schemes of gradual emancipation and the arousing of public opinion in opposition to the spread of slavery. In the Ordinance of 1784, a remarkable attempt was made by a Southerner, Thomas Jefferson, to exclude slavery from the western territories after 1800; and this proposal barely failed of adoption.[95] Three years later in the so-called Northwest

---

[94] George Tichnor Curtis, *Life of James Buchanan*, II, 283.

[95] Edward Channing, *History of the United States*, III, 539. Also see speech of Edward Everett, quoted in Livermore, *op. cit.*, pp. 15-18, and speech of James Iredell, *ibid.*, pp. 102-3. Channing, *op. cit.*, III, 539 n., cites P. L. Ford, *Writings*

Ordinance the anti-slavery principle was again recognized, and slavery was prohibited in the Northwest Territory, with a provision, however, for the return of fugitive slaves.[96] The entire Southern delegation voted for this Ordinance in 1787, which is not strange when we consider that throughout the history of the Continental Congress Southern representatives many times denounced slavery and the slave trade.[97]

In the Convention that assembled at Philadelphia in 1787 for the purpose of framing a constitution, great difficulties arose from diversity of views, though at first these did not assume a sectional form. In the controversies over the apportionment of representatives, navigation, and the slave trade, it appears that the Southern delegates may have been influenced by generous and patriotic motives, for the Northern States gained more advantages than they had expected by the encouragement provided toward their commerce and manufactures.[98] During this Convention, "not a voice was raised in unqualified defense and justification of slavery." Though the South Carolina delegates apologized somewhat for the institution, those from North Carolina, Virginia, and Maryland either "openly denounced it as criminal and disgraceful or freely admitted its evils."[99] The most scathing denunciation against the system of slavery that was delivered during the Convention came from George Mason of Virginia, who, in addition to being opposed to slavery, lamented greatly that the merchants of New England "had from a lust

---

of *Thomas Jefferson*, III, 429-30, as attributing the lack of attention to Jefferson's efforts "to the jealousy of New England historians and to the fact that at a later time it was desirable to divert public attention in the South away from Jefferson's earlier pronunciamento against negro slavery." See Goodloe, *op. cit.*, p. 72.

[96] C. E. Merriam, *A History of American Political Theories*, p. 203; also Channing, *op. cit.*, III, 546.

[97] Weeks, "Anti-Slavery Sentiment in the South," *Publications of the Southern History Association*, II (April, 1898), 89.

[98] Rhodes, *op. cit.*, I, 17; Cochin, *op. cit.*, pp. 8-9; Webster, *op. cit.*, V, 334.

[99] Weeks, "Anti-Slavery Sentiment in the South," *Publications of the Southern History Association*, II (April, 1898), 90.

of gain embarked in this nefarious traffic" known as the slave trade.[100] In the discussion of the latter, considerable difference of opinion among the delegates was manifest. The leaders from such Slave States as Maryland, Delaware, and Virginia opposed a continuance of the slave trade. The Carolinas and Georgia, since they needed slaves to cultivate the unhealthful rice swamps, desired that the trade continue. They were supported in this contention by that part of the New England delegation which represented the interests of those engaged in African trade. As a result of a compromise, the slave trade was to be allowed to continue until 1808, though Congress was given the power to levy a duty or tax not exceeding ten dollars "for each person imported up until that date."[101]

The question of the proper basis for representation in Congress brought forth another conflict. What was to be the status of the slaves in the Southern States? No argument was brought up in favor of granting them suffrage which would have been equivalent to placing them on the same political basis as the whites. However, many of the Southern delegates argued that all the slaves should be counted in determining population as a basis of representation.[102] Elbridge Gerry of Massachusetts, quite in opposition to the sentiment of that state fifty years later, insisted that slaves could be counted only as property and demanded "to know why South Carolina slaves should be represented when Massachusetts horses were not."[103] It was a Southern delegate, Williamson of North Carolina, who moved the counting of three-fifths of the slaves, which proposal finally formed the basis of the

---

[100] A. C. McLaughlin, *The Confederation and the Constitution, 1783-1789,* pp. 263-64.

[101] *Ibid.,* pp. 262-65. It is interesting to note that Massachusetts, New Hampshire, and Connecticut, whose merchants were actively engaged in the importation of slaves, joined with South Carolina and Georgia in insisting upon a few more years before the final prohibition. See Hawes, "Slavery in Mississippi," *Sewanee Review,* XXI (April, 1913), 225.

[102] McLaughlin, *op. cit.,* pp. 257-58.   [103] Channing, *op. cit.,* III, 511.

practical compromise which was adopted.[104] Taking the work of the Convention as a whole, it seems that the Southern States, after twenty years, lost what little advantage there was in the slave trade. But they gained an acknowledgment in the Constitution that slaves were property, being taxable the same as other articles of property; that fugitive slaves should be "delivered up" as property by the non-slaveholding states; and that, in case of servile insurrection, the Southern slaveholders should be protected in their rights of property by aid, when necessary, from the non-slaveholding states.[105] In submitting to the rule of reckoning five slaves as the equivalent of three whites in taxation and representation, the Southern States did not gain as much as had been expected in the matter of taxation. This was due to the fact that the expenses of the Federal Government were chiefly supported by the revenue from imports rather than from direct Federal taxes assessed in the states. Although they gained but little on this score, the Slave States lost in representation two-fifths of the slave population, which was not reckoned as a basis for the apportionment of representatives.[106]

It seems quite probable that from 1789 to 1820 the sentiment of the mass of people concerning slavery may be partially determined by the reflection of popular opinion in the congressional debates. Even prior to the slavery agitation during the Missouri struggle, many petitions dealing with slavery, abolition, manumission, and colonization were filed in both houses of Congress. Most of these early petitions were presented by the Society of Friends. The first, presented on February 11, 1790, evoked only mild protests from a few Southern representatives from the coastal districts of South Carolina and Georgia, and even the protests of these representatives were largely economic. They did not favor the agitation of the slavery question without "funds sufficient"

---

[104] McLaughlin, *op. cit.*, pp. 258-60.
[105] Fowler, *op. cit.*, p. 27.   [106] *Ibid.*, p. 28.

to compensate owners.[107] They also felt that congressional interference would reduce the value of that species of property and be injurious to their constituents.[108] Perhaps the recent revolution against English usurpation of rights was fresh in the mind of Representative Burke of South Carolina when he stated that he did not believe that "the rights of the Southern States" should be threatened to please the Quakers "who would be unaffected by the consequences."[109] This same view was expressed the following day in protesting against another petition, when Jackson of Georgia asked if it was a good policy to bring forward a business "likely to light up the flame of civil discord; for the people will resist one tyranny as soon as another."[110] Most of the arguments brought up against these petitions revolved around the question of the protection of property, the constitutionality of the petitions, and states' rights as opposed to the authority of the Federal Government.[111]

A committee instructed to report on the various Quaker petitions submitted its report on March 8, 1790. This committee had reached the conclusion that although Congress had the power to regulate the African trade, to provide for the humane treatment of the slaves, and to tax incoming slaves up to $10 per capita, that body, according to "a fair construction of the Constitution," was restrained from "interfering in the emancipation of slaves" or with the internal regulations of the states regarding slavery.[112] In the discussion that followed a few days later, Southern delegates, while zealously guarding their rights, were not unanimous in supporting slavery. White of Virginia, though aware that Congress had no

[107] *Annals of Congress*, 1st Cong., 1st sess., II, 1187. Hereafter cited as *Annals*.
[108] *Ibid.*, p. 1185.   [109] *Ibid.*, p. 1186.
[110] *Ibid.*, p. 1200; Jackson also added that the Southern States would not allow themselves to be "divested of their property without a struggle."
[111] *Ibid.*, pp. 1185-1202; see also "Early Congressional Discussions on Slavery," *DeBow's Review*, XXIII (July, 1857), 35-47.
[112] *Annals*, 1st Cong., 2 sess., II, 1414-16.

power in this matter, felt that in curbing slavery the essential
interests of the Southern States would not suffer.[113] Another
Virginia representative, Brown, enlarged upon the "pernicious
consequences" of Congressional interference, and thought
that "negro property will be annihilated" in time but felt
that it should be gradual.[114] On the other hand, Smith of
South Carolina resented the petition as a "very indecent attack on the character" of the Slave States and one "calculated
to fix a stigma of the blackest nature" upon the state that he
represented. This feeling of being unjustly attacked called
forth from Representative Smith one of the earliest defenses
of slavery in which he appealed to history and the Bible, ex-
pounded the evil effects of amalgamation, and wound up in a
support of states' rights.[115] He was supported by Representative Burke, one of his colleagues, who particularly stressed
the fact that the emancipation of slaves tended to make them
"wretched in the highest degree."[116]

Especially did the Southern representatives in Congress
resent the Society of Friends judging what was best for the
whole continent. Smith pointed out that when the Confederation was formed the North had adopted the South with her
slaves, and the South had adopted the North with her
Quakers.[117] Economically, the contentions of these two representatives as opposed to the majority of the Southern delegation may be explained by the necessity of slave labor in
their districts. It was pointed out that portions of South Carolina could "only be cultivated by slaves; the climate, the
nature of the soil, ancient habits, forbid the whites from per-
forming the labor." Removal of the slaves by emancipation
would result in "all the fertile rice fields and indigo swamps"
being deserted, and becoming "a wilderness. . . . Without
the rice swamps of Carolina, Charleston would decay," ruin-

[113] *Ibid.*, p. 1452.
[114] *Ibid.*
[116] *Ibid.*, p. 1452.
[115] *Ibid.*, p. 1457.
[117] *Ibid.*, p. 1458.

ing the commerce of that city and injuring the back country. "If you injure the Southern States, the injury would reach our Northern and Eastern brethren: for the States are links of one chain; if we break one, the whole must fall to pieces."[118] This continued to be the general position taken by Representative Smith, for on November 28, 1792, he spoke of a Quaker petition as "a mere rant and rhapsody of a meddling fanatic."[119]

Other abolition petitions were presented during 1794 and 1795, but were usually referred to a committee or tabled with very little discussion.[120] One interesting petition, illustrating a pro-slavery sentiment in a section which later became violently abolitionist, came from the Northwest Territory on April 25, 1796, praying "for permission to import slaves into that country from other States."[121] The Southern representatives did not favor this extension of the system and the petition was tabled.

In January, 1797, quite an extended discussion revolved around the question of a tax on slaves in connection with land and improvement taxes. Murray of Maryland stated that "he considered slaves in the Southern States as laborers" and unless provision was made for taxing laborers in the United States as a whole, he was opposed to the bill.[122] However, most of the representatives of the Southern States favored the tax on slaves with the land tax while those from the Northern States opposed it on the ground "that the land-holders in the Southern States would pay less than the land-holders in the parts of the Union where no slaves were kept."[123] In this connection, Brent of Virginia thought it "a very extraordinary thing that gentlemen who represented States where there were no slaves, should oppose a tax on

[118] *Ibid.*, pp. 1459-60—speech of Mr. Smith.

[119] *Ibid.*, 2nd Cong., 2 sess., I, 730.

[120] *Ibid.*, 3rd Cong., 1 sess., I, 249-50, 349, 448, 483; *Senate Proceedings* (1793-1795), pp. 36, 38, 64, 71, 72.   [121] *Annals*, 4th Cong., 1 sess., I, 1349.

[122] *Ibid.*, p. 1934.   [123] *Ibid.*, p. 1935.

that species of property, and that the Southern States where slavery existed, should be advocating that tax."[124] It is quite evident from the expressions of Southern Congressmen during this time that the majority of them looked upon the institution of slavery as an evil. A Virginian expressed the view that a person living where slavery did not exist "must enjoy reflecting, that his State was free from that evil."[125] A North Carolinian stated a very similar view by pointing out that "there was not a gentleman in North Carolina who did not wish there were no blacks in the country." He considered slaves as a misfortune, but "there was no way of getting rid of them."[126] The latter gentleman, though feeling as he did in opposition to slavery, resented the outside interference of Pennsylvania Quakers, whom he regarded as "warmakers" rather than "peace-makers" since they were "continually endeavoring in the Southern States to stir up insurrections amongst the negroes."[127] Probably most of the Southern representatives felt, as did Nicholas of Virginia, that it was not the "fault of the Southern States that Slavery was tolerated, but their misfortune; but to liberate their slaves at once, would be to act like madmen"; and such a step would be injurious to the whole United States. The South was unfortunately placed in a "situation which obliged them to hold slaves, but they did not wish to extend the mischief."[128]

During the period from 1800 to 1808, practically all of the discussions in Congress concerning slavery revolved around the question of the slave trade. In this connection, it is interesting to note the conflicting opinions of Northern and Southern representatives and to compare the sentiment at this time with that which existed forty or more years later. On April 26, 1800, a lengthy discussion took place concerning a

[124] *Ibid.*, 2 sess., II, 1939.

[125] *Ibid.*—speech of Mr. Page of Virginia.

[126] Mr. Macon of North Carolina speaking on November 30, 1797. *Ibid.*, 5th Cong., 2 sess., I, 661.   [127] *Ibid.*

[128] *Ibid.*, p. 665—speech of Mr. Nicholas on November 30, 1797.

Senate bill to prohibit the "carrying on the slave trade from the United States to any foreign country." A New England representative violently opposed the bill on the ground that the United States should enjoy this trade. He pointed out that "our distilleries and manufactures are lying idle for want of an extended commerce." Knowing that on the African coast "New England rum was much preferred to the best Jamaica spirits, and would fetch a better price," he felt that a profitable return should be made.[129] The Southern group favored the bill. Representative Nicholas, expressing the general sentiment, remarked upon the unfortunate condition of the Southern people who were obliged to keep slaves, and stated that the "people of the Southern States were wiping off the stain entailed upon them by their predecessors, in endeavoring to ameliorate the situation" as much as possible.[130]

By 1804 even the South Carolina delegation, no longer containing the fiery Smith, united with the other Southern Congressmen in advocating the restriction of slavery. In that year a bill for taxing imported slaves $10 per capita created a long debate. Representative Lowndes of South Carolina stated that rather than being friendly to a continuation of the slave trade, he thought that "the period has passed when the interests of the country required, and her policy dictated" this trade and felt that "an end should be put to it."[131] Huger of South Carolina expressed himself without hesitation as being "hostile to the importation of slaves" and pointed out that every representative from his state was opposed to the importation of slaves,[132] while one of his colleagues condemned it as a "horrid traffic."[133] Huger re-

[129] *Ibid.*, 6th Cong., 1 sess., I, 687—speech of Mr. Brown of Rhode Island.
[130] *Ibid.*—speech of Mr. Nicholas of Virginia.
[131] *Ibid.*, 8th Cong., 1 sess., I, 992—speech of Mr. Lowndes of South Carolina on February 14, 1804.
[132] *Ibid.*, p. 1006—speech on February 14, 1804.
[133] *Ibid.*, p. 1004—speech of Mr. Moore of South Carolina on February 14, 1804.

proached the North by pointing out that they had "kept
slaves as long as their interest dictated, and then got rid of
them." Feeling that the evil was decreasing in South Carolina, he went on to prophesy that if left alone the South
would work out some solution, but warned: "interfere and
you will only increase the evil; for, whenever the Government of the Union interferes in the peculiar concerns of a
State, it must excite jealousy and a spirit of resistance."[134]
The "New Abolitionists" of 1831, if they really had the interests of the slaves at heart, could have profited by considering this prophetic statement delivered by a Southerner in
1804.

During this discussion, the Yankee traders were condemned not only by the Southerners but even more severely
by representatives from some of the Northern States. A New
Yorker pointed out that the New Englanders continually
evaded the laws and bartered rum in Africa for slaves.[135] A
member from Pennsylvania pointed out that "numbers in the
Eastern States have been embarked, for some years past, in
the cruel traffic of slaves, and smuggling them into other
States." He feared that even then this group of New Englanders were preparing "to stimulate the barbarous tribes of
Africa to war against each other," and to violate every feeling
of humanity. He charged that they actually forged irons in
order that "they may have the infernal pleasure . . . of rivet-
ting them on the unfortunate men, women, and children, who
may fall into their hands."[136] Huger pointed out that "the
people to the North, who make the most noise on this subject,
are those, who when they go to the South, first hire, then
buy, and last of all turn out the severest masters among
us."[137] In contrast to a Kentuckian who felt that there was

[134] *Ibid.*, p. 1006.
[135] *Ibid.*, p. 1000—speech of Mr. Mitchel of New York on February 14, 1804.
[136] *Ibid.*, p. 997—speech of Mr. Bard of Pennsylvania on February 14, 1804.
[137] *Ibid.*, p. 1007—speech of Mr. Huger of South Carolina.

"not a member on the floor more inimical to slavery than he was"[138] a New Yorker favored the unbarring of "the door of the statute of limitations" in order to increase revenue.[139]

As a result of these debates in 1804 and 1805, there were some efforts in the form of petitions demanding that a constitutional amendment be passed which would allow Congress to deal with the slave trade before 1808. In fact the legislatures in Maryland, North Carolina, Massachusetts, New Hampshire, and Vermont passed resolutions favoring this movement. However, because of other pressing matters and the fact that it was only a short time until Congress would have such authority, nothing definite was done about it.[140] A movement in the opposite direction which should be mentioned is characterized by a petition from the Legislative Council and House of Representatives of the Indiana Territory "praying that the introduction of slaves into the said Territory may be permitted by Congress."[141]

A long discussion of the prohibition of the slave trade began in 1805 and culminated with the passing of an act in 1807 which was "to prohibit the importation of slaves into any port or place within the jurisdiction of the United States, from and after the first day of January, in the year of our Lord one thousand eight hundred and eight."[142] The efforts of the Yankee slave traders to make at least one last profitable excursion to the African coast brought forth a petition from "sundry merchants and others" of Charleston, South

[138] *Ibid.*, p. 1003—speech of Mr. Bedinger of Kentucky.

[139] *Ibid.*—speech of Mr. Mitchel of New York.

[140] See Edward Channing, *The Jeffersonian System, 1801-1811*, pp. 104-6; see also Mary S. Locke, *Anti-Slavery in America from the introduction of . . . to the prohibition . . . (1619-1808)*.

[141] *Annals*, 9th Cong., 1 sess., I, 294—presented December 18, 1805. Another petition for same was sent by the inhabitants of Randolph and St. Clair counties asking that the Territory be divided into two separate governments, "that slaves may be permitted, by law, to be brought into the said territory." *Ibid.*, p. 848.

[142] *Ibid.*, 2 sess., II, 486. See also 1 sess., I, 273-74, 347-49, 374-75, 397, 435-38, 440-44, 533, 854-55, 961.

Carolina, protesting that many vessels had cleared out of Charleston just before and just after the above law was passed; and praying that a "law might be passed affording them relief."[143] However, in spite of the passage of this act, slaves were smuggled into the United States from time to time. The only other mention of slavery that was made in Congress until well after the War of 1812 was in the form of a protest from South Carolina against the inefficiency of the Federal Government in enforcing the act.[144]

It is well to pause and consider some of the other elements of the period from 1800 to 1815 that affected the sectional alignment after the latter date. The acquisition of the vast territory west of the Mississippi known as Louisiana opened new and fertile lands that might be expected to increase the political power of the agricultural section as well as to divert much of the trade from New England to New Orleans. So embittered were the New England States against this territorial expansion westward that the legislature of Massachusetts in 1804 passed an act which declared that this acquisition of Louisiana by the Federal Government was sufficient cause for the dissolution of the Union.[145] In 1807,

---

[143] *Ibid.*, 10th Cong., 1 sess., I, 1243—petition presented by Mr. Marion of South Carolina on December 29, 1807. It might be pointed out that during the period 1804-1807, in which the ports of South Carolina were open to the slave trade, 202 vessels arrived at Charleston with slaves. Of this number 61 claimed to belong at Charleston; 70 to England; 59 to Rhode Island; 3 to Baltimore; 4 to Norfolk; 2 to Sweden; and 1 each to Boston, Connecticut, and France. The 61 that claimed Charleston as the home port were in reality owned either by New Englanders or in Great Britain. Of these 202 vessels, but 13 consignees were natives of Charleston; 88 from Rhode Island; 91 from Boston; and 10 from France.—Edward McGrady, Jr., "Address," *Southern Historical Society Papers,* XVI (1881), 250-51.

[144] *Annals,* 11th Cong., 3 sess., III, 1010. Mr. Cheves of South Carolina laid before the House two letters from Thomas Parker, District Attorney for the district of South Carolina, on the subject of "the inefficacy of certain provisions in the Act of March 1807, prohibiting the importation of slaves into the United States and their territories, and suggesting such amendments as in his opinion will remedy the defect."

[145] B. Munford, "Vindication of the South," *Southern Historical Society Papers,* XXVII (1899), 60. Also quotes Josiah Quincy (Mass.) concerning bill for admis-

the commercially inclined states of New England, with extreme Federalist views, represented Jefferson's embargo policy as a "diabolical scheme . . . to ruin New England's commerce,"[146] and protested violently against the Republican policies. The War of 1812 resulted in the destruction of a large portion of New England trade; so during the war the Massachusetts legislature issued a call for a convention of delegates from the other New England States to meet at Hartford in 1814 "to unite in such measures for our safety as the times demand and the principles of justice and the law of self-preservation will justify."[147] At this time the leaders in that section felt that Great Britain would capture the Mississippi Valley thereby insuring the loss of the agricultural Western States from the Union, and this would in turn of course weaken the South. It was thought that if the states south of the Potomac were sufficiently weakened they would of necessity "cling to those of the North, as the Connecticut vine to the tree which supports it."[148] This convention accepted as constitutional the doctrines of secession and nullification. The ending of the war and the resultant clearing up of the predicted calamities left this move of the Federalists without visible support and administered another great blow to the party which was already slowly dying.[149]

During the War of 1812 the loss of foreign trade and the great demand in this country for manufactured products caused literally thousands of small mills, manufacturing establishments, and other industrial plants to spring up in the

---

sion of first State from Louisiana Purchase as declaring: "It is my deliberate opinion that if this bill passes, the bonds of the Union are virtually dissolved; that the States which oppose it are morally free from their obligations, and that as it will be the right of all, so it will be the duty of some, to prepare definitely for separation."

[146] David S. Muzzey and J. A. Krout, *American History for Colleges*, pp. 156-57.   [147] *Ibid.*, p. 178.

[148] William O. Lynch, *Fifty Years of Party Warfare, 1789-1837*, p. 233.

[149] *Ibid.*, pp. 234-35. See also the discussion in K. C. Babcock, *The Rise of American Nationality, 1811-1819*, pp. 161-67.

East. The factory system was transplanted, through emigration, west of the Alleghenies in the Ohio Valley, thereby tying that section to industrialism. With the end of the war, the accumulated manufactured products of England were immediately dumped on the American market at an exceedingly low market price. Again the New England section, seeing their "infant industries" likely to be submerged in competition with Old World factories, set up a howl for relief. This time, most of the Southern leaders, particularly the younger ones like Clay and Calhoun, wishing to place the Union on a basis of economic independence, supported the Tariff of 1816 which was avowedly protective to the manufacturing interests. John Randolph was one of the few that realized the effect this would have upon the agricultural states. In opposing the nationalizing efforts of Clay and Calhoun he asked, "Upon whom do your impost duties bear? Upon whom bears the duty on coarse woolens and linens and blankets, upon salt, and all the necessaries of life? On poor men, and on slaveholders."[150] McDuffie of South Carolina vainly called attention to the fact that the high duties of this tariff favored the manufacturing interests at the expense of the farmers.[151] Using "internal improvements" as the complement to the protective tariff in his "American System" Clay was looking forward to tying the interests of the Western States with those of the Atlantic seaboard—providing protection against Europe for the manufacturers and at the same time granting a home market and better transportation to the farming group.[152]

Probably the first major sectional conflict growing out of the diverging social and economic interests of North and South came when Missouri applied for admission to the

[150] Henry Adams, *History of the United States*, IX, 113.

[151] Muzzey and Krout, *op. cit.*, p. 185.

[152] See discussion in S. E. Morison, *The Oxford History of the United States*, pp. 319-22.

Union in 1819. The question of admitting an additional state ordinarily would not have provoked a national disturbance, but in this instance it was fraught with underlying economic and political potentialities. Without going into detail it is necessary to consider more freely the vast changes that had been taking place since the War of 1812, to which reference has already been made.[153] From the rocky hills of New England and the soil-exhausted lands of the coastal South poured a continual stream of emigrants into the western territories. So swiftly did the western section grow that five states were added to the Union between 1812 and 1819.[154] The movement was so rapid that many of the Atlantic Seaboard States beheld the specter of gradual depopulation. Both the North and the South considered with anxious eyes the political possibilities to be found in this rising new section. With these new states and the possibility of several others, it could easily be seen that the West might contain the controlling vote necessary for either the North or the South to dictate the policies of the government. Since the election of 1800 and the consequent decline of the Federalist party, the policies of the United States had been determined by Jeffersonian Republicanism. Led by Virginia the South had controlled every national election. Nevertheless, the overbalancing of the population in favor of the North, whose western migrants had been replaced by European immigrants, caused alarm in the South and a minority consciousness which necessitated a tightening of sectional strength and the preservation of Southern equality in the Senate in order to maintain their integrity.[155] Unless the South could retain a position of

[153] See pp. 38-39.

[154] Louisiana (1812), Indiana (1816), Mississippi (1817), Illinois (1818), and Alabama (1819).

[155] In 1789, the population of the North and the South was approximately equal. In 1820 the Free States had 5,152,000 population and 105 members in the House of Representatives; the South had only 4,485,000 population with 81 members in the House. See Morison, *op. cit.*, p. 325.

equality in the Senate, the commercial and industrial section could arbitrarily pursue policies which would favor the manufacturing interests and work to the detriment of the agricultural states. Since 1802 the balance had been maintained by admitting alternately a Free and a Slave State. In 1818 each section controlled eleven states.

Therefore the Missouri struggle presented a possibility of new alignments, if not the origin of new parties. Rufus King, an old time Federalist, having finally decided that it would be impossible to rejuvenate the Federalist party, looked with expectancy to this opportunity of creating a schism in the Republican ranks and annexing one of the factions to the disorganized elements of Federalism.[156] Not only did King look forward to the formation of parties along geographical lines but also to the opportunity of personal leadership which a split over the admittance of Missouri might afford him. Though usually considered as anti-slavery in his opinion, at least the personal motive did not curb his views concerning slavery.[157] As one writer pointed out, King and the Federalist party "looked upon the agitation of the slavery question as the certain means of regaining political power; and so confident were they of success that a son of Rufus King had gone to Ohio and a son of Alexander Hamilton had gone to Illinois to be in position to avail themselves of it."[158] From this viewpoint it would seem that Federalist

[156] See discussion in article "The Black Race in North America," *Southern Literary Messenger*, XXI (November, 1855), 642-43.

[157] Lynch, *op. cit.*, pp. 268-69; also see "The Black Race in North America," *Southern Literary Messenger*, XXI (November, 1855), 642-43; Publicola (pseud.), "The Present Aspects of Abolitionism," *Southern Literary Messenger*, XIII (July, 1847), 430-31.

[158] Duff Green, *Facts and Suggestions Relative to Finance and Currency*, p. 33. It is supposed that Green refers to Edward King, the son of Rufus King who went to Ohio in 1815. He took an active part in politics and was elected to each branch of the Ohio Legislature, serving as Speaker of the House for two sessions. See Appleton's *Cyclopaedia of American Biography*, III, 544. William Stevens Hamilton, a son of Alexander Hamilton, migrated to Illinois where he was appointed

leaders had planned for several years before the Missouri controversy to organize an anti-slavery party in the Northwest. By alienating the interests of the agricultural West from the South, they could exert sectional political influence which would array the North against the South and give the former section a balance of power sufficient to govern both sections.[159] Daniel Pope Cook, on the advice of John Quincy Adams, migrated to Illinois in 1817 with the intention "of becoming a candidate for Congress for the purpose of agitating the slavery question."[160] Cook was successful in this effort for he was elected to Congress and took an active part in the fight for the restriction of slavery in the Missouri Compromise. As a son-in-law of Governor Ninian Edwards, a prominent lawyer and editor of the *Illinois Intelligencer*, he exerted an important influence in Illinois politics.[161] Cook, in his early agitation, published an anti-slavery pamphlet in which he drew "a disparaging picture of Southern society, of the habits, education, and general character of the Southern people; and he boldly declared the right of the slaves to rebel and make war on their masters!"[162]

Probably the best summary of this scheme on the part of the discredited Federalists to agitate slavery for political motives is given by James Williams, former United States minister to Turkey. He states that "It has ever been the aim of the manufacturing interests to enforce, under various pretenses, the payment of a portion of the earnings of the agriculturists into their coffers." For a short time this was done under the popular disguise of "protection of home productions." But as the South came to realize the real effects of the protective tariff this argument in behalf of home industry lost somewhat in popularity. And since the South and West

Surveyor of Public Lands. He later served as Colonel of the Illinois Volunteers in the Black Hawk War.—*Ibid.*, p. 60.

[159] *Ibid.*, p. 33.
[161] *Ibid.*, I, 714.

[160] *Ibid.*, p. 30.
[162] Green, *op. cit.*, p. 32.

were both largely agricultural in 1815 and outnumbered the industrialists, the latter realized the futility of waging a fight upon the direct issue of industrialism and agrarianism. As a result it can be pointed out that "the crusade against slavery, on the part of New England manufacturers, was designed, therefore, *to detach the great agricultural interests of the free States in the West from their natural allies, the Southern States.*" By dividing the opponents of their economic policies, the commercial states hoped to create between the South and the West "an irreconcilable feud upon a collateral issue" in order "to conquer them in detail." Viewing it from this angle the attack upon slavery by the New England group was for the purpose "of making allies and instruments of the agricultural States of the West," rather than from a sincere interest in destroying slavery, while the protective tariff was only a method of dividing "with the planters the earnings of slave labor."[163]

From these facts it is possible to understand better the explosive qualities of the elements underlying the admission of Missouri. The application of Missouri was met on February 13, 1819, by an amendment offered by Representative Talmadge of New York.[164] This amendment, which passed the House but was lost in the Senate, provided that no further slaves should be introduced into Missouri and required that all children subsequently born of slave parents were to be free at the age of twenty-five.[165] Since Congress adjourned without action upon this measure, the sectional issue was transferred to the people, where increasing bitterness and sectional passions were aroused. The notable speech of Rufus King in the Senate was widely circulated as a campaign document. In this the Federalist Senator had argued

---

[163] James Williams, *Letters on Slavery from the Old World*, p. 55. The italics are Williams'.

[164] *Annals*, 15th Cong., 2 sess., I, 1170.

[165] Morison, *op. cit.*, p. 326.

both the constitutionality and the expediency of excluding slavery from new states. In the latter argument he appealed to sectional prejudice by asserting that it was unjust to the North to create new slaveholding states the freemen of which had a relatively greater political representation than did freemen in the Northern States. He evaded the original compromise idea of the Constitution by arguing that the "three-fifths" ratio was applicable only to the original thirteen states. And finally King charged that the exclusion of slavery west of the Mississippi was necessary for the adequate defense of the country against assailants.

The natural result of King's sectional appeal was the creation of a feeling of alarm in the South. Southern leaders recognized the controversy as a struggle for political power between the East and the South. They realized that King's purpose was to break the power of the Southern States by the formation of a new type of Union in which Western States would be "admitted on terms of subordination," thereby aiding in perpetuating the Northern political domination.[166] The uniting of a free majority in the East and West and the restriction of the extension of slavery in the territories were expected to result in consigning the South to a minority position in the new Union.

In the next Congress Alabama was quickly admitted,[167] and the House of Representatives also passed a bill admitting Maine. The Senate, taking advantage of this opportunity for bargaining, combined the Maine bill with one for the unrestricted admission of Missouri. As voting strength was evenly divided in the Senate it looked as though a deadlock might be produced. However, Senator Thomas of Illinois, whose vote could have tied the Senate, proposed a compromise amendment which allowed Missouri to be admitted as a

[166] Frederick J. Turner, *Rise of the New West, 1819-1829*, pp. 157-60.
[167] December, 1819.

Slave State but prohibited slavery from the remainder of the Louisiana Purchase north of latitude 36° 30′.[168]

In this Senate debate Rufus King made another powerful sectional appeal, though his arguments were essentially the same as in the preceding Congress. William Pinkney of Maryland gave the best argument upholding the Southern position. His contentions were based largely on "state sovereignty" and the union of equal states. As each state was to be admitted on a basis of equality with the other members of the Union, then Congress had no right to subject it to special restrictions. If Congress could restrict slavery, then there would be nothing to hinder that legislative body "from plundering power after power at the expense of the new states" which might result in the squeezing of "a new-born sovereign state to the size of a pigmy."[169] In a great burst of oratory he pictured the future Union with some dominant states, others mere shadows of domestic sovereignty, with a resulting sectional overpowering of the minority by the majority.

During this same time the debate in the House increased in bitterness. The issue of slavery flamed brightly though most of the Southern representatives deplored its existence. Representative Reid of Georgia compared the South to the unfortunate man who "wears a cancer in his bosom."[170] It was argued that by spreading the institution of slavery over a wider area many of its evils would be mitigated. John Tyler of Virginia, portraying slavery as a "dark cloud," asked, "Will you permit the lightenings of its wrath to break upon the South when by the interposition of a wise system of legislation you may reduce it to a summer's cloud?"[171] Repre-

---

[168] Turner, *op. cit.*, pp. 160-61; Morison, *op. cit.*, p. 327.

[169] See speech of William Pinkney, *Annals*, 16th Cong., 1 sess., I, 389-417; partially quoted in Turner, *op. cit.*, p. 162.

[170] Representative Reid in *Annals*, 16th Cong., 1 sess., I, 1025.

[171] Speech of John Tyler, *ibid.*, p. 1391; also quoted in Turner, *op. cit.*, p. 163.

sentative Walker of North Carolina stated that "Slavery is an evil we have long deplored but cannot cure"; as the system had been inherited the "original sin" was not on the South. However, slavery being an "evil, the more diffusive, the lighter it will be felt, and wider it is extended the more equal the proportion of inconvenience."[172] The Southerners also urged that it was an injustice to restrict the citizens of the Slave States from migrating with their property to territories secured and owned by the entire Union.

Under the Northern attack, not all of the Southerners were content to deplore slavery and base their contentions upon constitutional rights. Pinckney of South Carolina was aroused in the second Missouri debate to defend the institution of slavery. His defense of the system was largely based on scriptural and social grounds. He condemned the contentions of the Northerners as being contrary to the will of God, for there was not "a single line in the Old and New Testament, either censuring or forbidding" slavery, while, on the other hand, "there are hundreds speaking of and recognizing it."[173] In addition he upheld the system as providing comfortable conditions which were conducive to the welfare and happiness of the slaves. Speaking of this he stated that "the great body of slaves are happier in their present condition than they could be in any other," and those attempting to grant them liberty "would be their greatest enemies."[174] As the sectional differences involved in this controversy became more apparent and as the verbal attacks aroused bitterness, we find threats of secession being exchanged and even leaders like Clay expecting to see new confederacies organized.[175]

[172] Representative Walker, *Annals,* 15th Cong., 2 sess., II, 1227.

[173] *Ibid.,* 16th Cong., 1 sess., II, 1324-25.

[174] *Ibid.*

[175] Turner, *op. cit.,* p. 164. Senator James Barbour of Virginia canvassed the Free State Senators concerning the possibility of dissolving the Union. Clay threatened to raise troops in Kentucky to defend the rights of Missouri. See Allan Nevins (editor), *The Diary of John Quincy Adams, 1794-1845,* pp. 227,

However, when the Senate's compromise proposal came to a vote in the House, the Southern representatives stood firm and by securing a few votes from Northern ranks were able to defeat the restrictionists' measure.[176] With the signing of the measure by President Monroe, it was thought that the controversy which threatened to split the Union was at least temporarily settled. Perhaps some even thought the question was permanently settled. However, this was not true of the leaders. During the entire contest Rufus King was primarily concerned with the political possibilities in the controversy. He firmly believed that the Missouri struggle would settle "forever the dominion of the Union."[177] Inasmuch as the compromise in 1821 did not actually settle the issue of political domination, it was necessary for the New England Federalists to prepare carefully for greater agitation, a more violent attack upon Southern institutions in order to discredit the South in the sight of the new Western States. In doing so, new party alignments would be created and the government could be dominated for the benefit of the commercial and industrial interests. Jefferson wrote that the settlement of the Missouri question by compromise was "a reprieve only, not a final sentence. A geographical line, coinciding with a marked principle, moral and political, once conceived and held up to the angry passions of men, will never be obliterated; and every new irritation will mark it deeper and deeper."[178] And John Quincy Adams thoughtfully confided to his diary that the question was but the "title page to a great tragic volume."[179]

Today the Missouri struggle may be viewed as the first skirmish, at most an early battle, in the lengthy campaign of

233; Everett Somerville Brown (editor), *The Missouri Compromises and Presidential Politics, 1820-1825*, pp. 11-14; also see Glover Moore, "Missouri Compromise Controversy" (unpublished thesis, Vanderbilt University).

[176] For the influence of Clay in carrying through the Compromise see Lynch, *op. cit.*, pp. 271-73.

[177] Turner, *op. cit.*, p. 173.

[178] *Ibid.*, p. 169.

[179] *Ibid.*

the commercial and manufacturing interests to secure political domination of the government for sectional aggrandizement. During the succeeding decade, leaders in both the North and the South realized the momentous importance of the issues involved and gradually began to consolidate their positions, to develop political philosophies in accord with their views, and to look to the future without knowing in what new forms the sectional issues might appear. The mass of people, however, did not realize the real significance of the struggle, if indeed they realized at all that the slavery issue would be again thrust to the front in the next decade. As already pointed out, anti-slavery sentiment continued to exist in the South and many schemes for gradual emancipation and colonization of the freed blacks received the support of the slaveholders from 1821 to 1831. Southern people continued their agricultural pursuits with the inherited system of slave labor not knowing that they would be subject to violent de-nunciation on the part of the "New Abolitionists" after 1831.

Chapter II

THE EXTREME ABOLITIONIST ATTACK

WITH the first issue of the *Liberator* on January 1, 1831, a new leader and a new theory appeared for those abolitionists, particularly in New England, who viewed slavery from an extreme, radical point of view. The editor, William Lloyd Garrison, had but recently toured the United States and "found contempt more bitter, opposition more active, detraction more relentless, prejudice more stubborn, and apathy more frozen" in New England concerning the institution than among the slaveholders themselves. From "the birthplace of liberty" he determined to attack the system of slavery until "every chain be broken, and every bondman set free!" Disregarding the views of others as well as their constitutional rights, Garrison declared: "Let Southern oppressors tremble—let their secret abettors tremble—let their Northern apologists tremble—let all the enemies of the persecuted blacks tremble," for the new leader had determined to be "as harsh as truth, and as uncompromising as justice." Avowing that he did "not wish to think, or speak, or write, with moderation" on such an urgent question, he concluded his salutatory address to the public with the oft-quoted warning that "I am in earnest—I will not equivocate—I will not excuse—I will not retreat a single inch—AND I WILL BE HEARD."[1]

Thus Garrison led the way to a new extreme on the left wing of anti-slavery tactics. Prior to this time Garrison had been a disciple of the well-known emancipationist and pub-

---

[1] The *Liberator*, I (January 1, 1831), 1, capitalization Garrison's, quoted in Garrisons, *op. cit.*, I, 224-25. See William Lloyd Garrison, *Selections from the Writings and Speeches of William Lloyd Garrison*, pp. 62-63.

lisher, Benjamin Lundy. The latter, a son of New Jersey Quakers, had in his youth become intensely interested in the possibility of ameliorating slave conditions in the South. As early as 1815, Lundy organized the Union Humane Society at St. Clairsville, Ohio, and a short time later aided Charles Osborne[2] in establishing the *Philanthropist* at Mt. Pleasant, Ohio. Lundy was in Missouri during the height of the controversy over the admission of that territory as a state, and while there he wrote many newspaper articles upon the evils of slavery. Returning to Ohio in 1820, he established in January, 1821, his own anti-slavery publication, known as the *Genius of Universal Emancipation*. Within a short time, Lundy was invited to Jonesborough, Tennessee, for the purpose of continuing the publication of the *Genius* in that locality. In doing so, Lundy stepped into the vacancy created by the death of Elihu Embree,[3] the editor of probably the earliest paper devoted exclusively to emancipation. Though Lundy found in Jonesborough a congenial atmosphere for the cause of emancipation, he moved his publication to Baltimore in 1824, with the hope of extending its influence. Lundy did not expect to secure the immediate abolition of slavery for he realized the racial problem involved in the free Negro element. In reality, he was deeply interested in colonizing the freed slaves. Negotiating with the governor

[2] Charles Osborne had previously been, with John Rankin, a leader in the organization of the Manumission Society of Tennessee. In 1835 Birney established an anti-slavery paper which also bore the name *Philanthropist*. It was published in Cincinnati. See sketch of Elihu Embree by Robert H. White in B. H. Murphy's reprint of *The Emancipator* (Nashville, Tenn., 1932), p. vii.

[3] *Ibid.*, pp. v-xi; Elihu Embree, born in Tennessee in 1782, was an iron manufacturer in East Tennessee. Though a slaveholder, Embree, after joining the Society of Friends in 1812, came to "a deep seated conviction that slavery was inhuman and morally wrong," aligned himself with the Manumission Society of Tennessee and became "the chief proponent of anti-slavery sentiment in East Tennessee." In 1819 he established at Jonesborough the *Manumission Intelligencer*, a weekly abolition newspaper. This was followed in April, 1820, by a monthly publication, *The Emancipator*. His death on Dec. 4, 1820, cut short publication of the latter, though Lundy's *Genius* might be called a successor. Embree's slaves were freed by his will. See Elijah Embree Hoss, *Elihu Embree, Abolitionist*.

of Hayti in 1825, he arranged for the settlement of emancipated blacks on the island of Hayti.[4] During the period
from 1820-1830, Lundy travelled over 5,000 miles on foot
and 20,000 by other means, visited nineteen states, made two
voyages to Hayti, and held over two hundred public meetings in the interest of emancipation.[5] Later he made at least
three journeys to Mexico and one to Canada in an attempt to
secure lands where emancipated slaves could be colonized.[6]
While in Boston in 1829 Lundy boarded at the same place
where young Garrison stayed. The latter was uninterested in
slavery at that time but later in the year he joined Lundy
in the editorship of the *Genius*, and Lundy set out on a
lecture tour. However, Garrison became entirely too radical,
was imprisoned, and Lundy returned to find that some articles had been printed which, to say the least, "did not entirely
meet" with his "approbation."[7] From their writings it can
readily be seen that Benjamin Lundy was an emancipationist
and colonizationist while Garrison was an outright abolitionist. Although realizing that the South was more interested in emancipation than the North, Garrison began his
agitation in the latter section and, instead of gratefully using
the favorable Southern sentiment, he soon stamped it out by
denunciation. This was in marked contrast to the example of
Lundy, who had exerted his greatest energies toward emancipation among the Slave States and from them received his
greatest support until the Garrisonian attack.[8]

[4] In 1828 he sent 88 slaves emancipated in Virginia and 119 from North
Carolina to Hayti. Another group was sent from Maryland in 1829. Thomas
Earle, *The Life, Travels, and Opinions of Benjamin Lundy*, p. 29.

[5] *Ibid.*, p. 240.   [6] *Ibid., passim.*

[7] *Ibid.*, pp. 29, 238. The imprisonment of Garrison occurred after his conviction for libel due to his denunciation of Francis Todd, a slave trader of Massachusetts.—Jesse Macy, *The Anti-Slavery Crusade*, p. 31.

[8] It might be pointed out that Lundy was in Mexico trying to secure a grant
of land for Negro colonization purposes during the early years of the attack of
the New Abolitionists. Upon his return in 1835, Lundy's later work was of
necessity, due to unfavorable reaction to the Garrisonian group in the South,
carried on in the North. In 1836 Lundy began the *National Enquirer* in Phil-

Garrison's uncompromising, partisan, sectional attitude has caused him to stand out as the foremost advocate of "New Abolitionism," the founder of a new sect.[9] Without perspective or sense of proportion, lacking a knowledge of the South and the problems revolving around slavery, Garrison led the abolition propagandists in their early efforts to discredit the Slave States. He assailed the system of slavery with such vituperation that the most humane slaveholders, when judged by his prejudiced and distorted description, took forms as terrible as the monsters of Greek mythology—cruel tyrants, murderers, thieves, and criminals. His uncompromising attitude was admirably expressed when he wrote that he considered it no part of his duty as editor, "to prove that the holding of slaves is criminal." Instead he took it for granted that the institution of slavery was "a crime—a damning crime" and therefore determined to direct his entire efforts "to the exposure of those who practise it." Without considering any possible errors or exaggerations he stated that "I retract nothing—I blot out nothing. My language is exactly such as suits me; it will displease many, I know—to displease them is my intention."[10]

Denunciation being his chief weapon, Garrison became even more fanatical as subsequent volumes of the *Liberator* appeared and were sent forth upon their deleterious mission. He was so zealous in his fanaticism that it became his religion; he spoke of himself and his followers as "soldiers of God," their "loins girt about with truth," while their feet were "shod with the preparation of the gospel of peace." A person would find that all without his "kingdom of God . . .

---

adelphia. This was taken over the following year by the Pennsylvania Anti-Slavery Society. Lundy moved to Illinois in 1838, and published irregularly the *Genius of Universal Emancipation* at Hennepin, Ill., and at Lowell. He died on Aug. 21, 1839.

[9] Herbert, *op. cit.*, p. 56.   [10] Garrisons, *op. cit.*, I, 227.

are dogs, and sorcerers, and whoremongers, and murderers, and idolators."[11]

Garrison's genius for organization soon rallied the supporters of the new sect in the East. These at first called themselves the "New Abolitionists,"[12] but were organized in 1832 as the New England Anti-Slavery Society. From this group many local societies were formed, and in December, 1833, in order to concentrate the agitation of the entire country, the New England group and the New York group led by the Tappans organized the American Anti-Slavery Society.[13] The object of the Society was the complete abolition of the institution of slavery in the United States. Its aim was to convince everyone that "slaveholding is a heinous crime in the sight of God, and that the duty, safety, and best interest of all concerned, require its immediate abandonment, without expatriation."[14]

Without waiting to perfect a complete organization, the delegates to the 1833 Anti-Slavery Convention immediately began their attack upon the slaveholders. The *Declaration of Sentiments* as well as the *Constitution* of the new organization plainly stated many charges against the South and these formed the basis for much of the later propaganda.[15] From the beginning the group showed a decided disrespect for the Constitution and laws of the United States, for they main-

[11] *Ibid.*, II, 202. See *ibid.*, p. 199, for the occasion for this manifesto.
[12] Herbert, *op. cit.*, pp. 58-59.   [13] Hart, *op. cit.*, pp. 183-84.
[14] Article II of the Constitution of the American Anti-Slavery Society. Quoted from *The Declaration of Sentiments and Constitution on the American Anti-Slavery Society*, drafted at Philadelphia on Dec. 6, 1833. Hereafter cited as *Declaration of Sentiments*.
[15] *Ibid.*, pp. 6-9; also see J. Mark Jacobson, *The Development of American Political Thought, A Documentary History*, p. 352. Some of the charges were that the slaves were treated "as marketable commodities, as goods and chattels, as brute beasts" who, without legal protection, were "plundered daily of the fruits of their toil." Also that the slaves were subjected to "licentious and murderous outrages"; often "ruthlessly torn asunder—the tender babe from the arms of its frantic mother —the broken-hearted wife from her weeping husband," all at the pleasure of "irresponsible tyrants."

tained that any law which admitted the right of slavery was "utterly null and void . . . and . . . therefore ought to be instantly abrogated."[16] Assuming that "SLAVERY IS A CRIME" and that a slave was "NOT AN ARTICLE TO BE SOLD," the American Anti-Slavery Society refused to consider any plan of emancipation which would grant the slightest compensation to the slaveowners.[17] In maintaining this premise, they denied to Southern planters the right which the fathers of the New England abolitionists had had in disposing of their slaves—the right of at least partial, if not full, compensation to prevent sustaining a severe financial loss on the property.[18]

Also, in their extreme views the abolitionists struck at the willingness of many Southern people to abolish slavery on condition that the freed blacks be removed, by regarding as "delusive, cruel and dangerous any scheme of expatriation" pretending to aid "in the emancipation of slaves," or in any way offering "a substitute for the immediate and total abolition of slavery."[19] The improvidence and criminality of freed blacks had caused many Southerners to hesitate before accepting plans for emancipation, and the desire for the removal of freed Negroes secured much Southern support for the Colonization Society. But the radical group of abolitionists offered continuous opposition to the colonizationists and this, of course, hampered the constructive work of the society.

As a means of accomplishing their aims and purposes, the abolitionists decided, in addition to the organization of auxiliary societies, to "send forth agents to lift up the voice of

[16] *Declaration of Sentiments*, pp. 8-9.

[17] *Ibid.*, p. 9. Capitalization in original.

[18] When slavery proved unprofitable in New England, many slaves were sold to Southern slaveholders. This was possible through a system of gradual emancipation over a period of years. Still others received compensation for freeing slaves. Because of the small number of slaves, and the method of disposing of them, the loss to Northern slaveholders was negligible. See Chapter I above.

[19] *Declaration of Sentiments*, pp. 8-9.

remonstrance, of warning, of entreaty, and of rebuke." The work of the agents was to be supplemented by the extensive circulation of "anti-slavery tracts and periodicals," by enlisting the "pulpit and the press" in the cause of freedom, by encouraging free labor, by attempting the "purification of the churches," and finally by sparing "no exertions nor means to bring the whole nation to speedy repentance."[20] The American Anti-Slavery Society became an important organ in spreading the propaganda of the abolitionists. The success of their agitators is shown by the rapid increase of local societies throughout the East. In 1835, there were 200; a year later more than 500; and by 1840, about 2,000 auxiliary societies had been formed, representing between 150,000 and 200,000 members.[21]

It was as organizer and agent for the American Anti-Slavery Society that Theodore Weld rapidly climbed to the leadership of the radical abolition movement.[22] Weld was a convert of Charles Grandison Finney, one of the greatest evangelists of the nineteenth century. With Finney and his "Holy Band" of evangelists Weld helped set the West on fire with religious fervor in the late twenties and early thirties.[23] Under the influence of Charles Stuart, a former British subject, Weld became a convert to "immediate" abolitionism in 1830,[24] and soon carried with him the leading young ministers who had been converted under Finney's evangelism. Weld, and to a great extent those who made up the "western abolitionists," though preaching in essence the same doctrine as that of Weld, for some years maintained a less violent tone than Garrison. In fact, their attitude was one of Christians attempting to convert the heathen—one of

[20] Ibid., p. 9; Jacobson, op. cit., p. 354; Garrison, op. cit., pp. 66-71.
[21] Hart, op. cit., p. 184. The income of the society also rose from $1,000 in 1834 to $47,000 in 1840. Also see Rhodes, op. cit., I, 59.
[22] Weld-Grimké Letters, I, 124-25.
[23] Gilbert H. Barnes, The Antislavery Impulse, pp. 12-13. Also Weld-Grimké Letters, Vol. I, passim.   [24] Barnes, op. cit., p. 33.

persuasion rather than denunciation.[25] As the movement grew and met with violent opposition, the Weld abolitionists, under the patronage of Arthur and Lewis Tappan of New York,[26] lost its tone of Christian charity. Invective replaced pleading, and such men as George Bourne who affiliated more closely with the Weld-Tappan-Grimké wing than with the Garrisonians reached new heights of denunciation. Weld was essentially the evangelist in method and the orator in temperament so that he committed very little to paper until many years later. It was he and not Garrison who was the greater organizer of the anti-slavery societies. From the central office in New York, under the control of Arthur Tappan, came the abolition petitions which Weld and his fellow agents of the American Anti-Slavery Society carried throughout the middle and western states during the famous congressional fight over the "gag rule."[27]

Barnes shows in a convincing fashion that the Tappan-Weld group were the real heads of the abolition crusade[28] and that hundreds and even thousands of abolition societies were under their control rather than that of Garrison. Finally, and contrary to tradition, Weld took an active and decisive part in politics.[29] Many of the Weld-Tappan abolitionists became political abolitionists.

The rapid growth of abolition sentiment in the North during this period was only a part of a larger movement which was sweeping over that section. Humanitarianism, idealism, and transcendentalism dominated the philosophy of the time and many idealistic religious or social reforms with strange doctrines found large numbers of adherents.

[25] *Ibid., passim.* Also *Weld-Grimké Letters, passim.*
[26] *Ibid.,* letters from Weld to Tappan and Tappan to Weld.
[27] Barnes, *op. cit.,* pp. 80-86, 94, 104-5, 107, 155.
[28] *Ibid., passim.*
[29] *Ibid.,* pp. 107, 134, 139, 177, 180-81, 183, 191-95; *Weld-Grimké Letters,* I, 175-76, petition to Congress written by Weld and II, 879-938, letters written by and to Weld while he was in Washington lobbying.

Abolitionism found its place among the other radical "isms" of the period, and these movements were in turn aided by the efforts of leading abolitionists like Garrison, Foster, Weld, the Grimké sisters, and others. At a somewhat later date the tendency of different abolitionists actively to sponsor women's rights, prohibition, anarchism, free-love, peace movements, and other characteristic schemes of the period created divisions within the anti-slavery ranks.[30] Socialistic and communistic ideas received favorable support in the North and were tried for a time in such experiments as those of Brook Farm and Icaria.[31] A similar experiment directly connected with emancipation had previously been attempted by New Englanders at the Nashoba Colony established in West Tennessee. This experiment included both whites and a few emancipated blacks, and was founded for the purpose of testing the "efficacy of the community system, as applicable to the promotion of emancipation and the improvement of the emancipated."[32] Frances Wright, a militant feminist and a leader in the colony, advocated an amalgamation of the races, which, of course, was offensive to the Southern whites.[33]

Religious sects like the Mormons and Millerites had many converts during this period. In the thirties the movement for women's rights also received a good start,[34] and was quickly allied with the drive for abolition. Lucretia Mott, a minister of the Society of Friends, took part in the proceedings of the American Anti-Slavery Convention in Philadelphia in 1833. Many of the Anti-Slavery Societies gradually

[30] *Ibid.*, I, 427-70. The Grimké sisters favored women's rights and Weld was opposed to bringing up the issue at this time.

[31] Merriam, *op. cit.*, pp. 216-17.

[32] Earle, *op. cit.*, p. 200, cites *Genius of Universal Emancipation*, Feb. 11, 1826. The colony was called "The Emancipating Labour Society of Shelby County, Tennessee," and ultimately proved a failure. The blacks were sent to Hayti.

[33] For an excellent discussion of the Nashoba experiment see Edd Winfield Parks, "Dreamer's Vision—Frances Wright at Nashoba, 1825-1830," *Tennessee Historical Magazine*, Ser. II, II (January, 1932), 75-86.

[34] Hart, *op. cit.*, pp. 15-16.

accepted women into active membership while a few separate women's organizations were formed.[35] Angelina and Sarah Grimké, as early agitators and speakers, had published a number of appeals to the women concerning slavery.[36] Lydia Maria Child became very active as an anti-slavery propagandist, while foreigners like Fanny Kemble and Fredrika Bremer "inflamed public opinion" by their indictment of slavery.[37] Probably the women leaders felt that their demands for political equality[38] would be greatly aided by the agitation of the slavery question. In joining their cause with that of abolition, it seems quite probable that the feminists expected the granting of their demands at the same time the Negroes were emancipated and given political rights.

It may be concluded that in the period of the thirties the environment of the North was conducive to the birth and development of various reforms, crusades, fanatical doctrines, and peculiar religious beliefs, many of which were entirely unpracticable and destined to a short life, but all of which were urged by their followers with an enthusiastic zeal and devotion which today seems both remarkable and pathetic. As one writer points out, the growth of abolitionism was "only one part of a great current of liberal and humanitarian

---

[35] Examples of separate women's organizations may be found in the Boston Female Anti-Slavery Society; the Female Anti-Slavery Society of Chatham Street Chapel (New York); and the Anti-Slavery Convention of American Women, first held in New York in May, 1837.

[36] Hart, op. cit., p. 179. For examples of their anti-slavery publications see Angelina Emily Grimké, Letters to Catherine E. Beecher, in Reply to an Essay on Slavery and Abolitionism (Boston, 1838), and Appeal to the Christian Women of the South (New York, 1836); Catherine H. Birney, The Grimké Sisters; Sarah and Angelina Grimké, the first American Women Advocates of Abolition and Woman's Rights (Boston, 1885); and Weld-Grimké Letters, I, 427-67.

[37] Hart, op. cit., p. 198. See Frances Anne Kemble, Journal of a Residence on a Georgia Plantation, 1838-1839; Fredrika Bremer, Homes of the New World. For an excellent biography of Frances Kemble see Leota Driver, Fanny Kemble.

[38] Hart, op. cit., p. 16, points out that they demanded woman suffrage in 1848. Also see Harriet Martineau, Society in America, Vol. II, Chap. IV, for a discussion of the reform movements.

sentiment that was sweeping over the country."[39] The merging of the anti-slavery agitation in many instances with the women's rights, temperance, religious revivals, world peace, and other movements causes the real significance of the former to be difficult at times to understand. The political undercurrent back of the anti-slavery agitation complicates the study and obscures the view still further.

It is well at this point to classify the larger groups of anti-slavery propagandists in order to distinguish certain characteristic methods and viewpoints. Because of the human element involved it is extremely difficult to do more than merely make a few broad generalizations concerning the various schools of anti-slavery thought. Certain active agitators supported the ideas of more than one group, while others changed their methods almost periodically. Many arrived at the same conclusions from entirely different lines of reasoning. Nevertheless, it seems that the anti-slavery propagandists may be classified under three general divisions. These schools of anti-slavery thought may be described as philosophical, political, and radical. Common to all was their consideration of slavery as an evil. All desired to attack slavery and to discredit the South but their methods and purposes were often quite different. The radical element, led by Garrison in the East and Theodore Weld in the West, to a great extent made possible the development of the other groups. The Garrisonian and Weld groups began the violent agitation which so aroused the South. It might be said that the radicals stirred up the agitation, the philosophical group attempted to place moral approval upon it, while the political abolitionists reaped the rewards after nearly thirty years of propaganda. Because the attack of the radicals led to reaction and later defense from the South and at the same time exerted a vast influence toward changing public opinion in the

[39] Merriam, *op. cit.*, p. 217.

North, considerable attention must be paid to the system of propaganda which they employed. But before describing the radical attack it will be well to summarize briefly the views of the other two schools of anti-slavery thought.

The philosophical abolitionists, led by scholars like William Ellery Channing and Francis Wayland, attacked slavery as an evil *per se*.[40] The arguments of this group were based upon a premise that man was a "Rational, Moral, Immortal Being," who inherently possessed certain natural rights.[41] From this viewpoint they attempted to show that slavery violated the rights necessary to moral beings and was therefore evil. In reality the philosophical abolitionists looked upon Southern slavery in the same way as they might have looked upon the enslavement of one white man by another.[42] Their theories were based upon the rights of all moral beings without regard for mental or physical disparities of the individuals; nor did they take into consideration the difference in the scale of civilization between the African and the Caucasian. Channing had early developed an abhorrence of slavery and in his essay on *Slavery* made a very thorough attack upon the ethical foundations of that institution. However, he had at first practically no sympathy with the radical group of abolitionists and felt that the solution of the slavery problem must come from the South.[43] Francis Wayland, like Dr. Channing, looked upon man as a moral being having certain rights and powers. In discussing the possible violations of liberties, Dr. Wayland pointed out that the "most common violation of personal liberty" by individuals existed in the

[40] *Ibid.*, pp. 217-21, gives a good summary of the theories of this group. Also see Jacobson, *op. cit.*, pp. 329, 335-41.

[41] See selection on "Slavery" from the *Works of William E. Channing*, reprinted in Jacobson, *op. cit.*, pp. 355-66. Channing's book on *Slavery* was published in Boston in 1835.

[42] This was the light in which many English abolitionists viewed slavery and was characteristic of groups that observed the workings of the institution from afar.   [43] Jacobson, *op. cit.*, p. 354.

"case of *Domestic Slavery*."[44] Wayland came to the same general conclusion as Channing but by a somewhat different route. His work on *The Elements of Moral Science* was, in reality, a text of philosophy and ethics, with the condemnation of slavery merely incidental to his treatment of moral philosophy.[45] Wayland was a Baptist minister, a leader in the church and president of Brown University for twenty years, while Channing was a Congregational minister and a leader of the Unitarian element of that Church. The two of them were the representative leaders of the philosophical abolitionists, and influenced greatly some of the leading educators and clergymen of the North. In fact these two men probably supplied many of the fundamental arguments of the propagandists among the radical and political abolitionists. However, it does not seem likely that the philosophical group exerted much influence upon the mass of people in the North. Nor did their arguments arouse a determined defense from the South, though several Southern scholars replied to the theories of Wayland and Channing.[46] In general, it might be said that insofar as the Southern people were concerned, only the radicals represented true anti-slavery opinion in the North.

It is quite difficult to separate the radical and political groups of anti-slavery leaders. Both were violent in their denunciation of slavery and the South. Their attacks were personal and specific rather than abstract theories. Both concentrated upon a Northern sectional appeal rather than offering to aid the South. Within the political division could be found all types of anti-slavery sentiment from the most conservative free-soiler to militant agitators of immediate abolition. In a general way, it might be concluded that the

[44] *Ibid.*, p. 373. Italics Wayland's.
[45] See sketch of life in Jacobson, *op. cit.*, p. 366.
[46] For examples see John Fletcher, *Studies on Slavery, in Easy Lessons;* Albert Taylor Bledsoe, *An Essay on Liberty and Slavery.*

political anti-slavery groups were largely represented by the development of the free-soil doctrine. This appealed to many people living in the Northwest and was inspired more from sectional economic motives than from a humanitarian desire to aid the Negro. For the most part, the politically-minded anti-slavery leaders did not allow themselves to be carried away by fanaticism. Basically a great many of them were as radical and violent as the Garrisonian abolitionists but they differed on the method of accomplishing their aims. As has been suggested, many of the leaders of the political group of the forties had been followers of Weld in the thirties.

Garrison or Weld might have continued to be the leader of both factions but for two reasons. First, in turning to other reformist doctrines of the period, such as the feminist movement, temperance, perfectionist theories, and others, Garrison in particular alienated many of his supporters who felt that the abolition issue had been submerged and obscured under other reforms. Garrison's insistence that all abolitionists should accept these other reforms as part of their program did not meet with the approval of many abolitionists, particularly those in the middle and northwestern states where Theodore Weld was so strong.[47] In the second place, Garrison's condemnation of the Constitution and his refusal to take part in the attempts to secure control of the government as a means of accomplishing emancipation conflicted with the aims of the political abolitionists. In 1839 an attempt was made to overthrow Garrison's leadership in the American Anti-Slavery Society. The attempt failed and both groups prepared for a contest in the next convention in 1840. By packing the Convention with his supporters, Garrison was able to retain nominal control.[48] But the failure of this attempt led to division and the formation of a new organization

[47] Hart, *op. cit.*, p. 200.
[48] *Ibid.*, pp. 200-1; also see discussion in Garrisons, *op. cit.*, III, 35.

known as the American and Foreign Anti-Slavery Society, largely controlled by Arthur and Lewis Tappan.

The new society was modeled on the British and Foreign Anti-Slavery Society of England and received considerable support from English abolitionists.[49] Within a few years the newly organized society, controlled by the political abolitionists, far outstripped the parent organization in both numbers and influence. The activities of the Garrisonian organization were curbed considerably by an immediate drop of its annual income to approximately one-seventh of what it had been the preceding year. For the next fifteen years the yearly income failed to go over $12,000.[50] The local societies, which had increased up until 1840, rapidly declined after the division of the two factions. Considering these facts, it will be of value to point out some of the features of Garrisonian fanaticism which led to his losing control of the main body of abolitionists.

Because the federal government did not immediately put an end to slavery and continued to aid the institution through the enforcement of the fugitive slave acts, the fanaticism of the Garrisonian group took the form of a denunciation of all governments. Garrison and J. H. Noyes became champions of a "non-resistance" or "no-government theory." An organized expression of this sentiment may be found in the New England Non-Resistance Society which advocated in 1838 that its members should not "acknowledge allegiance to any human government."[51] The members of this group proposed a sort of passive resistance which would not employ physical coercion either for or against their fellow men, which would not invoke the aid of judicial tribunals, and which in

[49] See evidences of the connection between anti-slavery leaders in England and America in the Tappan letters, published in Lewis Tappan, et al., A Side-Light on Anglo-American Relations, 1839-1858 (eds., A. H. Abel and F. J. Klingberg).

[50] See Hart, op. cit., p. 201. After the split the annual income of the American Anti-Slavery Society immediately dropped from $47,000 to $7,000.

[51] Merriam, op. cit., p. 210.

politics would refuse either to vote or to hold public office.[52] This theory was popular with socialistic organizations[53] and found religious support in the perfectionist movement, but it was not necessarily in favor among the politicians of the time. Many of the abolitionist leaders might be described as philosophical anarchists.

This same antagonism toward all forms of government was manifested by the Garrisonian group of abolitionists in their turning upon the American Constitution and in their disregard of all laws and common ties that bound the Union of the states together. By 1837 the American Anti-Slavery Society had adopted resolutions to the effect that "all those laws . . . admitting the right of slavery are, before God, NULL AND VOID."[54] For an official motto, the Society adopted the slogan of "No Union with Slaveholders."[55] The Ohio American Anti-Slavery Society in a series of resolutions condemned the framers of the Constitution as "base hypocrites" and advocated that their membership should not give that document either "sanction or allegiance" or uphold it by serving in public office or casting a vote.[56] The *Liberty Bell*, an abolitionist publication, after condemning the Union as an "atrocious compromise," a "libel on Democracy," which was "stained with human blood," rang out the imprecation "Accursed be the American Union."[57] The Indiana State Anti-Slavery Society advocated the "immediate abrogation of

[52] *Ibid.*, pp. 209-10.

[53] See J. H. Noyes, *History of American Socialism, passim.*

[54] Originally expressed in the Declaration of the American Anti-Slavery Convention of 1835, as quoted in *The South Vindicated from the Treason and Fanaticism of the Northern Abolitionists* (Philadelphia, 1836), p. 185; also quoted by A. J. Beveridge, *Abraham Lincoln, 1809-1858,* II, 28.

[55] *Ibid.* This motto appeared often in the *Liberator,* the *Anti-Slavery Bugle,* and other radical organs. The *Bugle* was the only paper west of the mountains to carry this slogan. *Anti-Slavery Bugle,* July 25, 1845.

[56] Resolutions of the Ohio American Anti-Slavery Society, quoted in the *Anti-Slavery Bugle,* June 20, 1845, p. 2.

[57] *Liberty Bell* (Boston, 1845); also in Beveridge, *op. cit.,* II, 28.

the Union"[58] in 1845, while the Southwestern Anti-Slavery Society favored severing connections "with the oppressor both in Church and in State," and occupying a firm stand on "No Union with Slaveholders."[59] The *Liberator* was a leader in this fanaticism, for in every issue of that incendiary publication Garrison, under the caption "The American Union," printed in large capitals the challenge: "YOUR COVENANT WITH DEATH SHALL BE ANNULLED AND YOUR AGREEMENT WITH HELL SHALL NOT STAND."[60]

In the forties and the fifties, many leading abolitionists among both the radical and political factions openly advocated the nullification of federal laws, the overthrow of the Constitution, and the dissolution of the Union. Much earlier a Garrisonian radical had lamented the fact that slavery could not be abolished because the legislative, judicial, and executive departments of the government were filled with *"perjured men-stealers."*[61] Another condemned the American people and their government for turning the "national capital" into a "human flesh-mart," and electing a "slave-breeder" as "chief magistrate."[62] Edmund Quincy in 1846 wrote that the only hope for either the slave or the free lay in "THE ABROGATION OF THE PRESENT PRO-SLAVERY CONSTITUTION, AND THE DISSOLUTION OF THE EXISTING SLAVEHOLDING UNION."[63] Henry C. Wright considered it his Christian

[58] Meeting of the Indiana Anti-Slavery Society held at Newport, Ind., Oct. 13, 1845, reported in the *Anti-Slavery Bugle*, Nov. 21, 1845, p. 1.

[59] The Southwestern Anti-Slavery Society (composed of Southern Ohio and Eastern Indiana) meeting in Cincinnati, Ohio, on Nov. 18, 1845, reported in the *Anti-Slavery Bugle*, Dec. 19, 1845, p. 2.   [60] Beveridge, *op. cit.*, II, 28.

[61] George Bourne, *Slavery Illustrated in its Effects upon Women and Domestic Society*, p. 19.

[62] S. S. Foster, *The Brotherhood of Thieves; or, A True Picture of the American Church and Clergy*, p. 3.

[63] Edmund Quincy of Dedham, Mass., in letter of Nov. 12, 1846, to Gerrit Smith. Capitalization Quincy's.

duty "to array the world against American Slavery, the American Church, and the American Republic, as the deadly foes of God and Man."[64] In 1857, Wendell Phillips expressed the general view of the radical abolitionists when he avowed "that this is a revolution" and "there is no Constitution left." He added that "the North must be educated to the consciousness that she must trample law under foot." Growing more enthusiastic, Phillips advocated that the state of Massachusetts nullify federal legislation by placing on her statute books the statement: "I will obey no slave law." This being done, he asserted that the next step would be to make the soil of Massachusetts so "hot that a slaveholder would sooner go down to his birthplace" in hell than to come to Massachusetts.[65] With various leaders taking such an extreme view it seemed inevitable that the anti-slavery ranks should be split in numerous factions as the lesser satellites followed their favorite abolitionist on one tangent or another.

Nor were the political abolitionists any less violent in their denunciation of the South. The charges of both factions became increasingly violent throughout the slavery controversy. Certain types of arguments used by the radicals were emphasized effectively by the political abolitionists. The argument that slavery was irreconcilable with American institutions is an example.[66] This was based largely on the equalitarian doctrine as enunciated by the Declaration of Independence. It was charged that slavery produced a ruling caste, a minority group of large slaveholders, who, through the constitutional provision for counting three-fifths of the slaves in computing the basis of congressional representation, controlled the destinies of the South and the nation.[67] It was

[64] Letter from Henry C. Wright to Garrison, quoted in the *Anti-Slavery Bugle*, Jan. 2, 1846, p. 1.
[65] Wendell Phillips' speech in New York in 1857, quoted in *DeBow's Review*, XXII (June, 1857), 665.   [66] See discussion in Beveridge, *op. cit.*, II, 21.
[67] *Ibid.* D. R. Hundley, *Social Relations in Our Southern States*, pp. 68-69,

asserted that this oligarchy, the "Slave Power," though composing only about one-thirtieth of the population, controlled the wealth of the country, while the remainder of the people were crushed and consequently consigned to poverty and ignorance.[68] It was described as a society so constituted that the political power necessarily resided in the group that contained the wealth, knowledge, and intelligence—"the small minority for whose exclusive benefit the system exists."[69] The abolitionists charged that this "satanic" group, "supported by the labor of four millions of slaves," ruled a population of five millions of whites, and a condition of society "more formidable for evil, more menacing to the best interests of the human race, it is difficult to perceive."[70] While these charges were not stressed by the radicals, they were turned into a potent and effective appeal by the political abolitionists.

The reputed oligarchical effect of slavery struck a responsive chord in the minds of those imbued with the frontier democracy of the Northwest. The political propaganda that the "Slave Power" was aggressively attempting to force the system of slavery upon the territories aroused the Northerners who looked forward to the possibility of migrating westward. Many who lacked a humanitarian desire to aid the Negro were greatly concerned over the possibility of economic competition with the slave. All of the charges of the radical abolitionists against the oligarchical "Slave Power,"

---

states that this reputed oligarchy was much hated by the conservative anti-slavery men of the North, and they were more influenced by this argument than any concerning the sin of slavery.

[68] Cairnes, *op. cit.*, p. 60. Rhodes, *op. cit.*, I, 345-46, states that "The political system of the South was an oligarchy under the Republican form." Also quotes Broderick's statement to the Senators that "Two hundred thousand men with pure white skins in South Carolina are now degraded and despised by thirty thousand aristocratic slaveholders."

[69] Cairnes, *op. cit.*, p. 60; Rhodes, *op. cit.*, I, 345.

[70] Cairnes, *op. cit.*, p. 63.

the assertions that slavery was inconsistent with American ideals and the Declaration of Independence, as well as the alleged conspiracies of the slaveholders to extend the empire of "King Cotton," all made clever propaganda which was skillfully used by the political abolitionists. The economic doctrine of free-soilism reached men that the emotional appeal on the evils of slavery could not reach. It must be remembered that not all of those who wished to forbid the extension of slavery into the territories were necessarily abolitionists, but all were anti-slavery in their views. Yet it was largely the propaganda of the abolitionists that aroused Northern opinion, established the Liberty and Free-Soil parties, and paved the way for Lincoln's election in 1860. Without the agitation of the radical and political abolitionists public opinion in the Northwest might not have been prepared for alliance with the industrial East. Politicians, carefully feeling the pulse of the masses, were glad to encourage the development of free-soil sentiment in order to alienate the South and bring about new party alignments.

Though it is difficult to trace changes of opinion among individual abolitionists, many of the earlier anti-slavery leaders, reacting favorably to the extreme views of Garrison and Weld in the thirties, aligned themselves with the radicals, aiding greatly in the rapid growth of the American Anti-Slavery Society, but later cast their lot with the political abolitionists. An example can be found in the life of James G. Birney. A Kentuckian by birth, Birney early became interested in the cause of gradual emancipation and colonization. Politically inclined, he served in the Kentucky General Assembly and later, upon moving to Alabama, became a member of the first legislature in that state. Buying land at Huntsville, Birney tried to be a success as a planter and slaveholder. However, due to the inexperience of himself and his slaves in cotton culture, combined with luxurious living and gambling, within a few years he found himself financially embarrassed. As a result he sold his plantation and slaves and devoted his time to law practice. Later he again became interested in emancipation and aided Josiah Polk in forming a colonization society at Huntsville in 1830. By 1832, however, the attack of the "New Abolitionists" had caused such organizations to become unpopular in the South, so Birney moved back to Kentucky to take a stand against slavery. Prior to this time Birney had been known as a friend of gradual emancipation, but during the next few years he fell under the influence of Theodore Weld[71] and resigned his connection with the Colonization Society and became identified with the abolition cause. After the beginning of the abolitionist attack, sentiment concerning emancipation changed radically in the slaveholding bluegrass region of Kentucky. By 1835 popular sentiment against Birney was so strong in Danville that he moved to Cincinnati in order to continue the publication of his *Philanthropist*. Public opinion was not favorable to the abolitionists at that time even on the north shore of the Ohio, so Birney moved to New York in 1837 and became secretary of the American Anti-Slavery Society. In that official capacity, he did a great deal toward shaping the policy of the organization. During the following two years 644 auxiliary societies were formed in addition to the 1,000 already existing. In one year more than 725,000 copies of the organization's official publications were issued. At the same time many lecturers were sent throughout the North to agitate the slavery question. Birney gave his personal attention to the legislative bodies, visiting every state legislature in the North, and influenced the passage of various resolutions against the extension of slavery. In doing so Birney gained a wide acquaintance in political circles and

[71] Barnes, *op. cit.*, p. 69.

perhaps laid the foundation for his leadership of the Liberty party a few years later.[72]

In general, abolition writers and speakers gave substantially the same arguments with but little variation except in the violence of the language used.[73] At the beginning of the "Abolition Crusade" the economic phase of the slavery question was neglected and the attack was based almost entirely upon moral and religious grounds.[74] However, the early emancipationists had, for the most part, merely denounced the system of slavery as an evil, while after 1831 the "New Abolitionists" launched a personal attack upon the slaveholders.[75] This period became a "sin-hunting" age, and the abolitionists expanded their denunciations of slavery by zealously searching for the evils which their vivid imaginations portrayed in the South. As Calhoun pointed out in 1837, "Abolitionism originated in that blind fanatical zeal which made one man believe that he was responsible for the sins of others," the same fanaticism that two hundred years before had "tied the victim that it could not convert to the stake."[76] A spirit of zealous desire to reform their neighbors again invaded New England. This view was expressed by an abolitionist who stated: "It is our duty in New England to 'come to the rescue'; and to divulge those awful corruptions" found among the slaveholders.[77]

Looking for sin the abolitionists, in their devout belief in themselves as chosen interpreters of divine law, asserted that the entire institution of slavery was sinful and accursed of God,[78] because it "assumes a power which Heaven denied,

---

[72] See sketches of Birney's life in *National Cyclopaedia of American Biography*, II, 312-13; Appleton's *Cyclopaedia of American Biography*, I, 267-69; William Birney, *James G. Birney and His Times, passim; Weld-Grimké Letters*, I, 156-62, 167-70.

[73] Beveridge, *op. cit.*, II, 20.   [74] *Ibid.*, pp. 20-21.

[75] See speech of Charles Sumner in the United States Senate on *The Barbarism of Slavery*, June 4, 1860.

[76] John C. Calhoun's speech of Dec. 27, 1837, in Beveridge, *op. cit.*, II, 20.

[77] Bourne, *op. cit.*, p. 24.   [78] Beveridge, *op. cit.*, II, 21.

while under its barbarous necromancy, borrowed from the Source of Evil, a man is changed into a chattel—a person withered into a thing—a soul shrunk into merchandise."[79] According to their theories, the black and white races were equal, and therefore any attempts of the laws of men to change the equality, or the brotherhood of the races, were direct violations of divine ordinances.[80] Slavery was magnified by their distorted perspective until it reached the proportions of a devastating evil that would gradually extend itself, crushing all good before it. They insisted that the institution of slavery was inherently an "unspeakable wrong" which, not content with "having invaded the human soul, and annihilated one of its most sacred attributes, in the persons of three millions of our fellow men; not satisfied with having killed the conscience, as far as it may be killed by human device, and human force, in an entire race," it now wished to multiply that race by the extension of slavery which would result in the "same unholy spoilation" being "committed forever."[81]

One of the very effective charges which the abolitionists used, and one that appealed to the sympathies of those who were not acquainted with actual conditions in the South, was that of non-recognition of slave marriages and the consequent separation of slave families. In the Slave States, the statutes recognized slaves as a species of property and therefore could not legally recognize their marriages.[82] With the exception of Louisiana, no Southern State had laws to prevent the possible separation of slave families.[83] Without taking into account the humane sentiment of the Southern people concern-

---

[79] Sumner, *op. cit.*, p. 5.   [80] Beveridge, *op. cit.*, II, 20-23.

[81] Speech delivered by Horace Mann in the House of Representatives, regarding slavery in the Territories; Horace Mann, *Slavery: Letters and Speeches*, p. 71.

[82] William Goodell, *The American Slave Code in Theory and Practice*, p. 24; Rhodes, *op. cit.*, I, 317.

[83] George M. Stroud, *A Sketch of the Laws Relating to Slavery in the Several States of the United States of America*, p. 82.

ing this, and failing to consider that thousands of slaves were married by a religious ceremony of which no legal record was made, the abolitionists suddenly became extremely legal-minded and through a strict interpretation of the statutes of the slave codes were enabled to draw upon their imaginations at length in portraying the supposed conditions in the South.

The anti-slavery press put forth its best efforts to convert the Northern people to the idea that the institution of slavery "annihilates the marriage relations."[84] One abolitionist, in writing of the abrogation of marriage by slavery, stated that to expect "moral purity from the slave" would be as irrational "as to pretend to change the Ethiopian's skin."[85] Yet, with remarkable inconsistency, only a very short space later, he remarked that the "colored Christian women" had the "most delicate virgin modesty" and the "most reserved chastity and faithfulness" which caused them great "agonies of con-science" when debased by civil jurisdiction and sanction of the slaveholder's church.[86] Another representative of the radical abolitionists shouted to the American people that "Ye have recklessly trampled under foot the sacred institution of marriage" through slavery which consigned "every sixth woman in the country to a life of hopeless concubinage and adultery."[87] This, he continued, had led to the turning of the District of Columbia "into a mart," where the "rich aris-tocrat" could lawfully sell "the poor man's wife for purposes of prostitution."[88]

Another radical agitator charged that when any sort of marriage ceremony was performed, instead of using the Lord's words "What God hath joined together, let not man put asunder," the Southern minister substituted his own adage of *"What slave-drivers join together, let men-stealers*

---

[84] *Anti-Slavery Bugle*, Feb. 13, 1846, p. 3. George Bourne, *op. cit.*, p. 38, makes a similar statement by saying that "slavery abrogates the law and institution of marriage."

[85] *Ibid.*, p. 40.

[86] *Ibid.*, p. 42.

[87] Foster, *op. cit.*, p. 25.

[88] *Ibid.*

put asunder."[89] Asserting that because of such a condition the South had been turned into "one vast brothel" he condemned the entire code of slave legislation as "diabolically contrived" for perpetrating "heinous crimes."[90] From the exaggerated accounts of the abolitionist literature, it would seem that as a direct result of the non-legal recognition of marriages slave families were continually being torn asunder; ruthlessly separated and sold, never to meet again.[91] There was not merely an occasional instance of "brothers, and sisters, parents and children, husbands and wives" being torn asunder, stated the anti-slavery tracts, but the "shrieks and the agony" of such "heart-rending scenes" were the daily occurrence in every neighborhood.[92] They charged that a sad "procession of manacled outcasts" could be observed upon every road in the South; victims "whose chains and mournful countenances tell us that they are exiled by force, from all that their hearts hold dear."[93]

Because of the lack of legal recognition of slave marriages, the abolitionists charged that the system of bondage sponsored the practice of "slave-breeding."[94] An English abolitionist asserted that the licentiousness resulting from the management of female slaves on a plantation where the object was "to rear as many as possible, like stock, for the southern market"[95] created a great moral evil. The *Anti-Slavery Bugle* charged that the "interests of slavery" forced the men and women "to commit adultery" and violate all social laws.[96] Charles Sumner thundered that under the slave laws "the ties that may be formed between slaves are all subject

---

[89] Bourne, *op. cit.*, p. 26.   [90] *Ibid.*, pp. 27, 45.

[91] J. Theophilus Kramer, *The Slave Auction*, *passim*.

[92] Wilson Armistead (compiler), *Leed's Anti-Slavery Tracts, or Five Hundred Thousand Strokes for Freedom*, Ser. 8, pp. 20-21. Hereafter cited as *Leed's Anti-Slavery Tracts*. Though this was English abolition propaganda, the work was widely distributed in America.   [93] *Ibid.*, p. 21.

[94] Rhodes, *op. cit.*, I, 317; Beveridge, *op. cit.* II, 16.

[95] Martineau, *op. cit.*, II, 81.

[96] *Anti-Slavery Bugle*, Feb. 13, 1846, p. 2.

to the selfish interests and lusts of the master, whose license knows no check."[97] It was charged that when Negro women were being advertised for sale, the value of one would be greatly enhanced by the announcement that she was "very prolific in her generating qualities."[98] For the most part, in their elaboration upon this evil, the abolitionists merely reasserted their contentions concerning the immorality of the South and the charge of miscegenation, which will be discussed subsequently.

One of the favorite methods of propaganda which the abolitionists resorted to as a means of discrediting the South was the printing of extracts and advertisements, supposedly taken from Southern newspapers, from which they portrayed many cruelties and much inhuman treatment as being the lot of the slaves. Runaway slave advertisements were an effective feature of this type of abolition propaganda. As an example of the numerous "extracts" reprinted in the anti-slavery tracts and newspapers, it might be well to quote only a few as typical of thousands distributed over the North.

"Ranaway, a negro woman and two children; a few days before she went off I burnt her with a hot iron, on the left side of her face. I tried to make the letter M."[99]

"Ranaway, my man Fountain—has *holes in his ears,* a *scar* on the right side of his forehead—has been *shot in the hind parts of his legs*—is marked on the back with the whip."[100]

[97] *Op. cit.,* p. 5.

[98] Goodell, *op. cit.,* p. 84; Rhodes, *op. cit.,* I, 317.

[99] Quoted from Abolitionist paper by *DeBow's Review,* VII (November, 1849), 384-85. A Northern man writing an article upon the subject in that issue states "that these pretended extracts from Southern runaway slave advertisements never existed except in the brain of some mischief-maker, I will not believe until I see the original."

[100] Foster, *op. cit.,* p. 65. Charles Sumner, in a speech in the U. S. Senate on June 4, 1860, quotes this advertisement, which he attributed to the *Georgia Messenger.* However, it had appeared in Foster's work sixteen years before. Sumner commented on the extract as follows: "Holes in the ears; scar on the forehead; shot in the legs; and the mark of the lash on his back! Such are the tokens by which a slavemaster proposes to identify his slave."—P. 14. The italics in the above-quoted advertisement are Foster's.

"Was committed to jail, a negro man—says his name is Josiah: his back very much scarred by the whip, and *branded on the thigh and hips, in three or four places,* thus, J.M.—the *rim of his right ear has been bit or cut off.*"[101]

The editor of the *Indiana Freeman,* after quoting a series of these "extracts" allegedly taken from "Southern papers," stated that "a favorite method of marking slaves so that they may be recognized is by knocking out their front teeth." As an afterthought he adds that "this form of cruelty is mild in comparison to others frequently resorted to."[102]

Such articles appearing in the anti-slavery press were only a part of a widespread attempt of the abolitionist group to discredit the South in general. Under the heading of "Southern Outrages," their newspaper correspondents and pamphleteers gave increased publicity to any crimes committed in the Southern States, in order to make such occurrences the basis of proof for their many assertions concerning the brutality and moral degradation of the South. By ignoring similar crimes in the Northern section, they expected, and correctly so, as it turned out, that the attention of the nation would be concentrated upon the iniquities of the agricultural section, the evils of slavery, and the complete downfall of law and order in the South, thereby discrediting, through contrast with the inspired apostles of abolitionism, the entire South—its life, economic institutions, political leadership, and culture.

The innumerable printed accounts of alleged atrocities published under the headings of "Southern Outrages" covered every phase of brutality from allowing hogs to devour Negro babies before the eyes of a "frantic but helpless

---

[101] Foster, *op. cit.,* p. 64. This abolition pamphlet lists a large number of alleged extracts, which he states are from "Southern newspapers, and are only a very few of the many thousands of similar ones, which blacken the columns of the Southern press." *Ibid.,* pp. 62-68.

[102] Editor of the *Indiana Freeman* quoted in an article on "Slavery at the South," *DeBow's Review,* VII (November, 1849), 386.

Mother"[103] to the drowning in a wholesale lot of a group of six hundred slaves.[104] Pamphlets vividly described slaves escaping and bravely defying their pursuers to the point of death.[105] Stories of horror supposed to come from the lips of fugitive slaves were given wide publicity. The *Herald of Freedom* gave a particularly striking example of this type of propaganda. Speaking of a fugitive slave, an article stated that the "poor fellow" had just arrived from the "very head-quarters of Satan's Kingdom—where the orgies of Hell" were performed by "*earthly* devils." The condition of the slave was described as being "battered with the damnable whip and paddle," branded in the arm, and shot in the leg, by his "pious" master, a "Baptist cannibal." Laboring at the "rice swamp" for six months while dragging an "iron ball of fifty pounds" had caused the shackles to tear the flesh from the bone.[106] The entire galaxy of mob riots, killings, lynchings, burnings, and other atrocities published as "Southern Outrages" by the abolitionist press can be compared only with the "waving the bloody shirt" type of propaganda in the years of Reconstruction or to the more recent crusade of certain Northern elements to turn attention to the alleged political and judicial discriminations against the Negro in the South.

Nor did the abolitionists limit their campaign of propaganda against the South to a mere listing of alleged "Southern Outrages." In the deluge of violent abolitionist literature and denunciatory speeches following Garrison's example, which were promoted by the sentiments of the American

[103] *Anti-Slavery Bugle*, Aug. 28, 1846, p. 1. The "Startling Facts" column lists a sordid and ridiculous article concerning a slave girl forced to work while in "pains of parturition," who gave birth to a child on the bare ground, only to have the infant torn and eaten by a "ravenous old sow."

[104] *Ibid.*, Oct. 1, 1847.

[105] Foster, *op. cit.*, pp. 66-67, pictures a slave drowning while holding his captors at bay.

[106] *Herald of Freedom* article reprinted in *Anti-Slavery Bugle*, Jan. 2, 1846, p. 1.

Anti-Slavery Society,[107] the most scathing attack was upon the slaveholders themselves. The aristocracy of the South, whose culture and hospitality had so favorably impressed visitors, were condemned by the abolitionists as criminals of the vilest type—thieves, robbers, man-stealers, and tyrants, who were the enemies of all civilization.[108] Southern society was condemned as "artificial and deceitful" by George Bourne, who charged that it was merely an "amalgamation of polished suavity and furious haughtiness, of splendid prodigality and squalid penury," where luxurious living on one hand was contrasted with "half starvation and entire nakedness" on the other, whose pretensions to the "most scrupulous refinement" was combined with "ferocity and licentiousness."[109] One Northern minister, charging that slavery at the South had produced a "bowie-knife style of civilization," deprecated the lack of intellectual refinement among the slaveholders and argued that the "barbarous institution" barred progress, education, and religion thus causing the South to reach a lower state of degradation with each succeeding generation.[110] It was charged that the states that were proverbial for Southern chivalry had been converted into mere "breeding estates," their youth "corrupted" with false honor and idleness,[111] their civilization tottering until the entire section had become the "nurse of riot and lawlessness, and assassination—its symbols, the Whip, the Pistol, and the Knife!"[112] With the premise that violence was the foundation of slavery, the abolitionists in thousands of pamphlets, newspaper articles, and speeches charged that brutality and vulgarity were manifest among the slaveholders with the result that the moral and

[107] *Declaration of Sentiments*, p. 9.

[108] Beveridge, *op. cit.*, II, 5-12, 20-21.   [109] Bourne, *op. cit.*, p. 93.

[110] Sermon of Dr. Bushnell of Hartford, Conn., in Mann, *op. cit.*, pp. 50-52.

[111] Editorial in *Zion's Herald*, quoted in both the *Liberator* and the *Anti-Slavery Bugle;* see the latter for Oct. 24, 1845.

[112] Article in the *Charter Oak*, reprinted in the *Anti-Slavery Bugle*, Aug. 7, 1846, p. 1.

ethical standards of these Southerners were barbarous in the extreme.[113]

The system which reduced Southern society to brutality resulted, according to the theories of the fanatics, in inflicting on the slaves all the tortures and barbaric cruelties that the "irresponsible tyrants" could conceive. In order to drive men and women to "heart-breaking and endless toil,"[114] it was asserted that the slaveholder applied the knotted scourge "until the blood runs down their lacerated bodies in streams."[115] In order to secure absolute obedience to his will, they accused the master of inflicting a multitude of cruelties, of whipping the slaves "until death ensues" or driving them to "hard labour" without sufficient "food or rest, until they sink down and die." Whenever slaves fled to escape their sufferings, they were "followed into their hiding places, and put to death."[116]

Miss Harriet Martineau, an English spinster who travelled in America, and whose preconceived ideas on slavery and her gloomy moral outlook caused her to seek the worst possible exceptions in order to condemn the South in general, discussed the brutality of slavery at length in her several volumes.[117] She described the cruelty of the slaveholders by stating that "it is well known that the most savage violences that are now heard of in the world take place in the Southern and Western states of America. Burning alive, cutting the

[113] For examples see Sumner, *op. cit.*, p. 13; Martineau, *op. cit.*, II, 82; *Leed's Anti-Slavery Tracts*; Mann, *op. cit.*, pp. 50-52; Bourne, *op. cit.*, pp. 53-55; and practically all of the abolitionist magazines, of which the *Anti-Slavery Bugle* is an example.   [114] Beveridge, *op. cit.*, II, 22.

[115] *Leed's Anti-Slavery Tracts*, Ser. 31, pp. 3-4.

[116] *Ibid.* Another tract describes a slave receiving a thousand lashes on the bare back. In another instance an overseer took a slave mother and "stripped her as naked as the day she was born, fastened a rope around her two hands and ordered two other slaves . . . to pull her up so that her extremities would be about two feet from the ground; and this overseer, with his terrible lash, whipped this poor ill-fated creature to the extent of three hundred lashes. He literally 'cut her to pieces,' as he had said he would do."—Ser. 46, p. 2.

[117] Harriet Martineau, *Retrospect of Western Travel*, and *Society in America*.

heart out, and sticking it on the point of a knife, and other such diabolical deeds; the result of the deepest hatred of which the human heart is capable, are heard of only there."[118]

Practically all of the abolitionist writers and speakers waxed eloquent through the use of many descriptive adjectives in this particular phase of the attack. The many narratives of floggings and cruel punishments to be found in the hundreds of tracts and pamphlets as well as in the abolition newspapers of the time vary but little in their descriptions. In studying this type of propaganda, the reader is impressed with the view that either the abolitionists drew upon New England history to supplement their imaginations, or the slaveholders took their cue from the seventeenth-century Puritans, for many of the descriptions of Southern cruelty scattered by the abolitionists could, by inserting white nonconformists for black slaves, be substituted for the history of New England church discipline of two hundred years before. One writer stated that the slaves were placed in a pillory, the body stripped naked and exposed "for the operation of the slave-driver and his merciless hireling, the *flayer general*."[119] After the skin was literally lashed off, it was charged that the "slave-doctor's panacea, salt, vinegar and other equally mollifying ingredients," was applied.[120]

Charges were made that the slaves, after being subjected to such barbarous treatment, were half starved and underfed, with hovels unfit for beasts as their only shelter from inclement weather.[121] One of the anti-slavery tracts, which may

[118] *Ibid.*, II, 82.

[119] Bourne, *op. cit.*, p. 54; italics Bourne's.

[120] *Ibid.* Bourne also describes a public whipping of a negro woman by stating that the "shrieking creature" was "uncovered to her loins" fastened in a pillory in the public square and severely whipped. A New York traveler, the alleged witness of the act, according to Bourne, "could not command his unutterable emotions longer than to see three or four strokes inflicted . . . wondering to himself how it was that the woman's breasts were preserved from being cut to pieces . . . doubting almost whether such a forcible application of the slave-drivers prodigious whip, would not almost sever her body in two parts." [121] Beveridge, *op. cit.*, II, 22.

be considered as rather typical of the hundreds of thousands that were widely distributed for the purpose of enlightening the Northern people upon the cruelty of domestic slavery, described the condition of the slaves as follows:

. . . they are overworked, under-fed, wretchedly clad and lodged, and have insufficient sleep; that they are often made to wear round their necks iron collars armed with prongs, to drag heavy chains and weights at their feet while working in the field, and to wear yokes, and bells and iron horns; that they are often kept confined in the stocks day and night for weeks together, made to wear gags in their mouths for hours or days, have some of their front teeth torn out or broken off, that they may be easily detected when they run away; that they are frequently flogged with terrible severity, have red pepper rubbed into their lacerated flesh, and hot brine, spirits of turpentine, etc., poured over the gashes to increase the torture; that they are often stripped naked, their backs and limbs cut with knives, bruised and mangled by scores and hundreds of blows with the paddle, and terribly torn by the claws of cats drawn over them by their tormentors; that they are often hunted with bloodhounds, and shot down like beasts, or torn to pieces by dogs; that they are often suspended by the arms, and whipped and beaten till they faint, and, when revived by restoratives beaten again till they faint, and sometimes till they die; that their ears are often cut off, their eyes knocked out, their bones broken, their flesh branded with red hot irons; that they are maimed, mutilated and burned to death over slow fires, *are undeniable facts.*[122]

The above condemnation of the methods of the slave-holders is no more severe in its language than many other similar tracts and pamphlets that were written and distributed widely throughout the North by the abolitionists. In fact, it is quite conservative in comparison with some.[123]

[122] *Leed's Anti-Slavery Tracts*, Ser. 7, pp. 7-12.

[123] Weld (comp.), *American Slavery as it is: The Testimony of a Thousand Witnesses*, an abolition pamphlet, issued in 1839, by the *American Anti-Slavery Society*, is supposedly compiled from the numerous accounts of many who claimed to be eyewitnesses of ghastly atrocities in the South.

Not content with declaring that all Southern society was corrupted with brutality and violence, the extreme abolitionists boldly condemned all slaveholders as robbers, thieves, and man-stealers.[124] It remained for Stephen Symonds Foster, one of the early extremists and a born agitator and reformer, to carry this charge to the vilest depths of denunciation. Foster, a Dartmouth graduate, became interested in anti-slavery during his college career. Though he entered a seminary to prepare for the ministry, he felt that the churches were not what they should be and soon severed his relationship with organized religion altogether. He was a close friend of Garrison and accompanied the latter on many lecture tours. Though awkward and ungainly in personal appearance, Foster had a wonderful voice and his influence was very great during the early years of the abolition crusade. Foster detested religious bodies but would often interrupt their services in order to ask permission to speak on slavery. This very unusual method resulted in his being thrown out and roughly handled on numerous occasions, but he felt that it was worth while because it drew attention to him and his work. In common with many of the other agitators of the time, Foster was tremendously interested in other reforms. He particularly advocated world peace, woman suffrage, supported all labor organizations in their demands for rights, and was an energetic worker for temperance. As a means of protesting the fact that women were denied political rights, he often refused to pay his taxes, thereby necessitating the buying of his property by friends at the ensuing sheriff's sale. Quite enthusiastically supporting every reform movement which gave opportunity for extreme views, he seemed to favor the most unusual and spectacular methods of promoting his cause. Nor was this characteristic trait of fanaticism curbed by his marriage to Abigail Kelly, an outstanding aboli-

[124] Beveridge, *op. cit.*, II, 21.

tionist lecturer and one of the leaders in the movement for women's rights. Though essentially belonging to the radical group of abolitionists, Foster was not opposed to political action and was an active propagandist against the pro-slavery tendencies of the Democratic and Whig parties.[125] His charge that all slaveholders were thieves and his specific denunciation of religious organizations in his book entitled *The Brotherhood of Thieves* was considered "one of the most vitriolic works of the anti-slavery era."[126] This work, in spite of its extreme nature, was so widely distributed by the abolitionists that twenty editions were necessary.

Foster argued that the whites and the blacks were equal in their rights. Therefore the slaveholder had no right to compel the slave to labor. He completely denied the right of one person to purchase or inherit another's body or to take the fruits of his labor. Inasmuch as the slaveholder laid his "felonious hands on the body and soul of his equal brother," charged Foster, then the slave was "converted into an article of merchandise," and robbed of himself. Therefore the master was nothing but a "kidnapper, or a man-thief."[127] Others charged that the system of slavery in the South not only crushed the "bodies and souls" of three million of "God's children," but also in doing so changed them into property and plundered them of every right.[128] In taking away the products of slave labor, it was asserted that all slaveholders became "freebooters" and as such were much more "despicable . . . than the common horse-thief."[129] Basing their contention on the fact that the African slave trade was considered as piracy, the abolitionists charged that it was "piracy the wide world over" and that the American slaveholder was

---

[125] Foster, *op. cit., passim;* also see Chap. VIII below.

[126] *Dictionary of American Biography,* IV, 558-59, gives an excellent sketch of Foster's life.   [127] Foster, *op. cit.,* p. 10.

[128] Article in the *Charter Oak,* reprinted in the *Anti-Slavery Bugle,* Aug. 7, 1846.   [129] Foster, *op. cit.,* p. 9.

guilty "of a crime which, if committed on a foreign coast, he must expiate on the gallows."[130]

In addition to being thieves of the worst type, the abolitionists asserted that the slaveholders were also murderers. One writer based his contentions upon the idea that a person "may commit murder without actually taking life" and that "the intention constitutes the crime" and argued that "the crime of which every slaveholder is guilty" was murder. He charged that the slave had no alternative but "submission or death" and therefore if he did not choose death he submitted to a "protracted torture more horrible than death." It was stated that the slaveholders kept the instruments of murder, the dirk, the pistol, and the bowie knife, at their pillows with "a troop of bloodhounds standing sentry at every door!" This condition alone, argued the abolitionists—with "burnished steel" ready "to drink the lifeblood of outraged innocence"— branded all slaveholders as murderers.[131] Other abolitionists went even further in their accusations. A widely distributed anti-slavery tract emphatically stated that the slaves were driven so hard in their labor that it was a common practice to work them to death in five years on the sugar plantations and to kill them off every seven years in the cotton fields.[132]

The principal charge of the abolitionist indictment—the "ultimate depth of vileness," as expressed by a recent historian,[133] and one that was repeatedly insisted upon by all abolition writers and speakers—was the charge of miscegenation, the illicit intercourse between the whites and blacks, which they asserted was forced upon the Negro and mulatto girls and women. "The South," shouted Wendell Phillips, "is one great brothel, where half a million women are flogged

[130] *Ibid.*, p. 11.   [131] *Ibid.*

[132] *Leed's Anti-Slavery Tracts*, ser. 2, p. 1; also see Kemble, *op. cit.*, p. 389, for such statements. For the origin of this charge see U. B. Phillips, *American Negro Slavery*, p. 382.   [133] Beveridge, *op. cit.*, II, 23.

to prostitution."[134] Phillips probably resembled Garrison more than any other man, particularly in the "fierceness and mercilessness of his attacks."[135] With his great oratory, entirely uncurbed by any necessity of adhering to facts, Phillips became a powerful factor in the abolitionist attack. However, he was not alone in his condemnation of the South in broad statements concerning miscegenation. It was argued that inasmuch as slave women were "property" then their bodies were used for satisfaction of the "unbridled lusts" of the slaveholders.[136] That acidulous spinster, Miss Martineau, took pleasure in repeating the vilest examples of this charge as the foundation of her chapter upon the "Morals of Slavery." She went so far as to state that "every man who resides on his plantation may have his harem, and has every inducement of custom and pecuniary gain to tempt him to the common practice."[137] Again she asserted that "the licentiousness of the South takes women of color for its victims,"[138] and according to her declaration a wife of a Southern planter confided that she was "only the chief slave of the harem."[139]

Another feminist leader and abolitionist, Lydia Maria Child, followed the example of Miss Martineau and scornfully asserted that the Southerners favored Negro slavery because of their "love of unbridled licentiousness and despotic control."[140] Mrs. Child early became one of the leading women abolitionists when she published in 1833 *An Appeal in Favor of that Class of Americans Called Africans*. She and her husband edited the *National Anti-Slavery Standard*, a weekly abolition publication in New York, from 1841-1849.

[134] Speech delivered in Boston, Jan. 27, 1853, before the 21st annual meeting of the Massachusetts Anti-Slavery Society. Wendell Phillips, *Speeches, Lectures, Letters*, 1st ser., pp. 8-9, 108-9.

[135] Hart, *op. cit.*, p. 185.   [136] Foster, *op. cit.*, p. 9.

[137] Martineau, *Society in America*, II, 87.

[138] Martineau, *Retrospect of Western Travel*, I, 234.

[139] Martineau, *Society in America*, II, 81.

[140] Lydia Maria Child, *Anti-Slavery Catechism*, p. 5, quoted by Beveridge, *op. cit.*, II, 24.

Always alert for a spectacular opportunity, she later gained considerable notoriety by requesting Governor Wise of Virginia to allow her to nurse John Brown after the latter was wounded at Harpers Ferry. Using the ensuing correspondence for publicity purposes to aid the abolition cause, she issued a pamphlet which reached a circulation of 300,000 copies.[141] Like many other women abolitionists, Mrs. Child seemed to take the "holier-than-thou" sectional attitude and condemned Southern society as the very essence of immorality.[142]

Asserting an alleged "incontrovertible" fact that a single man in the Northern States lived "in purity," his morals were contrasted with those of the single slaveholder who, it was charged, surrendered to the "ordinary instincts of humanity" by having "seven to ten women at his command."[143] It was charged that all slave women were "doomed to a life of universal prostitution and concubinage."[144] The quadroon girls of New Orleans were brought up for the express purpose of being what their mothers were—"the mistresses of white gentlemen."[145] Every young Southerner, according to the accusations, early selected his quadroon partner and the illegitimate connection often lasted even after his marriage to a white lady.[146] It was charged that the merchants and political leaders of the South regularly bought "warranted virgins" expressly for concubinage and the "manufacture of light colored slaves."[147]

In the many abolitionist pamphlets and books that make charges of miscegenation, it was the common practice to assert that the slave girl was virtuous and only submitted to

[141] See sketch of Mrs. Child in *Dictionary of American Biography*, IV, 67-69. The pamphlet mentioned above is entitled *Correspondence between Lydia Maria Child and Gov. Wise and Mrs. Mason of Virginia.*

[142] See her abolition pamphlet on *Anti-Slavery Catechism, passim.*

[143] Bourne, *op. cit.*, p. 76.   [144] Beveridge, *op. cit.*, II, 24.

[145] Martineau, *Society in America*, II, 80.

[146] *Ibid.*, pp. 80-82.   [147] Bourne, *op. cit.*, pp. 50, 62-63.

the "lusts" of her master after continually being flogged to the point of death.[148] The "Daughters of the North" were implored to *remember the degraded slave daughter*," who, in spite of chasteness and modesty, was unprotected and subject "to every insult and outrage which any pale-faced libertine may choose to inflict." It was asserted that her brother, in many instances, was forced by the slaveholder to be the "unwilling witness of her ruin."[149] It was charged that the "licentiousness of the masters" had so degraded Southern society that only its dissolution could be looked forward to with hopefulness.[150] Stephen S. Foster went even farther in condemning the slaveholders in general by shouting, *"Rape* is his crime! death his desert!"[151]

The charge was made that in addition to the inherent licentiousness of the slaveowners which resulted in the defiling of female slaves, the Southern planters considered it to their advantage to do so. George Bourne asserted that the masters "transformed their debauchery into a virtue" by pleading that it was "expedient and proper" that every slave girl should early admit "to her embraces her master or his son." The purpose of this, as stated by the abolitionists, was to secure the "lasting affections of the young woman" by having her first child to be the "known offspring of her owner."[152] It was asserted that some plantation owners had "carnally known at a very early age, every female slave" on the plantation and that their affection for their owners was attributable to these facts.[153] So anxious were some masters

---

[148] *Ibid.*, pp. 50, 59-61, 66-67. See also such works as Martineau, *Society in America*, Vol. II, chapter on "Morals of Slavery"; Foster, *op. cit., passim;* and Leed's *Anti-Slavery Tracts.*

[149] *Anti-Slavery Bugle*, May 15, 1846; italics in *Bugle.* In this connection Foster condemned the Southerners as "wretches" who prostituted the slave women and as deserving an "epithet compared with which adultery is spotless innocence." *Op. cit.*, p. 9.

[150] Martineau, *Society in America*, II, 82.

[151] Foster, *op. cit.*, p. 10; italics Foster's.

[152] Bourne, *op. cit.*, p. 59.   [153] *Ibid.*, pp. 59-60.

in exercising this prerogative, the abolitionists maintained, that dire and merciless punishment would be meted out to any slave that frustrated them.[154]

According to the abolitionists, the lusts of the slaveholder did not in any way surpass his greed,[155] for instead of keeping his illegitimate children near him he sold them into slavery. Miss Martineau asserted that in the South the mixture of the races "is hourly encouraged" and that the planters would "sell their own offspring to fill their purses."[156] It was charged that the "blood of orators, statesmen, generals, and even presidents, flows in the veins of thousands who are bought and sold like mules and horses."[157] Another extremist vowed that among Southern white men "amalgamation with colored women is the rule; and abstinence from illicit intercourse with them, is the exception."[158] And he further asserted that the only racial prejudice manifest among the slaveholders was in regard to free blacks, for they had "no disgust for the female slave who suckles their children or who brings forth light-colored offsprings to be nurtured as merchantable cattle."[159] The laws declaring that children of slaves should follow the condition of their mothers, led to the practice "of planters selling and bequeathing their own children," maintained one belligerent feminist.[160] An antislavery publication stated that it was nothing unusual "for

[154] *Ibid.*, p. 61. Gives example of a master's ferocity upon being frustrated by having discovered a prior association of a Negro girl with another slave. Before her eyes her lover was "mercilessly scourged for having dared to interfere with the prior right, as they allege, of the slave-driver, or his son, or the overseer, or some other debauchee to whom she may have been promised at a time specified. Then in her delicate condition she is divested of her clothing, and her only friend, whose mutual affection constituted the sole cordial amid their degradation in the house of bondage, is obliged to whip her, and if he does not strike hard enough, and draw sufficient blood, the deficiency is measured out upon himself." After which she is defiled "before her lover's face."

[155] See discussion in Beveridge, *op. cit.*, II, 24.

[156] Martineau, *Society in America*, II, 81.

[157] Beveridge, *op. cit.*, II, 24.

[158] Bourne, *op. cit.*, pp. 96-97.   [159] *Ibid.*, p. 96.

[160] Martineau, *Society in America*, II, 77.

slaveholders to sell their own children as slaves. Brothers
traffic in the bodies of their fathers, sons, and daughters."[161]
In order to stir up sectional strife on this subject appeals were
made to the women of the North. *"Christian daughters"*
were questioned whether they would allow their sister to
be "placed on the auction block and sold for a domestic
Seraglio." *"Christian Mothers"* were asked to consider their
feelings if their babes were torn from them "by the ruthless
hand of the slave driver."[162]

Of all the fanatical abolitionists, the Reverend George
Bourne went to the extreme upon this subject. Bourne, an
English clergyman and abolitionist, early began his anti-
slavery agitation while serving as pastor of a Presbyterian
church in South River, Virginia. In 1816 he published a
work entitled *The Book and Slavery Irreconcilable*,[163] which
caused a Presbyterian council to condemn him on a charge of
heresy. Compelled to leave the Southern States, he jour-
neyed North and was in Quebec from 1825 to 1828. Having
what seemed to be an "anti" complex, he became violently
opposed to Catholicism while in Canada, so he broke away
from the Presbyterian Church and became a member of the
Dutch Reformed Church. Since he was one of the first advocates of immediate emancipation of slaves, Bourne was a
suitable delegate to the Convention which formed the American Anti-Slavery Society in 1833. Naturally of a belligerent
nature, he was entirely out of patience with the later policy
of "non-resistance" advocated by some of the abolitionists,
and believed in carrying out violent methods to secure re-

[161] *Leed's Anti-Slavery Tracts*, ser. 2, p. 5.

[162] *Anti-Slavery Bugle*, May 15, 1846, p. 2; italics in *Bugle*.

[163] George Bourne, *The Book and Slavery Irreconcilable, with Animadversions
upon Dr. Smith's Philosophy.* Some of his later publications are: *An Address to
the Presbyterian Church, Enforcing the Duty of Excluding all Slaveholders from
the "Communion of Saints"; Man-Stealing and Slavery Denounced by the Presbyterian and Methodist Churches; Picture of Slavery in the United States of America; Slavery Illustrated in its Effects upon Women and Domestic Society;* and *A
Condensed Anti-Slavery Bible Argument: by a citizen of Virginia.*

form. Unlike many of the Garrisonian group, Bourne was
entirely opposed to the movement for "woman's rights."[164]
However, he was of the opinion that because of the institution of slavery in the South, the women of that section were
submerged in a den of iniquity and corruption and were too
timid to protest against the evils of the system.[165] As he did
not believe that women had a right to speak for themselves,
Bourne decided that it was his duty "to draw aside the veil
which conceals the grand slaveholding 'mystery of iniquity' "
and for the sake of the Southern women "to depict that 'working of Satan' " which crushed them "with agony and degradation." It was with zealous fanaticism that he intended,
through the abolition of slavery, to reform the South in such
a way as to protect "female purity," restore "connubial obligations" by preventing and abolishing "all domestic relations
. . . at the impulse of lascivious desires and pecuniary demands," and forever prohibit "a million women" from constituting "one vast harem where men-stealers may prowl,
corrupt, and destroy."[166]

Garrison stated in the *Liberator* that "Bourne thunders
and lightens,"[167] and this statement was no doubt correct, for
an actual electrical storm could not have produced a more
terrific shock upon the Southerners than some of his outrageous statements. He charged that "all the old families"
among the slaveowners had many "colored relatives" though
all "ties of consanguinity" were denied even in instances
where there could be no dispute. Under such a system he
contended that the master would have carnal knowledge of
his slaves and later defile his own daughters, his son often
defiling his own sisters and their mother, until the whole
domestic society would be commingled into an "indiscrim-
inate assemblage of unnatural monsters" who would destroy

---

[164] *Dictionary of American Biography*, II, 485.
[165] Bourne, *Slavery Illustrated in its Effects upon Women* . . ., pp. 22-23.
[166] *Ibid.*, p. 24.   [167] Garrisons, *op. cit.*, I, 461.

God's laws and humanity, and degrade women "to the lowest abyss of pollution and iniquity."[168]

Bourne considered American slavery "as the everflowing fountain of all uncleanness"[169] which destroyed the "moral purity of the youth of both sexes."[170] He charged many times that the adult blacks labored both in the fields and in domestic service completely nude thereby corrupting the "innocence and virtue" of Southern youth.[171] Also it was asserted that "adulterous intercourse" with slave girls was so constant and flagrant that wives and daughters were continually affronted with this evidence of degeneracy on the part of husbands and fathers.[172] In fact, it was stated that the "pernicious" custom was so prevalent that the inns and hotels of the South kept a number of mulatto girls for the benefit of guests at night, which of course, was attributed directly to the practices of slavery.[173]

The most objectionable of Bourne's contentions was his charge that miscegenation with the blacks was not confined to Southern men, but that Southern women were also guilty. He argued that the "harem-like" seclusion in which Southern girls were reared, combined with their "artificial" character, rendered them the easy prey of their colored attendant, "who ensnares the white female youth into an unhallowed acquaintance with the surrounding iniquity or into an unlawful connection with her colored brother."[174] Asserting that the "colored women exult in the prospect that their boys might dishonor their tyrant's children as he injured and debased them," Bourne described in detail a revolting instance of such an occurrence, yet in such general terms as to lead the

[168] Bourne, *Slavery Illustrated in its Effects upon Women* . . ., p. 24.

[169] *Ibid.*, p. 22.

[170] *Ibid.*, p. 90.   [171] *Ibid.*, pp. 90-98.

[172] *Ibid.*, pp. 22-23. Bourne narrates an instance in which the slaveowner's wife, informed of her husband's defiling of female slaves, "sacrificed her feelings, and often witnessed her husband scourging and abusing his female slaves."— Pp. 66-67.

[173] *Ibid.*, p. 56.   [174] *Ibid.*, p. 75.

reader to believe it was the common practice in every slave-owner's household.[175] It was asserted that as a result of such common practices, Southern young men invariably visited the Northern States to secure wives, knowing that in choosing a Southern girl they would get only "a vitiated constitution, the remains of her attachment for her father's niggers."[176] He appealed to Northern "puritan brides" not to be misled into marrying a slaveholder by picturing her "disillusionment" at finding herself as only the "most favored slave of the planter's 'gang.'"[177] Nor were the older women of the South neglected in the abolitionist attack. It was asserted that many were "cruel and most terrific scourgers," who in their debasement, tacitly sanctioned "the violation of the seventh commandment," and in many instances operated houses of ill fame at a profit "by inviting sexual intercourse between their guests and their female slaves."[178] Due to these things, Bourne charged that Southern women were even worse than "female seducers and panderers for debauchees" as they were "privy to all the violations which pass around them." Prophesying a revolution of the blacks for their liberty, at which time the Lord would again display

> "That wonder-working arm which broke
> From Israel's neck the Egyptian yoke"

Bourne stated that "Southern women may be assured that they will have no adequate defenders from the North."[179]

Not even the ministers and the churches of the South were allowed to escape in the violent and wholesale attack of the "New Abolitionists." Garrison stated that "at the South, slaves and slaveholders, the masters and their victims, the spoilers and the spoiled, make up the *Christian* church."[180]

---

[175] *Ibid.*, pp. 70-75.   [176] *Ibid.*, p. 77.

[177] *Ibid.*, p. 80. See similar view of Martineau that the Southern wife was only "the chief of the harem."—*Society in America*, II, 81.

[178] Bourne, *Slavery Illustrated in its Effects upon Women* . . ., pp. 55, 65-66.

[179] *Ibid.*, pp. 101-2.   [180] Garrisons, *op. cit.*, II, 480.

According to Frederick Douglass, a free Negro and follower of Garrison, there existed in the Slave States a system of religion, propounded by ministers, whose mockery and hypocrisy could inspire only loathing rather than an inspiration to higher ideals and spirituality. A tract which quoted him stated that "they have men-stealers for ministers, women whippers for missionaries, and cradle plunderers for church members." While the gong of the auctioneer and the bell of the church chimed together, it was charged that the cries of the "heart-broken" slaves were drowned out by the "religious shouts" of their pious masters and the "clanking of the fetters and the rattling of the chains" sounded with "the pious psalm and solemn prayer in church." It was asserted that the slaveholder "gives his blood-stained gold to support the pulpit, and the pulpit, in return, covers his infernal business with the garb of Christianity. There we behold religion and robbery the allies of each other."[181]

The vitriolic Bourne, embittered by his earlier expulsion from a Virginia church, was even more radical than Douglass and turned the full force of his vocabulary into the vilification of his former colleagues. He charged that the Southern pulpits were often filled by "man-stealing, girl-selling, pimping, and slave-manufacturing preachers," while the churches over which these ministers presided were "synagogues of Satan."[182] In his opinion, it would be far better *"to transfer the inmate from the State prison, and the pander from the brothel to the pulpit"* than to permit a Southern minister "to teach us righteousness and purity" in a Northern church.[183] The *Religious Telescope,* allegedly a religious journal of the

---

[181] Frederick Douglass quoted in *Leed's Anti-Slavery Tracts,* ser. 19, p. 7.

[182] Beveridge, *op. cit.,* II, 25. See also Foster, *op. cit.,* pp. 7-8. Foster states that the "American church and clergy, as a body," were "thieves, adulterers, man-stealers, pirates, and murderers."

[183] Bourne, *Slavery Illustrated in its Effects upon Women . . .,* pp. 116-17; italics Bourne's.

North, assailed Southern ministers in general by stating that the "holiest men in the South" sanctioned "slaveholding and slave-breeding." The same publication condemned the Methodist Church in particular, charging that it had "slave-breeders" for bishops.[184] It was charged that "Southern institutions" comprised a compound of "man-stealing, lewdness, and cruelty,"[185] yet were upheld by "slave-manufacturing preachers."[186] Southern ministers were accused of living in luxury upon "money filched from the toil" of their "fellow-citizens," their wealth being wrung from "the moans and blood" of their own church members.[187] Without attempting to give any proof, a leading abolition agitator declared that Southern ministers wished to perpetuate slavery "for the purpose of supplying themselves with concubines from among its hapless victims."[188] Another propagandist accused a Southern minister of selling his own daughter to a neighboring planter for service as a concubine, a transaction by which the clergyman profited to the extent of $600.[189] The abolitionist assault upon the clergy of the South seems to have been more violent than their attack upon any other group of men. This may explain, to some extent, the determined stand which Southern ministers later took in defending and justifying Southern institutions. Certainly the wholesale condemnation and unjustified personal attack upon this group of religious

---

[184] *Religious Telescope*, quoted by the *Anti-Slavery Bugle*, Aug. 7, 1846, p. 1. It should be remembered that by this date the Methodist Church had already split into Northern and Southern branches.

[185] Bourne, *Slavery Illustrated in its Effects upon Women* . . ., p. 92.

[186] *Ibid.*, p. 105; similar statements may be found on pp. 93, 116-17.

[187] *Ibid.*, p. 20.

[188] Foster, *op. cit.*, p. 69; similar statement on pp. 7-8.

[189] Bourne, *Slavery Illustrated in its Effects upon Women* . . ., pp. 64-65, cites an example of a free colored preacher, who had bought his own children, then later, through the evil influence of the slave-holding type of religion, was induced to sell his daughter to a planter. Bourne insists that the planter wanted the girl for concubinage purposes and that the sale was made over the protests of the virtuous and religious daughter.

leaders created a smoldering resentment that required only a short time to burst into a flame which several generations would not extinguish.[190]

Led by Bourne, Foster and Garrison, the abolitionists did not confine their attack to the ministers alone but also denounced the membership of the various churches, both collectively and individually. As early as 1834 Garrison commented in the *Liberator* upon the churches being the "stronghold of slavery."[191] Based upon such a conclusion, the attack carried on by the "New Abolitionists," many of whom were entirely unidentified with any organized church or religion, was violent to an extreme. It was charged that the Southern churches were but confederations between the ministers, their congregations, and "hordes of robbers and pimps," for the purpose of dividing "the infernal spoils."[192] Incendiary magazines were established largely to overthrow the Southern churches. An example may be shown in the *Anti-Slavery Bugle,* which stated in its first issue, as a fundamental part of its objective, that the attack upon the "monster" of slavery would be concentrated upon "his refuge and hiding place—the Church."[193] Bourne asserted that religion was impossible in the South because of the "vast consociation of hypocrites and sinners" where *"gangs of men-thieves are consistent members of the church of God."*[194] A leading radical abolitionist, in writing of the immorality of Southern churches, charged that the "demons in hell" would not rape their "fellow-demons" as did many of the clergy "their own

[190] See similar conclusion in Beveridge, *op. cit.*, II, 25-26.

[191] This occurred after the Baptist Board of Foreign Missions refused to promote immediate emancipation in 1834. See quotations from the *Liberator,* in Garrisons, *op. cit.*, II, 480.

[192] Bourne, *Slavery Illustrated in its Effects upon Women* . . ., p. 112.

[193] *Anti-Slavery Bugle,* June 20, 1845, no. 1; this publication was started at New Lisbon, Ohio, by the Ohio American Anti-Slavery Society as a weekly. It was later published at Salem, Ohio.

[194] Bourne, *Slavery Illustrated in its Effects upon Women* . . ., pp. 118-19; italics Bourne's.

church members."[195] Anti-slavery meetings in the North
were reported in the abolitionist press as proving that "the
priests of this country are liars, thieves, adulterers, man-
stealers, pirates, and murderers."[196] Wendell Phillips deliberately used his powers of oratory to attack the church as
an evil, condemning religious organizations because of their
pro-slavery attitude.[197]

Among the radical abolitionists who condemned the
American churches, none was more rabid than Stephen S.
Foster. In portraying Garrison as the leading exponent of
abolitionism, historians seem to have neglected propagandists
like Foster and Bourne. Though lacking a newspaper in which
to leave historical evidence and failing to inspire definitive
biographers, these two radicals were constant and untiring
agitators. Their publications were widely distributed and
were violent even in comparison to extreme Garrisonism.
Through personal work in conventions and anti-slavery meetings these men, particularly Foster, aided greatly in arousing
Northern public sentiment against the South, and their vehement declarations naturally created much resentment among
the Southerners. This was particularly true in the case of
Foster's denunciation of the ministers and churches. Having
thoroughly repudiated his former theological training and
connection with all forms of organized religion, Foster emphasized this brand of abolition propaganda. Not content to
denounce the churches collectively, he picked out the individual denominations for specific vilification. As a result of
the General Conference of the Methodist Episcopal Church
failing to condemn slavery in 1836 and 1840, Foster wrote
that the denomination was *"a conclave of incarnate fiends"*

[195] Foster, *op. cit.*, pp. 9-10.

[196] Report of anti-slavery meeting at West Middleton, Penn., in the *Anti-Slavery Bugle*, May 15, 1846. This was one of a series of meetings that were held by Stephen S. Foster and his wife, the former Abigail Kelly.

[197] Wendell Phillips, speech delivered at the Fifteenth Annual Meeting of the American Anti-Slavery Society, printed in the *Anti-Slavery Bugle*, June 8, 1849.

where every "*intelligent* communicant" was worse and more infamous, according to the eyes of God, "than the common prostitute, the pickpocket, or the assassin."[198] Although allegedly speaking with "love" and "kindness," he charged that the Methodist Church was "more corrupt than any house of ill-fame in the city of New York," citing as his proof that within that denomination fifty thousand females were "inevitably doomed to lives of prostitution" under the penalty of scourging and death.[199] His fellow agitator, the Reverend George Bourne, had previously enunciated the same doctrine by condemning the Methodist conferences as proclaiming the "debasement of twelve hundred thousand American women, as victims of ungovernable lust," as a part of their "*bible doctrine.*"[200] In what Foster insisted was "a true but painful picture" of American churches, he condemned them as subsisting upon "ROBBERY" and "THEFT," while within the organization they plundered the cradle, robbed youthful lovers of their brides, and sold their "own sisters in the church for the SERAGLIO," in order to obtain money to purchase "BIBLES for the heathen!"[201] The attack upon the Church was not confined to a few pamphlets and books, but was agitated in anti-slavery meetings throughout the North. The *Anti-Slavery Bugle,* in reporting one of a series of such meetings, stated that the Methodist Church was the "most wicked church of the country—the most diabolical of all the associations of our nation."[202]

If such be possible, Foster was as violent in his denunciation of the Baptist Church as of the Methodist. Speaking of the Baptist Church in general, he stated that it had sanctioned

---

[198] Foster, *op. cit.,* p. 40; italics Foster's.

[199] *Ibid.,* pp. 68-69, 72.

[200] Bourne, *Slavery Illustrated in its Effects upon Women* . . ., p. 32; italics Bourne's.

[201] Foster, *op. cit.,* pp. 71-72; capitalization Foster's.

[202] *Anti-Slavery Bugle,* May 15, 1846. Report of meeting at West Middleton, Penn.

every crime which had been "perpetrated by depraved mortals."[203] Among other crimes of that denomination, he asserted that they had annihilated marriage, "legalized adultery and rape" in the most odious forms, and forced "thousands of the female members" of the church to become "BREEDERS on their plantation," thereby sanctioning a "system of forced concubinage and adultery."[204] Even the good sisters of the church were not allowed to escape the fiery denunciation, for Foster specifically charged that every intelligent woman in the Baptist Church was *an adulteress at heart.*[205] Going still farther in his personal attack, he selected Dr. Furman, one of the great Baptist leaders in South Carolina, in order to give vent to his spleen, and suggested that some of the slaves belonging to that eminent clergyman were his own children.[206] Still unsatisfied, he crowned his derogatory remarks by stating that the most distinguished ministers of the Baptist Church " 'have given a boy for a harlot, and sold a girl for wine, that they might drink!'— nay, who have even *sold* GIRLS *for wine for their communion* table!!"[207]

A similar condemnation was placed at the doors of the Presbyterian and the Congregational churches. It was asserted that a large number of the ministers in these denominations gained their "subsistence by preaching sermons, making prayers, and stealing babes!"[208] Charging that the "spiritual guides" of the Presbyterian Church claimed and appropriated the wives and daughters of their neighbors, Foster argued that thousands among the membership of this church stocked their plantations with their religious sisters and engaged themselves in "raising *boys* and *girls* from these

---

[203] Foster, *op. cit.*, p. 55.   [204] *Ibid.*

[205] *Ibid.*, p. 56; italics Foster's. See also Bourne, *Slavery Illustrated in its Effects upon Women* . . ., p. 31, for condemnation of the Baptist Church.

[206] Foster, *op. cit.*, p. 53.

[207] *Ibid.*, pp. 56-57; italics and capitalization Foster's.

[208] *Ibid.*, p. 41.

breeders," the offspring being used for rice and cotton culture.[209]   Bourne, perhaps mulling over his expulsion as a
clergyman of the Presbyterian Church some twenty years before, denounced the ministers of that religious body as baptiz-
ing the "offspring of adultery and incest" under the direction
of their General Assembly and upon the "Christian pretensions of fornicators, adulterers, and the unclean of every
degree and name."[210]

The Episcopal Church was pointed out as "an inveterate
enemy of abolition," whose ministers and members were
"slave-claimants," and whose general abusive treatment of
Negroes "rivalled even the Methodist Church," this last
statement evidently being sufficient condemnation within itself according to Foster's viewpoint.[211] The Unitarians and
the Universalists were denounced as abettors in the crime of
stripping the slave of his rights and "plundering his domestic
hearthstone."[212] Even the Freewill Baptists and the Society
of Friends, denominations ordinarily considered as anti-
slavery, did not escape the virulent pen of Foster.[213] Though
not emphasizing this method of attack to the extent exhibited
by his abolition satellites, Garrison also condemned the various religious denominations as protecting slavery, sponsor-
ing "man-stealing," and usurping the "prerogatives of the
Almighty!"[214]

Northern churches were included in the abolitionist attack upon religious organizations, but only to the extent to
which they were united with the slaveholding churches of
the South. "Christian women" of the North were implored
not "to hold the communion of the gospel with slave-drivers"

[209] *Ibid.*, pp. 41-42; italics Foster's.

[210] Bourne, *Slavery Illustrated in its Effects upon Women* . . ., p. 59.

[211] Foster, *op. cit.*, p. 56. See Bourne, *Slavery Illustrated in its Effects upon Women* . . ., p. 31, for Episcopal condemnation.

[212] Foster, *op. cit.*, p. 59.

[213] *Ibid.* These denominations were denounced because of their inconsistency in disapproving slavery and then aiding in the election of "manstealers to fill the highest offices in the government."   [214] Garrisons, *op. cit.*, II, 480.

and not to allow "slaveholders" to preach.[215] "Christian
Mothers" in the North were entreated to think of the
"wretched slave Mother," whose child was not her own, and
who was "robbed of all the endearments of domestic life—in
ignorance and darkness—she toils, she suffers, she dies—with
none to pity, none to aid."[216] Then it was pointed out that
slavery could not be blotted out so long as any slaveholder's profession of religion was recognized by Northern
churches.[217] It was argued that as long as Christian women
of the North recognized and admitted slaveholders into
church fellowship, they were virtually approving "the debasement and pollution" of their sex, and were an accessory
"to all the rapes and lewdness" found in the "slave-driver's
domains."[218] Foster generally condemned the churches in
both sections, and, by stigmatizing them as "The Brotherhood of Thieves" because of their communion with slaveholders, exerted influence for the alienation of the Northern
group from the South.[219] As the religious attack gained
strength, the radical abolitionists preached upon the duty of
Northern Christians to destroy the "diabolical system of
slavery." In line with this doctrine, they denounced anyone
belonging to a "pro-slavery Church, or of one that is in fellowship with a pro-slavery Church."[220] Certainly such agitation on the part of the abolitionists was not, to say the least,
conducive toward inspiring brotherly love and Christian fellowship between the churches of the North and of the
South.[221] The question was agitated in various church conferences and assemblies from about 1835 and became particularly violent in the forties. In 1844 the Methodist Epis-

---

[215] Bourne, *Slavery Illustrated in its Effects upon Women* . . ., p. 126.
[216] *Anti-Slavery Bugle,* May 15, 1846, p. 2; italics in *Bugle.*
[217] Bourne, *Slavery Illustrated in its Effects upon Women* . . ., p. 18.
[218] *Ibid.,* p. 127.   [219] Foster, *op. cit., passim.*
[220] *Anti-Slavery Bugle,* Nov. 28, 1845.
[221] Similar conclusion given by A. B. Hart, *Slavery and Abolition, 1831-
1841,* p. 214.

copal Church split over the question of a bishop owning slaves, and the division of the sections was completed by 1846.[222] After considerable agitation over slavery from 1835-1837, the Presbyterian Church split over a doctrinal question in 1838, the Old-School group gradually becoming pro-slavery.[223] The Baptist Church abruptly split into Northern and Southern branches in 1845.[224] It seems quite probable that the bitterness aroused among Southern churches as a result of the unjustified attack of the Bourne-Foster-Garrison group of abolitionists, as well as that animosity engendered by the later War and Reconstruction, has caused these church divisions to be maintained to the present day.

In viewing the radical abolitionist attack upon the South after approximately a hundred years, it seems that the violence of the propaganda appealed only to the sectional interests of the North and merely served to antagonize and alienate the South. If the abolitionists were genuinely interested in ameliorating the condition of the slaves, why did they fail to make use of the anti-slavery sentiment among the Southern people? Instead of using Southern opinion, which might have aided the cause of emancipation, the radicals soon smothered it under an avalanche of vituperation. If the abolitionists really hoped to benefit the Negroes, their attack was a failure because of their incendiary propaganda which necessitated greater coercion and stringent discipline from the slaveholders and left the blacks totally unprepared for freedom when the day of emancipation came. On the other hand, if it was the intention of the abolitionists to discredit the

---

[222] Macy, *op. cit.*, p. 84. Also see J. M. Buckley, *History of Methodists in the United States*, pp. 403-5. For an official Northern account of this, provided by the Northern Conference of 1848, see Rev. Charles Elliott, *History of the Great Secession from the Methodist Episcopal Church*, *passim*. See also Lucius C. Matlack, *The History of American Slavery and Methodism*, and his *The Anti-Slavery Struggle and Triumph in the Methodist Episcopal Church*.

[223] Hart, *Slavery and Abolition*, p. 214; Macy, *op. cit.*, p. 84.

[224] *Ibid.*

Southern agricultural states, to create new sectional and political alignments, to encourage the development of sectional bitterness and hatred, and either to dissolve the government or allow its domination by Eastern industrialism, their tactics were highly successful. But first it is necessary to consider the immediate reactions resulting from this tidal wave of abolition propaganda.

CHAPTER III

IMMEDIATE REACTIONS

ASTOUNDED as they were by the violence of the extreme attack instituted by the Garrisonian and Weld abolitionists, the Southern people were nevertheless slow to change from their view that slavery was a regrettable evil and a racial problem of such magnitude as to render futile their efforts toward a solution. During the decade following the Missouri Compromise, possibly a few of the Southern leaders, realizing the real significance of the ensuing sectional contest for political domination, ceased to condemn or apologize for the peculiar institution of the South. Perhaps still others, as a result of the pecuniary gain which seemed to emanate from cotton produced with slave labor or because they recognized the futility of the numerous proposed schemes of manumission and colonization, merely remained silent upon the subject of slavery. Yet, from the evidence at hand, it seems that in 1831 the majority of the Southerners would have welcomed emancipation had a satisfactory method, one not injurious to the whites and providing for the removal of the freed blacks, been presented. Although they wished to be rid of the evil they hesitated to give up their "young and valuable negroes" because of the severe monetary loss, nor were they willing to "set adrift the aged and helpless," as in many instances they were deeply attached to them.[1] The universal opinion seemed to be that the entire African race should be removed, for the Southerners felt the responsibility of leaving to their posterity "the ills, which from the existence of slavery in our state, they themselves

[1] Susan D. Smedes, *A Southern Planter*, p. 149. See also Hawes, "Slavery in Mississippi," *Sewanee Review*, XXI (1913), 227.

have long felt."[2] Although many of the Southern planters
doubted the advisability of the system of slavery,[3] none at
this time attempted to justify it except on the score of necessity.[4]

It must be remembered that, in 1831, the massacre and
wholesale butchery of the white population of Santo Domingo by emancipated Negroes and mulattoes was still fresh
in the minds of the Southern people.[5] The striking contrast
of the peace, order, and general prosperity of the island while
slavery prevailed, as compared with the destruction, bloody
butchery, the general desolation and resultant economic chaos
that followed emancipation in Santo Domingo, had created a
profound and lasting impression upon the minds of those
living in close proximity to the blacks in the Slave States.[6]
In addition to the massacre in Santo Domingo, the same racial
antagonisms had, at various times and on a smaller scale,
threatened the peaceful existence of the South. The uprising
in 1800, known as "Gabriel's Attempt,"[7] the plot of a free
Negro, Denmark Vesey, in Charleston in 1822,[8] and a slave
rising in lower Louisiana in 1829 brought potential dangers
of servile insurrections close home and to a great extent
created a general feeling of alarm.[9] The *Maryville* (Tennessee) *Intelligencer* stated that the Southern whites were
"emphatically surrounded . . . by a dangerous class of beings

[2] Extract from the *Petersburg* (Virginia) *Intelligencer*, quoted in *Niles Weekly
Register*, XLI (1831), 266. Mississippi passed a law in 1831 requiring that all
adult free Negroes should leave the state.—Sydnor, *op. cit.*, p. 203.

[3] Edward Channing, *History of the United States*, V, 159.

[4] *Pro-Slavery Argument*, p. 179; Rhodes, *op. cit.*, I, 366-67. The essays on
slavery by Harper, Hammond, Simms, and Dew were published under the title of
Pro-Slavery Argument in Charleston in 1852. In 1860 another edition known as
Cotton is King, and Pro-Slavery Arguments was edited by Professor E. N. Elliott.
This work included also sketches by Stringfellow, Hodge, Bledsoe, Cartwright, as
well as Christy's former work, *Cotton is King*.

[5] Herbert, *op. cit.*, p. 80.   [6] *Ibid.*; Beveridge, *op. cit.*, II, 17-18.

[7] James Curtis Ballagh, *A History of Slavery in Virginia*, p. 92.

[8] Beveridge, *op. cit.*, II, 17.

[9] *Niles Weekly Register*, XXXVI (1829), 53.

—degraded, stupid savages, who would repeat Santo Domingo."[10]   Although they were apt to deny it, one writer asserted that many Southerners lived under a "habitual sense of danger" because even a well-cared-for slave population when "coerced into obedience" was a constant threat and a potential source of insecurity.[11]

Even prior to the violent abolition crusade, a sensation had been produced in the South during the winter of 1829-1830 by the distribution of *Walker's Appeal,* a pamphlet written and printed by an obscure free Negro of Boston. Walker addressed his appeal to all colored people and advocated the overthrow of the whites by insurrection and bloodshed as a religious duty. The pamphlet dwelt at length upon the numerical superiority of the blacks and their greater bravery in battle.[12] This pamphlet was circulated in various parts of the South and may have had some influence in stirring the slaves to discontent and revolt.[13] Coming before the fanaticism of the "New Abolitionists" this type of incendiary material did not meet with the approval of Benjamin Lundy who stated that it was an attempt to arouse the "worst passions of human nature" by inflaming the minds of the blacks.[14] As the pamphlet is known to have reached Virginia, it seems quite probable that it may have influenced the diseased mind of Nat Turner.[15]

In August, 1831, Nat Turner, an educated Negro preacher, felt that he was called to deliver his race from bondage. Looked upon by the blacks as a prophet, Turner, by means of omens, an eclipse of the sun, and his own misconception of the Scriptures,[16] inspired his superstitious fellow slaves to accept his leadership and by dramatically describing his spiritual visions and supernatural communion with

---

[10] Quoted in Beveridge, *op. cit.,* II, 17.   [11] Kemble, *op. cit.,* p. 379.
[12] Quoted in Garrisons, *op. cit.,* I, 159-62.
[13] Hart, *Slavery and Abolition,* p. 217.   [14] Earle, *op. cit.,* pp. 237-38.
[15] *Ibid.,* p. 237; Hart, *Slavery and Abolition,* pp. 217-18.
[16] Ballagh, *op. cit.,* pp. 93-94.

the Holy Spirit urged them to emulate the gory triumph of their brethren on the island of Santo Domingo.[17] Planning his insurrection carefully for a time when many homes were open and when most of the male population of the county was attending a religious gathering in North Carolina, Turner and his followers fell upon the whites in Southampton County, Virginia, on the night of August 22.[18] Gathering arms and recruits as they went from house to house, the massacre continued nearly forty-eight hours, during which time sixty-one whites, nearly all of them women and children, were brutally murdered. There seems to have been only one authentic case of a violation of a white woman,[19] though the Negroes, inspired by the fanatical Turner, reverted to the tactics of their ferocious African ancestors, bathed their arms in blood, and committed many savage barbarities before the bloody work was checked.[20] It might be pointed out in passing that of the some forty blacks who took part in the massacre, practically all were given an impartial trial, and of the twenty-one convicted only thirteen were executed. Both free Negro and slave testimony was admitted by the Court during the trial.[21]

[17] Rhodes, *op. cit.*, I, 56; Beveridge, *op. cit.*, II, 16.

[18] Ballagh, *op. cit.*, p. 93.

[19] *Ibid.* A recent publication, Harry Haywood and Milton Howard, *Lynching* (published under the direction of the Labor Research Association, N. Y., 1932), p. 8, states that the Negroes were not known "as rapists until 1830 at the time of the Abolition Crusade," and that the charge has often been made since that time. It is interesting to note that this atrocity by Negroes increased after the circulation of such incendiary material as *Walker's Appeal* and Garrison's *Liberator*. It should be pointed out, though, that the above-quoted statement from *Lynching* is not entirely correct. For early rape cases among the slaves see Flanders, *op. cit.*, p. 255. However, the cases listed are more numerous after 1831.—*Ibid.*, pp. 245, 255, 267-69. As a result of the emphasis placed upon racial equality by the abolitionists from 1830-1860, by the Freedmen's Bureau and Union Leagues during the Reconstruction period, and the more recent activities of the Communists in inciting the Negro, rape cases have become increasingly common.

[20] Beveridge, *op. cit.*, II, 16-17; Rhodes, *op. cit.*, I, 56.

[21] Ballagh, *op. cit.*, pp. 93-94. For a full account of the Nat Turner Insurrection see William S. Drewry, *The Southampton Insurrection, passim.* See also the

The effect of this tragedy in the form of a servile revolt was immediate and the retribution was great.[22] Though at first it was believed that the Southampton insurrection was merely the result of an insane man's influence over the credulous and superstitious slaves, the fact that it came but a few months after the founding of the *Liberator* caused a later view to develop that Turner had been influenced by Northern abolitionists who were believed to be the instigators of the horrible affair.[23] This view, of course, had a tendency to arouse the South against the work of the "New Abolitionists" and to unite Southern opinion against the circulation of antislavery newspapers, in opposition to the education of Negroes, and to create antagonism against any scheme of emancipation unless accompanied by expatriation.[24]

Though the insurrection alarmed the entire South,[25] Virginia was naturally most interested in finding some means of preventing a similar occurrence in the future. Governor Floyd expressed the opinion that Negro preachers were a constant source of trouble when incited by abolitionist doctrines. Speaking to the Virginia legislature in December, 1831, the Governor pointed out that there was reason to believe that "unrestrained fanatics" from other states had influenced the action of Nat Turner,[26] and he urged legislation providing for more repressive slave laws and the expulsion of free Negroes. These proposals resulted in the heated and

---

Richmond Enquirer, Aug. 30, 1831; the *Richmond Whig*, Sept. 26, 1831; and the *Norfolk Herald*, 1831. Also Joshua Coffin, *An Account of Some of the Principal Slave Insurrections, passim*.

[22] Rhodes, *op. cit.*, I, 56.   [23] Beveridge, *op. cit.*, II, 16-17.

[24] Earle, *op. cit.*, pp. 246-47. This biographer takes the view that the Southern press, attributing the insurrectionary plots to the *Genius of Universal Emancipation* and the *Liberator*, probably rendered it impracticable for Lundy to continue the former publication at Washington.

[25] See Stephen B. Weeks, "The Slave Insurrection in Virginia," *Magazine of American History*, XXV (1891), 457-58.

[26] Message of Governor Floyd to the General Assembly of Virginia on Dec. 6, 1831.—Beveridge, *op. cit.*, II, 17.

picturesque "Virginia Debates" during the winter of 1831-1832.

Notwithstanding the recent crusade of Garrison and Weld, and the more recent tragedy at Southampton, probably more outstanding and momentous expressions of Southern sentiment in favor of emancipation occurred in the notable debates of the Virginia legislature than at any other one time. Though these anti-slavery views did not take the form of legislation for the manumission of the slaves, it may at least be concluded that the abolitionist attack had not by that time stifled all anti-slavery sentiment in the South or turned it into righteous wrath. The subject of slavery was still open for discussion in the Slave States and the evils and merits of the institution were given careful consideration and deliberation.

Professor Thomas Dew, in reporting the debate, stated that though most of the legislators were young and relatively inexperienced, the debates "transcended" his expectations and the interest was so great that "multitudes" thronged to the capital.[27] In their great "zeal for discussion," the members "set aside all prudential considerations" in regard to the possible effect of their anti-slavery utterances upon the Negroes following the Nat Turner insurrection, and openly discussed the subject "before the world."[28]

Some of the advocates of emancipation were quite vehement in their denunciation of the system of slavery. Charles J. Faulkner indignantly exclaimed: "Does not the slaveholder," while enjoying the benefits of slave labor, "reflect upon the deep injury and incalculable loss which the possession of that property inflicts upon the true interests of the country? Slavery, it is admitted is an evil."[29] He denounced the economic effect of slavery and its consequent pressure against the best interests of the state by asserting: "it banishes

[27] *Pro-Slavery Argument*, pp. 291-92.   [28] *Ibid.*, p. 293.
[29] Charles J. Faulkner, in the Virginia House of Delegates, Jan. 20, 1832, quoted by Abbott, *op. cit.*, p. 149.

free white labor—it exterminates the mechanic, the artisan, the manufacturer" by depriving them of their means of earning a living.[30]   Another delegate charged that slavery was not only an evil but was also a "mildew" which had "blighted every region" that it had touched.[31]   Still another pointed out that the resources of the entire state had been paralyzed by the "withering, devastating influence of our present system."[32]   Slavery, it was asserted, converted the "energy of a community into indolence, its power into imbecility, its efficiency into weakness."[33]   Because of the very injurious effect of the institution of slavery, it was argued that society demanded the extermination of the system of bondage, in order to protect the interests of humanity.   "Must the country languish, droop, and die, that the slaveholder may flourish?"[34] was the question hurled at the delegates defending slavery.   Mere pecuniary gains could not be compared with the "great interests of the common weal" nor should all rights be made subservient to one.   The middle classes, rather than being subordinate to the slaveholding group, should have their rights—"rights incompatible with the existence of slavery."[35]   Viewing slavery as an evil, they felt that *every year's delay but augments the difficulties of this great business and weakens our ability to compass it.*"[36]   It seems that the anti-slavery delegates took the general view that a crisis had been reached and the remedy of the evil, which would be emancipation, presented fewer difficulties at that time than it would at a later date.

Three main propositions were brought forward by the anti-slavery representatives as possible means of emancipating the slaves and relieving the dangerous situation in the state.

[30] *Ibid.*

[31] Mr. Brodnax, quoted by Olmsted, *op. cit.*, I, 320.

[32] Speech of Mr. Summers quoted in *ibid.*, p. 321.

[33] Speech of Mr. Faulkner, in Abbott, *op. cit.*, p. 149.

[34] Olmsted, *op. cit.*, I, 320.   [35] *Ibid.*

[36] *Ibid.*, p. 321, speech of Mr. Summers; italics in Olmsted.

First, the members of the tidewater counties urged the deportation of the entire mass of blacks and suggested that this might be a means of Christianizing the heathen. This proposition was objected to from an economic standpoint since the slaves represented approximately one-third of the wealth of the entire state.[37] At an average price of $200 each, the slave population of Virginia represented an outlay of $94,000,000, and, as land values were thought to be dependent upon the institution of slavery, the actual loss from emancipation and deportation would be represented by a far greater sum.[38]

A second proposal dealt with the deportation and colonization in Africa of the increase in the slave population. By deporting approximately 6,000 Negroes per year at the expense of the state, it was expected that slavery would gradually decline and that Virginia would eventually be free of her black population. This solution was urged by those who thought that the profits accruing from the interstate slave trade were the incentive that encouraged the retention of slavery. This plan did not receive general support among the delegates because the value of the Negroes combined with their transportation would cost the state approximately $1,380,000 per year, while the domestic slave trade removed the surplus slaves without cost to the Commonwealth.[39]

Still another plan for remedying the evil was proposed by Thomas Jefferson Randolph, who advocated the maintaining of the slaves until they became of age, at which time they were to be hired out until they could pay their transportation from America. This plan was severely criticized and, as Pro-

[37] One-half of the wealth of the tidewater counties of Virginia was invested in slaves. This region would also have had the greatest problem of the free blacks upon emancipation.

[38] Ballagh, *op. cit.*, p. 138; also see article by the same author on "Anti-Slavery Sentiment in Virginia," *South Atlantic Quarterly*, I (April, 1902), 107.

[39] Ballagh, *History of Slavery in Virginia*, p. 138; also his "Anti-Slavery Sentiment in Virginia," *South Atlantic Quarterly*, I (April, 1902), 107-10; Thomas R. Dew, *Review of the Debate in the Virginia Legislature of 1831 and 1832*, pp. 358-60, 377-78.

fessor Dew points out, "Scarcely anyone in the Legislature—
we believe not even the author himself—entirely approved of
this plan."[40] It was objected to because it placed too great
a burden upon the slaveholders, it violated property rights,
and, as it did not begin to operate until 1840, it would probably result in the removal of many slaveholders to other states,
thereby sacrificing much landed property as well as slave
property.[41]

The efforts of the advocates of emancipation in the Virginia General Assembly were weakened by their inability to
agree upon any practical scheme of emancipation or to combine in their attempt to eliminate satisfactorily the evil of the
free Negro. This failure to present a united front strength-
ened the position of the pro-slavery group and the emancipation proposals were defeated by a small majority. Although
a desire and willingness on the part of the Virginia delegates
to abolish slavery was not wanting, unfortunately a satisfactory method of accomplishing emancipation eluded them.
Therefore the same insurmountable problems that had confronted the South in all previous attempts to eliminate the
evils of slavery prevented a solution in 1831-1832. The effect
of this failure was the creation of a feeling among Virginians
as well as other Southerners that "the negro, slave or free,
was an incubus, hopelessly immovable," while, on the other
hand, among the "Northern abolitionists, now in the first
freshness of their zeal," it inspired "an aggressiveness that
inflamed resentment and prevented a future calm consideration of the problem."[42]

We may conclude from the opinions expressed during the
Virginia Debates that the impossibility of emancipating the
slaves without economic destruction, the expense of deporta-

[40] *Ibid.*, p. 381.

[41] *Ibid.*, pp. 381-82; Ballagh, *History of Slavery in Virginia*, pp. 138-39.

[42] *Ibid.*, p. 139; and "Anti-Slavery Sentiment in Virginia," *South Atlantic Quarterly*, I (April, 1902), 115.

tion, and the lack of a suitable location to which to send the Negro were all towering obstacles that barred the way of the South in its efforts to abolish slavery. Yet the remarkable debates, the open discussion of all the phases of the subject in the winter of 1831-1832, stands out as the last great demonstration of Southern sentiment in its protest against the evils of slavery.[43] Although at that time many of the delegates boldly advocated emancipation and denounced slavery as an evil, by 1835 few could be found in the South who would express, openly at least, such opinions. The cause of this rapid and complete change of Southern thought and feeling was the violent abolition assault which began as an organized movement in 1819 but flared up with fiery intensity in 1831.[44]

Immediately after the attack of the radical abolitionists upon the slaveholders, and the consequent revolt led by Nat Turner, the Southern people were filled with consternation and dismay. Rumors of plots, insurrections, and even massacres of the white population in certain sections of the black belt reached gigantic proportions as they were magnified by vivid imaginations.[45] The South was stirred to its very foundation, for many looked upon the Southampton tragedy as but an example on a small scale of the wholesale destruction that would be the fate of the South if the slaves were freed or if the abolitionists were allowed to continue their distribution of incendiary literature.[46] This view, translated into practical operation by the legislatures of various states, resulted in more stringent laws which discriminated against the slaves, free Negroes, and mulattoes. Negroes were not allowed to hold meetings and their instruction was either forbidden or limited by statutes. In North Carolina, for

[43] Olmsted, *op. cit.*, I, 319.

[44] Beveridge, *op. cit.*, II, 18. Also see Chap. II above, which deals with the abolitionist attack.

[45] Ballagh, "Anti-Slavery Sentiment in Virginia," *South Atlantic Quarterly*, I (April, 1902), 115.

[46] Herbert, *op. cit.*, p. 80; Beveridge, *op. cit.*, II, 17-19.

example, no slaves were allowed to employ their time as freemen, while all Negroes, either free or slave, were forbidden to preach, peddle without license, or to own or make a deadly weapon.[47] Due to cases of "insubordination" among the slaves, "traceable . . . to abolition movements," the legislative authorities found it expedient "to infuse new vigor into the police" and to pass laws regulating the conduct of the slaves.[48] The reason that these stringent laws necessarily had to be enforced was the "suspicion eternally attached to the slave himself—the suspicion that a Nat Turner might be in every family."[49] Henry Berry, alarmed by a similar view, predicted that "a *death struggle must come between the two classes, in which one or the other will be extinguished forever.*"[50] Therefore it can be pointed out that the first reaction of the South to the abolition assault and the atrocious event in August, 1831, had a tendency to check the doctrine of emancipation which had previously been gaining a dominant place in Southern sentiment. The effect of the attack, then, was to cause more restrictions to be placed upon the Negroes rather than to promote the interests of abolition.[51]

Nor were the Southerners alone in their astonished opposition to the tactics of the Garrisonian group, for many thoughtful people in the North were alarmed at the shocking potentialities of this group's drastic utterances. Immediately after the attack upon the South, various outstanding leaders

[47] Weeks, "The Slave Insurrection in Virginia," *Magazine of American History*, XXV (1891), 457.

[48] Henry Clay, speech in U. S. Senate, Feb. 7, 1839, quoted in Calvin Colton, *Life, Correspondence and Speeches of Henry Clay*, VI, 154; Beveridge, *op. cit.*, II, 30.

[49] James McDowell, Jr., speaking in the Virginia House of Delegates in 1832, quoted by Coffin, *op. cit.*, pp. 32-33.

[50] Henry Berry in Virginia Legislature in 1832, quoted by Coffin, *op. cit.*, pp. 32-33, and Beveridge, *op. cit.*, II, 17; italics given in the latter.

[51] Weeks, "The Slave Insurrection in Virginia," *Magazine of American History*, XXV (1891), 457; Smedes, *op. cit.*, p. 312; Beverly B. Munford, *Virginia's Attitude Toward Slavery and Secession*, p. 114.

in the North denounced the purpose and methods of the
"New Abolitionists." One of the most familiar expressions of
this widespread opposition to the abolitionists was the Faneuil
Hall meeting in Boston on August 31, 1835. The general
spirit of this meeting belittled the number of agitators and
accused them of wishing to "scatter among our Southern
brethren firebrands, arrows, and death" and of attempting to
force the abolition of slavery by emotional appeals to the
"terror of the masters and the passions of the slaves."[52] The
methods of the abolitionists were denounced at this meeting
with "indignation and disgust," while the city of Boston expressed her "eagerness to lead in bowing to the Southern demand for a general Northern manifesto against the abolitionists."[53] It was pointed out that a number of foreign
abolitionists travelled through the South for the express purpose of observing the most evil, sordid side of slavery. Aided
by fertile imaginations, these invaders portrayed many unim-
portant events as crimes unequalled in the annals of history
under the heading of "Southern Outrages." The Bostonians
emphatically denounced such abolition propaganda as an "in-
trusion upon our domestic relations," performed by "alien
emissaries," who were supported "by the funds of a foreign
people."[54] Briefly, the Faneuil Hall meeting exposed all
abolitionists "to public odium as disorganizers," who sought
"constitutional ends by unconstitutional means," and aimed
"to excite servile insurrection under the pretext of enlightening the masters." They charged that the American abolitionists had called to their aid "hereditary enemies of the republic," a further toleration of whom would mean the
"speedy end of the Union between the States."[55]

On the day after the meeting, the *Liberator* appeared
with the comment that Faneuil Hall had been "turned into
a worse than Augean stable, by the pollutions of a pro-slavery

[52] Garrisons, *op. cit.*, I, 495-96.   [53] *Ibid.*, p. 495.
[54] *Ibid.*, pp. 495-96.   [55] *Ibid.*, p. 500.

meeting held for the first time within its venerable walls."
Garrison charged that the Hall should no longer be called
the "CRADLE OF LIBERTY" but instead should receive
the appellation of the "REFUGE OF SLAVERY."[56] This
attitude on the part of Garrison only served to incense the
citizens of Boston even more against the work and spirit of
the abolitionists.[57]

In other Northern cities mobs strenuously objected to the
more fanatical abolitionists holding meetings or publishing
incendiary literature. A series of anti-abolition riots occurred
in New York from July 7 to July 11, 1834.[58] Lewis Tappan,
a prominent New York merchant, was attacked and his home
wrecked by an angry mob.[59] Tappan, formerly an active colonizationist, had joined the radical abolitionist group in 1833.
Later Lewis Tappan, with his brother Arthur, became leaders
in organizing the American and Foreign Anti-Slavery Society[60] and as has been mentioned before were coöperating
with Theodore Weld. So bitter was sentiment in 1834
against such abolitionists that the action of the mob was
justified on the theory that the "abolitionists are endeavoring
to carry out their wild notions with a high hand."[61]

[56] *Ibid.*, p. 502—capitals Garrison's.

[57] James Schouler, *History of the United States of America under the Constitution 1783-1861*, IV, 217.

[58] These riots are described in contemporary newspapers. *Niles Weekly Register*, XLVI (1834), 357-60, quotes the *New York Daily Advocate*, the *New York
Commercial Advertiser*, and the *New York American*, of July 8, 1834, concerning
the riots of July 7th.

[59] Hart, *Slavery and Abolition*, pp. 189, 246.

[60] See the Tappan papers, reprinted in Tappan, *op. cit.*, p. 315, *et passim.* For
a very partisan biography see Lewis Tappan, *The Life of Arthur Tappan*, and
Clarence W. Bowen, *Arthur and Lewis Tappan.* See also *Weld-Grimké Letters*, I
and II, *passim.*

[61] *Niles Weekly Register*, XLVI (1834), 332. At a meeting held in Tammany
Hall on July 20, 1835, resolutions were adopted which stated that the question of
the evils of slavery belonged "solely to the States in which it is tolerated." Another
resolution stated that the South should not indulge in "any serious apprehensions
that the efforts of the abolitionists, can seriously affect public opinion even in the
North."—*Ibid.*, XLVIII (1835), 382.

Anti-abolition sentiment forced the closing of the school of Miss Prudence Crandall at Canterbury, Connecticut. Miss Crandall was indicted and imprisoned for admitting Negro girls into her institution on an equal basis with the whites. The legal foundation of her indictment came from an act of the Connecticut Legislature of May 24, 1833, which prohibited Negro instruction without the consent of local authorities. This resulted in the closing of the school.[62] Negro instruction without segregation was but a logical result of the abolitionist program. Two years later Oberlin College opened its doors to Negro students and became a center of abolitionist activity in the Northwest.[63]

Despite the Quaker influence, pro-slavery sentiment was so prevalent in Philadelphia in 1834 that mobs attacked and in some instances destroyed approximately forty-four homes of abolitionists.[64] The arrival of George Thompson, an English abolition agitator, precipitated another riot in Boston. He had been imported by his friend Garrison for the purpose of arousing public sentiment against slavery and influencing action through the state legislatures and Congress.[65] Thompson, while on an "inflammatory tour" to agitate the slavery question, asserted that the slaves had the right to cut their masters' throats.[66] The announcement that this British disturber was scheduled to address a meeting of the Female Anti-Slavery Society in Boston was the signal for a protest. The "patriotic citizens" of that city offered $100 as a reward to the first person to "lay violent hands on Thompson" and to facilitate his being brought "to the tar-kettle before

[62] Hart, *Slavery and Abolition*, p. 245. See also the rather lengthy account of the trial of Prudence Crandall in William Jay, *An Inquiry into the Character and Tendency of the American Colonization and American Anti-Slavery Societies*, pp. 30-47.

[63] See introductory note in *A Classified Catalogue of the Collection of Anti-Slavery Propaganda in the Oberlin College Library* (Oberlin, 1932), p. v.

[64] Hart, *Slavery and Abolition*, p. 249.

[65] *Ibid.*, p. 246.   [66] Schouler, *op. cit.*, IV, 217-18.

dark."[67] A group of approximately five thousand persons gathered to break up the meeting and mob the English agitator.[68] Thompson wisely failed to attend the meeting and the mob, refusing to be pacified by the mayor, captured Garrison and dragged him through the city streets with a rope around his neck.[69] The latter only escaped serious physical injury when a few influential men got him away from the mob, placed him in jail for protection, and finally allowed him to leave the city.[70] The unfavorable sentiment aroused by mob action forced the Boston officials to provide sufficient protection to abolition meetings after that date.[71]

Similar scenes took place throughout the North. A series of riots was started in Utica, New York, to prevent the formation of an anti-slavery society, but ended with no more damage than the destruction of an abolitionist press.[72] The organization of this society was completed at the home of Gerrit Smith, a former colonizationist who had by 1835 become an active apostle of the Garrisonian group. After his conversion to the fanaticism of the "New Abolitionists," Smith liberally supported the anti-slavery societies in a financial way, aided fugitive slaves, and later became a leading political abolitionist, being influential in the formation of the Liberty party in 1839.[73]

In Cincinnati, James G. Birney, moving north of the Ohio in 1835 to establish his anti-slavery paper, found that the mayor and the city authorities were opposed to its publication. Later mob violence threatened the destruction of his

[67] Hart, *Slavery and Abolition*, p. 247, quotes from a handbill distributed over the city.   [68] Schouler, *op. cit.*, IV, 218.

[69] *Ibid.*, also Hart, *Slavery and Abolition*, p. 247.

[70] Schouler, *op. cit.*, IV, 218; Hart, *Slavery and Abolition*, pp. 247-48. As a result of these mobs, Thompson was forced to end his tour and was smuggled out of the country on a sailing vessel.

[71] *Ibid.*, p. 248.   [72] *Ibid.*

[73] *Ibid.*, pp. 189-90, 248. See also Octavius B. Frothingham, *Gerrit Smith—A Biography*.

press and of his life.[74] Still farther west, a mob in St. Louis completely demolished the office of the *Observer*, an anti-slavery publication edited by Elijah P. Lovejoy. The latter moved his publication across the river to Alton, Illinois. Twice after settling in his new location, Lovejoy's offices were looted and his presses were destroyed and thrown in the river. Despite repeated warnings, Lovejoy continued to issue his paper containing violent abolition literature. Finally on the night of November 7, 1837, a mob attacked the building in which was stored the anti-slavery press. Though at first they were repulsed with several casualties by the guns of the defenders, they later returned and in the ensuing battle killed Elijah Lovejoy. Though several Alton citizens were indicted for taking part in the mob's action, the jury returned a verdict of not guilty.[75]

Southerners, with the possible exception of a few who were able to pierce the future and predict the consequences, were deeply gratified to learn of the violent opposition to the abolitionists in the North. A majority thought that the mobs who from 1835 to 1838 prevented anti-slavery meetings and destroyed the printing presses and property of the fanatical abolitionists, were true representatives of public opinion and therefore guaranteed the security of Southern social and economic life.[76]

However, the judgment of the South was not correct in

[74] See the *National Cyclopaedia of American Biography*, II, 312-13; Appleton's *Cyclopaedia of American Biography*, I, 267-69; William Birney, *op. cit.*

[75] Practically all of the accounts of the Alton mob are bitterly partisan. Anti-slavery newspapers gave it wide publicity and continued to refer to it for many years. One extremely partisan sketch is given in Frank A. Flower, *History of the Republican Party*, pp. 47-59, who, of course, places the entire blame upon pro-Southern Democrats. See also Henry Tanner, *An Account of the Life, Trials, and Perils of Rev. Elijah P. Lovejoy, who was killed by a Pro-Slavery Mob at Alton, Ill. on the night of Nov. 7, 1837* (Chicago, 1881), and Joseph C. and Owen Lovejoy, *Memoir of Rev. Elijah P. Lovejoy; who was murdered in defence of the Liberty of the Press at Alton, Ill., Nov. 7, 1837* (New York, 1837), for examples of anti-slavery partisanship and propaganda methods.

[76] Herbert, *op. cit.*, pp. 84-92.

this supposition, for the mobbing of abolitionists and the consequent lawless violence which followed the denunciation of that despised sect by Northern newspapers and political leaders proved to be an extremely disastrous boomerang to the Southern cause.[77] The reaction against mob violence, combined with the growing sentiment in the North against slavery, and the realization of the sectional issues involved, brought about a tremendous change in public opinion over the entire North within the next few years. Many Northerners, including influential leaders who had not previously either supported the radicals or approved of their methods, soon inclined favorably toward abolitionism.[78] For example, the great pulpit orator, Dr. William E. Channing, had stated prior to the Faneuil Hall mob that the influence of the abolitionist attack had been *"wholly evil"* upon the South by stirring up *"bitter passions, and a fierce fanaticism"* through the use of *"vituperation."*[79] However, after the series of riots and mob violence, Dr. Channing wrote that the abolitionists had become *"sufferers for the liberty of thought, speech and press,"* and in maintaining themselves against violent aggressions upon liberty they deserved *"a place among its honorable defenders."*[80] John Quincy Adams was another prominent leader who, though not entirely in accord with the early methods of the Garrisonian group, became one of their most ardent defenders in the halls of Congress.[81] In this connection, it must be remembered that Adams was conscious of the possible political results of the abolition crusade against the South.[82]

Without pointing out the many similar individual changes, it may be concluded that many conservative Northerners were

[77] *Ibid.*, pp. 84-85.
[78] *Ibid.*, p. 90; Schouler, *op. cit.*, IV, 219.
[79] Herbert, *op. cit.*, p. 87; italics given in Herbert.
[80] *Ibid.*, p. 88; italics in Herbert.   [81] *Ibid.*, pp. 90-92.
[82] See Chap. I; also Green, *op. cit.*, pp. 30-33.

influenced by these factors which contributed to the change in public opinion. This was particularly true of those groups which were not especially interested in the pros and cons of the slavery question. Though not favorable to the fanatical abolitionists in the beginning, they began to look upon the radical group, not as the attackers of the South, but as martyrs for freedom of speech and press. As a result of this reaction various conservatives became affiliated with the "New Abolitionists" as their defenders and eulogists.[83] To the minds of these, Garrison became the "apostle and martyr of emancipation."[84] With this view they not only allowed the attack of the abolitionists to continue unmolested, but they soon began to encourage it.[85] This abrupt change in Northern opinion concerning the doctrines of abolitionism increased the numbers and resources of the anti-slavery societies and encouraged the radical abolitionists to greater depths of vituperation.[86]

As the people of the South gradually awoke from their lethargy during the years from 1831 to 1836 and as they viewed the new tendency of Northern sentiment, they went even further than merely passing more stringent slave laws— they accepted the challenge of the abolitionists. During the Virginia Debates, they had openly discussed the subject of slavery, its advantages and its evils, rather than denouncing the abolitionists. From that time, however, organized expressions of emancipation sentiment in the South subsided, and it is possible to trace the developments and detect the steps that led to a Southern defense of their civilization. Abundant proof might be presented to show that this change was due almost entirely to the effect of the abolition crusade.[87] A writer in *DeBow's Review* stated that the attack of

---

[83] Herbert, *op. cit.*, p. 90; Schouler, *op. cit.*, IV, 219-20.
[84] *Ibid.*   [85] *Ibid.*
[86] Hart, *Slavery and Abolition*, p. 250.
[87] Many of the contemporary writers, both North and South, made statements

the abolitionists had "done more to retard the progress of Christianity, civilization, comfort and happiness among the slaves than all the other causes put together."[88] Even Daniel Webster, in speaking of the abolitionists, charged that "they attempted to arouse, and did arouse, very strong feeling" by agitating the slavery question and turning the North against the South. He pointed out that, as a result of their agitation, "the bonds of the slaves were bound more firmly than before." Webster argued that everything done by "these agitating people" had been "not to enlarge, but to restrain, not to set free, but to bind faster, the slave population of the South."[89] In 1836 Edmund Ruffin, an intelligent and influential Southerner, wrote that, though the South had nothing to fear from slavery itself, both the "South, *and the Union*" had "everything to fear, (and danger far greater than from servile insurrections) from the restless, mad, and *sustained* action of Northern abolitionists."[90]

As early as 1833 the *Charleston Courier* pointed out to the "Boston editor" that slavery, as it existed in the South "in a mild and parental form," was not "a curse" but an absolute necessity for Southern agriculture and a "great source of their prosperity, wealth and happiness."[91] In the same year the *Charleston Mercury* pointed out that the Southern people would not sanction the suggestion that Southern slavery was "an evil to be deprecated."[92] In 1835 Governor McDuffie of

---

giving this viewpoint. For one example see article in the *True Democrat*, reprinted in the *Anti-Slavery Bugle*, June 15, 1849, p. 1, which states that at the basis of Southern agitation "rests the Northern [agitation] . . . when that began, there was not in the South, as a whole, any thought or action, however distant, on the subject." See also Sydnor, *op. cit.*, pp. 243-48.

[88] *DeBow's Review*, VII (September, 1849), 221; this particular article was written "by a northern man." See also Smedes, *op. cit.*, p. 312.

[89] Daniel Webster quoted by John Douglas Van Horne, *The Southern Attitude Toward Slavery*, pamphlet reprinted from the *Sewanee Review*, XXIX (July, 1921), 15. See also Marshal Hall, *The Two-Fold Slavery of the United States*, pp. 51-52.

[90] Craven, *op. cit.*, pp. 106-7; italics given in Craven.

[91] Jenkins, *op. cit.*, p. 77.   [92] *Ibid.*, pp. 77-78.

South Carolina issued his famous message in which he contended that slavery was a blessing to both the white and black races.[93]

This gradual change in Southern sentiment was not the aggressiveness of a "slave Power," as the abolitionists often charged, but was merely the logical result of the abolitionist attack launched upon them. The safety of the South was jeopardized and therefore some move was necessary as a means of self-preservation. Governor Gayle, in his protest to the Alabama legislature in 1835, stated that the abolitionists were distributing incendiary pamphlets, tracts, and pictures among the slaves, "calculated to render them dissatisfied" and for the purpose of inciting them "to rebellion against their masters." Such literature was a means of introducing the "bloody scenes" of a drama which was being plotted by the "dark spirit of fanaticism" for the ruin of the South. Governor Gayle also pointed out that the Southern people looked upon slavery as their own peculiar institution which had been in existence prior to the drafting of the Constitution and which had been "sanctioned, ratified, and confirmed by that instrument."[94] Knowing the effects of emancipation and being deeply impressed by the horrible calamities of a servile and domestic revolt which would be the inevitable result of the abolitionists arousing the slaves, the Southern people in self-defense resolved to permit no discussion of the subject of slavery. And by means of laws they hoped to prohibit the distribution of incendiary literature which might incite the blacks to massacre the white population.

An admirable statement of the view that was later prevalent over the entire South was expressed by Chancellor Wil-

---

[93] Gov. McDuffie's message "on the slavery question" in 1835, reprinted in *American History Leaflets*, No. 10.

[94] Thomas M. Owen, "An Alabama Protest against Abolitionism in 1835," *Gulf States Historical Magazine*, II (July, 1903), 30-31, quotes extract from Governor Gayle's message to the Alabama legislature; taken from the *Journal of the Alabama House of Representatives*, 17th sess., November, 1835, pp. 12-14.

liam Harper of South Carolina when he said: "If we are tyrants, cruel, unjust, oppressive, let us humble ourselves and repent in the sight of Heaven," in order that the foul stains "may be cleansed, and we enabled to stand erect as having common claims to humanity with our fellow-men." On the other hand, if the Southern people were "nothing of all this"; if they committed "no injustice or cruelty"; or if the maintenance of their institutions was "essential to our prosperity, our character, our safety, and the safety of all that is dear to us, let us enlighten our minds and fortify our hearts to defend them."[95]

Using such a sentiment as a foundation for their efforts, Southern writers, scholars, ministers, and public leaders really began seriously to study the question of slavery—its historical background, its biblical associations, and the social and economic significance of this peculiar institution.[96] From these studies came the South's answer to the charges of the abolitionists. Southern leaders objected vigorously to the methods and the alleged sincerity of the abolitionists. These objections may be classified into three general but nevertheless distinct groups. First, it was only natural that the spirit of men should rebel against such "wholesale vituperation and calumny" as was embodied in the attack of the Northern abolitionists. Next, they objected to the obstacles which the abolitionists themselves placed in the way of providing the slaves a degree of education, religious training, and the consequent raising of the Negroes' standards of civilization. Numerous inflammable pamphlets, filled with pictures and arguments to incite the blacks to revolt, which the abolitionists continually circulated among the slaves, forced the South to place restrictions upon the education of all Negroes. Lastly, the South objected to the abolitionists by denying the sincerity of their "professed sympathy" for the slaves "as

---

[95] *Pro-Slavery Argument*, p. 2.   [96] *Ibid.*, p. 169.

evidenced by the antipathy" which Northerners exhibited toward the free Negroes.[97] The South had good reason to doubt the sincerity of those who clamored so loudly for loosening the fetters of the slaves when these same abolition-ists treated the free Negroes as outcasts and forced them to a life of wretchedness in the North. It was pointed out that in theory the fanatical attack of the abolition-crusaders was to free the slaves, whereas in reality it was "the spoilation of their neighbors." One writer stated: "Had the proposition come from the wild Arabs . . . I might have comprehended the modest proposal; but coming from those whose energy for business is proverbial . . . I confess it is beyond my puny imagination to fathom." It was preposterous to the South-erners that those whose ancestors had profited by the slave trade and later "profitably removed slavery from their borders" should demand complete and immediate abolition in the South without any adequate pecuniary offers for the sacri-fice proposed. Had the abolitionists considered the proposi-tion carefully they should have known that "in every epithet heaped upon their Southern countrymen, they were riveting a fresh bolt for the slave's fetters."[98]

The South, composed of an agricultural people seeking to pursue their own destinies under their own social and eco-nomic system, largely desired to be left alone and was not aggressively seeking to extend the system of bondage as charged by the abolitionists. Or, in the words of Edmund Rhett, the Southern people merely wished the opportunity of rearing their children for "some other purpose than to make them vulgar, fanatical, cheating Yankees."[99] A slow amel-ioration of the conditions of the slaves in the South had been developing until halted by the abolition agitation.[100] Had

[97] Henry Anthony Murray, *Lands of the Slave and the Free*, p. 358.
[98] *Ibid.*, pp. 355-56.
[99] William H. Russell, *My Diary, North and South*, p. 60.
[100] Beveridge, *op. cit.*, II, 32; see also Cotton, *op. cit.*, VI, 154.

not the "assaults of the abolitionists" stopped this improvement of slave conditions it is quite probable that it would
have developed into some form of peonage. This regulating
and improving of the status of the blacks, combined with un-
profitableness of slave labor in certain areas of the South,
would have led eventually to complete emancipation.[101] Certainly, as a result of the more diversified agriculture in Kentucky, Tennessee, and Virginia, slave labor was declining and
those states would have taken steps toward "prospective
emancipation" had it not been for the interference of outside
abolitionists.[102]

It was pointed out that, with their social system, the
Southerners were able "to cultivate the arts, the graces, and
accomplishments of life, to develop science," and to apply
themselves to the duties and affairs of the government even
while they were accomplishing the great work of saving a
race from barbarism.[103] As they began to realize that their
social and economic structure was being undermined, and that
they as individuals were being unjustly attacked, it was only
natural that the Southern people studied the question of
slavery carefully and viewed its effect from a different angle.
The investigation of slavery which followed the "violent assaults" of the abolitionists resulted in the "firm and settled
conviction" among Southerners that "duty to the slave as
well as the master" prohibited the disturbing of the relationship between the two races.[104] And with this conviction came
what might be called a counterattack, but what was in reality
a sincere defense of what the Southern people considered as
one of their inalienable rights. It was expressed by Jefferson

---

[101] Beveridge, *op. cit.*, II, 32.

[102] "The Black Race in North America," *Southern Literary Messenger*, XXI
(November, 1855), 680. See similar view in Hall, *op. cit.*, pp. 51-52.

[103] Russell, *op. cit.*, p. 48, quotes Edmund Rhett.

[104] Beveridge, *op. cit.*, II, 33, quotes letter of Judge Joseph Henry Lumpkin to
Howell Cobb, Jan. 21, 1848, reprinted in *Report of the American Historical Association*, II (1911), 94-95.

Davis in 1850 when he stated that "We of the South stand now, as we have always stood, upon the defensive. We raised not this question; but when raised, it is our duty to defend ourselves."[105] Subsequent chapters will show that in their defense they at first merely answered the outrageous charges of the abolitionists, but that as they delved deeper into the subject a new philosophy of slavery was developed, part of which to this day forms the "central theme of Southern History."[106]

[105] Jefferson Davis, in speech on Jan. 10, 1850, in Dunbar Rowland, *Jefferson Davis, Constitutionalist, His Letters, Papers, and Speeches,* I, 252.

[106] See discussions in subsequent chapters.

CHAPTER IV

SOUTHERN DEFENSE

RECOVERING from their first shock at the violence and injustice of the abolitionist attack, Southerners resolved to defend themselves and their way of living.[1] The passage of repressive slave laws had been accomplished with a view to preventing the South from being turned into a second Santo Domingo. Abolition literature was suppressed to prevent the recruiting of future Nat Turners to repeat countless Southampton tragedies. In pursuance of this policy the Southerners appealed to their Northern neighbors to aid in the suppression of the incendiary material of the fanatics.[2] But these were only minor results of the radical abolition attack. Much more important, in the light of later events, was the Southern defense of slavery.

A few political leaders had believed since the Missouri controversy that the agitation of the slavery issue was but an entering wedge by which the political control of the federal government might be secured for the industrial section to the detriment of the agricultural South. Though the leaders viewed the struggle in this light, the mass of Southerners were slow to grasp the real significance of the agitation and the movement had spread rapidly before they became thoroughly alarmed at the possible consequences of such radical proposals. Only when they realized that, in addition to the attack upon their personal rights, the abolitionists were undermining the social and economic foundations of Southern civilization did the Southerners rally to the defense of their institutions. In doing so they discarded their earlier anti-

---

[1] See Chap. III. [2] Beveridge, *op. cit.*, II, 32.

slavery views[3] and prepared to answer the charges made by the abolitionists. Then were the politicians joined by the literary, educational, and religious leaders in formulating the doctrines that dominated Southern thought for many years.

The entire controversy may be described as a great debate between the representatives of industry and agriculture. The industrial section, as represented vocally by the abolitionists, advocated a complete change in the social and economic organization of the neighboring agricultural section. To accomplish this they proposed the complete overthrow of the labor system of the South. Their emotional appeal was founded on the declaration that the South's labor system was an unmitigated evil. The burden of proof, the necessity of attacking an established principle, an institution that had survived for countless ages, was upon the shoulders of the abolitionists. No debating ethics governed this contest, for first the abolitionists and later the pro-slavery group denounced their opponents in the most scathing terms. Nor was it conducted for academic recognition or forensic exercise, for in the background lay a worthy prize—political domination by which one section might exploit the other for economic gain. The outcome of the complete change proposed by the abolitionists naturally caused the first efforts of the Southern leaders to take the form of refuting the charges of their opponents. A deluge of pamphlets, books, addresses, and periodicals, almost equalling the voluminous works of the abolitionist press, sent forth the data and arguments that were to substantiate the Southern position. The debate grew hotter, and thousands in each section, viewing the contest with eyes blurred by personal interests, were no longer content to remain as part of the audience but entered actively into the forum. As each new group was drawn into the camp of one side or the other, their numbers were carefully computed and

[3] See Chap. I.

filed away for future use by those men interested in controlling the block of votes that wielded the balance of power.[4]

Not only were the people of the South prepared to refute
the charges of the abolitionists but they were ready to point
out the fact that either defense or complete submergence were
the only alternatives. A people characterized by a "quick and
fiery temperament" would naturally resent the "wholesale
slander" upon such "devout Christians as thousands of the
slaveholders." It is not surprising that the loyal citizens of
the Slave States should feel "aggrieved, slandered, and ill-
treated" and in their excitement use harsh language toward
the Northern States. The Southern people would be expected
to object "to any interference by the people of the Northern
States, or those of other nations" with what they considered
"their constitutional rights."[5]

The charges made by abolitionists that slavery sponsored
violence and inspired brutality and viciousness among the
overseers and planters were vigorously denounced by the defenders of the system as being grossly exaggerated. Miss
Martineau had boldly asserted that it was a common practice
for the planters to kill off their slaves by overwork in five to
seven years.[6] Such statements, according to Hammond, were
lies resulting from the research and ingenuity of the abolitionists, aided by the "inventions of runaway slaves," the
latter being unrivaled masters of the art of "improvising
falsehoods." Exaggerations, reinforced by a few "highly
colored" instances that had occurred half a century before,
had allowed the fanatical abolitionists to shock the world with

[4] See somewhat similar view in John Henry Hopkins, *A Scriptural, Ecclesiastical, and Historical View of Slavery*, pp. 17-18.

[5] "Slavery at the South," *DeBow's Review*, VII (November, 1849), 384-85.

[6] Martineau, *Society in America*, II, 29; Kemble, *op. cit.*, p. 389, makes a sim-
ilar statement regarding sugar plantations. It must be remembered that the
Georgia plantation described by Miss Kemble was not typical as it was owned by a
Northern man and operated under a system of absentee ownership. Also see U. B.
Phillips, *American Negro Slavery*, p. 382.

"a small number of pretended instances" of Southern barbarity.[7]

The innumerable assertions of abolitionists concerning the use of "thumb screws" and other inhumane forms of punishment were emphatically denied. It was pointed out that only in extreme cases of turbulent and vicious slaves did the masters make a practice of flogging and then with less severity than charged by the abolitionists. Only runaways and known criminals were chained and it was the common practice to confine criminals the world over.[8] Simms admitted that in occasional instances the slaves suffered "wrongs, blows, brutalities, and loss of life," but denied that these risks were peculiar to slavery. Therefore, such offenses should be charged to the system of slavery only when proof was given that the "free states and communities enjoy exemption from them."[9] It was also pointed out that the abolitionists had overlooked Southern laws which effectually protected the slave from such outrages. Courts redressed wanton injuries against the slave while the murder of a Negro, either slave or free, was punishable by death.[10]

It was stated by the defenders of slavery that a large portion of the alleged atrocities of the slaveholders were perpetrated by foreigners, the Scotch and English making the most cruel masters with New England Yankees a close second.[11] Even Mrs. Stowe admitted this in her work of abolitionist fiction by describing the "most heartless, bloody, brutal, gross, loathsome" wretch as a Yankee planter. Despite this fact she had attempted to portray him as the example of the masters found upon Louisiana plantations.[12]

[7] *Pro-Slavery Argument,* p. 127.

[8] *Ibid.,* pp. 127-29; George S. Sawyer, *Southern Institutes: or, An Inquiry into the Origin and Early Prevalence of Slavery and the Slave Trade,* p. 213.

[9] *Pro-Slavery Argument,* p. 216.

[10] *Ibid.,* pp. 215-16. [11] *Ibid.,* p. 127.

[12] *Ibid.* Simms has reference to Harriet Beecher Stowe, *Uncle Tom's Cabin.* This work of fiction, in which we find all the isolated examples of the cruelties of

Certainly such brutal outrages were uncommon in the South, for during the notable Virginia Debates of 1831-1832 not even the most fervid advocate of emancipation had charged or even insinuated that the slaves of Virginia were not treated kindly.[13] In the trial of Nat Turner, following the Southampton tragedy, none of the witnesses, not even Nat, submitted testimony to show that cruel treatment had been a contributing cause of the insurrection.[14] In contrast to the abolitionists' accusations, it was pointed out that many people who were acquainted with conditions in the slaveholding communities testified to the rareness of cruelty there, because of the fact that slaveholders were "more keenly alive to the noblest sentiments of generosity and honor" and came nearer to having the "highest refinements of feeling" than most men.[15]

It was readily admitted that when the Negroes committed offenses some form of punishment was necessary for the sake of discipline, but this was merely in accord with criminal laws in all sections.[16] To confine a Negro overnight or to deprive him of going to a dance was often sufficient punishment because of the gregarious instinct of the blacks which caused a dread of solitude. This method of discipline, according to one slaveholder, was more effective than flogging.[17] Even in confinement, chains and irons were rarely used, except in the case of runaways, when of course they were necessary to prevent the slave from absconding.[18] Northern and foreign visitors had been favorably impressed by the patience that the slaveowners displayed toward their

---

slavery portrayed as typical of the system, went into many editions, was widely quoted by the abolitionist press, and greatly influenced public opinion in the North against slavery and the South.   [13] *Pro-Slavery Argument*, p. 459.

[14] Ballagh, *History of Slavery in Virginia*, p. 94.

[15] *Niles Weekly Register*, XLVII (Sept. 27, 1834), 60.

[16] *Pro-Slavery Argument*, pp. 127-30.

[17] *DeBow's Review*, XI (October, 1851), 390.

[18] *Pro-Slavery Argument*, p. 129.

slaves regarding trivial but exasperating offenses.[19] Southerners resented greatly the exaggeration of the abolitionists
as to the cruelty and degradation of slave punishments. The
pro-slavery writers protested against this by pointing out that
the punishments accorded to slaves were far less severe than
those meted out for the same offenses in the North or in England.[20] Governor Hammond substantiated this argument by
pointing out that for the crime of stealing a pig an Englishman would be "transported—torn from wife, children, parents, and sent to the antipodes, infamous, and an outcast
forever," while a slave for the same crime would perhaps get
"forty stripes." For burglary an Englishman might be hung,
while a slave would receive only a few lashes or a short confinement for the same offense.[21]

Southerners argued that the majority of the Northern
people had the wrong impression of the system of slavery as
practiced in the South. This misconception of slavery was
the result of abolition propaganda. It was pointed out that to
those who depended upon abolition propaganda as a source
of information, slavery meant tyranny, cruelty, oppression,
and every burden that tended toward making those in bondage suffer and hopelessly repine. Regarding this point, it
was boldly asserted that "if slavery means anything of that
nature, then slavery does not exist" in the Southern States.
The Northern people were being misled by the term "slavery," for, to those acquainted with the patriarchal system of
the South, it was "precisely the kind of slavery to which
every abolitionist in the country *dooms his wife and children.*"[22]

[19] Martineau, *Society in America*, II, 75.

[20] Beveridge, *op. cit.*, II, 37.   [21] *Pro-Slavery Argument*, p. 130.

[22] *DeBow's Review*, VII (September, 1849), 216. This article, signed "by a
northern man," goes on to state that the author would feel "just as guilty of
meddling" where he had no right in trying to take away the control of a man
over his wife and children as he would in trying to "free the Southern slaves."
In doing so he would be transferring the slave from "a state of comparative happiness and reducing him to a state of absolute misery." Italics in *DeBow's*.

In their concession that there were isolated examples of a few cruel masters and overseers, just as there were bad men everywhere, the defenders of slavery emphatically denied that this was inherently a result of the institution of slavery.[23] Chancellor Harper declared that the "miscreant" guilty of wanton cruelty not only violated the "law of God and humanity" but also endangered the welfare of his country and cast a shadow upon the character of "his fellow-citizens."[24] The slaveholder, asserted Hammond, was "responsible to God," to the community in which he lived, and to the civil laws for his actions. Therefore he was legally and morally prevented from killing, maiming, severely punishing, or even overworking his slaves.[25] It was pointed out that masters who abused or mistreated their slaves lost the respect of their community and were universally despised and hated in the South.[26] According to this view public opinion alone was sufficient to prevent the cruel practices which Miss Martineau implied were common occurrences in the South.[27]

Not only from a moral and legal responsibility, but also from an economical, common-sense point of view, the planters were obligated to provide good food, sufficient clothing, and comfortable homes for the slaves, as a means of promoting their interests.[28] Simms declared that it was the policy of slaveholders to prolong the Negro's life, preserve his health and strength, and provide contentment. These things were accomplished, according to Simms, by supplying the necessities of life, requiring moderate tasks, and allowing more leisure time to slaves than was usually allotted to free laborers in other sections.[29] In regard to this considerate care of the

---

[23] *Pro-Slavery Argument*, pp. 65, 123-35.

[24] *Ibid.*, p. 65.   [25] *Ibid.*, p. 123.

[26] *Ibid.*, pp. 123-24; also *DeBow's Review*, VII (November, 1849), 384.

[27] See charge made by Martineau, *Society in America*, II, 29; see also Olmsted, *op. cit.*, I, 108; *Niles Weekly Register*, XLVII (September, 1834), pp. 59-60.

[28] Abbott, *op. cit.*, p. 169.

[29] *Pro-Slavery Argument*, p. 215. See also the "Rules enforced on the Rice

health of slaves, a citizen of Mississippi wrote in *DeBow's Review* that "the great object is to prevent diseases and prolong the useful laboring period of the negro's life. Thus does interest point out the humane course."[30]

The conditions portrayed by the defenders of slavery were quite different from the picture of half-starved, naked slaves, shivering under the chill of a cold rain, and lacking sufficient food or rest to sustain life in their miserable bodies, as described in the abolition propaganda.[31] Care was taken to show that the slaveholders were extremely considerate in providing sanitary living quarters for the slaves.[32] The slave quarters on most plantations were neat, clean, roomy cabins, conducive to healthful living.[33] Some planters were so concerned about the health of the slaves that they provided sheds in the fields to shelter the Negroes during inclement weather.[34] All of these provisions took additional time and expense, but the attitude of the slaveholder, as expressed by one, was that he would rather sustain this loss than "suffer the slave's exposure to the elements."[35] During illness, slaves were given medical attention, often by the same doctor who

Plantation of P. C. Weston of S. C.," which state that the first object of the proprietor and overseer was to see to the "care and well being of the negroes." Quoted in *DeBow's Review*, XXII (January, 1857), 38-44, in article on "Management of a Southern Plantation."

[30] "The Negro" by a citizen of Mississippi, *DeBow's Review*, III (May, 1847), 419-20.

[31] See charges made in *Leed's Anti-Slavery Tracts*, and other abolitionist material.

[32] "The Negro," *DeBow's Review*, III (May, 1847), 419-20, states that "Houses for negroes should be elevated at least two feet above the earth, with good plank flooring, weather proof, and with capacious windows and doors for ventilation, a large fireplace, and wood convenient. A negro house should never be crowded. . . . Good water is essential . . . should not allow bayou, or spring, or well water to be taken into the field."

[33] Olmsted, *op. cit.*, I, 47; also "The Negro," *DeBow's Review*, III (May, 1847), 419.

[34] "Management of Negroes upon Southern Estates," *DeBow's Review*, X (June, 1851), 624.

[35] "The Negro," *DeBow's Review*, III (May, 1847), 420.

attended the planter's own family.[36] Dental care was provided for the slaves from time to time.[37] On the larger plantations, hospitals were even provided with clean, well-ventilated rooms, and adequate accommodations for the needs of the plantation.[38] Even Miss Martineau credited a wealthy planter with having sufficient kindness to risk his life by nursing and bathing with his own hands slaves that were stricken with cholera.[39]

Not only did natural kindness and humane principles condemn the maltreatment of slaves, but the large monetary investment involved furnished a strong incentive for taking care of such valuable property.[40] All of the Southern advocates of slavery agreed that interest alone, regardless of sentiment, demanded that the slaves be well treated and that leniency be shown them since profitable results from slave labor could be obtained in no other way.[41]

This attitude would cause the master to provide a sufficient supply of good simple food. Since underfeeding would promote theft, create discontent, and lessen the effectiveness of the slave labor, the Negroes were given an abundant supply of nourishing food. Regular allowances of approximately four pounds of meat and a peck of corn meal were distributed to each slave during each week.[42] These staples were usually

[36] Olmsted, op. cit., I, 438-39; George Fitzhugh, Sociology for the South, or The Failure of Free Society, p. 246.   [37] Beveridge, op. cit., II, 38 n.

[38] Sir Charles Lyell, A Second Visit to the United States of North America, I, 264.

[39] Martineau, Society in America, II, 74.

[40] Abbott, op. cit., p. 169, states that the master cared for sick slaves "tenderly. . . . These slaves are worth fifteen hundred dollars perhaps, and their lives and health are not to be trifled with."

[41] John Perkins, "Relation of Master and Slaves in Louisiana and the South," DeBow's Review, XV (September, 1853), 275-77; Pro-Slavery Argument, p. 30.

[42] "Management of Negroes upon Southern Estates," DeBow's Review, X (June, 1851), 623-24; Taylor, op. cit., p. 89, cites the Farmers' Journal of May, 1853, in which a contributor states that he gave slaves in winter "five pounds of pork, clear of bone, and a peck of meal; and in the summer we reduce the allowance of each one pound of meat and give a quart of molasses instead." See also U. B.

supplemented with field peas, beans, melons, pumpkins, corn, and various other vegetables in season. These additions to the regular allowance were either supplied from the master's garden or, as was the case upon many plantations, each slave family had its patch of vegetables for its own use.[43] In many instances the slaves were permitted to raise poultry and pigs and these formed a valuable supplement to the rations.[44] In numerous reports and articles concerning plantation management the defenders of slavery pointed out that the abolitionist charge of starving the slaves was utterly false.[45] Not only were the slaves well fed on all plantations, but in some instances specific amounts were provided in the plantation budgets for additional luxuries in the form of sugar, molasses, and other delicacies.[46]

It was assumed that the humanitarian principles and personal interests of the masters impelled them to grant the slaves a comfortable living. The scarcity of complaints on this score justified the assumption.[47] This was also borne out by Olmsted, a Northern traveler who, after visiting the South, wrote that if a master failed to provide well for his slaves, he received the name of "nigger-killer" and lost the respect of the community.[48] To insure sufficient food for the

---

Phillips, *American Negro Slavery*, pp. 261-90; Sydnor, *op. cit.*, pp. 23-44; and Flanders, *op. cit.*, pp. 133-81, for discussions of care of slaves.

[43] Olmsted, *op. cit.*, I, 120-21. One farmer stated that he gave his food out daily, "one half pound to each hand that goes to the field, large or small," and "bread and vegetables without stint, the latter being prepared in my own garden, and dealt out to the best advantage, endeavoring to have something for every day in the year."—*DeBow's Review*, XXIII (October, 1857), 370.

[44] "Management of Negroes upon Southern Estates," *DeBow's Review*, X (June, 1851), 623-24.

[45] *DeBow's Review* carried many articles concerning this. For example see issues X (June, 1851), 623-24; VII (November, 1849), 380-83; XXIII (October, 1857), 370; XIX (September, 1855), 258-63; XVIII (June, 1855), 713-19.

[46] *Ibid.*, XXIII (October, 1857), 372.

[47] Ballagh, *History of Slavery in Virginia*, p. 102.

[48] Olmsted, *op. cit.*, I, 120-21. Olmsted stated that the slaves were well provided for, having a sufficient supply of meal, pork, vegetables, etc.

slaves many of the Southern States regulated the minimum rations by law;[49] evidently the abolitionists had overlooked this fact.

Economic interest also prevented the use of slave labor in such unhealthful and dangerous labor as "ditching, trenching, clearing waste lands, and hewing down forests," which was usually done by Irish labor gangs under contractors.[50] The reason for this, as expressed by one overseer, was that it was more profitable "to have the Irish do it, who would cost nothing to the planter, if they died, than to use up good field hands in such severe employment."[51]

Having refuted the abolitionist charges of the slaves being poorly housed and ill-fed, the pro-slavery group proceeded to point out that the slaves were far from being the naked wretches described in the anti-slavery press. Many examples were given to illustrate the fact that the slaves were comfortably clothed in both summer and winter.[52] In addition to being of economic importance, it was a matter of pride with all plantation owners to display a group of healthy well-clothed Negroes. It was asserted that this pride of ownership that manifested itself in the favorable appearance of the slaves reached such heights that a Southern lady took pleasure in advising and directing her servants in order that they might present a respectable appearance. A grotesque or ill-fashioned garment on a female slave appearing in public was sure to be the subject of comment from the lady's neighbors.[53] Indeed, it was stated that some of these "colored

[49] Louisiana required meat to be furnished while North Carolina fixed a daily allowance of corn. Other states had legislation providing that sufficient food be given to preserve the health of the slaves. See discussion of this in Rhodes, *op. cit.*, I, 306.   [50] Russell, *op. cit.*, p. 104.

[51] *Ibid.*, Olmsted, *op. cit.*, I, 101, gives similar example.

[52] See *DeBow's Review*, "Management of Negroes upon Southern Estates," X (June, 1851), 623-24; Nehemiah Adams, *A Southside View of Slavery*, pp. 29-31; Olmsted, *op. cit.*, I, 438-39.

[53] Nehemiah Adams, *op. cit.*, pp. 31-32.

ladies" were so well dressed "after the latest Parisian mode" that they "would have produced a decided sensation in any European drawing room."[54] A Northern visitor in the South asserted that his "previous images of slaves were destroyed" by seeing slave women in clothes that "would have been creditable to the population of any town at the North."[55] In connection with these assertions, it might be well to point out that though the slaves were adequately clothed most of their garments were plain and often made upon the plantation by the mistress, the housekeeper, or domestic servants. On the smaller plantations the women members of the family were often seriously inconvenienced by the necessary drudgery of providing clothing for the slaves. In some instances, of course, clothing was imported from the North or England.[56] At least it may be concluded that in general the dress of the slave reflected credit upon the masters and compared favorably to that of the laboring classes in other parts of the world.[57]

In refuting the specific charges of the abolitionists concerning the ill-treatment of slaves in the South, the pro-slavery writers did not depend alone upon mere denials of the anti-slavery assertions. They also referred to the views of many Northern and foreign visitors who had been favorably impressed by the general appearance of the plantations and slave life. This, of course, did not include Harriet Martineau. It was asserted that Miss Martineau, who viewed all things in the South through a "blackened glass," needed the "helping hand of that benign occulist, Truth," to give her

[54] Beveridge, *op. cit.*, II, 40. Olmsted, *op. cit.*, I, 28-29, speaks of there being more well-dressed colored people on the streets of Richmond, Va., than whites. He states that some wore "the finest French cloths, embroidered waistcoats, patent-leather shoes, resplendent brooches, silk hats, kid gloves, and *eau de mille fleurs.*"

[55] Nehemiah Adams, *op. cit.*, p. 32.

[56] See discussion in Ballagh, *History of Slavery in Virginia*, p. 103.

[57] "Management of Negroes upon Southern Estates," *DeBow's Review*, X (June, 1851), 623-24; Nehemiah Adams, *op. cit.*, pp. 29-31.

eyes clearer vision.[58] On the other hand, Nehemiah Adams, a New England clergyman who went South expecting to hear the clanking of chains and the wails of three millions of slaves, found conditions good and the slaves a happy contented group of people.[59] In spite of his original anti-slavery sentiment, this New Englander, after careful examination of the system of slavery while in actual contact with the institution, became converted to the Southern point of view. Although previously a contributor to abolition societies, after viewing the effects of the violent abolitionist attack upon the South, Adams condemned the Northern anti-slavery societies for distributing incendiary material among the slaves. He explained the lack of anti-slavery sentiment in the South after 1832, the prohibition of abolition publications from the mails, the more stringent slave laws, and the Southern defense of slavery purely as the natural and direct result of the abolition attack upon the South. Nothing was more evident in the mind of a Northerner in the South, according to his statement, "than the vast injury" which had "resulted from Northern interferences" in Southern domestic affairs.[60] Frederick Law Olmsted, in his various journeys over the Slave States, found that the Negroes were well treated and provided with comfortable quarters.[61] Foreign visitors like Lady Wortley were impressed by the contentment of the Southern slaves.[62] Fredrika Bremer believed that with good masters the slaves enjoyed better conditions than did the poor laboring classes in many parts of the Old World.[63] After travelling in the United States for some time, Charles Mackay was convinced that the slaves were "better clad, fed, and cared for

---

[58] *Pro-Slavery Argument*, p. 215.

[59] Nehemiah Adams, *op. cit.*, pp. 9, 10, 18.

[60] *Ibid.*, pp. 7, 11, 106, 107, 108, 110. See also the discussion of this point in Ballagh, *History of Slavery in Virginia*, pp. 141-42.

[61] Olmsted, *op. cit.*, I, 47; also Olmsted's *A Journey in the Back Country*, p. 15.

[62] Rhodes, *op. cit.*, I, 373.   [63] Bremer, *op. cit.*, I, 296.

than the agricultural laborers of Europe or the shop toilers and seamstresses of London and Liverpool."[64]

Not content merely to refute the abolitionist charges of maltreatment of slaves by pointing out the facts and referring to observations of visitors, the pro-slavery writers went so far as to return the challenge. The Southerners demanded and insisted upon an investigation, declaring that crimes of all descriptions, brutality, murder, and violence occurred less frequently in the Slave States than in the North and that the Negro was less often the sufferer than the white man.[65] Maintaining the benefits of the patriarchal system of agriculture practiced in the South, the defenders of slavery challenged the abolitionists to a comparison of the conditions of labor in the Slave States with those in the industrial centers of the North and Europe.[66]

Basing their counterattack upon the premise that slavery existed wherever a man is compelled to labor at the will of another, the Southern defenders were emphatic in their denunciation of the "slavery" of the free laborers of the North and England as being a greater evil than the type practiced in the South.[67] DeBow's Review asked whether it was better for an individual to be well fed, adequately clothed, comfortably housed, and cared for during infancy, illness, and old age, as provided by the patriarchal system of the South, or to live in the damp, crowded cellars, fireless dens, and the squalid wretchedness of the tenements in the industrial sections of New and Old England.[68] It was the group familiar with the horrors of the latter description that filled the world

[64] Charles Mackay, Life and Liberty in America, I, 311; also quoted by Rhodes, op. cit., I, 373.
[65] Pro-Slavery Argument, p. 216; also see Thomas R. Dew, "Address on the Influence of the Republican System of Government upon Literature and Development of Character," Southern Literary Messenger, II (March, 1836), 278.
[66] Pro-Slavery Argument, pp. 30-31.   [67] Ibid., pp. 52-53.
[68] "Negro Slavery at the South," DeBow's Review, VII (September, 1849), 222.

with "clamor, concerning the injustice and cruelty of slavery."[69] The existing inequalities, the degradation, the discontent, the misery of their conditions caused the industrial slaves of the North to feel more acutely the "mockery that calls them free."[70] It was asserted that the hard life of the peasants of Europe and the factory workers of England, rather than making them happy and contented as the slaves of the South, had left its stamp upon their "starved and emaciated forms . . . sickly countenances . . . toil worn . . . crooked spines . . . swelled joints and contorted limbs, clothed in a scanty supply of filthy rags that were hardly sufficient to harbor vermin," much less cover "the nakedness of proud anti-slavery England's freemen!"[71]

Perhaps due to the great activity of various English abolitionists like Harriet Martineau, George Thompson, Henry Wright, and others, the Southern counterattack on this point concentrated upon the evils of English industrialism. The defenders of slavery were well aware of the close connection between the English abolition movement and the slavery agitation in America.[72] The leading abolitionists in both countries were in constant touch with each other and with the progress of the entire movement.[73] Not only did the English abolitionists continually exchange letters with Tappan, Leavitt, and others, but they also maintained a correspondence with the Society of Friends, the American Colonization So-

[69] *Pro-Slavery Argument*, pp. 54-55.

[70] *Ibid.*, pp. 55-56. From this Chancellor Harper reaches the conclusion that the African slave, a different and inferior race, "not tantalized" with freedom, did not resent the barriers between his condition and his master's as the Northern laborer would the comparison with the capitalistic group.

[71] "Negro Slavery at the South," *DeBow's Review*, VII (September, 1849), 222.

[72] T. C. Thornton, *An Inquiry into the History of Slavery*, pp. 343-44; *DeBow's Review*, VII (September, 1849), 221; letter of Duff Green to J. C. Calhoun, Aug. 2, 1842, J. C. Calhoun, *Correspondence of John C. Calhoun* (edited by J. Franklin Jameson), p. 846 (hereafter cited as *Correspondence*).

[73] Tappan, *A Side-Light on Anglo-American Relations*, p. 11.

ciety, the American Anti-Slavery Society, and later the American and Foreign Anti-Slavery Society.[74] In addition to such correspondence, practically all English newspapers had one or more correspondents in the United States.[75] After many years of agitation on the part of men like Wilberforce and Sir Thomas Buxton, the slaves in the British colonies were freed by the "Emancipation Act" of August, 1833,[76] only about four months prior to the formation of the American Anti-Slavery Society. The success of the English abolition movement exerted a powerful influence upon the Garrisonian movement in the United States. Various English agitators, no longer having a job or outlet for their fanaticism at home, migrated to America.[77] Vast amounts of English propaganda in the form of thousands of tracts, pamphlets, and books on slavery were dumped into America to aid the cause of emancipation.[78] In addition to the propaganda sent directly, the English abolitionists also supplied many Irish and other emigrants to the United States with anti-slavery tracts before their embarkation.[79] Various English philanthropists contributed monetary aid to the American abolition crusade.[80] American abolitionists like Garrison, Harriet Beecher Stowe, Charles Sumner, and others were stimulated by the aid of the English.[81] On the other hand, it was largely due to the activities of the American abolitionists that the anti-slavery sentiment in England was kept alive long after slavery had been abolished in the British dominions. The two groups exchanged anti-slavery pub-

[74] *Ibid.*, p. 24. [75] *Ibid.*

[76] It should be pointed out that Parliament provided that £20,000,000 were to be paid as compensation to the owners. The act was to take effect on April 1, 1834.

[77] See discussion in Frank J. Klingberg, *The Anti-Slavery Movement in England: A Study of English Humanitarianism*, p. 305.

[78] *Ibid.*, pp. 305-6.

[79] Tappan, *A Side-Light on Anglo-American Relations*, pp. 30-31.

[80] *Ibid.*, p. 45. [81] Klingberg, *op. cit.*, p. 306.

lications.[82] More than a million copies of *Uncle Tom's Cabin* were sold in England during the first year of its publication while only one hundred and fifty thousand copies were sold in the United States during the same time.[83] American abolitionists visited England and attempted to arouse sentiment in that country against the Slave States and against the Federal Government of the United States.[84] When the American Anti-Slavery Society divided in 1839-1840, the influence of English abolitionism could readily be found in the new organization. The English abolitionist, John Scoble, later reported on the work of the American and Foreign Anti-Slavery Society by stating that "a comparison of its Constitution with that of the *British (&) Foreign Anti-Slavery Society* will show that they completely harmonize in principles, object, and modes of operation."[85] It may be concluded that there was a direct connection between the activities of some of the American radicals and their fellow agitators in England.

The abolition attack of the English group was neither forgotten nor neglected by the Southern defenders of slavery. Asserting that "English arrogance and ignorance" were masking under the name of "abolition," one writer in *DeBow's Review* charged that the English were deliberately seeking "to throw a fire-brand into the explosive magazine of southern excitability, for the hidden purpose of blowing up the Union."[86] Other pro-slavery writers were more interested in denouncing the evils among English industrial centers. Parliamentary reports describing the conditions under which

[82] Tappan, *A Side-Light on Anglo-American Relations*, p. 24; George Thompson, after his visit to America in 1834-1835, returned to England with approximately 2,400 distinct publications on slavery in America.

[83] Klingberg, *op. cit.*, p. 306.

[84] Thornton, *op. cit.*, pp. 343-44, quotes letter from Englishman.

[85] John Scoble to Committee of the British and Foreign Anti-Slavery Society, Feb. 14, 1853, reprinted in Tappan, *A Side-Light on Anglo-American Relations*, p. 315.

[86] "Negro Slavery at the South," *DeBow's Review*, VII (September, 1849), 221.

English children labored were quoted by Southern writers.
Boys from eight to twelve years of age were forced to drag
barrows "on all fours, with a dog belt and chain," through
the mud and muck of the mines.[87] These reports were quoted
to show that the intense suffering, brutal cruelty, long hours,
and degraded conditions of child laborers in England were in
direct contrast to the happy life of the slave children. Hammond pointed out that in many instances English children
worked over twelve hours a day for a mere pittance of two
dollars and fifty cents per month. After working these long
hours in the mine pits, if the child laborers complained of
their bloody, torn skin, they were beaten severely.[88] English
abolitionists were challenged to deny the facts presented by
these Parliamentary reports of laboring conditions in their
own country. It was implied that instead of conducting an
unjustified attack upon the South to emancipate the African,
the English abolitionists should have been interested in
ameliorating the conditions under which their own countrymen labored. Governor Hammond declared to them that
"your *fellow-citizens*, are more miserable and degraded,
morally and physically, than our slaves," and if the English
laborers could be "elevated to the condition" of Southern
Negroes, it would be "a most glorious act of emancipation."[89]

Nor did the defenders of slavery neglect the evils of the
rising industrialism of the Northern and Eastern sections of
the United States. It was asserted that the misery and poverty of industrial cities could find no parallel in the agricultural sections. The "wonder-working abolitionists" were
admonished that "justice, as well as charity, begins at
home."[90] It was charged by one familiar with conditions in

---

[87] *Pro-Slavery Argument*, pp. 135-36.   [88] *Ibid.*, p. 136.

[89] *Ibid.*, p. 135; italics Hammond's. See also *DeBow's Review*, VII (September,
1849), 222; Hundley, *op. cit.*, pp. 66-67; Sawyer, *op. cit.*, p. 225; Williams,
op. cit., pp. 86-95.

[90] *The North and South, or Slavery and its Contrasts*, anonymous publication
by "the author of Way-marks in the life of a Wanderer, etc.," p. 14. This work,

both sections that no harder master could be found anywhere than "poverty." This "hard tyrant," found in the factory settlements of the North, exposed his white slaves to "every species of cruelty," forced them to labor beyond their capacities, and allowed thousands to "drag out a miserable life." Unable to secure sufficient "bread" for their existence, it was asserted that many free laborers were forced to "pine and sicken and starve in loathsome cellars, in filthy courts and vile alleys."[91] It was contended that thousands of white children worked fourteen or more hours per day in the mills, shops, and factories of the North, at an age when the black children of the South were "enjoying all the sweets of luxurious idleness."[92] In contrast to the happy life of slave children, the children of the "great cities" of the North were portrayed as having insufficient clothing, "feet bare; their backs bowed" under the weight of heavy burdens, "features sharp and pinched," and "tortured, goaded, and lashed" in an industrial system that forced poverty upon the mass and provided wealth only for the few.[93] The defenders of slavery felt that the abolitionists were really making a "mockery of human wrong and outrage" by harping upon the "worst ills of negro slavery" when contrasted with "this white bondage—a bondage from which there is no relief but death."[94] To emancipate the slaves of the South would re-

written largely as a counter document to Harriet Beecher Stowe's *Uncle Tom's Cabin*, shows the conditions of the "white slaves" of the North as being considerably more miserable than those of the Southern Negro slaves. A good portion of the book traces the history and life of a family confronted with laboring conditions in the Northern cities. This is purported by the author to be "A Tale of Real Life." Cited hereafter as *The North and South*.

[91] *Ibid.*, p. 12.

[92] "Slavery in the Southern States," *Southern Literary Messenger*, IX (1843), 736-44; quoted by Beveridge, *op. cit.*, II, 44.

[93] *The North and South*, pp. 13-14; *Pro-Slavery Argument*, pp. 54-56.

[94] *The North and South*, p. 21, quotes a Philadelphia editor. Also see Williams, *op. cit.*, pp. 89-90, for similar view as quoted from Southey in his description of the condition of free laborers in England.

sult in eradicating one evil, only to be overwhelmed by "others of tenfold greater magnitude."[95]

According to the abolitionist doctrine, the oppressed victims of the institution of slavery, upon being emancipated, should have immediately taken their places on a basis of equality with the white population. It was pointed out by the defenders of slavery that the reverse had been true in every instance where slaves had been freed. Though the abolitionists demanded immediate emancipation, they did nothing to elevate the status of the free Negro of the North. It was argued that a great many slaves that had been given their freedom and sent North found life there so miserable and degrading that, longing "like fatherless Israelites, for the fleshpots of slavery," they returned of their own accord to the South.[96] The assertion was made that the "noble-hearted abolitionists" had but little real sympathy for their "downtrodden colored brethren" if the condition of this "idle, worthless, and improvident race" residing in "abodes of sin and debauchery" in Northern cities was any indication.[97] According to reports the free Negroes, due to the unkind treatment afforded them, the inability to secure work on account of race prejudices, and their natural inferiority, were segregated, despised, and, in general, hated throughout the North.[98]

Nor were the conditions surrounding the free blacks much better in the South. In that section, the free Negro, rather than feeling superior to his brothers in bondage, found himself in the inferior position. The slaves of the wealthy and

[95] *The North and South*, p. 24. In connection with the general Southern position on the contrast of Northern and Southern laboring conditions see also George Fitzhugh, *Cannibals All! or, Slaves without Masters*, *passim*.

[96] Olmsted, *op. cit.*, I, 144.   [97] *The North and South*, pp. 15-16.

[98] *Pro-Slavery Argument*, pp. 212-13; see also Michael Chevalier, *Society, Manners and Politics in the United States*, p. 361; William Chambers, *Things as They Are in America*, pp. 129, 131-33, 300; and D. W. Mitchell, *Ten Years in the United States*, p. 250.

aristocratic Southern planters prided themselves upon having a more honorable position in life than their free brethren. Their view of the matter was admirably stated by one who asserted that they were *"dirty, free niggers!—got nobody to take care of them."*[99] From the reports concerning the status of free blacks in both sections, it would seem that their condition was not one to be envied even by the slaves. Professor Dew, speaking of free Negroes in general, stated that they were considered as the "most worthless and indolent" of citizens throughout the entire Union and were looked upon "as the very drones and pests of society."[100] A similar opinion was expressed by Judge Conrad, who pointed out that the free Negroes as a group were the "most ignorant, voluptuous, idle, vicious, impoverished, and degraded population" of the entire country. He asserted that this element of the population had "sunk lower than the Southern slaves," thereby constituting but "melancholy proof of the advantages of abolition."[101]

In direct contrast to the condition of the free Negroes in both sections and to the misery and degradation of the poverty-stricken laborers of the industrial cities of the North, the defenders of slavery pointed out the favorable aspects of the Southern system of slave labor.[102] They referred to the testimony of many visitors as evidence that instead of having

[99] Olmsted, *op. cit.*, I, 144; italics in Olmsted.

[100] Thomas R. Dew, "Slavery in the Virginia Legislature of 1831-1832," *De-Bow's Review*, XX (March, 1856), 269.

[101] T. R. R. Cobb, *An Inquiry into the Law of Negro Slavery in the United States of America, to which is prefixed, An Historical Sketch of Slavery*, p. 40.

[102] Williams, *op. cit.*, pp. 146-47. The *Anti-Slavery Bugle*, April 24, 1846, p. 3, reprinted a statement from the *Richmond Whig* which stated: "If the slanderers of the South will condescend to travel through this wicked Commonwealth, they will find a race of men, more contented, happy, and kindly treated, than any other class of laborers in the world. They will find them well fed, well clothed, tenderly nursed in sickness and comfortably supported in old age. Let them contrast this condition of things with that of the free blacks and poor whites of the Northern States."

a Negro population of overburdened, driven, stupid, melancholy heathens, crazed by abuse, the slaves were, for the most part, happy and contented.[103] James Kirke Paulding testified that "of all the varieties of the human race or of human condition" he had observed, "the African slave of the South" best realized "the idea of happiness." This Northern writer described the Negro slave as the "most light-hearted, sportive, dancing, laughing being in the world," filled with an exuberance of mirth that "could only come from the heart."[104] William Thompson, a Scotch weaver, found the slaves contented and, after living for many weeks on cotton plantations, asserted that he had not seen "one fifth of the real suffering" to be found in the industrial districts of England.[105] Charles Mackay, another traveler in the South, was so impressed with the happiness and the comfort of the slaves that he felt convinced that their life would have excited the envy of many of Great Britain's freemen.[106] Still another traveler, Frederick Law Olmsted, found the Southern Negroes a laughing, happy group, characterized by a love of music and good-natured enjoyment of simple amusements.[107] A former abolitionist, Nehemiah Adams, came South with the theory that involuntary servitude made its victims perpetually miserable and tried to "persuade" himself that they were, but he was finally forced to conclude that the slaves,

[103] See view of Nehemiah Adams before and after visiting the South as expressed in his *Southside View of Slavery*, pp. 28-32.

[104] Beveridge, *op. cit.*, II, 41. Paulding's work, published in 1836, is largely a defense of slavery. Though a Northern writer of Dutch ancestry, he had observed slavery in New York in his youth and later in Virginia. His main arguments for the retention of slavery were the biblical recognition, the evils that would result from emancipation, property rights of owners, the favorable conditions of slave labor as contrasted to the conditions of free laborers in the North and England, and the fanaticism of the abolitionists. See the life of this author by A. L. Herold, *James Kirke Paulding: Versatile American*, pp. 114-15, *et passim*.

[105] Lyell, *op. cit.*, II, 29; also quoted by Beveridge, *op. cit.*, II, 44 n.

[106] Mackay, *op. cit.*, I, 311; also cited by Rhodes, *op. cit.*, I, 373.

[107] Olmsted, *Seaboard Slave States*, II, 19-20, 194-96, 209.

judging by their freedom from care, their boisterous spirits, and light-hearted gayety, were the happiest people in the world.[108]

In addition to the statements of visitors in the South concerning the contentment of the slaves, the pro-slavery writers were also quite vehement in their assertions on this point. Professor Dew declared in 1832 that "a merrier being does not exist on the face of the globe, than the negro slave of the United States."[109]   Governor McDuffie, in his message to the South Carolina Legislature in 1835, asserted that "there is not upon the face of the earth, any class of people, high or low, so perfectly free from care and anxiety."[110]   It was pointed out that this freedom from anxiety was a result of the slaves' knowledge that under all circumstances, even in the extremity of old age, the masters would provide kind treatment and comfortable accommodations rather than drive them to beggary. The statement was made that the only danger of creating exceptions to the happiness, cheerfulness, and contentment of the Southern slaves was when "those foreign intruders and fatal ministers of mischief, the emancipationists, like their arch-prototype in the Garden of Eden," actuated by similar motives, tempted the Negroes "to aspire above the conditions" to which they had been "assigned by Providence."[111] This same view was expressed by Governor Hammond when he stated that the "slaves are the happiest three millions of human beings on whom the sun shines" but added that into their "Eden is coming Satan in the guise of an abolitionist."[112] By bringing forth such statements, corroborated by the descriptions of travelers, the Southerners were able to show vividly the best side of slave life and thereby create a stronger impression of the evils of emancipa-

---

[108] Nehemiah Adams, *op. cit.*, pp. 28-30.   [109] *Pro-Slavery Argument*, p. 459.
[110] Governor McDuffie quoted in Hart, *Source-Book of American History*, document 95, p. 247.
[111] *Ibid.*   [112] *Pro-Slavery Argument*, p. 133.

tion. Certainly the free Negroes and factory laborers of the North had only a dubious freedom to invite the envy of the Southern agricultural workers.

The defenders of slavery did not rely alone upon their own assertions or upon the comments of visitors to refute the charges of the abolitionists; they also referred to statistical records. According to census reports the Negro population increased in about the same rapid proportion as the whites. If the abolitionist charges that the slaves were driven to endless toil, half starved, poorly clad, cruelly beaten, and killed off every seven years were true, why did the slave population continue to increase so prodigiously?[113] The very fact that this group of alleged "miserable wretches" increased rapidly emphatically refuted the charge that they were universally ill-treated and starved.[114] Pointing out that since the black population could not be recruited by immigration from abroad, Hammond asserted that the equal comparative increase combined with the greater longevity of Negroes outweighed "a thousand abolition falsehoods, in favor of the leniency and providence" exerted in the management of Southern slaves.[115] Mortality lists were used to prove that the death rate among the slaves in the South was much lower than among the blacks enjoying the "abstract delights of liberty" in Northern cities.[116] Even when an epidemic of cholera in 1836 doubled the slave death rate in Charleston, South Carolina, it was pointed out that "slavery and cholera combined" were less destructive to the Negro than liberty

---

[113] See charges of abolitionists in Chap. II. Also see similar expression in Beveridge, *op. cit.*, II, 43.

[114] According to the *U. S. Census*, the slave population increased after the prohibition of the slave trade in 1808 as follows: 1810—1,191,364; 1820—1,538,-038; 1830—2,009,043; 1840—2,487,455; 1850—3,204,318. From these figures it is evident that the slave population had more than doubled in 30 years.

[115] *Pro-Slavery Argument*, p. 131.

[116] Josiah Nott, "Statistics of Southern Slave Population," *DeBow's Review*, IV (November, 1847), 275-91, shows that the average mortality in Philadelphia among Negro population was 1 in 26, in Charleston, 1 in 44.

and climate in Boston.[117] Not only was the mortality rate among slaves low, but it was also pointed out that cases of insanity and suicide were almost unknown among them. If they were really in "abject misery, goaded by constant injuries," and outraged and tormented as depicted by the abolitionists, it seemed only reasonable to expect a large number of suicides and insanity cases.[118]

Concerning the abolition charge that families were continually being torn apart, Southern defenders of slavery conceded the fact that slave families were occasionally separated but condemned the inferences drawn by the abolitionists as grossly exaggerated and untrue. It was stated that these few instances occurred through the force of circumstances caused by the death or failure of a planter and the consequent disposition of his property.[119] It was pointed out that division of slave families was carefully guarded against as a result of the interest, religion, and humanity of the slaveholders.[120] Sir Charles Lyell found several planters that refused to sell their slaves when such a separation would result.[121] The affection alone of the masters for their slaves prevented many planters from selling their Negroes except when forced to do so by the "pressure of extreme necessity."[122] Governor Hammond stated that it was always "an object of prime consideration" among the slaveholders to keep the families together whenever possible.[123] Southern writers also brought out the fact that family ties were not as strong among the Negroes as among the whites.[124] The slaves lacked domestic affections, regarded marriage with indifference, and were practi-

---

[117] *Ibid.*, p. 279. The mortality rate among free Negroes in Boston was 1 in 15; in Charleston during cholera epidemic, 1 in 19.

[118] *Pro-Slavery Argument*, pp. 131-32.

[119] *Ibid.*, p. 132.

[120] Charles C. Jones, *Religious Instruction of the Negroes in the United States*, p. 133.   [121] Lyell, *op. cit.*, I, 209-10.

[122] William Chambers, *American Slavery and Color*, p. 116.

[123] *Pro-Slavery Argument*, p. 132.   [124] *Ibid.*, p. 133.

cally insensible to ties of kindred.[125] This was shown by their
promptly forgetting their domestic associations when separated, and singing, dancing, and playing the banjo even
when before the auction block or on the way to distant plantations.[126] Regardless of this, however, the defenders of
slavery did not feel that the South should be condemned for
the separation of families when the same evil occurred in
every free state under various conditions and circumstances.
In fact, it was estimated that there were more slave families
in the South whose members had enjoyed uninterrupted communion without losing a single member, except by the process
of nature, than among the same number of civilized people
elsewhere.[127]

One of the abolitionist charges that had appealed strongly
to many religious New Englanders was that the slaves were
denied scriptural instruction in the South. To the minds of
these Northerners the benighted Africans were surrounded
by the vilest immorality without the enlightening benefits of
religion. Such charges were easily refuted by Southern
writers by merely referring to the numerous instances in
which the slaves were encouraged in their religious work.
Not only were extensive provisions made for the enlighten-
ment and regeneration of the slaves religiously, but it was
indicated by the defenders of the system that the number of
conversions among the Southern slaves was proportionately
far larger than among the free blacks in the North.[128] Inasmuch as the potency of religion humanized and softened the
institution of slavery, it was asserted that it was to the interest
of the slaveholder, in addition to his religious duty, to furnish scriptural instruction and spiritual guidance to his
slaves.[129]

[125] *Ibid.*, pp. 56-57.
[126] Beveridge, *op. cit.*, II, 52.   [127] *Pro-Slavery Argument*, p. 133.
[128] "Domestic Slavery Considered as a Scriptural Institution," *Southern Literary
Messenger*, XI (September, 1845), 516.
[129] *Ibid.*, pp. 513-28; also see *Pro-Slavery Argument*, p. 133.

The probable basis of the abolitionist charge that the slaves could not obtain religious instruction may be found in the various state laws prohibiting the teaching of slaves to read and write and preventing Negroes from having meetings unless a white man was present. In their interpretation of these laws, the Garrisonian abolitionists leaped to the conclusion that it would be impossible for a Southern Negro to read the Bible or to attend religious services. However, it should be pointed out in this connection that the churches very early began a movement for Christianizing the African.[130] This type of missionary work among the Negroes continued on through the abolition crusade. Nevertheless, the movement came into conflict with the state laws after the abolitionist attack. As we have seen, more repressive slave laws resulted from the attack of the Garrisonian abolitionists upon the institutions of the South.[131] These laws were justified by the Southerners on the basis that the incendiary material distributed by the abolitionists made them necessary. The education of the Negroes had to be curbed and their assemblies supervised to prevent possible conspiracies inspired by abolitionists. It was denied by the Southern leaders that

[130] As early as 1673 Richard Baxter published his *Christian Directory* which contained a chapter on "Directions to those Masters in Foreign Plantations who have Negroes and other Slaves; being a solution of several cases about them." See William Orme (editor), *The Practical Works of Reverend William Baxter*, Vol. IV, Chap. XIV. Charles C. Jones, *op. cit.*, p. 7, states this work was "productive of much good on the Plantations." In 1685, Morgan Godwyn implored James II to endeavor to propagate the gospel in the colonies. See his *Trade Preferred Before Religion and Christ made to give place to Mammon*. The Society for the Propagation of the Gospel in Foreign Parts sent out many missionaries. To aid the work of this society, the Bishop of London wrote two letters, of which about 10,000 copies were distributed in the American colonies and exerted great influence. See *The Bishop of London's Letter to the Masters and Mistresses of Families in the English Plantations Abroad: Exhorting them to encourage and promote the Instruction of their Negroes in the Christian Faith*. Also, *The Bishop of London's Letter to the Missionaries in the English Plantations: Exhorting them to give their assistance toward the Negroes of their several Parishes in the Christian Faith*. See Charles C. Jones, *op. cit.*, p. 15; Jenkins, *op. cit.*, pp. 14-15.

[131] See Chap. III.

these laws hindered the spread of true religion to any appreciable extent.[132]

The Southern churches took the position that in granting the slaves religious instruction they were not in any way interfering with slavery as an institution. In fact, the churches looked upon the system of slavery as a patriarchal institution, and realized a twofold religious duty as a result of it. This took the form first of instructing the masters as to their duties, responsibilities, and obligations growing out of the system of servitude.[133] The second obligation of the church was to enlighten the slaves through Christian instructions as to their duties toward their masters on earth as well as to their Heavenly Master.[134] As the people of the South gradually realized that the slaves could be instructed along religious lines without being faced with the menace of abolitionism, this missionary movement gained increasing support. This increase of interest was probably due in part to the intense study of the Scriptures that was almost universal in the South following the abolitionist attack.[135] Religious instruction of the slaves was sponsored by the churches, advocated by the religious periodicals,[136] aided by the ministers, and

[132] In this connection see W. B. Seabrook, *An Essay on the Management of Slaves and especially their Religious Instruction;* also Jenkins, *op. cit.,* p. 212.

[133] See Rev. J. H. Thornwell, *The Rights and Duties of Masters.* This was "A Sermon preached at the dedication of a Church erected in Charleston, S. C., for the Benefit and Instruction of the Colored Population, May 26, 1850." Also Holland N. McTyeire, *Duties of Masters to Servants: three Premium Essays* and *Duties of Christian Masters;* and John Bailey Adger, *The Christian Doctrine of Human Rights and Slavery.* It seems quite probable that the above collections of sermons had wide circulation and influence.

[134] See George Washington Freeman, *The Rights and Duties of Slaveholders;* also Jones, *op. cit.,* p. 67.

[135] The South studied the Scriptures as part of their defense of slavery. See Chap. V.

[136] Among the periodicals that openly advocated the instruction of the Negroes along religious lines we find: *The Christian Index* (Baptist); *The Charleston Observer* (Presbyterian); *The Gospel Messenger* (Episcopal); *The Southern Christian Advocate* (Methodist); *The Western Seminary; The New Orleans Observer;* and *The Southern Churchman.* See Jones, *op. cit.,* p. 67.

finally taken up by an awakening public sentiment until it virtually became a crusade within itself. All of the leading Southern churches established missions upon the larger plantations and enrolled slaves among their membership. It should be pointed out that this movement for the establishment of missions began before the Garrisonian attack,[137] and was handicapped for a few years by the repressive laws following 1831, but later became so general that by 1845 a meeting of all denominations was held in Charleston for the purpose of discussing methods of giving the slaves religious instruction and means of coöperating in the endeavor.[138]

In their refutation of the abolitionist charges, the defenders of slavery pointed out that many of the planters hired clergymen for the purpose of ministering to the colored flocks and in many instances required the slaves to be present each Sabbath morning and evening at family prayers.[139] Over practically the entire South the slaves had the same opportunity of attending religious services which the whites enjoyed, and the galleries in most churches were turned over to them.[140] In addition, the slaves also had many churches of their own and their services were described as "an example of decorum" by a visiting Northern minister.[141] The Negro members of the congregation were of special interest and both the ministers and plantation missionaries made particular efforts to provide the slaves with the proper religious instruction. In fact, many special sermons were preached in the en-

---

[137] Rev. James H. McNeilly, *Religion and Slavery*, pp. 34-35, places 1829 as the beginning of the movement to spread the gospel upon the larger Southern plantations.

[138] *Proceedings of the Meeting in Charleston, S. C.*, May, 1845, cited by Jenkins, *op. cit.*, p. 213.

[139] "Management of Negroes," *DeBow's Review*, XI (October, 1851), 371; see also Beveridge, *op. cit.*, II, 48.

[140] *Pro-Slavery Argument*, p. 133; see also various articles in magazines like *DeBow's Review*, VII (September, 1849), 220-21; X (June, 1851), 625.

[141] Nehemiah Adams, *op. cit.*, pp. 24-29.

deavor to explain Christianity to the Negro and to exhort the latter to fulfill loyally his position in the social structure.[142]

It was asserted that those people who believed that slavery was *"accursed of God,"* and existed in the South in an orgy of sinful horror would be surprised, upon visiting the South, to find the Sabbath better kept by all classes than in "puritan New England."[143] The slaveholders recognized the fact that they were responsible to the world for the humane treatment of the slaves, "whom God" had placed in their hands, and were obligated to give the Negroes an opportunity for religious instruction and spiritual development.[144] From this realization they felt that if they failed in this duty the consequences would be visited upon the masters rather than upon the slaves.[145] As evidence of their successful efforts in the performance of their duty, the defenders of slavery pointed out that approximately half a million slaves belonged to Southern churches, which was a far greater number than belonged to the Christian churches in all heathen countries.[146] Thus, in their refutation, they laid the foundation of the later justification of the system of slavery as a great Christianizing institution.[147]

The charge that slavery was in direct violation of American principles was vigorously denied by Southern leaders. The preamble to the Declaration of Independence was not intended to apply to Negro slaves, the Southerners declared. Jefferson and the other slaveholders who signed the doc-

---

[142] Many of these sermons were compiled and published with special catechisms explaining Christianity in simple terms for the Negro. For a list, see Jenkins, *op. cit.*, p. 214 n.

[143] "Negro Slavery at the South," *DeBow's Review*, VII (September, 1849), 220-21.

[144] *Pro-Slavery Argument*, p. 134.   [145] *Ibid.*, p. 37.

[146] Hundley, *op. cit.*, p. 297; Sawyer, *op. cit.*, pp. 218-19; see also the discussion of the missionary work and gospel on the plantations given in W. P. Harrison (compiler), *The Gospel Among the Slaves*, pp. 117-96.

[147] See Chap. VII.

ument would have emancipated their slaves if the Declaration had applied to bondsmen.[148] Simms pointed out, "The democracy which they asserted not only recognized, but insisted upon inequalities."[149] Instead of declaring the "fitness of all men for any place," it merely meant that each individual should enjoy the position to which he was "justly entitled," by reason of his moral, intellectual, or physical resources.[150] It was denied that all men were in reality born equal. Instead it was stated that the diversity of men increased the inequality throughout life as the various factors of strength, weakness, wealth, poverty, knowledge, ignorance, and other elements exerted their influence.[151] The "inalienable rights" were violated every day by laws and court procedure for the betterment of society.[152] It was asserted that society recognized no natural rights of man except within the compliance of its laws. These laws required from each individual the *application of his mental and physical energies, to the improvement of the passive world around him.*"[153] With the proof of superiority would come a superior position and increased rights.[154]

According to these views the rights of human beings were not fixed but fluctuated in quantity according to a graduated scale. The intelligence and education of man to a great extent determined his ascent. As a man gradually worked up the scale, the number of rights would increase, but the number of individuals possessing them would diminish. From this view it was asserted that slavery was not inconsistent with human rights. The Negro slave occupied such a place and fulfilled such duties as were commensurate with his capacities. Unless the minimum rights of the slave could be proved to be out of proportion to his capacity, then slavery

[148] Beveridge, *op. cit.*, II, 53.
[149] *Pro-Slavery Argument*, p. 258.
[150] *Ibid.*, pp. 252-57, 258.
[151] *Ibid.*, p. 6.
[152] *Ibid.*, p. 259.
[153] *Ibid.*, p. 260; italics Simms'.
[154] *Ibid.*

could not be charged with doing him an injustice.[155] African slaves were suited to the position of laborers in society. Since all primitive nations had been subjected to long periods of bondage, the system as practiced in the South was not only natural, but actually elevated and improved the Negro race.[156] As a result of the slaves fulfilling their proper place in society the cause of liberty was sponsored instead of handicapped. As proof it was pointed out that the "spirit of liberty and equality" glowed with the greatest of intensity in the hearts of "masters of slaves."[157] It was therefore maintained that the enslavement of the black race in the United States was "THE PRICE AMERICA" had "PAID FOR HER LIBERTY, CIVIL AND RELIGIOUS, AND HUMANLY SPEAKING, THESE BLESSINGS WOULD HAVE BEEN UNATTAINABLE WITHOUT THEIR AID."[158]

Concerning the charge of the radical abolitionists with regard to miscegenation and the promiscuity of licentious sexual intercourse in the South, the defenders of slavery stated that they regretted that the topic could not be avoided.[159] Since, however, "learned old maids" like Miss Martineau had stressed the charge, since "folios" had been written on it, and because an abolitionist clergyman had stigmatized the South as a "brothel," it was necessary to answer the charges.[160] Because many female abolitionists had con-

---

[155] For a discussion of these arguments see Jenkins, *op. cit.*, pp. 214-15.

[156] *Pro-Slavery Argument*, pp. 260-63.

[157] Dew, "Address on the Influence of the Republican System of Government upon Literature and the Development of Character," *Southern Literary Messenger*, II (March, 1836), 280.

[158] "The Black Race in North America," *Southern Literary Messenger*, XXI (November, 1855), 647; capitalization in *Messenger*.

[159] *Pro-Slavery Argument*, pp. 117-18.

[160] *Ibid.*, pp. 117-19. Hammond states, however, that he should not feel any "delicacy" in discussing a question to which they had been "invited and challenged by clergymen and virgins." See Chap. II, above, for the various charges made by the abolitionists.

stantly recurred to this topic with an "insatiable relish," and with the clergymen no less violent, Governor Hammond wondered whether " 'Such rage without betrays the fires within' " or if the abolitionists being " 'without sin' " were the first to "cast stones."[161]

Though admitting that the charges were based on partial truth, the defenders of slavery denounced the abolitionist assertions as being unjust and "atrociously" exaggerating conditions in the South.[162] Though denouncing sexual immorality as an evil in any country, the defenders of slavery expressed the opinion that the condition was not due to the effects of slavery so much as to the temperament and sensuality of the African. The Negro was "strongly inclined to polygamy" and the females were rather proud of such connections.[163]

The Southern writers accused the abolitionists of being extremely contradictory. It was asserted that "one of your heavy charges has been, that we regard and treat these people as brutes," yet in speaking of miscegenation, "you now charge us with habitually taking them to our bosoms."[164] In refutation of the latter charge the abolitionists were referred to the court records, to the newspapers, and to accounts of those who actually knew conditions, to prove that the evil of licentiousness did not pervade the South as in other regions.[165] It was pointed out that the laws and public sentiment in the South, combined with the natural repugnance of the white man toward association with colored women, rather effectively discouraged miscegenation.[166]

As a means of counterattack, rather than condoning evils of miscegenation, the Southerners pointed out the fact that,

---

[161] *Pro-Slavery Argument*, pp. 117-18.   [162] *Ibid.*, pp. 119, 229-30.

[163] Sawyer, *op. cit.*, p. 221; Lyell, *op. cit.*, I, 271-73; also cited by Beveridge, *op. cit.*, II, 52.

[164] *Pro-Slavery Argument*, p. 119; also *DeBow's Review*, VII (December, 1849), 493.

[165] *Pro-Slavery Argument*, p. 118.   [166] *Ibid.*, pp. 118-20.

though the abolitionists had written many volumes upon the licentiousness of the South, they had failed to mention conditions in other sections. It was asserted that the only fair method of judging the vices of slavery would be to compare conditions in the South with those in the North.[167] Only if the Free States were free from the evils of sex immorality could the Slave States be condemned for its existence. It was argued that it was a great error to condemn the South as a brothel resulting from slavery when the immorality in that section could not be compared with the licentiousness of the seventy thousand prostitutes in London, the ten thousand in New York, or the same relative proportion existing in other Northern industrial cities.[168] Frederick Law Olmsted, after interviewing Southerners who had lived in the North and Northerners who had lived in the South, concluded that though the opportunities for licentiousness were greater in the South, the evils of licentiousness were far greater and the effect more "captivating, irresistible, and ruinous" in the North.[169] Therefore, rather than increasing the evil, the presence of a subjugated people in the South appealed to the pride of caste and prevented the promiscuous intercourse that was practiced in the North. As no laws, human or divine, had been able to prevent a few "brutes and debauchees" from defiling themselves, why should the entire population of the Southern States be condemned for a few exceptions, asked the pro-slavery writers.[170]

Although the evil was one to be apologized for in any region, it was asserted that the South at least had the advantage of having a race which had not been lifted into sensibilities, "the possession of which brings, with indulgence in vice, the consciousness of degradation."[171] Unlike the prostitution

[167] *Ibid.*, p. 230.

[168] *Ibid.*, p. 41; p. 229, cites the report of the Commissioners of the Magdalen Asylum concerning the number of professional prostitutes in New York.

[169] Olmsted, *Seaboard Slave States*, II, 250-51.

[170] *Pro-Slavery Argument*, pp. 41, 119.   [171] *Ibid.*, p. 230.

of the North, it did not debase the civilized, and it scarcely affected the mind or altered the social status of the Negro. The lowly Negro of the agricultural section supplied the place which, in the industrial North, was filled by "factory and serving girls."[172] Though deprecating the existence of a few Southern brothels, Chancellor Harper charged that the inmates of these houses were imported from the cities of the Free States. He asserted that in return for the many benefits which the slavery of the South furnished to the industrial states, the latter furnished the South with a supply of "thieves and prostitutes."[173] As a result of slavery, it was concluded that among the white population there were "fewer cases of divorce, separation . . . seduction, rape and bastardy" in the South than "among any other five millions of people on the civilized earth."[174] It should be pointed out that the defenders of slavery, on the whole, handled this "disgusting topic" with repugnance and regret.[175]

The charges which George Bourne and others of the more fanatical abolitionists made upon the morals of Southern women were not mentioned by the defenders of slavery. The purity of the Southern women was the glory of the South. Their modesty, beauty, and ladylike decorum made them the "model women of the age" in the opinion of at least one writer who favorably contrasted them with the women of the North.[176] While the slanderous charges of the abolitionists in this connection were silently ignored, they were not overlooked or forgotten, but instead caused the fires of undying hatred to smolder with intense heat in the hearts of Southern people.[177]

It may be concluded that the defenders of slavery, following the change in Southern opinion resulting from the

---

[172] *Ibid.*, pp. 229-30.

[173] *Ibid.*, p. 44.

[174] *Ibid.*, pp. 118-19.

[175] *Ibid.*, pp. 120, 230.

[176] Hundley, *op. cit.*, p. 72; also quoted by Beveridge, *op. cit.*, II, 53.

[177] See similar view in *ibid.*

crusade of the Garrisonian abolitionists, at first merely refuted the charges of their antagonists. They frankly admitted
the partial truth in some of the charges but vigorously protested against exaggerations and false conclusions. They invariably denied all exaggerations in the form of "Southern
Outrages" which were hurled upon the Southern people by
the radicals. They often challenged the abolitionists, both in
the North and in England, to compare actual conditions in
their own sections with those of the South before condemning
any evil as the direct result of slavery. In doing so they built
a strong case in favor of Southern agrarian civilization against
the industrialism of the North and East. In their refutation
of abolitionist charges it was necessary that the Southern defenders carefully study the question of slavery from all an-
gles. In doing so many arguments were brought to light for
the protection of their constitutional rights and Southern
institutions. In their defense of slavery as a cornerstone of
the Southern civilization, the system took on a new meaning
and their arguments changed from a stubborn defense into an
aggressive justification which was later incorporated into a
Southern philosophy.

CHAPTER V

HISTORICAL AND SCRIPTURAL JUSTIFICATION

PROBABLY no group in the South was more astounded by the violence of the abolition propaganda than were the clergy and laity of Southern churches. To be called a "Brotherhood of thieves" by Stephen S. Foster and condemned as a "brothel" by Wendell Phillips aroused this group to indignation. The personal attack upon the ministers of the South naturally caused that group to defend themselves and to justify Southern institutions through the use of the Scriptures. Though the South in general had, prior to 1831, looked upon the institution of slavery as an evil, they had not necessarily considered it as a sin. George Whitefield, one of the earliest Methodists, owned slaves and had pointed out in 1751 that the Bible recognized slavery.[1] Jonathan Edwards, though one of the foremost theologians of his day, had also been a slaveholder.[2] Such religious leaders did not consider the system of slavery as inherently sinful.

At various times before 1831, when Southern institutions were attacked, biblical authorities pointed out that slavery was recognized in the Scriptures. Following the attack upon the South during the Missouri controversy and the consequent abolition propaganda developing out of this movement, several Southerners mildly defended the institution of slavery. As early as 1823 Dr. Frederick Dalcho issued a pamphlet which proved, through an elaborate scriptural argument, that the possession of slaves was not an unchristian act.[3]

[1] Letter of Whitefield to Wesley, March 22, 1751, quoted in Whitefield, *Letters*, II, 404, and L. Tyerman, *The Life and Times of John Wesley*, II, 132.

[2] Beveridge, *op. cit.*, II, 54-55.

[3] Frederick Dalcho, *Practical Considerations founded on the Scriptures relative to the Slave Population of South Carolina.*

Dr. Richard Furman, one of the leading Baptist ministers, stated the position of that denomination in 1823 by pointing out that the "just and humane masters" who ruled their slaves "according to christian principles" could not be charged with moral evil nor with acting contrary to the spirit of Christianity.[4] Dr. Thomas Cooper of South Carolina College pointed out in 1826 that slavery was not forbidden in the Bible and that the institution had existed in various forms since ancient times. Even at this early date, Cooper attributed the anti-slavery agitation and propaganda arising from the Missouri controversy to "sectional interest," "blind sentimentalism and philanthropy."[5]

The flood of abolition propaganda after 1831 and the increase of anti-slavery sentiment in the North had the effect of solidifying public opinion in the South concerning slavery. Having previously looked upon slavery as a regrettable but necessary evil, few Southerners had ever considered the institution in the light of a scriptural blessing until they had investigated it after the Garrisonian attack. The previous apologies for the system made by the Southerners had neither justified the institution as a blessing of God nor condemned

[4] Richard Furman, *Exposition of the Views of the Baptists relative to the Colored Population of the United States in a Communication to the Governor of South Carolina*, p. 12.

[5] Dumas Malone, *The Public Life of Thomas Cooper, 1783-1839*, p. 288, summarizes the views of Cooper on slavery. See Thomas Cooper, *On the Constitution of the United States, and the Questions that have arisen under it*, pp. 45-49. It is interesting to note the change in Cooper's attitude. While in England, he had been violently opposed to slavery and had written pamphlets against the slave trade. When first settling in the United States, he did not consider the Southern States as a place of residence due to their system of slave labor. Later settling in South Carolina, Cooper completely adopted "the traditional Southern attitude toward the negro." Living in a Slave State, he soon came to realize the necessity of slavery if the blacks were to remain. His biblical defense of slavery was only part of his justification on social, racial, and other grounds. He was one of the early Southern leaders to realize the sectional significance of the slavery agitation during the Missouri struggle. As President of South Carolina College, he influenced the later pro-slavery writings of William Harper, who was a member of the board of trustees and James H. Hammond, a student in the College. Malone, *op. cit.*, pp. 76, 284-89.

it as an inherent sin. Perhaps the South would have continued to apologize for slavery but for the denunciations of the abolitionists which led to an investigation of the actual benefits and evils of the institution. A concentration of the abolition propaganda upon the charge that slavery *per se* was wrong reacted to cause Southern leaders to take the opposite view.

With this reversal of sentiment, Southern men began to propose and maintain that "slavery, *per se,* is right"; that the abstract principles of slavery were right, being based upon "a fundamental principle of the social state and that domestic slavery as an institution" was "fully justified by the conditions and circumstances."[6] It was pointed out that if slaveholding was criminal the Southerners should seek every means to rid themselves of the evil.[7] Since no one could justify himself for committing a known sin, the Southern people began to blame themselves for ever assuming the position that "slavery is wrong in the abstract," for by doing so they had been assuming that a person might be compelled to sin.[8] From this they reasoned that if nothing could justify an enlightened people in committing sin, therefore by assuming slavery to be an evil they had been violating the laws of God and humanity by remaining slaveholders.[9] As a result of this viewpoint many attempts on the part of some to apologize for domestic slavery were condemned on the basis that only the conduct of bad men might find apologists, while the conduct of good men should be justified. Maintaining that the South was either right or wrong in supporting the institution of slavery, they asserted that apologies should not be made on the ground of necessity, nor claimed on the ground of ignorance.[10]

[6] William Andrew Smith, *Lectures on the Philosophy and Practice of Slavery,* pp. 11-12.

[7] *Pro-Slavery Argument,* p. 2.   [8] Smith, *op. cit.,* p. 12.

[9] *Pro-Slavery Argument,* p. 2.   [10] Smith, *op. cit.,* pp. 13-14.

This view was the reverse of the Southern position prior to the abolition crusade, so it became necessary to explain the reason for their previous views on this topic. The ascendancy of the earlier opinion on slavery was said to be the result of training and environment. Early in American history Thomas Jefferson had denounced slavery as sinful. The Southerners claimed that this "grossly offensive error" was probably the only doctrine of Jefferson which New England adopted and that, owing to the prominence given by the Puritans to higher educational institutions and the fact that New England soil was not favorable to agricultural pursuits, the citizens of these states had supplied most of the textbooks for schools and colleges. As a result, the sinfulness-of-slavery view became diffused throughout the textbooks and influenced the sentiments of the entire country.[11] It was pointed out that even the literary institutions and pulpits of the South had aided in propagating that error. In view of these facts, it could hardly be considered a matter of surprise that the people in both the North and the South had the impression that something was wrong with the system of domestic slavery.[12]

With the breaking away from the old conceptions as a result of the awakening of Southern thought, slavery became a blessing in the eyes of its defenders. Slaveowners declared that the practice of slavery in other countries, the influence of the system on civilization as recorded by the annals of history, and the Holy Scriptures contributed evidence to establish this new viewpoint. As a result of this idea, they maintained that slavery as it existed in the United States was in all respects morally right, economically beneficial, and

[11] *Ibid.*, pp. 15, 16.

[12] *Ibid.*, p. 17; Hopkins, *op. cit.*, pp. 18-19. Dr. Hopkins was Bishop of the Diocese of Vermont, and though a Northerner defended the scriptural foundation of the institution of slavery. This particular work was addressed to the Rt. Rev. Delonzo Potter, Bishop of the Protestant Episcopal Church in the Diocese of Pennsylvania.

socially necessary.[13] On this assumption slavery was not inconsistent with justice, reason, or religion.[14] In the maintenance of these views, the most important arguments used in the Southern justification of slavery were promulgated by Southern leaders. In this chapter the Southern contention that the institution was morally right because of its biblical foundation will be discussed. It should, however, be pointed out in this connection that this scriptural justification played an important part in the establishment of the new philosophy of slavery among the Southerners.

The widespread scriptural justification of slavery from 1831 to 1860 resulted from the abolitionist attack. It grew largely from the abolition charge that slavery was "a damnable sin" and from the personal vituperation launched upon Southern ministers. As the Southern leaders and people turned to the Holy Scriptures many passages recognizing the existence of slavery were brought to light. And since the abolitionists were hard pressed to refute the scriptural quotations, a fierce verbal controversy raged between the North and the South over the sinfulness of slavery.[15] Practically all of the ministers, denominational conferences, and religious publications of the South boldly took the stand that the Bible advocated slavery. Many Southern ministers now upheld the earlier views of Dr. Furman and George Whitefield.[16] And numerous debates upon the question of slavery were held between the ministers of the North and those of the South.[17]

Judging from their writings, it seems that Southern ministers were united in their scriptural justification of slavery. Rev. J. C. Postell, of Orangeburg, South Carolina,

[13] See discussion in Beveridge, *op. cit.*, II, 33.

[14] A. S. Roane, "Reply to Abolition Objections to Slavery," *DeBow's Review*, XX (June, 1856), 647.   [15] Beveridge, *op. cit.*, II, 2-52.

[16] Furman, *op. cit.*, p. 12; Tyerman, *op. cit.*, II, 132.

[17] Rev. Richard Fuller and Rev. Francis Wayland, *Domestic Slavery Considered as a Scriptural Institution*; Rev. J. Blanchard and N. L. Rice, *A Debate on Slavery*.

argued that slavery was *"not a moral evil,"* inasmuch as it had *"existed in all the ages"* and was "supported by the Bible."[18] Another South Carolinian, Dr. Dalcho, an Episcopal minister, stated that slavery was "not forbidden in the divine law" and it was therefore left to each individual's judgment as to whether he cared to own slaves or not.[19] Rev. Josiah Priest, feeling that the question of slavery had been agitated by sectional "busybodies" of the North, wrote a lengthy and scholarly biblical defense of the institution.[20] Dr. George D. Armstrong, pastor of the Presbyterian Church of Norfolk, Virginia, wrote a similar work in which he stressed the arguments from the New Testament.[21] Dr. Thornton Stringfellow, realizing that slavery had been condemned as a sin, felt the necessity of examining the Scriptures to determine the truth of the charge. He concluded that slavery was not *"in the sight of God"* what it was *"in the sight of the Abolitionists."*[22] With the increase of public interest in the slavery controversy many ministers, both North and South, expressed themselves in books, pamphlets, and articles upon the various aspects of this question.[23]

[18] Rev. J. C. Postell, quoted by Foster, *op. cit.*, p. 38; italics Foster's.
[19] Dr. Dalcho, quoted in *Leed's Anti-Slavery Tracts*, ser. 8, p. 24.
[20] Josiah Priest, *Biblical Defense of Slavery, or The Origin, History, and Fortunes of the Negro Race.*
[21] George D. Armstrong, *The Christian Doctrine of Slavery.*
[22] Thornton Stringfellow, *Scriptural and Statistical View of Slavery*, p. 101; italics Stringfellow's.
[23] Rev. George B. Cheever, *The Guilt of Slavery and the Crime of Slaveholding Demonstrated from the Hebrew and Greek Scriptures*; also *Responsibility of Church and Ministry respecting the Sin of Slavery*; Howell Cobb, *A Scriptural Examination of the Institution of Slavery in the United States, with its Objects and Purpose*; George Duffield, *A Sermon on American Slavery, its Nature and Duties of Christians in Relation to it*; H. D. Ganse, *Bible Slaveholding not Sinful*; Reuben Hatch, *Bible Servitude reexamined; with special reference to Pro-Slavery Interpretation*; Jonas Hartzel, *Bible Vindicated, A series of Essays on American Slavery*; John Hersey, *An Appeal to Christians on the Subject of Slavery*; John Richter Jones, *Slavery Sanctioned by the Bible*; Rev. Enoch Pond, *Slavery and the Bible*; Rev. M. J. Raphall, *Bible View of Slavery, A Discourse*; Rev. F. A. Ross, *Position of the Southern Church in Relation to Slavery*; also Ross' volume on *Slavery Ordained by God*; Albert Barnes, *An Inquiry into the Scriptural Views of*

Nor did the Southern ministers lack support from some of their Northern brethren in their scriptural justification of slavery. Rev. Wilbur Fiske, D.D., President of Wesleyan University, Connecticut; Rev. John Henry Hopkins, the Episcopal Bishop of the Diocese of Vermont; Rev. Nathan Lord, D.D., President of Dartmouth College; and many ministers of less importance in the North through their sermons and writings showed the biblical and Christian basis for slavery.[24] Dr. Moses Stuart, Professor in the Theological Seminary of Andover, Massachusetts, in response to a letter from President Fiske in 1836, stated that "the precepts of the New Testament respecting the demeanor of slaves and their masters beyond all question, recognized the existence of slavery." He continued by pointing out that as the slaveholders were in part "believing masters," the Bible therefore recognized that the relation might "still exist salva fide, salva ecclesia [i.e., without violating the Christian faith or the Church]."[25] And a Jewish rabbi of New York, M. J. Raphall, though not friendly to slavery, in either the abstract or its practical workings, felt it his duty to point out in sermons that the institution was not condemned as a sin in the Scriptures. He went even further by asserting that the Bible

---

Slavery; Rev. Phillip Schaff, *Slavery and the Bible, A Tract for the Times*; Joseph Parish Thompson, *Teaching of the New Testament on Slavery*; idem, *A Fugitive Slave Law tried by the Old and New Testaments*; Isaac V. A. Brown, *Slavery Irreconcilable with Christianity and Sound Reason, or An Anti-Slavery Bible Argument*; Rev. George Bourne, *A Condensed Anti-Slavery Bible Argument*; also *The Book and Slavery Irreconcilable*; Chas. Eliot, *The Bible and Slavery; in which the Arabic and Mosaic Discipline is considered in connection with the most Ancient Forms of Slavery; and the Pauline Code on Slavery as related to Roman Slavery and the Discipline of Apostolic Churches.* There are other books and pamphlets of similar nature, though the ones cited thus far in this chapter are among the most important.

[24] See Nathan Lord, *A Letter of Inquiry to Ministers of the Gospel of all Denominations on Slavery*, and *A Northern Presbyter's Second Letter to the Ministers of the Gospel of all Denominations on Slavery.* These were anti-abolition pamphlets. See also Hopkins, *op. cit.*, and similar view expressed by Beveridge, *op. cit.*, II, 56.

[25] Dr. Moses Stuart, quoted in *Leed's Anti-Slavery Tracts*, ser. 8, p. 25.

not only sanctioned slavery, but authorized the protection of slaves as property.[26] John Richter Jones, a layman of Pennsylvania, feeling the responsibility of Northern Christians, denounced the abolition propaganda as "principles furnished by infidel sophists," and appealed to all churchmen to search the Scriptures in order to prevent being misled concerning the institution of slavery. His views, as expressed in a pamphlet entitled *Slavery Sanctioned by the Bible*, constituted a strong biblical argument in favor of the institution.[27] The Southern cause was also aided by Professor Hodge of the Princeton Theological Seminary (Presbyterian), who in April, 1836, published an article in the *Biblical Repertory* which pointed out that during the time of Jesus Christ "slavery in its worse forms prevailed over the entire world." He charged that the assumption that slaveholding was criminal was "not only an error" but it was "an error fraught with evil consequences."[28] Therefore it may be concluded that many of the conservative Northern ministers, though not in favor of slavery personally, aided the Southern defense through their scriptural arguments.

Not only did individual leaders of various denominations express such views, but many resolutions advocating the same ideas were issued by church organizations. The General Conference of the Methodist Episcopal Church adopted a resolution in 1836, eight years before its schism over slavery, which stated that body's opposition "to modern abolitionism" and disclaimed "any right, wish or intention to interfere in the civil and political relation between master and slave" as it

---

[26] Raphall, *op. cit.*, pp. 18-19, 24-31, 38.

[27] Pp. 3-4.

[28] Professor Hodge, quoted in *Leed's Anti-Slavery Tracts,* ser. 8, p. 24. The purpose in quoting so many of the religious leaders and organizations is to illustrate one of the methods of the abolitionists. By quoting church leaders as defenders of slavery, the abolitionists were able, through propaganda, to stir up dissensions within the ranks of the church organizations. They were hoping probably to cause division in the church over the slavery controversy.

existed in the South.[29] This Conference, held in Cincinnati, and the first following the formation of the American Anti-Slavery Society, also condemned two of its members for lecturing on the topic of modern abolitionism. In support of the position assumed by the General Conference, the Ohio Annual Conference stated in a resolution that "those brethren of the north who *resist the abolition movement with firmness and moderation,* are the true friends of the church, to the slaves of the South and to the Constitution of our common country."[30] This stand was confirmed by the New York Annual Conference. In the same year the Georgia Annual Conference unanimously resolved "that slavery, as it exists in the United States, *is not a moral evil.*"[31]

The Missionary Society of the South Carolina Methodist Conference, through its Board of Managers, denounced the "principles and practices of the abolitionists, in toto" and stated its belief that the Holy Scriptures "so far from giving any countenance to this illusion, do, unequivocally, authorize the relation of master and slaves."[32] Also in 1836, the synods of South Carolina and Georgia resolved unanimously that "abolition societies and the principles on which they are founded, in the United States, are inconsistent with the rights of slaveholders, and the great principles of all political institutions."[33] The Charleston Union Presbytery on April 7, 1836, resolved that "the holding of slaves, so far from being a SIN in the sight of God, is nowhere condemned in his holy Word" and that slavery was "in accordance with the example

[29] Foster, *op. cit.,* p. 36, quotes resolutions of Methodist General Conference held in Cincinnati, May, 1836. Points out that it was adopted by a vote of 120 to 14; also see *Leed's Anti-Slavery Tracts,* ser. 8, p. 23.

[30] Foster, *op. cit.,* p. 36, quotes Ohio Annual Conference; italics Foster's.

[31] *Ibid.* Foster quotes New York and Georgia Annual conferences; italics Foster's.

[32] *Leed's Anti-Slavery Tracts,* ser. 8, p. 23, quotes the action of the Board of Managers of the South Carolina Conference.

[33] *Ibid.*

and consistent with the precepts of patriarchs, apostles, and prophets."[34] The Hopewell Presbytery of South Carolina issued a document affirming that slavery had always existed "in the church of God from the time of Abraham . . ." and pointed out that the system was not only recognized in both the Old and New Testaments, but that its duties were clearly defined. The group further asserted that emancipation was not mentioned in the Bible "among the duties of master to the slave."[35] Even a Northern magazine, *The Quarterly Christian Spectator* of New Haven, Connecticut, an organ of the Congregational Church, admitted in 1838 that the "Bible contains no explicit prohibition of slavery" and recognizes not only "such a constitution of Society," but also "lends its authority to enforce the mutual obligations resulting from that constitution."[36] These examples of the actions of the various synods and conferences in refusing to condemn slavery, and at times rebuking the abolitionists, created an even more violent attack upon the Church by men like Bourne, Foster, Pillsbury, and Birney.[37] As anti-slavery sentiment gradually increased during the forties, the agitation of the slavery question within the various denominations created a quarrel which led to the division of some into Northern and Southern branches. Other denominations narrowly avoided division.

The Southerners also argued that slavery had existed in various forms since the dawn of history. They pointed out that slavery had been an element in the growth of civilization —a system "honored by antiquity, guarded by law, upheld by

[34] *Ibid.*
[35] *Ibid.*
[36] *Ibid.*, p. 24.
[37] In addition to the previously cited works of Foster and Bourne, see also Parker Pillsbury, *The Church as it is, or the Forlorn Hope of Slavery*. This pamphlet is almost identical with that written by James G. Birney, entitled *The American Churches, the Bulwarks of American Slavery*. Birney also wrote a pamphlet entitled *The Sinfulness of Slaveholding in all Circumstances, Tested by Reason and Scripture*.

truth," and sanctioned by the Divine Master.[38] Thus did
the Southern defenders connect the biblical arguments with
the annals of history. Briefly, their evidence brought out the
fact that the Negro, from the earliest records, had been in a
position of servility.[39] Unable to build a civilization in
Africa, the Negroes had made progress only through enslavement. The Southerners had only to point to history to show
that, in addition to African slavery, ancient records proved
that slavery was the normal condition of a large portion of
mankind. Under their interpretation of historical facts, much
of modern civilization was based upon the institution of
slavery.[40] They contended that the ancient system of villen-
age in England, the organization of serfdom in Russia, the
establishment of peonage in Mexico, and domestic slavery in
the colonies of North America were but different phases of
the same institution.[41]

The historical and scriptural appeal made by the Southerners to defend slavery, the concurrence of various denominational conferences, and the support given by conservative
ministers of the North brought forth increased efforts on the
part of the more radical abolition ministers. Many of these
like Bourne, Foster, and Henry C. Wright had completely
severed their connection with religious organizations. The
radical group defined biblical passages in such a way as to
bring out an opposite interpretation to that established by the
pro-slavery writers. One of the anti-slavery ministers argued
that the pro-slavery interpretation confounded the *"Free or
non-chattel servitude* so frequently alluded to in the Scriptures, with *chattel slavery."*[42] Another charged that "not
only is slavery not instituted in the Bible, *it finds no support*

[38] "Domestic Slavery Considered as a Scriptural Institution," *Southern Literary
Messenger*, XI (September, 1845), 516.
[39] John Campbell, *Negro Mania, An Examination of the Falsely Assumed
Equality of the Races of Men*, p. 421.
[40] *Pro-Slavery Argument*, pp. 294-95.   [41] Smith, *op. cit.*, p. 40.
[42] Hatch, *op. cit.*, p. 10; italics Hatch's.

or sanction there."[43] Reuben Hatch, in his *Bible Servitude reexamined,* based his argument upon three propositions. These were:

1. God's Book, the Bible, must be consistent.
2. God's Book must agree with the great law of love.
3. God's Book must be consistent with natural right.

He then argued that chattel slavery violated the second and third propositions and therefore invariably caused a violation of the first. From this he reached a conclusion that the servitude of biblical times was quite different from that found in the Slave States of America.[44]

Another Northern minister, George B. Cheever, vigorously denounced slavery as a crime according to the Bible. As a basis for his argument, the book of Jeremiah was cited as showing God's wrath against slavery.[45] This passage reads as follows:

"Therefore thus saith the LORD; Ye have not hearkened unto me, in proclaiming liberty, every one to his brother, and every man to his neighbour: behold, I proclaim a liberty for you, saith the LORD, to the sword, to the pestilence, and to the famine; and I will make you be removed into all the kingdoms of the earth."[46]

As an example of the criminal characteristics of slavery, Cheever argued that slaveholding was the same as manstealing.[47] Albert Barnes, feeling that a Northern citizen owed a "duty to his Southern brethren" to enlighten them upon the evils of slavery, wrote a lengthy *Inquiry into the Scriptural Views of Slavery.* Barnes argued, in common with other anti-slavery writers, that, according to the Scripture, "[God]

[43] Pond, *op. cit.,* p. 3; italics Pond's. This writer gives practically no proof for this assertion.   [44] Hatch, *op. cit.,* pp. 10, 15-27.
    [45] George B. Cheever, *God Against Slavery! and the Freedom and Duty of the Pulpit to Rebuke it, as a Sin against God,* pp. 136-37. Cheever was a pastor of the Church of Puritans.   [46] Jeremiah, 34:17.
    [47] Cheever, *God Against Slavery,* pp. 127-30.

hath made of one blood all nations of men for to dwell
on all the face of the earth,"[48] thereby definitely establishing
the equality of all races.[49] He based his attack largely upon
the abstract principles of slavery as being evil, though he denied any relation between the patriarchal form of the institution in the Bible with the system as practiced in the Southern
States.[50] One alleged difference was that the slaves of Egypt
were held by the government rather than by individuals.[51]
Many of the contentions made by Barnes revolved around
the argument that the Bible prohibited many evils that were
inherent in slavery. It was asserted that since the Bible prohibited stealing, oppression, withholding of wages and instruction, then the Scriptures did not sanction slavery which
violated these prohibitions.[52] Southern ministers emphatically denied such interpretations placed upon the Scriptures
by Barnes and others. In fact, Dr. Armstrong, of Norfolk,
Virginia, published a book not only for the purpose of giving
a "faithful exhibition" of the biblical doctrines of slavery but
also to refute the "false glosses" presented by "Dr. Barnes."[53]

In general it seems that the Southern arguments for the
biblical justification of slavery may be classified under certain
points expressed in the form of syllogism as follows:

1. Whatever God has sanctioned among any people cannot
    be in itself a sin.
2. God did expressly sanction slavery among the Hebrews.
3. Therefore slavery cannot be in itself a sin.[54]

In their discussion of God's sanction of the institution of
slavery most of the Southerners divided their arguments into
two groups, passages taken from the Old Testament and

[48] Acts, 17:26.
[49] Albert Barnes, *op. cit.*, p. 344.   [50] *Ibid.*, pp. 60-61.
[51] *Ibid.*, pp. 81-96.   [52] *Ibid.*, pp. 355-61.
[53] Armstrong, *op. cit.*, pp. iii-iv (Preface). The arguments in this work will
be cited from time to time in connection with the general biblical justification of
the South.
[54] See statement of Rev. Fuller in Fuller and Wayland, *op. cit.*, p. 182.

those from the New. They felt that if the system of slavery was sanctioned in both Testaments, and not prohibited in either, then it must be in accord with God's Word. If it were in accord with the Word of God, then the logical conclusion would necessarily be that the holding of slaves was not sinful.

From the Old Testament, pro-slavery writers found many passages that not only proved that slavery existed among the patriarchs but that it had the sanction of the Divine Master. They went so far as to state that the Scriptures proved that this form of servitude was especially ordained for the members of the Negro race.[55] From the Book of Genesis, the story of Noah was unfolded and portrayed as the basis of this contention. Of the three sons of Noah—Shem, Japheth, and Ham—two of them were radically different in constitution and appearance. It was pointed out that Japheth was "a *blue* eyed white man," while Ham was "a woolly headed, black eyed black man."[56] This difference in types was in accordance with God's plan for the change in the climate, humidity, and topography of the earth following the flood, the black man being adapted for populating the tropical, humid portions of the earth.[57] It was pointed out that after the flood had subsided and the land was again tilled to produce crops, Noah became drunk from imbibing a quantity of wine and, while he was asleep in his tent, Ham invaded the sacredness of his father's rest, and much to the horror of his brothers, observed the nakedness of Noah in repose and ridiculed his father.[58] When old Noah learned of the conduct of his youngest son, he was "deeply grieved on account of the reckless impiety of Ham, as well as offended on his own personal behalf."[59] So incensed was Noah by this act of Ham that, in a spirit of

[55] Priest, *op. cit.*, pp. 1-75.

[56] *Ibid.*, pp. 76-81; italics in Priest.   [57] *Ibid.*

[58] Genesis, 9:21-22; "And he [Noah] drank of the wine, and was drunken; and he was uncovered within his tent. And Ham, the father of Canaan, saw the nakedness of his father, and told his two brethren without."

[59] Priest, *op. cit.*, pp. 90-91.

prophecy, he pronounced a terrible curse upon all of the descendants of Ham. Many writers quoted this curse of Noah which is found in Genesis and reads as follows:

24. And Noah awoke from his wine, and knew what his younger son had done unto him.

25. And he said, Cursed *be* Canaan; a servant of servants shall he be unto his brethren.

26. And he said, Blessed *be* the LORD God of Shem; and Canaan shall be his servant.

27. God shall enlarge Japheth, and he shall dwell in the tents of Shem; and Canaan shall be his servant.[60]

Therefore it was asserted that the curse of Noah, as a "*judicial* act of God" against the children of Ham, was placed upon the entire black race as a result of their wickedness and depravity.[61] This view was concurred in by some of the Northern clergy, the Rev. Phillip Schaff stating in this connection that slavery was, from the beginning, a "punishment and curse."[62] Rabbi M. J. Raphall, of New York, concluded that slavery must have existed even prior to the flood or otherwise Noah would not have known of it.[63] A Northern bishop stated that God, "foreseeing" the degradation of the Negro race, ordained the blacks to slavery because "*he judged it to be their fittest condition.*"[64]

After a study of this scripture, Southerners no longer censured themselves for holding African Negroes as slaves, for they felt that the blacks were destined to such an existence by the Almighty. Inasmuch as a slave was under obligations to obey the master, therefore the latter had the right to demand and enforce his obedience. Nor could the slaveholder be

---

[60] Genesis, 9:24-27; quoted in Priest, *op. cit.*, p. 91; Stringfellow, *op. cit.*, pp. 8-9; Fletcher, *op. cit.*, pp. 464-65. Canaan was the son of Ham. Therefore the curse of bondage was inherited by all of Ham's posterity.

[61] Priest, *op. cit.*, p. 104.

[62] Schaff, *op. cit.*, pp. 4-7.   [63] Raphall, *op. cit.*, pp. 18-19.

[64] Hopkins, *op. cit.*, p. 7; italics in Hopkins. For similar views as expressed by a Northern layman, see J. R. Jones, *op. cit.*, pp. 11-13.

considered a "robber" or a "murderer" and "man-stealer" by intelligent persons merely because he claimed from the slave the obedience and fidelity that the Word of God commanded the slave to render.[65] Governor Hammond wrote in 1845 that it was impossible to consider that "Slavery is contrary to the will of God."[66] He expressed the opinion of the South by adding that *We accept the Bible terms as the definition of our Slavery, and its precepts as the guide of our conduct.*[67]

As part of their argument that the Old Testament sanctioned slavery, the pro-slavery writers also pointed to the existence of the institution in the time of Abraham and other patriarchs. Among the enumerated property acquired by Abraham in Egypt, it was found that he had "sheep, and oxen, and he asses, and menservants, and maidservants, and she asses, and camels."[68] In order to rescue Lot after the capture of Sodom, Abraham armed three hundred and eighteen of his slaves for pursuing the enemy.[69] In addition to the slaves born in the household of Abraham, he had others that were "bought with money."[70] It was pointed out that Sarai, the wife of Abraham, had a "handmaid, an Egyptian," whose name was Hagar.[71] The latter had a son by Abraham, which caused her to despise Sarai. Later Sarai told Abraham to "cast out this bondwoman and her son: for the son of this

---

[65] Bledsoe, *op. cit.*, pp. 168, 189.

[66] *Pro-Slavery Argument*, p. 107.   [67] *Ibid.*, p. 108; italics Hammond's.

[68] Genesis, 12:16; quoted by J. R. Jones, *op. cit.*, p. 13. Also see Schaff, *op. cit.*, pp. 7-10, for discussion of the patriarchal forms of slavery.

[69] Genesis, 14:14 states that "And when Abram heard that his brother was taken captive, he armed his trained *servants*, born in his own house, three hundred and eighteen, and pursued them unto Dan." Quoted by J. R. Jones, *op. cit.*, p. 13. The Southerners and the Northern ministers that agreed on the biblical sanction of slavery always maintained that the translation of servant from the Greek and Hebrew had originally meant slave.

[70] Alexander McCaine, *Slavery defended from Scripture against the Attacks of the Abolitionists*, p. 5. See Genesis 17:12, which in reference to circumcision states "he that is born in the house, or bought with money of any stranger, which is not of thy seed."

[71] Genesis, 16:1. See McCaine, *op. cit.*, p. 6.

bondwoman shall not be heir with my son. . . ."[72] Many
biblical passages were quoted to show that the slaves of Abraham were inherited by Isaac and later by Jacob.[73] Even the
meek and patient Job had numbered many slaves among his
"very great household."[74]

Having pointed out that slavery was sanctioned by divine
authority during the patriarchal age, the biblical defenders
turned to the Mosaic age to ascertain if the same proposition
held true. In connection with this study of the period from
the time of Moses until the birth of Christ, one writer asserted that slavery was sanctioned in the "only national constitution emanating from the Almighty."[75] The divine laws
established during this period governed the Jewish Commonwealth for approximately fifteen hundred years. During this
time, though various prophets reproved the people for their
sins, it was charged that there was no denunciation uttered
against the "system of involuntary slavery."[76] Among the
great moral principles and laws which God delivered to
Moses, the biblical defenders of slavery turned to one of the
Ten Commandments as an example of the Lord's recognition
of the system of human servitude. One of these commandments stated: "Thou shalt not covet thy neighbour's house,
thou shalt not covet thy neighbour's wife, nor his man-
servant, nor his maidservant, nor his ox, nor his ass, nor
anything that *is* thy neighbour's."[77] This passage was used
as a basis for the argument that slaves were recognized as the
exclusive property of the owner. The fact that under this

[72] Genesis, 21:10; quoted by J. R. Jones, *op. cit.*, p. 14. See also discussion of
this point in Stringfellow, *op. cit.*, pp. 12-15.

[73] Genesis, 26:13-14; 30:43; 32:5—quoted by J. R. Jones, *op. cit.*, p. 14;
Stringfellow, *op. cit.*, pp. 15-17; McCaine, *op. cit.*, p. 6.

[74] *Ibid.*, p. 3, and *Pro-Slavery Argument*, p. 542, italics in both. See also
Job, 1:1-3.

[75] Stringfellow, *op. cit.*, p. 25.   [76] *Ibid.*, p. 28.

[77] Exodus, 20:17, quoted in *Pro-Slavery Argument*, p. 105; Smith, *op. cit.*, p.
139; Hopkins, *op. cit.*, p. 8; J. R. Jones, *op. cit.*, pp. 11-18.

great law a man's servants were consecrated as his property and guaranteed for his exclusive benefit gave new confidence to the slaveholders of the South.[78] Because of the biblical sanction and protection of slave property, Professor Dew emphatically denied that the Southern planters committed "any offence in holding slaves."[79]

The fact that God's chosen people, the children of Israel, had slaves under the Mosaic law led to the assertion that the system was established for them through the wisdom of God.[80] The assertion was made that slavery was "a peculiar institution" in the Jewish Commonwealth just as it was among the Slave States of America.[81] In order to prove this theory the defenders of slavery presented the slave laws of the Israelites as evidence. The Hebrews had two types of slaves. The first type consisted of people of other nationalities who were either bought or captured in war. The second type was composed of Hebrews who had lost their liberty by the various means known to Mosaic law.[82]

It was shown by the pro-slavery writers that under the scriptural laws a Hebrew might lose his liberty and become a domestic slave in six different ways.[83] The right of a man to sell his liberty in cases of extreme poverty was recognized by the Bible.[84] The passage stating "if a man sell his daughter to be a maidservant" was cited as an example proving that a father might sell his children.[85] In the event that a man was unable to pay his creditors, the law provided that not only might he sell himself, but also his family. The Southern Negroes endured no more anguish at separation than did the widow that cried out "my husband is dead, and the creditor

---

[78] *Pro-Slavery Argument*, pp. 106-7.

[79] *Ibid.*, p. 451.   [80] Hopkins, *op. cit.*, p. 8.

[81] J. R. Jones, *op. cit.*, p. 15.   [82] McCaine, *op. cit.*, p. 9.

[83] Smith, *op. cit.*, p. 140; McCaine, *op. cit.*, pp. 9-10; J. R. Jones, *op. cit.*, pp. 15-16, give these various methods of becoming a slave according to Hebrew law.

[84] Leviticus, 25:39.   [85] Exodus, 21:7.

is come to take unto him my two sons to be bondsmen."[86] Conviction for theft might result in a Hebrew being sold if he was unable to pay the fine prescribed by law. In this instance the sale would be made for the profit of the man who had been robbed.[87] The enslavement of prisoners of war was cited as a fifth example of Hebrew slavery.[88] Still another method of enslavement resulted from the selling of a person to one of his own race after the payment of a ransom.[89]

The Mosaic laws were also referred to by various anti-slavery writers who interpreted them as condemning the institution of slavery. One law, found in Exodus, was particularly emphasized by the abolitionists. This passage stated: "And he that stealeth a man, and selleth him, or if he be found in his hand, he shall surely be put to death."[90] This law, according to the views of the abolitionists, prohibited all forms of human slavery. Albert Barnes interpreted the term "stealeth" to mean *"stealing, selling,* and *holding* 'a man.' "[91] The fallacy in the logic of the abolitionists on this point was noted by a Northern writer. John Richter Jones asserted that instead of the passage being against slavery, it actually proved the legal existence of slavery in the Jewish community. He argued that "if property in slaves had not been recognized" this prohibition against "stealing a man" would have been an utterly "useless" piece of legislation.[92] Another passage which was constantly used in the North as a basis of the attack upon the fugitive slave laws may be found in the Book of

[86] II Kings, 4:1; Matthew, 18:25. "But forasmuch as he had not wherewith to pay, his Lord commanded him to be sold, and his wife, and children, and all that he had, and payment to be made."

[87] Exodus, 22:3. "If he have nothing, then he shall be sold for theft."

[88] II Chronicles, 12:8. This passage in speaking of prisoners of war states that "nevertheless they shall be his servants; that they may know my service, and the service of the kingdoms of the countries."

[89] Smith, *op. cit.*, pp. 139-41; also see discussion of Jewish slavery in Schaff, *op. cit.*, pp. 10-15.

[90] Exodus, 21:16; quoted by Albert Barnes, *op. cit.*, pp. 118, 119.

[91] *Ibid.*, p. 120; italics Barnes'.　　　　[92] J. R. Jones, *op. cit.*, p. 17.

Deuteronomy. This portion of the Mosaic legislation on slavery reads as follows:

15. Thou shalt not deliver unto his master the servant who is escaped from his master unto thee.

16. He shall dwell with thee, *even* among you, in that place which he shall choose in one of thy gates, where it liketh him best: thou shalt not oppress him.[93]

Thousands of sermons and many abolitionist appeals to the "higher-law" in order to stir Northern sentiment against the rendition clauses of the Constitution had their foundation upon these biblical passages.[94] It was pointed out by the pro-slavery writers that these passages applied to instances where slaves had escaped from *"foreign heathen masters"* and did not apply to the slaves of the Hebrews.[95] Therefore, the application of this biblical law to American slavery could not apply among the states within the United States, since they were considered as part of one nation. In fact, a Northern writer asserted that if this was the basis of the "higher-law" doctrine, then the Northern conscience was a "baseless fabric."[96]

Biblical history recorded that the children of Israel, while under the special protection of Jehovah, conquered the land of Canaan and enslaved one entire tribe by making them "hewers of wood and drawers of water."[97] In order to obtain an adequate number of slaves, the Hebrews were permitted to purchase additional ones from the heathens, for the biblical law stated that "Both thy bondmen, and thy bondmaids, which thou shalt have, *shall be* of the heathen that are round about you; of them shall ye buy bondmen and bondmaids."[98] Another source of supply was from the "chil-

[93] Deuteronomy, 23:15-16, quoted by Albert Barnes, *op. cit.*, p. 140; J. R. Jones, *op. cit.*, p. 17; Hopkins, *op. cit.*, p. 11.

[94] J. R. Jones, *op. cit.*, p. 17.

[95] Hopkins, *op. cit.*, p. 11; italics in Hopkins.

[96] J. R. Jones, *op. cit.*, p. 17.

[97] *Pro-Slavery Argument*, p. 452.   [98] Leviticus, 25:44.

dren of the strangers that do sojourn among you, of them
shall ye buy, and of their families that *are* with you, which
they begat in your land: and they shall be your possession."[99]
In addition to permitting these people to be enslaved for a
short time, the biblical law stated that "ye shall take them
as an inheritance for your children after you, to inherit *them*
for a possession; they shall be your bondmen for ever: but
over your brethren the children of Israel, ye shall not rule
over one another with rigour."[100] Therefore, the pro-slavery
group concluded that inasmuch as slavery was sanctioned
during the patriarchal age and was recognized as a legal institution under Mosaic law, then their argument that slavery
existed among the Hebrews had a firm biblical foundation.[101]

From this conclusion the biblical defenders of slavery
turned to the New Testament to determine whether Christ
and the apostles reversed under the gospel dispensation the
recognition of slavery as it existed under Mosaic law. After
carefully examining the New Testament, it was asserted that
they were unable to find "a single passage at all calculated to
disturb the conscience of an honest slaveholder."[102] The basis
of Southern contentions was formed on the proposition that
"Jesus Christ recognized" slavery as an institution that "was
lawful among men, and regulated its relative duties."[103] If
it could be proved that the early conception of slavery was
sanctioned by Christ, through His apostles, then the Southern
case for biblical justification would be established, for "what
God ordains, and Christ sanctifies, should surely command
the respect and toleration of man."[104] One of the best New

[99] *Ibid.*, vs. 45.

[100] *Ibid.*, vs. 46, quoted by Smith, *op. cit.*, p. 141; Ross, *Slavery Ordained by
God*, p. 63, 148.

[101] *Pro-Slavery Argument*, pp. 451-52; Hopkins, *op. cit.*, pp. 5-12; McCaine,
op. cit., pp. 18-19; Matthew Estes, *A Defence of Negro Slavery as it exists in the
United States*, pp. 21-31.   [102] *Pro-Slavery Argument*, p. 452.

[103] Stringfellow, *op. cit.*, p. 34.   [104] *Pro-Slavery Argument*, p. 108.

Testament arguments in favor of slavery was presented by a Virginia pastor[105] and may be summarized as follows:

1. Though numerous sins were catalogued and condemned by Christ and His apostles, Slaveholding does not appear in any catalogue of sins or disciplinable offences given us in the New Testament.[106]

2. All the books of the New Testament were written in the slaveholding states, and were originally addressed to persons and churches in slaveholding states: One of them —the epistle to Philemon—is addressed to a slaveholder.[107]

3. The condition of slaves in Judea, in our Lord's day, was no better than it now is in our Southern States, whilst in all other countries it was greatly worse.[108]

4. Slavery and the relations which it established are frequently spoken of, and yet more often referred to, by Christ and His Apostles.[109]

This author reached the conclusion that slavery was not only sanctioned in the Bible but that *"Christian slavery"* was God's method of gradually raising the degraded African from the "debasing effects of generations of sin."[110] Therefore the "great duty of the South" was not, according to God's Word, "emancipation, but improvement." He denounced the anti-slavery conclusions of Dr. Albert Barnes as sounding like a "Fourth-of-July oration of some beardless Sophomore," instead of the writings of a man of wisdom.[111]

[105] Armstrong, *op. cit., passim.* Dr. Armstrong was pastor of the Presbyterian Church at Norfolk, Virginia.

[106] *Ibid.,* p. 9. Illustrates by the cataloguing of sins and offenses in the Scriptures as cited in Romans 1:29-31; Galatians, 5:19-21; Matthew, 15:19; Mark, 7:21-22; I Corinthians, 5:11; 6:9-10; Ephesians 5:5; Colossians, 3:8-9; I Timothy, 1:9-10; II Timothy, 3:2-4; Revelations, 21:8; 22:15.

[107] Armstrong, *op. cit.,* p. 10.

[108] *Ibid.,* p. 11.

[109] *Ibid.,* p. 13. The three quotations above were all italicized in Armstrong. In connection with number 4, he quoted and cited a number of biblical passages.

[110] *Ibid.,* pp. 131-34; italics in Armstrong.

[111] *Ibid.,* p. 132.

With the growing interest in the biblical phase of the slavery issue, Southerners read their Bibles zealously, searching for passages which defended their position. According to Professor Dew, they greatly admired the Saviour who, in his meekness and humbleness, did not meddle with the established institutions of mankind that had been permitted by the Father.[112] Josiah Priest pointed out that the New Testament did not condemn slavery but agreed favorably with "the curse of Noah and the law of Moses" by its "absolute recognition of the practice" of "enslaving the negro race."[113] This fact, according to J. R. Jones, was generally admitted even among the anti-slavery writers.[114] Phillip Schaff asserted that neither Jesus nor His disciples interfered in any way with slavery as an economic or political question.[115] Dew pointed out that at the time Jesus was born the most horrible forms of slavery existed throughout the world—"slavery a thousand times more cruel" than that practiced in the Slave States of America.[116] Though there were sixty million slaves under the jurisdiction of the Roman Empire when He began teaching, neither Jesus nor His apostles encouraged insurrection, fostered discontent among the slaves, denounced the character of slaveholders, appealed to "passions and prejudices of men" concerning the "abuses of slavery," or even suggested "immediate emancipation."[117] These biblical and historical facts were used by various pro-slavery writers as an argument that slavery was recognized in the New Testament.[118] As one writer concluded: what a difference would have been made in the prosperity and unity of the United States "if the eloquent and pertinacious declaimers against slavery had been willing to follow their Saviour's example!"[119]

[112] *Pro-Slavery Argument*, p. 452. [113] *Op. cit.*, p. 323.
[114] *Op. cit.*, pp. 24-25. [115] *Op. cit.*, p. 19.
[116] *Pro-Slavery Argument*, p. 452; J. R. Jones, *op. cit.*, p. 25.
[117] See *Pro-Slavery Argument*, p. 452, for discussion of this point. For quotations see Schaff, *op. cit.*, p. 19; also Hopkins, *op. cit.*, p. 12.
[118] Armstrong, *op. cit.*, pp. 11-13; J. R. Jones, *op. cit.*, pp. 24-25.
[119] Hopkins, *op. cit.*, p. 12.

The fact that Jesus exhorted the slaves to implicit obedience and fidelity was used as a weapon to strike at the methods of the abolitionists. A Northern layman asserted that if "denunciation of slaveholding is a moral duty now," it was much more so during the time of Christ, because of the greater barbarity of the earlier period.[120] Bishop Hopkins carefully pointed out that the Saviour rebuked the "sanctimonious Pharisees," denounced the "infidel Sadducees" and the "hypocritical Scribes," drove the money-changers from the temple, yet uttered no word against the slaveholder. Though proclaiming Himself as the friend of the poor and lowly, Jesus did not advocate the abolition of slavery. Thus did this Northern bishop contrast the action of Christ on one hand with the "loud and bitter denunciations of our antislavery preachers and politicians," who called *themselves Christians,*" on the other.[121] A similar thought had been voiced from the South when Professor Dew stated that the practice of the Redeemer rebuked the conduct of his "nominal disciples" of the nineteenth century, who sought to "destroy the contentment of the slaves, to rouse their deadly passions, to break up the deep foundations of society, and to lead on to a night of darkness and confusion."[122]

In proof of these contentions, the defenders of slavery turned to passages in the New Testament. This portion of the Bible, they asserted, admonished slaves to obedience and nowhere condemned the slaveholders.[123] Instead of condemning slavery, Christ and the apostles had actually promulgated what might be called a "code of reciprocal duties" for both slaves and masters.[124] Slaves were instructed to "be obedient to them that are *your* masters according to the flesh, with fear and trembling, in singleness of your heart, as unto

---

[120] J. R. Jones, *op. cit.,* p. 25.

[121] Hopkins, *op. cit.,* pp. 15-16; italics in Hopkins.

[122] *Pro-Slavery Argument,* p. 452.

[123] *Ibid.,* p. 453.   [124] J. R. Jones, *op. cit.,* p. 26.

Christ."[125] On the other hand masters were charged to "do the same things unto them, forbearing threatening: knowing that your Master also is in heaven; neither is there respect of persons with him."[126] In Paul's Epistle to Titus, the latter was instructed to "*Exhort* servants to be obedient unto their own masters, *and* to please *them* well in all *things;* not answering again"; "Not purloining, but shewing all good fidelity; that they may adorn the doctrine of God our Saviour in all things."[127] It was pointed out that in another Epistle of Paul "servants under the yoke" were instructed to honor their masters while anyone who should "teach otherwise," (interpreted by pro-slavery writers to mean the abolitionists) did not "consent . . . to the words of our Lord Jesus Christ," and were "proud, knowing nothing."[128] Considering this statement of Paul, John Richter Jones charged that the Northern abolitionists would have prohibited such a "dough-faced" apostle from entering their pulpits.[129]

The Southerners argued that the apostles, instead of en-couraging slaves to revolt under cruel treatment, actually commanded them to be faithful and obedient even to unkind masters. Peter said: "Servants, *be* subject to *your* masters with all fear; not only to the good and gentle, but also to the froward."[130] As a reward for such obedience, the same apos-tle wrote that "what glory *is it*, if, when ye be buffeted for your faults, ye shall take it patiently? but if, when ye do well, and suffer *for it*, ye take it patiently, this *is* acceptable with God."[131] These passages are typical of the many that

---

[125] Ephesians, 6:5, quoted in Stringfellow, *op. cit.*, p. 38; J. R. Jones, *op. cit.*, p. 26. It might be pointed out that this passage was used many times as the text of sermons preached to slaves.

[126] Ephesians, 6:9, quoted by J. R. Jones, *op. cit.*, p. 26; Stringfellow, *op. cit.*, p. 38.

[127] Titus, 2:9-10, quoted by J. R. Jones, *op. cit.*, p. 26; Fletcher, *op. cit.*, pp. 573-74.

[128] J. R. Jones, *op. cit.*, p. 27, quotes from I Timothy, 6:1-4; *Pro-Slavery Argu-ment*, p. 453; also Sawyer, *op. cit.*, p. 113.   [129] *Op. cit.*, p. 27.

[130] I Peter, 2:18, quoted in *Pro-Slavery Argument*, p. 453.

[131] *Ibid.* quotes I Peter, 2:20.

were cited and quoted by pro-slavery writers in order to amass evidence to prove their proposition that slavery was sanctioned by apostolic example.[132]

Biblical quotations were used to prove that not only were slaveholders received into the Christian church by the apostles, but that at least one, Philemon, was considered as a "co-worker" and "fellow-minister."[133] Certainly such conduct on the part of the apostles was not in accordance with the doctrines of "no communion with slaveholders" enunciated by abolition groups led by men like George Bourne, Stephen Foster and Henry Wright. Not content with receiving slaveholders into the church, Paul violated abolitionist doctrines to an even greater extent by sending a fugitive slave back to his master,[134] wrote George Armstrong. The fact that this slave, Onesimus, was sent back to Philemon by the apostle, was held up as a splendid example of the duty of Northern people concerning fugitive slaves. Bishop Hopkins felt that Paul was evidently not an abolitionist or he would have written Philemon, rebuking him "for the awful sin of holding a fellowman in bondage," and charging him "as a solemn duty, to emancipate his slaves, at the peril of his soul."[135] If the abolitionists were correct in condemning slavery as a sin, then, according to George Sawyer, the Saviour and His disciples would have advised the slaves to run away instead of counseling them to be obedient and faithful.[136] If emancipation accomplished such beneficial results, why did the apostle John predict that there would be "both free and bond" at the end of the world?[137] Many similar

[132] See Fletcher, *op. cit.*, pp. 559-85; Armstrong, *op. cit.*, pp. 18-101; Stringfellow, *op. cit.*, pp. 37-52; Hopkins, *op. cit.*, pp. 13-16; J. R. Jones, *op. cit.*, pp. 24-28.

[133] Armstrong, *op. cit.*, pp. 21-32; Hopkins, *op. cit.*, p. 16.

[134] See Philemon, 10-19, quoted in Armstrong, *op. cit.*, pp. 33-34, and either quoted or referred to in the biblical arguments of many other Southern writers.

[135] Hopkins, *op. cit.*, p. 16. Similar sarcasm is used in Bledsoe, *op. cit.*, p. 195.

[136] Sawyer, *op. cit.*, pp. 104-18.   [137] Hundley, *op. cit.*, p. 323.

statements, substantiated by scriptural passages, were used by
the Southerners in their biblical justification of slavery. So
numerous were the scriptural arguments that only a brief sur-
vey and the quoting of typical and often-used passages from
the Bible are possible here. The general conclusion of all the
biblical arguments in favor of slavery was probably best expressed by Dr. Richard Fuller when he stated: "WHAT
GOD SANCTIONED IN THE OLD TESTAMENT,
AND PERMITTED IN THE NEW, CANNOT BE
SIN."[138]

Being able to corroborate their arguments with passages
of Scripture, the Southern people realized as never before the
benefits accruing from their social system. Southern leaders
wished to justify their position and prove to the world that
slavery was divinely ordained. Though denying the alleged
sinfulness of slavery, they felt that even if the system should
be an evil, then the Southern people would accept the responsibility, and it was not the business of outsiders to interfere in the domestic affairs of the South.[139] They maintained
that the thrusting of the slavery problem upon the South
during colonial times had created a situation which could not
be solved by emancipation. As a result of this fact, they asserted that "self-support and self-preservation" demanded
the continuance of the system of slavery.[140] According to
Professor Dew, this placing of slavery in the Southern States
was the entrusting of the slaveholders with the "five talents";
all masters, therefore, having the responsibility of usefully
applying, to the best advantage, these blessings which had
been placed in their hands. Dew admonished slaveholders
to remember the exhortations of the apostle: "Masters, give
unto *your* servants that which is just and equal; knowing

---

[138] Fuller and Wayland, *op. cit.*, p. 170; capitalization Fuller's.

[139] Beveridge, *op. cit.*, II, 55.

[140] "Domestic Slavery Considered as A Scriptural Institution," *Southern Literary Messenger*, XI (September, 1845), 518.

that ye also have a Master in heaven."[141] By accepting the
responsibilities thrust upon them as a result of the patriarchal
form of slavery and by applying the system to promote
civilization and Christianity, he predicted that the masters
might expect on the judgment day to hear the "welcome
plaudit": "Well done, thou good and faithful servant, thou
hast been faithful over a few things, I will make thee ruler
over many things; enter thou into the joy of thy Lord."[142]
With this new conception of the responsibilities of slaveholding came a greater realization on the part of the Southern
people of the Christianizing possibilities of slavery. Bishop
Elliott of Georgia asserted that, regardless of how the rest of
the world might judge the Slave States, the Southern people
conscientiously believed slavery "to be a great missionary
institution."[143] It was felt that God had intended that slavery, though a "seeming evil," should be in reality a "blessing," by means of which the degraded and ignorant African
might be educated, Christianized, and elevated to a higher
scale of civilization.[144] This sentiment, as it developed over
the South, probably did much toward ameliorating slave conditions, an improvement previously prevented by the anti-
slavery agitation in the early thirties.

As the controversy over the biblical sanction of slavery
reached a climax, the anti-slavery group, in the face of undeniable scriptural arguments, were forced to denounce as being incorrectly translated the many passages of the Old and
New Testaments which recognized and approved slavery.[145]
Some Northern ministers contended that the Greek noun
"doulos" did not mean slave but "one who serves."[146] In

[141] Colossians, 4:1, quoted in *Pro-Slavery Argument*, p. 454.
[142] *Ibid.*   [143] Jenkins, *op. cit.*, pp. 217-18.
[144] *Ibid.* See discussion of this same view in Armstrong, *op. cit.*, in his chapter
on "God's Work in God's Way," pp. 131-48.
[145] See Blanchard and Rice, *op. cit.*, pp. 103, 108, 135, 138; William Jay, *An
Examination of the Mosaic Law of Servitude, passim*; William Henry Brisbane.
Slaveholding Examined in the Light of the Holy Bible, passim.
[146] *Ibid.*, pp. iv-v,

refutation, the Southern writers traced the origin of both the Greek and Hebrew terms, both literally and phonetically, to prove that it meant a "slave unconditionally."[147] The Southerners pounced upon the weakening position of the anti-slavery contenders by emphasizing the view that infidelity in the North was a direct result of the agitation of the fanatics against slavery. It was asserted that the latter group were seeking an "abolition Bible, an abolition Constitution for the United States, and an abolition God."[148] They argued that the anti-slavery propaganda had resulted in many Northern ministers of the gospel being brought to the verge of denying the Bible because it sanctioned slavery.[149] Southern ministers had previously professed their willingness to accept the decision that slavery was a sin if the system was denounced as criminal in the Word of God. Since the Bible had substantiated their arguments and convictions, they now looked down upon the abolitionists who *"deny the Bible, and set up in its place a law of their own making."*[150]

That the Southern charges of infidelity as applied to the abolitionists were literally true is indicated by the fact that a Massachusetts abolitionist stated in the London Abolition Convention that if the Bible sanctioned slavery, he was quite ready to *"throw it from him,* and learn again his religion and philosophy from the flowers of the fields."[151] In a meeting

[147] Fletcher, *op. cit.,* pp. 510, 511-637. This author devotes a great deal of space to explaining the original Greek and Hebrew terms of the Bible. See also Armstrong, *op. cit.,* pp. 18-21.

[148] Ross, *Slavery Ordained by God,* pp. 96-97.

[149] *Ibid.,* p. 98.

[150] *Pro-Slavery Argument,* p. 109; italics Hammond's. See similar view expressed in Joseph C. Stiles, *Modern Reform Examined; or, The Union of North and South on the Subject of Slavery,* p. 98. Though born a Southerner, Rev. Stiles was pastor of the Mercer Street Presbyterian Church in New York for several years, and at the time of writing, was pastor of the Congregational Church in New Haven, Conn.

[151] G. Bradburn, speech in the London Abolition Convention reprinted in the *Pennsylvania Freeman,* No. 204, August 6, 1840; quoted by Priest, *op. cit.,* pp. 293-94; italics in Priest.

of the Anti-Slavery Convention held in Boston in May, 1850, William Lloyd Garrison offered a series of resolutions. Among those reprinted in the *Liberator* was one stating that if the Bible sanctioned slavery it opposed the "self-evident truth that 'all men are created equal' " and therefore "*the Bible is a self-evident falsehood*" and should be considered as an "enemy . . . of the progress of the human race in liberty, justice, and goodness."[152] Certainly by this time Garrison had accepted the doctrine of his disciples—Foster, Birney, and Pillsbury—for in 1852 he declared "that the American *Church* is the mighty bulwark of American slavery, the haughty corrupt, implacable, and impious foe of the Anti-Slavery movement." As such, he considered that "its pretensions to Christianity are the boldest effrontery and the vilest imposture."[153] Henry C. Wright, a former Congregational minister, in speaking of the biblical sanction of slavery, shouted "shame on such a God. I defy him, I scorn him, he is not my God."[154] This same abolitionist stated in a letter to Henry Ward Beecher that the anti-slavery cause would triumph, "but only on the ruins of the American Church." With this victory he asserted that "what this nation calls God" would be hurled "forever from his throne of blood; simply because that God has staked his claim to our worship on the support of slavery."[155] Wright became so violent in an anti-slavery meeting that he denounced the pro-slavery God as a "phantom," and stated that he would "fasten the

[152] *Liberator*, June 7, 1850, quoted in Stiles, *op. cit.*, p. 275; italics in Stiles.

[153] Resolution offered by William Lloyd Garrison at the New England Anti-Slavery Convention, May, 1852; quoted in Stiles, *op. cit.*, p. 276. This view of Garrison is in accord with Foster, *op. cit.*; James G. Birney, *The American Churches, The Bulwarks of American Slavery*, and Pillsbury, *op. cit.*

[154] Henry C. Wright, speech before the New England Anti-Slavery Convention in Boston, May 28, 1850; reprinted in the *Liberator*, June 7, 1850 and partially quoted in Stiles, *op. cit.*, pp. 274-75. Wright had been pastor of the Congregational Church at West Newbury, Mass., but at this time was not affiliated with any religious organization.

[155] Wright to Beecher, May 21, 1851; published in *Liberator*, June 20, 1851; quoted in Stiles, *op. cit.*, pp. 275-76.

chain upon the heel of such a God . . . discard the phantom
. . . and liberate the slave."[156] This speech was greeted by
both cheers and hisses. A Connecticut pastor, in speaking of
the "Church which sustains slavery" asserted that he would
"welcome the bolt, whether it come from heaven or from
hell, which shall destroy it."[157] Much earlier than any of
these, George Bourne had condemned the use of the Bible
for sanctioning slavery as the last *"refuge of lies."*[158]

An interesting change in sentiment in both sections resulted from this phase of the slavery controversy. Previous
to the abolition crusade, the Northern section, influenced by
New England Puritanism, was thought to be more religious-
minded than the planters of the Southern States. Whether
this was literally true or not, the anti-slavery agitation after
1831, followed by the Southern defense, certainly placed a
new emphasis upon scriptural study in both sections. During
the controversy the Southern people found in both the Old
and New Testaments a firm foundation for the defense of
their civilization. The history of the patriarchs, conditions
under Mosaic law, and the teachings of Christ and His apostles all illuminated the slave system of the South in a new
light. The slaveholder became satisfied, as never before, that
the relation of the master and the slave was sanctioned by
the Bible. In doing so he realized anew his obligations to
the Word of God. Rather than defend his position upon
theories of infidelity, he could justify it with the Holy Scriptures. The Northern abolitionists, on the other hand, when
hard pressed to meet the scriptural arguments, allowed their
extreme emotionalism either to deny God and the divine inspiration of the Bible or to rewrite the latter with anti-slavery
interpretations. Though they had denounced the Constitution
on the basis of a "higher-law" doctrine, they inconsistently

---

[156] *Ibid.*, p. 275, quotes Henry C. Wright, in New England Anti-Slavery Convention in May, 1850.   [157] *Ibid.*, p. 276.
[158] Bourne, *Slavery Illustrated in its Effects upon Women* . . ., p. 28.

revoked their own "higher-law" by substituting a still superior law of nature when it was found that the Bible sanctioned slavery. Though Garrison had initiated his attack by considering himself and his followers "soldiers of God,"[159] their emotional fanaticism carried them to the point of denying their former alleged leader. As a result of the biblical recognition of slavery, much of their most bitter propaganda was turned against the clergy and the church. It seems quite probable that the emphasis placed upon the Bible during the controversy led to a wave of infidelity and atheism in the North and created a spirit of religious revival in the South. In speaking of this tendency toward religion in the South, at least one writer rejoiced in the anti-slavery agitation because it had stirred the "stagnant waters" of Southern minds and left them "greatly purified."[160]

[159] See Chap. II.
[160] Ross, *Slavery Ordained by God,* p. 103.

CHAPTER VI

ECONOMIC JUSTIFICATION

WHILE engaged in their attack upon the agricultural states, the abolitionists, the sectional politicians, and the moral reformers were so intent upon condemning the moral and social aspects of slavery and in keeping pace with the political developments that they failed to give much consideration to the economic and monetary problems connected with the plantation system.[1] Judging from the controversial literature of the period, it seems that the radical group of abolitionists stressed the moral aspects more than the economic phase of slavery, while the pro-slavery writers treated these elements as of equal importance in their justification of the institution. Certainly the economic phase of the slavery controversy should not be neglected, as it formed a background for many arguments. In fact, much of the development of those commonwealths comprising the Southern agricultural states was based upon the production of certain staples, which in turn had their roots in the firm economic basis of the system of servitude known as Negro slavery. The agricultural organization of the Southern States must be borne in mind as a background for an understanding of the economic justification of slavery and for a correct interpretation of the sectional rivalries behind the slavery controversy.[2]

In common with the scriptural and social advocates of slavery, the economists among the pro-slavery writers turned to the practices of antiquity, as recorded by the annals of history, for a starting point of their justification. The necessity

[1] James D. Hill, "Some Economic Aspects of Slavery," *South Atlantic Quarterly*, XXVI (January, 1927), 161.

[2] See William E. Dodd, *Jefferson Davis*, pp. 55-56.

for this type of argument was partly the result of the abolitionist charge that slave labor was unproductive.[3] In their reply, the Southerners declared that in all countries slave labor was more effective than free for certain types of production. In China where, in spite of the denseness of population, the slave labor had for centuries stood its ground against the free, the slave districts were largely determined by latitude and the agricultural products.[4] It was asserted that in the wheat-growing sections there were no slaves, but that in the warmer areas, where rice, cotton, and sugar cane were the staple crops, slaves were found to be an economic necessity.[5] Professor Dew pointed to the vast production necessary to support the immense armies placed in the field by the tribes of Judah and Israel, as recorded by biblical history, to prove the effectiveness of slave labor during early times.[6] In the modern period of history it was necessary to look no farther than the records of the early American colonies to view the productiveness of slave labor. It was pointed out that prior to the Revolutionary War, the Southern colonies using slave labor were the most prosperous and wealthy among the English colonies of the New World.[7] The abolitionists had charged that the distressed economic conditions of the Southern States during the late twenties were the direct result of the ineffectiveness of slave labor. In answer to this charge, Dew explained that the unequal operation of the Federal Government, through sectional legislation, had produced an economic depression in the agricultural states. He argued that the Northern section, being unable to com-

---

[3] *Pro-Slavery Argument*, p. 482.

[4] *Ibid.*, p. 484.   [5] *Ibid.*, pp. 484-85.

[6] *Ibid.*, p. 485. Professor Dew points out that the Kings of Judah and Israel had armies approximating 1,200,000 men.—II Chronicles, Chap. 13. Jehosaphat, of Judah, later had an army of 1,160,000 men.—II Chronicles, Chap. 17; these vast armies had to be supplied with food and provisions. The pro-slavery writers maintained that slaves produced the required provisions.

[7] *Pro-Slavery Argument*, p. 486.

pete with the South in agricultural production, had turned to manufacturing. In order to protect these new industries, Dew charged that the New England section formed a coalition with the West, by means of which a high protective tariff was passed. The West supported this alliance in return for a portion of the federal funds to be used for internal improvements. Dew asserted that this sectional legislation, which gave a bounty to Northern labor and industry at the expense of the South, had produced the agricultural depression rather than the slave system of the Southern States.[8]

Several economic factors, conducive to early sectionalism, should be pointed out in this connection. The vast tracts of fertile lands found in the Southern colonies created a demand for labor far in excess of the supply. This scarcity of labor in the New World was partially solved first by indentured servants and later by Negro slaves. During the early colonial period, with abundant crops, high prices, and cheap slaves, the planters were tempted to increase their acreage and labor supply in order to reap greater profits. This, as is quite evident, led to a vicious economic circle in which the planter bought more land and slaves to produce more tobacco to make larger profits which in turn secured additional land and slaves. The Yankee skipper's cycle of rum for slaves, slaves for molasses, and molasses for rum, was similar but far more profitable. The great difference was that the Southern planter placed his profits back in the plantations and as a rule never accumulated surplus for any other form of investment. On the other hand, the New England trader always sold the surplus slaves that represented profits and thriftily laid up his savings for investment in commerce or industry.[9] Naturally, then, the latter would be interested in forms of legislation favorable to industry and commerce. Such sectional legisla-

[8] *Ibid.*, pp. 486-87.
[9] See U. B. Phillips, "Economic Cost of Slaveholding in the Cotton States," *Political Science Quarterly*, XX (1905), 258-60, for discussion of these facts.

tion would inevitably work to the disadvantage of the "land poor" Southern planter.

It was admitted by Southern writers that, from a superficial view, slave labor was more expensive than free.[10] It was a fallacy to suppose that the work of slaves was unpaid labor as some of the abolitionists had charged. The initial cost of the slave, which was rather large, had to be paid before the planter could receive any return whatsoever. In addition to this first investment, the slave had to be well fed and adequately clothed in order to conserve health and life. Too, the master accorded to the children and the old, infirm slaves the same kind treatment as he did the workers, and this class of ineffectives became an economic burden.[11] During the entire life of the slave, the planter had the risk of losing his total investment through death by injury or illness. From this viewpoint, it was admitted that slave labor was more expensive than following the example of free countries in hiring a worker for the "smallest pittance" needed "to keep soul and body together and rags on his back." In admitting this, Hammond asserted that the free labor system cared for the worker only during "actual employment" and forced him to be "dependent at all other times on alms."[12]

Even though under certain conditions free labor was cheaper than that of slaves, it was argued that this did not necessarily prove that it would be cheaper for the Southern people, situated as they were. It was an accepted fact that free labor could not be procured or used to the best advantage in the South.[13] This was due to several factors: first, to the idea that white men could not successfully work under the unhealthful conditions that prevailed in the lower

[10] Olmsted, *Seaboard Slave States,* I, 111; also Hill, "Some Economic Aspects of Slavery," *South Atlantic Quarterly,* XXVI (January, 1927), 174.

[11] See U. B. Phillips, "Economic Cost of Slaveholding in the Cotton States," *Political Science Quarterly,* XX (1905), 258.

[12] *Pro-Slavery Argument,* p. 121.   [13] *Ibid.,* p. 122.

South;[14] second, to the natural aversion of free labor to work in competition with slaves; third, to the fact that the large tracts of unoccupied land tempted the white laborers to establish their own plantations rather than to be contented as hired laborers;[15] and last, to the fact that the sparseness of the population necessarily demanded slave labor for extensive cultivation.[16] On account of these factors, it was asserted that the Southern States must be contented with more expensive labor with the "consoling reflection" that what was lost to them was gained by humanity.[17]

Regardless of these admissions concerning the greater expense of slave labor to the individual planter, the Southern writers denied that their labor system was more expensive to the state or to the community. They boldly asserted that the great cost of labor under the institution of slavery was more than compensated by certain beneficial results. The staples cultivated upon Southern plantations required about the same amount of labor each season, thereby creating no inconvenience in retaining workers the year around. On the other hand, under a free labor system, a strike for higher wages at certain periods of cultivation and harvest would insure the destruction of rice and cotton crops.[18] The truth of this argument was substantiated by a foreign visitor. Sir Charles Lyell told of a Louisiana planter who employed white laborers on a sugar plantation to excellent advantage until harvest time, a crucial period in the production of that staple, when all the white hands struck for double pay, thereby placing the owner in the dilemma of either acceding to their demands or losing the crop.[19] Southern economists realized

[14] See discussion of this point in Hill, "Some Economic Aspects of Slavery," *South Atlantic Quarterly*, XXVI (January, 1927), 174.

[15] See discussion of this point in U. B. Phillips, "Economic Cost of Slaveholding in the Cotton States," *Political Science Quarterly*, XX (1905), 258.

[16] *Pro-Slavery Argument*, p. 122.

[17] *Ibid.*   [18] *Ibid.*, p. 87.

[19] Hill, "Some Economic Aspects of Slavery," *South Atlantic Quarterly*, XXVI (January, 1927), 175.

that the use of free labor might easily result in expensive
strikes which would be disastrous to the individual planters
and the communities.[20] From this viewpoint, the slave system seemed an investment for the security of labor. The
additional expense attached to slave labor seemed small in
comparison to the possible terrific monetary loss which might
result from all hands striking during the harvest season of
tobacco, rice, or sugar cane, when a few days' delay would
mean the difference between a bumper crop and a total loss.
The fact that slavery suffered no economic waste from strikes
was used as a strong argument in favor of the system.[21]

Freedom from strikes was only one industrial ill that the
labor organization of the South eliminated. Many industrial
evils of the North were attributed to the conflict between
capital and labor. John Fletcher pointed out that capital and
labor existed in one of two relations, either "congenerous or
antagonistic."[22] Under the organization of a free labor system, the interests of the capitalists and workers were diamet-
rically opposed to each other. The tendency therefore was
for capital to exploit the workers until they continually
reached a lower point of poverty and degradation. The conditions surrounding the factory workers of the North and
England were pointed out as illustrations of the results of
the industrial exploitation of free labor.[23]

Such was not the situation in the Southern agricultural
states. It was felt that Negro slavery was the most effective
and at the same time the most simple solution of the labor
problem. Thomas R. R. Cobb pointed out that this solution
reconciled the interests of labor and capital while at the same
time it protected each "from the encroachments and oppressions of the others."[24] Slavery reconciled these divergent in-

[20] *Ibid.*; also William Harper, "Memoir on Slavery," *DeBow's Review*, X
(January, 1851), 59.

[21] *Pro-Slavery Argument*, pp. 87-88.   [22] Fletcher, *op. cit.*, p. 219.

[23] *Pro-Slavery Argument*, pp. 30-31, 135-45.

[24] Thomas R. R. Cobb, *op. cit.*, p. 214.

terests by transforming labor into capital, thereby eliminating the basic foundations for conflict by making identical the interests of both.[25] Instead of conflicting, it was asserted that under the benign influence of Southern slavery, capital and labor were "beautifully" blended, harmonized, and made into one. Because the value of the slaves constituted a large portion of the wealth of the South, the capital of the agricultural states was mingled and united with the interests of their labor. It was maintained that this unity counteracted "all those social, moral, material, and political evils which affect the North and West."[26] The emphasis placed by pro-slavery writers upon the contrast between the effects of free and slave labor systems may have had its foundation on this viewpoint.[27] Fletcher was quite surprised that "the sympathies of the abolitionists" were not turned from the analogous relationship of capital and labor in the South "to a consideration of that morass of misery into which the worn-out, broken tools of labour are thrown, with cruel heartlessness, where capital and labour are antagonistic."[28]

The comparative insignificance of a pauper class in the South was pointed out as another result of the slave labor system which benefited the state and community without being too detrimental to the individual planter: Thomas Cobb stated

[25] See discussion of this in Fletcher, *op. cit.*, pp. 219-20; Calhoun stated in 1837, that "It is impossible with us that the conflict can take place between labor and capital, which makes it so difficult to establish and maintain free institutions in all wealthy and highly civilized nations where such institutions as ours do not exist." Also discusses the patriarchal form of the slavery system where "labor, and capital is equally represented and perfectly harmonized." John C. Calhoun in speech on the States Rights' Resolutions in regard to abolition, in U. S. Senate, on Dec. 27, 1837, in *The Works of John C. Calhoun*, III, 180.

[26] "American Slavery in 1857," *Southern Literary Messenger*, XXV (August, 1857), 82.

[27] For a rather lengthy poetic defense of the slave labor system through contrast with free labor, see William J. Grayson, *The Hireling and the Slave, and Other Poems;* also Elwood Fisher, "The North and the South," *DeBow's Review*, VII (October, 1849), 315. For examples of actual comparisons made by pro-slavery writers see Chap. IV, *supra*, on "Southern Defense."

[28] Fletcher, *op. cit.*, p. 220.

that "Slavery is a protection from *pauperism*, the bane for which the wisdom of man has not yet prepared an antidote."[29] It was declared that the industrial system of the North, with its conflicting interests of capital and labor, created a large number of paupers which constituted a "monument and record of *free labour*."[30] Southern writers contended that paupers in the North were supported by the community at large. The "hired agents" administering the system in the industrial section lacked the "interested care and economy—not to speak of humanity," that characterized the Southern solution of the same problem where each planter took care of his own ineffectives.[31] Because of this fact, Governor Hammond asserted that the Northern means of providing for the numerous paupers were "both more expensive to those who pay, and less beneficial to those who receive its bounties."[32] It was expected that the immediate emancipation of the slaves would effect a similar result at the South. Chancellor Harper estimated that the practical effect of the abolitionists' policies would change half the population of the Slave States into paupers,[33] a prophecy largely fulfilled by later events.

Notwithstanding the beneficial economic results accruing from the institution of slavery, or the arguments concerning the superiority of free white laborers over black slaves, the South was faced with an actual condition involving thousands of Negro laborers. Lacking a supply of white laborers, the Southern agricultural states could only depend upon their Negro slaves for the production of rice, tobacco, sugar cane, and cotton. Therefore, the important question in their minds was "*the relative amounts of labor*" that might be "*obtained from slaves before and after their emancipation.*" Since the South would be unable to deport the freed blacks upon eman-

[29] Thomas R. R. Cobb, *op. cit.*, p. 214; italics Cobb's.
[30] Fletcher, *op. cit.*, p. 220; italics Fletcher's.
[31] *Pro-Slavery Argument*, p. 122.
[32] *Ibid.*   [33] *Ibid.*, p. 89.

cipation, this question was of basic importance. After carefully surveying the work of free Negroes in various parts of the world, the Southern writers were ready to rest their arguments upon the proposition that the slaves, economically as well as morally, were *"entirely unfit for a state of freedom among the whites."*[34] From the economic viewpoint, the Southern arguments upon this proposition were based upon past experiments in emancipation in both the United States and in other countries.

Beginning with conditions as they existed in the United States, the pro-slavery group pointed out that it was a well-known fact that slave labor was "vastly more efficient and productive than the labor of free blacks," the latter being considered as "the most worthless and indolent of citizens" and looked upon throughout the Union as the "very *drones* and *pests* of society."[35] Though the colored population in the North enjoyed the *"blessings* of freedom," and had ample opportunities for education and progress, yet they remained "an idle, worthless, and improvident race."[36] It was asserted that even the abolitionists generally kept white servants because the blacks were too impudent and lazy.[37] The unproductiveness of the free Negro resulted in placing a "considerable burden upon the laboring and producing citizens."[38] The pro-slavery writers insisted that not only did the destitution of the free blacks of the North and South illustrate their indolence, but the experience of other countries also furnished abundant testimony to this fact.[39]

It was pointed out that the free Negroes of the West Indies were averse to all forms of productive labor and would

---

[34] *Ibid.*, pp. 421-22; italics Dew's.   [35] *Ibid.*, p. 422; italics Dew's.
[36] *The North and South, or Slavery and Its Contrasts*, p. 15.
[37] *Ibid.*, pp. 15-17.
[38] J. H. Van Evrie, *Negroes and Negro "Slavery": The First An Inferior Race: The Latter its Normal Condition*, p. 312.
[39] *Pro-Slavery Argument*, p. 423; see also Priest, *op. cit.*, pp. 352-53; Fisher, "The North and the South," *DeBow's Review*, VII (October, 1849), 314.

exert themselves only in order to supply their immediate or most urgent needs.[40] The report of the Committee of the Privy Council in Great Britain upon the conditions in Jamaica and Barbados was used as evidence to substantiate the Southern contentions. This report, in common with those from other colonies, stated that the free Negroes would not work for wages, were not interested in freedom, and yet had all the vices of slaves.[41] Though the citizens of Great Britain had been taxed approximately five hundred million dollars to carry out the British "anti-slavery" policy, the Negroes, instead of being uplifted with liberty, had fallen to a still lower depth of economic and moral degradation.[42] Dr. Van Evrie charged that this anti-slavery policy of England was a "monstrous delusion" which had been represented as the "noblest philanthropy."[43] He asserted that the English aristocracy taxed the laborers of England "to carry on a policy at war with liberty in America." By striving to tear down racial distinctions which God placed upon the black and white men, Van Evrie felt that the British aristocracy were attempting to distract attention from their own man-made social distinctions in order to preserve the latter. By legislation they forced the Negro to be elevated and the white man to be lowered until the two reached a common level. He argued that by the equalizing of the blacks and whites in the insular possessions the British Government had followed a policy which curbed labor and production and tended toward destroying the white race and civilization.[44] Economically

---

[40] *Pro-Slavery Argument*, p. 423.   [41] *Ibid.*, pp. 423-24.
[42] Van Evrie, *op. cit.*, p. 324.   [43] *Ibid.*
[44] *Ibid.*, pp. 321-23, 329. Dr. Van Evrie believed that Great Britain expected that her emancipation policy would be followed by the freeing of the slaves in the United States. He argued that this policy was a conspiracy by which England hoped to strike at the very fundamentals of American Government. Under the abolitionist policy, liberty and equality would be reduced to an absurdity through the elevation of an inferior race to economic, social and political equality. With such a distorted transformation, Van Evrie felt that the fundamental principles of republican government would disappear in the United States as it had in the British West

this seemed to be true in the case of Jamaica. In cotton alone the British exports from her West Indies possessions dropped from 1,708,764 pounds in the year prior to emancipation to 427,529 pounds in 1840.[45] The pro-slavery writers quoted actual reports of abolitionist missionaries and English newspapers to prove the economic degradation of Jamaica. Approximately twenty years after emancipation, the London *Times* declared that the blacks on the island "instead of becoming intelligent husbandmen" had become "vagrants and squatters."[46] Though the island itself was very fertile, under a system of free black labor, production steadily declined and the population was described as "the most wretched-looking Negroes to be seen on the face of the earth."[47] From all reports, it seemed quite evident that British emancipation in the West Indies, regardless of motives, had failed in achieving any economic benefits for either blacks or whites.

Another emancipation experiment, used to substantiate the Southern contention that the Negro slaves were "economically . . . unfit for freedom," was to be found in the Island of Hayti.[48] Statistical reports were used to show the tremendous decline in productiveness resulting from emancipation. Under French rule and the stability of a slave labor system in 1789, the sugar exported from the island amounted to more than 672,000,000 pounds; after the bloody revolt in which the slaves obtained their liberty, the production de-

---

Indies. This view was, of course, contrary to the economic interpretation of British actions by other pro-slavery writers. Calhoun and others considered the anti-slavery policy of Great Britain a result of commercial rivalry, through which England was willing to sacrifice the economic welfare of her colonial possessions in the West Indies in order to monopolize tropical products in the East Indies.

[45] David Christy, *Cotton is King*, table of statistics on pp. 205-6. See n. 75, *infra*, for further title and fuller description of this book and its author.

[46] *Ibid.*, p. 140, quotes London *Times* of 1853.

[47] *Ibid.*, p. 143, quotes Bishop Kip in 1853. Also quotes reports of missionaries of the American Missionary Association, Annual Report of the American and Foreign Anti-Slavery Society and other sources on the same point. *Ibid.*, pp. 133-43. [48] *Pro-Slavery Argument*, p. 433.

clined steadily until in 1806 it was only 47,516,531 pounds; in 1825 it was 2,020 pounds, and by 1832 production had diminished to such an extent that no sugar was exported.[49] In 1825 the value of all the exports was only $8,000,000, a decrease of $1,000,000 since 1822, while the revenue of the island was considerably below public expenditures.[50] Haytian exports which amounted to $125,000,000 in 1789 were reduced to less than one-tenth that amount by 1849.[51] Southern writers argued that this experiment in emancipation, conducted for forty years under favorable circumstances, was sufficient evidence to "convince and overwhelm the most skeptical, as to the unproductiveness of slave labor converted into free."[52] Considering the disastrous economic results of these experiments in emancipation, the pro-slavery group viewed with alarm the possible translation of the same conditions in the Southern States.

With a feeling that slave labor, from an economic point of view, was far superior to free Negro labor, the Southern slaveholders realized that immediate emancipation would bring dire consequences upon the South.[53] Disastrous economic effects upon one section of the Union would naturally react unfavorably upon the other. Therefore, Southern economists studied carefully the probable effects of the abolitionist policy upon both the North and the South.

In the first place, the large monetary loss resulting from the possible emancipation of the slaves appalled the Southerners. A large portion of Southern capital was invested in that type of property. In 1850 the lower South alone, includ-

---

[49] Bledsoe, *op. cit.*, p. 279. [50] *Pro-Slavery Argument*, p. 432.

[51] Fisher, "The North and the South," *DeBow's Review*, VII (October, 1849), 314.

[52] *Pro-Slavery Argument*, p. 432; see also Priest, *op. cit.*, pp. 352-53; article on "Free Negroes in Hayti," *DeBow's Review*, XXVII (November, 1859), 526-49, describes Hayti in 1789 as "the brightest jewel in the French Crown," having "two thirds of the exterior commerce of France." P. 530 gives a table of exports from Hayti, 1789-1841, which shows a terrific drop in production.

[53] *Pro-Slavery Argument*, p. 433.

ing the states of South Carolina, Georgia, Alabama, Mississippi, Louisiana, and Texas, supported a slave population of
1,723,358. The value of these slaves amounted to $689,343,-
200. The value of all the land and improvements in these
states was only $450,939,711.[54] Ten years later the capital
invested in slaves had practically doubled as a result of increased numbers and higher prices. To follow the policy
advocated by the American abolitionists would be to destroy
completely this vast amount of invested wealth. In demanding immediate emancipation without compensation the abolitionist group in the United States even went beyond the
emancipation policy of Great Britain, which had compensated
the slaveowners in the British dominions. Dr. Bledsoe
charged that the abolitionists expected the South to sacrifice
"twelve hundred millions of dollars," the estimated value of
the slave property, upon the "altar of abolitionism." He asserted that such an "enormous robbery" would have aroused
the South to "righteous indignation" and compelled the
slaveholders to make some move for the protection of their
property even if emancipation produced no injurious results
other than the economic loss.[55] These slaves had been hon-
estly acquired and much of the original cost had been paid to
Yankee traders. Despite the protection assured by the Constitution, the radical group of abolitionists demanded the
complete annihilation of this species of property without substituting any other form. Southerners argued that upon
emancipation, the Negroes, worth millions as slaves, "would
become worthless to themselves and nuisances to society."[56]
Such an extreme measure, from an economic standpoint,
would completely bankrupt the South.

[54] See discussion of this point in Hill, "Some Economic Aspects of Slavery,"
South Atlantic Quarterly, XXVI (January, 1927), 165-66.

[55] Bledsoe, *op. cit.*, pp. 285-87; also see Fisher, "The North and the South,"
DeBow's Review, VII (October, 1849), 313.

[56] Bledsoe, *op. cit.*, p. 287; also see Publicola (pseud.), "The Present Aspects
of Abolitionism," *Southern Literary Messenger*, XIII (July, 1847), 431.

Following closely upon the destruction of the capital invested in slaves, the South faced another great economic loss. The ineffectiveness of free Negro labor, the inadequate supply of white laborers, and the abundance of land would combine to destroy the extensive cultivation of Southern staples. Without the discipline and organization of the slave labor system, the blacks would be worthless, while white laborers could not be procured because of the sparseness of population and their tendency to become independent landowners.[57] Unable to secure a sufficient labor supply, the cultivation of rice, tobacco, sugar cane, and especially cotton would be seriously curtailed, thereby creating an immediate and rapid decline in land values.

The valueless lands in the British West Indies after emancipation were cited as an example of what might be expected from the same program in the South.[58] The planters, bankrupted by the annihilation of slave property and the consequent destruction of land values, would be unable to continue agricultural pursuits in the South. It was felt that such conditions would result in many slaveowners migrating to other sections. As early as 1832 Professor Dew asserted that "slave labor" was the "Atlas" that upheld the whole Southern economic system by giving value through the cultivation of the soil. Applying this fact specifically to his native state, he predicted that if the slave population were eliminated, "the worn soils of Virginia would not bear the paltry price of government lands . . . and the Old Dominion will be a 'waste of howling wilderness; the grass shall be seen growing in the streets, and the foxes peeping from their holes.' "[59] Two years later, Professor Ingraham, a Northern-born opponent of slavery, wrote that Mississippi would "revert to the aboriginal possessors" upon the freeing of the slaves and the consequent destruction of cotton production and withdrawal

[57] *Pro-Slavery Argument*, pp. 86-87.
[58] Bledsoe, *op. cit.*, p. 287.   [59] *Pro-Slavery Argument*, p. 358.

of the planters. He asserted that, with the annihilation of this combination, "every southern state might be bought for a song."[60] The Southern writers contended that emancipation would in a very few years turn the "most beautiful garden-spots" of that section into a "jungle," relieved only by an occasional "forlorn plantation."[61] Without a doubt they felt that the "poverty and distress, bankruptcy and ruin" that prevailed in the "once flourishing British colonies" after the abolition of slavery would be reproduced on a larger scale if "the fatal experiment of emancipation" was tried in the South.[62]

Aside from the utter poverty and misery to which the South would be reduced, the Southern leaders declared that the effects of emancipation would also be detrimental to the North, since the desolation would spread over the entire country. The first and most obvious result of the slave's acquiring freedom would be the rapid decline in the cultivation of the Southern staples. The effect of this, they announced, would be to destroy, at one blow, between two-thirds and three-fourths of the foreign commerce of the United States.[63] Not only did slavery provide for the subsistence of millions of Negroes but the pro-slavery writers maintained that the institution also provided employment for millions of freemen residing in other states of the Union. With the destruction of Southern agriculture it was declared that the Northern manufacturers would be without a market,

[60] Joseph Holt Ingraham, *The Southwest*, II, 91. Ingraham was a native of Maine, a sailor, a participant in a South American Revolution. He became a professor of languages in a Southern school. At the time of the above publication he was opposed to slavery and even more so to the abolitionists. After living for several years in the South he became a strong supporter of the institution of slavery.

[61] Bledsoe, *op. cit.*, p. 287. The *Charleston Courier*, July 25, 1833, stated that without slavery "their fertile fields would become a wilderness and a desert."

[62] Bledsoe, *op. cit.*, pp. 287-88.

[63] *Pro-Slavery Argument*, pp. 87, 486; *DeBow's Review*, X (January, 1851), 59. See also Kettell, "The Future of the South," *DeBow's Review*, X (February, 1851), 137. He states that "few persons reflect upon the immense superstructure of wealth and power which is reared upon the foundation of American slave culture

their factories would be forced to close their doors, and their laborers would become destitute from want and misery.[64] It was argued that slavery produced a diversity of industrial "pursuits and products," supplied markets, supported trade and manufacturers, occasioned "mutuality of independence," and prevented "undue rivalry and competition between the two sections."[65] Those who justified slavery argued that emancipation would necessarily cause Northern and Southern "pursuits and products" to become similar, consequently causing trade and intercourse to cease, since one section would not furnish a market for the other. Under such a condition competition and rivalries would arise that would result in "a useless and cumbrous Union" being "dissolved."[66] Much of the prosperity and luxury of the North was attributed to the

---

of cotton. United States trade is practically based upon that industry." The following table is taken from the same article:

	Southern Produce Exported	Value of Production
Cotton, raw	71,984,616	$105,600,000
Cotton, manufactures	4,734,424	100,000,000
Tobacco	9,951,223	15,000,000
Rice	2,631,557	3,000,000
Naval Stores	1,142,713	2,000,000
Sugar	23,037	12,396,150
Hemp	5,633	695,840
Provisions from New Orleans	3,523,809	
Other Southern Articles	6,000,000	$238,691,990
Total	99,997,012	

North and Western Exports........... 34,903,221
Total U. S. Exports................. 134,900,233

Note: These statistics were for the year 1850. Amount of exports much higher in proportion by 1860.

[64] *Pro-Slavery Argument*, pp. 86-88. A writer in 1854 pointed out that cotton, rice and tobacco constituted three fourths of the exports of the U. S. The vast increase of production in the Southern States was accomplished by slave labor. He stated that "to the North this vast production has been the Aladdin's lamp—and the negroes of the South have been the genii of its prosperity—have built its palaces and supplied its wealth." See article "A Few Thoughts on Slavery," *Southern Literary Messenger*, XX (April, 1854), 196.

[65] George Fitzhugh, "The Conservative Principle," *DeBow's Review*, XXII (April, 1857), 429.

[66] *Ibid.*, p. 430; also Sawyer, *op. cit.*, pp. 371-72.

fact that the industrial section was able to exchange its manufactured articles for the products of slave labor, the latter finding a ready market in Europe.[67]

Not only was slavery beneficial to America, declared Southern writers, but it had also given "existence to hundreds of thousands, and the means of comfortable subsistence to millions" upon the continent of Europe.[68] *Blackwood's Magazine* in 1853 admitted Europe's dependence upon slave labor by stating that the increased demand for cotton "has placed the internal peace—we may say subsistence of millions, in every manufacturing country of Europe—within the power of an oligarchy of planters."[69] It seemed evident that the products of slave labor constituted the basis of a large portion of the world's wealth, so the pro-slavery writers boldly declared that the prosperity and civilization of both Europe and the United States depended greatly upon the institution of slavery.[70] They asserted that slavery had thus enabled the world to obtain cheap and serviceable clothing, thereby inspiring a taste for comfort, and consequently contributing more than anything within modern times to the progress of civilization.[71] The Southerners argued that to follow the schemes of the abolitionists and free the Negro slaves of the South would result in a decline in the necessary products of slave labor and would thus affect the commerce and disturb the peace of the entire world.[72] George Fitzhugh maintained that while "African slavery" was "not king," through its influence upon the commercial prosperity of the world it became the "pacificator and grand conservator of the peace of nations."[73]

[67] *Pro-Slavery Argument*, p. 88.   [68] *Ibid.*, pp. 88-89.

[69] *Blackwood's Magazine*, LXXIII (January, 1853), quoted by Christy, *op. cit.*, p. 46.

[70] See discussion in Hawes, "Slavery in Mississippi," *Sewanee Review*, XXI (April, 1913), 226-27.   [71] *Pro-Slavery Argument*, p. 88.

[72] *Ibid.*, pp. 86-89, 428-33; Bledsoe, *op. cit.*, pp. 284-92.

[73] Fitzhugh, "The Conservative Principle," *DeBow's Review*, XXII (April, 1857), 430.

These various economic arguments portraying the benefits of slave labor, the economic chaos that followed abolition experiments, and the continual demand for more and more cotton by the industrial centers of America and Europe created among the Southern people an ever greater realization of the blessings of slavery and a dawning knowledge of the significant economic weapon which that institution had placed in their hands.[74] It remained for a Northern writer to sum up the economic arguments which justified the importance of slavery in world affairs and especially its importance in the cultivation of American cotton, on which the factories of the world depended, and to popularize them under a slogan that struck a responsive chord among the Southern people. David Christy, ardent colonizationist and opponent of both slavery and abolitionism, who lived on the border between free and slave territory, adequately pointed out the dependence of the world upon the Southern staple in his famous work entitled *Cotton is King*.[75]

Christy contended that emancipation in the United States had been checked and slavery extended through the influence of three factors. According to his argument, these factors were first, the failure of the freed Negroes to improve themselves with the advantages afforded by emancipation; second, the increased values imparted to slave labor and slave products; and finally, the mistaken policies of the abolitionist

---

[74] A. A. Smith, "A Southern Confederacy," *DeBow's Review*, XXVI (May, 1859), 578, states that "In cotton, the South possesses a weapon more formidable than all the inventions of modern warfare."

[75] *Cotton is King; or the culture of Cotton, and its Relation to Agriculture, Manufactures and Commerce; to the Free Colored People; and to Those Who Hold that Slavery is in itself Sinful.* The first edition was published anonymously "by an American." Later editions bear Christy's name. In 1860, it was incorporated as an important contribution to a larger work of essays by Southern writers known as *Cotton is King and Pro-Slavery Arguments*, edited by Professor E. N. Elliott of Planter's College, Mississippi. At the time of writing Christy was living in Cincinnati, Ohio. He had previously been an agent of the Colonization Society.

group.[76] From the standpoint of the economic justification of slavery, the importance of Christy's work lies in his summarizing in terms of concrete facts the fundamental arguments in both Europe and America, proving the dependence of Northern and European factories upon Southern cotton at that date. The "Cotton is King" doctrine, soon shortened to "King Cotton," fitted snugly as the keystone of the previous economic arguments in support of slavery propounded by the Southerners. Having maintained for a number of years that slave labor was necessary for the production of Southern staples, the "King Cotton" idea took its proper place to fill out a logical conclusion. The arguments revolving around this doctrine may be summarized in the form of a syllogism as follows:

1. The cultivation of cotton is dependent upon the system of Negro slavery.
2. The world is dependent upon cotton, therefore:
3. The world is dependent upon Negro slavery.

Under the leadership of men like Senator James H. Hammond of South Carolina and J. D. B. DeBow, editor of *DeBow's Review*, a widely circulated Southern industrial and literary journal, the "King Cotton" doctrine was accepted enthusiastically and occupied a dominant position in the Southern philosophy of slavery. Still later this sentiment was to become a powerful argument for the success of secession and to form the foundation of the diplomatic relations of the Confederacy.[77]

It was only natural that the Southern economic justification of slavery should be based largely upon the importance of cotton. In value the cotton crop amounted to more than

---

[76] *Ibid.*, p. 184, *et passim.*

[77] Frank L. Owsley, *King Cotton Diplomacy*, pp. 1-25. Dr. Owsley gives an excellent summary of the development of the King Cotton philosophy and shows its relationship to Confederate diplomacy.

that of rice and sugar combined.[78] It constituted the most important export of the United States. In 1854 two-thirds of
the cotton and tobacco crops, both products of slave labor,
were exported in comparison to the one forty-sixth of all
other agricultural products exported.[79] However, this fact
was not detrimental to the other agricultural sections of the
United States, for, as it was pointed out, the provisions and
cattle of the free states supplied the slave plantations of the
South with those commodities, thereby binding their market to
the slave system. A destruction of slavery would, therefore,
destroy the market for many other agricultural products.[80]

Christy pointed out that disregarding such products of
slave labor as tobacco, rice, and sugar, the value of the raw
cotton alone reached the grand total of $109,456,404 in
1853.[81] While the cotton exports were stressed in showing
the dependence of Europe upon that staple, the importance
of the increase in the domestic consumption of cotton products
was not neglected by the Southern economists. The fact that
cotton consumption in the United States had increased nearly
600 per cent from 1830 to 1850 demanded consideration.
During this same period the per capita consumption had practically tripled.[82] In spite of the enormous value of cotton
products in the early fifties, the pro-slavery writers declared

[78] J. D. B. DeBow, *Industrial Resources of the Southern and Western States*,
III, 419.
[79] Christy, *op. cit.*, p. 42; see also table in n. 63 of this chapter.
[80] Christy, *op. cit.*, pp. 42-43.
[81] *Ibid.*, p. 48. Most of this raw cotton was destined for Great Britain. Its
distribution was as follows: Great Britain, 768,596,498 lbs.; Continent of Europe,
335,271,434 lbs.; to countries on American continent, 7,702,438 lbs. The total
exported for that year was 1,111,570,370 lbs.; entire crop amounted to 1,600,-
000,000 lbs.; this left 488,429,630 lbs. for home consumption. The value of the
cotton exports nearly doubled in the period 1850-1853.
[82] Kettell, "The Future of the South," *DeBow's Review*, X (February, 1851),
143. The following table is from this article:

Year	Cotton (lbs.)	Population	Per capita (lbs.)
1830	50,804,800	12,866,020	12
1840	118,357,200	17,069,453	21
1850	283,107,600	22,000,000	32¼

that the climax of the production and demand for the staple was far from being reached.

Southern economists insisted that the demand for cotton would continue to increase since half of the world did not yet realize the practical superiority of that staple over hemp, flax, bark, wool, and silk in the fabrication of cloth for different purposes.[83] They declared that within the space of a few years "six hundred millions of people" would be "clothed chiefly in cotton," requiring millions of bales annually, while household, agricultural, commercial, and mechanical purposes would demand a similar quantity.[84] The Southern writers asserted that the most vivid imaginations could hardly visualize the immense proportions to which the industry might extend or the tremendous influence it might wield over the destinies of nations.[85]

The industrialization of England and the consequent demands for raw materials placed the Slave States of America in a strategic position to secure a monopoly of the cotton production. An almost unlimited supply of fertile lands, the labor supply controlled and stabilized, the production of a high quality product, and proximity to market enabled the South to outdistance all other competitors in that trade. Foreseeing the increased demand for the staple, Great Britain had made "the most vigorous efforts to promote its cultivation in her own tropical possessions."[86] Her West Indian policy turned out to be a dismal failure and successive attempts to secure the fiber from Egypt and India met with little success.[87] Cotton could be produced in those countries, but production and transportation costs were greater while the raw material itself was of shorter fiber and poorer quality

[83] *Ibid.*

[84] R. Abbey, "Cotton and the Cotton Plantings," *DeBow's Review*, III (January, 1847), 1-2.

[85] *Ibid.*, p. 2.   [86] Christy, *op. cit.*, p. 45.

[87] I. T. Danson, "Connection between American Slavery and British Cotton Manufacture," *DeBow's Review*, XXII (March, 1857), 265.

than that exported from America. In spite of all attempts to encourage its production in the various parts of the United Kingdom, the supply could not in any way keep pace with the demand with the result that the English industries became increasingly dependent upon the Slave States. Early in the fifties a million workers were employed in the cotton mills and subsidiary industries in England, while by 1860 between 4,000,000 and 5,000,000 people were dependent upon the cotton industry.[88] England's alarm at her dependence upon the Southern States for such a vital industry stimulated and firmly entrenched the South's faith in the "King Cotton" doctrine and in the economic necessity of slavery.

Behind the demand for cotton, always forming the dark background for the white fiber of that staple, was the necessity of Negro labor in its production. The Southerners declared that "slavery is essential to our existence as producers of what Europe requires."[89] Without the use of slave labor, doubt was expressed as to whether the exportation of cotton would have increased to any appreciable extent or have been of sufficient importance to inspire the inventive genius of Eli Whitney to construct the cotton gin.[90] George Fitzhugh boldly declared that "slavery makes Europe dependent upon us" for food, clothing, and the maintenance of her commerce and manufacturers.[91]

The Southern contention that England was dependent upon cotton produced by slave labor was not without foundation. Arguments and assertions of pro-slavery writers were often corroborated by statements of foreign economists and newspapers. As only one example among many, it may be pointed out that the *London Economist* in 1850 stated that "the lives of nearly two millions of our countrymen are de-

[88] Owsley, *op. cit.*, pp. 8-9.   [89] Russell, *op. cit.*, p. 181.

[90] M. Tarver, "Domestic Manufacturers in the South and West," *DeBow's Review*, III (March, 1847), 193.

[91] Fitzhugh, "The Conservative Principle," *DeBow's Review*, XXII (April, 1857), 430.

pendent upon the cotton crops of America," to such an extent that "should any dire calamity befall the land of cotton, a thousand of our merchant ships would rot idly in docks; ten thousand mills must stop their busy looms; two thousand thousand mouths would starve, for lack of food to feed them."[92] Other English publications like the London *Times* and *Blackwood's Magazine* expressed similar views, while men like John Chapman and Henry Ashworth warned England of the possible consequences of this dependence upon Southern cotton.[93] Receiving such foreign support for their arguments, the South's confidence in the "King Cotton" doctrine increased steadily until it reached a point where the Southern people, led by Hammond, DeBow, and others, were willing to found a new government upon the necessity existing in the North and Europe for the great staple of Southern soil. "Destroy the production of cotton at the South and you will almost ruin Europe and America," boasted a Mississippian;[94] while Fitzhugh predicted: "Blot out negro slavery, and you arrest the trade of the world."[95]

Because the monopoly of cotton production imparted an economic value to slave labor, the Southern leaders felt that the institution of slavery would continue to exist as long as their monopoly of the markets of the world was maintained.[96] Therefore the foundation of their economic argument rested upon cotton. "King Cotton" had no evidence that Negroes could cultivate cotton except "in the capacity of slaves."[97] The enervating climatic conditions making cotton culture unhealthful for whites in tropical sections and the indolence of free blacks forced the "King" to employ the use of Negro slaves. It seemed only logical that slavery would flourish so long as the demand for cotton existed or increased.

[92] *London Economist*, 1850, quoted by Christy, *op. cit.*, pp. 46-47.
[93] Owsley, *op. cit.*, pp. 6-11.   [94] Estes, *op. cit.*, p. 159.
[95] Fitzhugh, "The Conservative Principle," *DeBow's Review*, XXII (April, 1857), 429-30.
[96] Christy, *op. cit.*, pp. 184-85.   [97] *Ibid.*, p. 187.

With great confidence in the supremacy of "King Cotton," the Southern writers became increasingly enthusiastic in portraying his "wondrous powers." "His Majesty," firmly placed on a throne of cotton, was viewed as a conqueror who had the "citizens of the world . . . dragging forward his chariot, and shouting aloud his praise!"[98] From among the many passages dealing with the "King Cotton" theory found in contemporary books, newspapers, and periodicals by various writers, the following is quoted as typical of the most enthusiastic expressions of the supporters of the "King."

Great and incalculable is the wondrous power of cotton! It earns the poor man's bread, and fills the rich man's pocket. It covers the newborn infant, and forms our garment for the grave. . . . The hopes and fears of millions born and unborn, cluster around those unsightly cotton bales. It permeates through every department of civilized and, it may be, uncivilized life.

It invents cotton gins, and spinning jennies, and lifts inventive genius to immortality. It quickens slow moving industry, and sharpens hungry avarice. Roaring waterfalls and puffing steam sing poems to its attenuating fibre, and clattering looms attune their notes in harmony. It enlarges the boundaries of science and adorns art. It fills the imaginations of poets and divines and constructs cunning platforms for statesmen and politicians. It institutes oligarchies and perpetuates them while it binds up with its tough fibre the great democratic heart, and shields it from destruction. It freights the ships of commerce, and sends a missionary to every clime, and in the hour of danger it barricades our cities and nobly protects us from pillage and booty. More than this it has made salubrious and fragrant the once abodes of hideous reptiles and miasma, and perhaps not least of all, has raised up more than three millions of the children of Ham to an elevation above their sable brothers which challenges comparison in history. Wonderful! Most wonderful! is the power of cotton! The universe is but a cotton mill, elaborating the necessities of man.[99]

[98] *Ibid.*, pp. 186-87.
[99] D. D. Deming, "The Power of Cotton," *DeBow's Review*, XXII (May, 1857), 540-43.

Such was the extreme Southern view of the great power of cotton, inevitably bound with the institution of slavery, without which "the advancing civilization" would "receive a shock that must retard" progress for many years.[100]   To understand the relationship of this doctrine to Negro slavery, it is necessary always to bear in mind that many Southerners firmly believed that cotton culture required an adequate supply of strictly controlled black laborers.[101]   There seems to be no doubt that this phase of the Southern philosophy played an important part in shaping the policies of the Southern people during the slavery controversy.

Basing their contentions upon these economic arguments many writers charged the abolitionists with mistaken policies and outright inconsistencies.   David Christy, in maintaining his "Cotton is King" doctrine, asserted that slavery was upheld by a *"tri-partite alliance"* composed of Southern planters, Western farmers, and English manufacturers.[102]   According to this view, the Western farmers furnished grain, cattle, and other supplies to the planters.   The planters in turn furnished the raw materials needed by the English manufacturers, the latter supplying the planters with manufactured articles. Thus the Southern planters, who were dependent upon slave labor for their agricultural system, supported and made prosperous the other two economic groups.   These groups were benefited by a free trade policy and injured by a protective tariff.   Christy pointed out that the abolitionists were allied with and in sympathy with England.   Being in agreement with England on the slavery question, Christy charged that the abolitionists also agreed on the free trade policy advo-

---

[100] Christy, *op. cit.*, pp. 122-23.

[101] See letter of J. B. Davis to Calhoun, July 22, 1848, as an example. Davis stated that "The deplorable condition of agriculture in the hot climates of Europe, Asia, Africa and America, when black labour is not employed, illustrates one fact, that no *white* man can labour in the *hot* sun of the South, and the *free black man will* not."—Calhoun, *Correspondence*, p. 1178.

[102] Christy, *op. cit.*, p. 188; italics Christy's.

cated by the British without understanding its effect upon American slavery. Therefore he concluded that as the abolitionists were allied with the English manufacturers they, in reality, inconsistently created a *"quadruple"* alliance out of the former tripartite arrangement.[103]

In following the lead of their English brethren, he charged that the American abolitionists were again led into a mistaken policy. The English emancipationists had exerted their efforts to convince Parliament that in addition to eliminating the evils of slavery, emancipation would be economically beneficial to the commerce and prosperity of the empire. In that case the English Parliament had the power to act. The American abolitionists neglected the economic phases of the question and issued their propaganda largely for consumption in the free states. They also erred in failing to grasp the difference between the English and American systems of government. Congress, unlike Parliament, had no power to overthrow slavery. Only the legislatures of the Slave States, representing their constituents, the slaveholders, had that power in America. Instead of pointing out the economic benefits of emancipation to the slaveholders, who alone had the power of emancipation, Christy charged that the American abolitionists antagonized that group from the beginning by denouncing them as thieves, murderers, and criminals. In other words, they attacked those who had the power of emancipation and made their appeal on moral grounds to those groups that had no constitutional power to interfere. Nor was this their final inconsistency. For while condemning the slaveholder as robber they placed themselves in the position of persons that seemingly did not allow their right hands to know what their left hands were doing. To the slaveholders, the abolitionist appeared with one hand held high as an exhorter, haranguer, and propagandist, while

[103] *Ibid.*, pp. 108-28, 188; italics Christy's.

"from beneath his cloak of seeming sanctity" the other hand reached out "to clutch the products of the very robbery he was professing to condemn!"[104]

Concerning this inconsistency, many Southern writers ridiculed the anti-slavery manufacturers and merchants of the North for manufacturing and selling to the planters the alleged symbols of slave discipline—the handcuffs, shackles, chains, and whips. Were not Northern hands outstretched to receive the "blood-stained" money produced by the wickedness of the slavery which they condemned?[105] Why didn't Northern church members and anti-slavery philanthropists refuse to purchase cotton, sugar, rice, and other Southern products that were "sprinkled with blood, as you say, from the lash of the driver?"[106] Surely if the system of slavery was a sin, the opponents of the institution could at least prove their sincerity by refusing to use any of the staples produced by slave labor. Southern writers declared that rather than do this, the men of Boston, New York, London, and Paris, who had branded the slaveholder as "a pirate, a kidnapper, a murderer, a demon, fit only for hell," continued to buy cotton in such immense quantities that the prices of slaves soared higher and higher.[107] Ross denounced such inconsistency among the abolitionists by writing: "O ye hypocrites! ye denounce slavery; then ye bid it live, not die;—in that ye buy sugar, rice, tobacco, and, above all, cotton! Ye hypocrites! ye abuse the devil, then fall down and worship him."[108]

[104] *Ibid.*, p. 167.

[105] Ross, *Slavery Ordained by God*, pp. 16-17. See also the discussion in Beveridge, *op. cit.*, II, 57.

[106] Ross, *Slavery Ordained by God*, p. 17.   [107] *Ibid.*, p. 76.

[108] *Ibid.*, pp. 76-77. Ross continues by stating: "Ye hypocrites,—ye New England hypocrites,—ye Old England hypocrites,—ye French hypocrites,—ye Uncle Tom's Cabin hypocrites,—ye Beecher hypocrites—Oh your holy twaddle stinks in the nostrils of God, and he commands me to lash you with my scorn, and his scorn, so long as ye gabble about the sin of slavery, and then bow down to me, and buy and spin cotton, and thus work for me as truly as my slaves! . . . in your unitarianism and neology and all modes of infidelity, ye are rejecting and crucifying the Son of God."

Such was the bitter denunciation of the South for the inconsistency of the abolitionists in their moral and economic views.

The Southern economic justification of the slave system,
faith in the power of cotton, and the enormous possibilities of
economic loss involved in immediate emancipation must be
considered as important factors in the development of Southern opinion before 1860. Viewing the slavery agitation nearly
a hundred years later, it seems regrettable that the abolitionists did not reason more with the planters concerning the
possible economic evils involved in the system of slave labor.
Certainly such a course could not have aroused as great antagonism as the abolitionist policy of moral condemnation of
everything Southern and the propagation of sentimental
stories about the sad plight of imaginary heroes like Uncle
Tom and Eliza. The vicious onslaught of the radical abolitionist had a tendency to blind the Southern people to any
possible evils of their institutions by engendering within them
deep-set prejudices that hindered a careful and impartial
analysis of the problem. The marshaling of the forces of industrialism for the purpose of reconstructing the social and
economic organization of an agrarian civilization could hardly
have been expected to have any result other than conflict.
While it seems likely that many Southerners realized that
slavery created certain economic handicaps, the system was
justified on the ground that white men could not work under
the semi-tropical conditions of the lower South[109] and the
presence of an inferior race necessarily created an economic
burden which could be most easily remedied or diminished
through the system of Negro slavery. Had some plan been
offered by which the slaveowners could have been compensated for the tremendous loss in property resulting from
emancipation, part of the Southern economic justification
would have been without foundation. This the abolitionists

[109] Priest, *op. cit.*, p. 352; also see discussion in Hill, "Some Economic Aspects
of Slavery," *South Atlantic Quarterly*, XXVI (January, 1927), 174-76.

would not concede and emancipation was therefore considered to be disastrous in its economic effect.

Today the South's belief in the supreme power of "King Cotton" seems remarkable when viewed in the light of the overproduction of that staple within recent years and the consequent drop of prices to a new low level. However, it is not so strange if the worldwide economic conditions during the period from 1830 to 1860 are considered. The rapid industrialization of the North, of England, and of the continent of Europe demanded an increased supply of raw products. The Southern States had a practical monopoly upon the supply of cotton. England tried in vain to avert dependence upon the South by attempting to secure cotton from various other parts of the world. Yet the plantation system of the Slave States continued to produce a higher quality fiber at a lower cost than could be produced in Brazil, India, or Egypt. During this period English newspapers and statesmen continually admitted that the welfare of a large portion of Britain's industrial population depended upon American cotton. The South realized also that cotton supplied many factories in the industrialized eastern part of the United States. In turn the North depended upon the Slave States to consume a large portion of their manufactured articles of various types. What the South failed to realize was that this dependence was mutual. The Southern States, almost exclusively devoted to certain staples—namely, cotton, rice, tobacco, and sugar cane—were dependent upon the North and Europe for most of their manufactured articles and in many instances for food products. When conditions seemed to necessitate a policy of secession, the South hoped for a peaceful separation. If this could not be accomplished, then the South expected victory through the intervention of foreign powers. The basis of this expectation rested largely upon their belief in the need of American cotton in England and France. They failed to realize that a great oversupply of cotton in those countries might greatly weaken the power of "King Cotton."[110]

In addition to these other factors, the evils of the free blacks after emancipation created the possibility of economic chaos. Yet, unwilling to consider this, the radical group of abolitionists continually fought and condemned the colonization movement which sought to rid the country of these freed Negroes. Added to the economic consequences of abolition was the question of racial adjustments following emancipation which always loomed as a dark cloud shadowing Southern thought. Slavery as a necessary social relationship under which two completely diverse races might live and prosper together held an even firmer grip on Southern opinion than did the economic benefits of the institution. The justification of slavery as a social necessity, a most important factor in determining Southern opinion and Southern history, will be discussed in the next chapter.

[110] Owsley, *op. cit.*, pp. 1-51, 562-78.

Chapter VII

SOCIAL JUSTIFICATION

"*THE negro question lies far deeper than the Slavery question.*"[1] This statement, though voiced by a Northern minister, expressed a fundamental truth concerning the problem of the Southern Slave States which the abolitionists either failed to recognize or intentionally ignored. The freeing of the African race was not, to the Southern people, merely an academic question nor the subject of a moral crusade. Instead, the possible results of emancipation faced them as a stark reality, clearly outlined by many potentialities. Two diverse races, of almost equal numbers, lived within the same area and formed the economic and social structure of Southern civilization. Could these two races dwell together without friction under any form of social relationship besides slavery? This question was of vital importance to Southern whites. In this regard the social aspect of slavery was closely connected with the economic problem. Economically, the South had to choose not between Negro slave labor and free white labor, but between Negro slaves and free black laborers.[2] Socially, the problem was similar and the choice lay between disciplined slaves and the menace of uncontrolled, barbarous free blacks. As Calhoun pointed out in 1837, the question was much more than a "mere naked question of master and slave," for it involved an institution which was considered "essential to the peace and existence" of the Slave States.[3]

The South disclaimed all responsibility for the origin of

---

[1] Schaff, *op. cit.*, p. 31; italics Schaff's.   [2] See Chap. VI.

[3] *Works*, III, 179—speech on the States Rights' Resolutions in regard to abolition, delivered in U. S. Senate, Dec. 27, 1837.

this race problem. African slaves were imported to America by the mother country without "consulting the colonies supplied" and despite their "frequent protests."[4] Many years later a Southern minister explained this by asserting that God, moving in His mysterious way, "allowed England, and her Puritan sons at the North, from the love of gain, to become the willing instruments, to force African slaves upon the Cavaliers of the South."[5] Certainly the burden of "civilizing and christianizing" a group of "degraded savages" was not a responsibility ordinarily sought after.[6] Neither did the Negro desire to be transplanted to another continent. Yet it was pointed out that upon the arrival of a slave vessel the Negro had only two choices—"deliverance from his loathsome dungeon by the planter, or protracted and daily increasing suffering, to terminate in death."[7] Both being the victims of circumstances, the slave accepted service with the planter in lieu of a worse fate, while the latter accepted the "great responsibility" devolving upon him in the position of master.[8] In contrast to the benevolent treatment of the slaves by the Southern colonists it was pointed out that the Yankee skippers pocketed the profits of the slave trade but failed to bear their share of "the burden of training and elevating" the African savages.[9] Slavery in spite of the opposition of certain leaders spread through the Southern colonies until it reached alarming proportions. All Southern attempts to eliminate slavery without creating even greater race problems had failed. Many Southerners realized this and accepted the institution as one inherited from their fathers, though they sponsored various colonization schemes and societies as methods of ameliorating conditions. Certainly the generation of Southerners attacked by the Garrisonian abolitionists had nothing to do with the origin of the problem.

[4] Fuller and Wayland, *op. cit.*, p. 131.   [5] Stringfellow, *op. cit.*, p. 144.
[6] *Ibid.*   [7] Fuller and Wayland, *op. cit.*, p. 131.
[8] Stringfellow, *op. cit.*, p. 144.   [9] *Ibid.*

But they were vitally concerned as to the social significance of any proposed schemes of solution.

As a late authority on American slavery has pointed out, despite many diversities the white people of the South were and still are united "with a common resolve indomitably maintained—that it shall be and remain *a white man's country*."[10] On this premise both the slaveholding and the non-slaveholding elements of the population were conscious of the necessity of maintaining white supremacy and civilization.[11] This consciousness, though not always expressed, formed what Professor Phillips called the "central theme of Southern history."[12] This "theme" constantly recurred throughout the social justification of the institution of slavery either as a direct expression or as a powerful undercurrent dominating Southern thought. Without an understanding of this important factor, the unanimity of Southern opinion concerning slavery after the abolitionist attack cannot be fully explained. With a knowledge of this "central theme," it is possible to gain a greater appreciation and understanding of

[10] Ulrich Bonnell Phillips, "The Central Theme of Southern History," *American Historical Review*, XXXIV (October, 1928), 31; italics Phillips'.

[11] Robert J. Walker, "Appeal for the Union," *DeBow's Review*, XXI (December, 1856), 589-602. Walker stated that "In all the slave states there is a large majority of voters who are non-slaveholders; but they are devoted to the institutions of the South—they would defend it with their lives—and on this question the South are a united people."—Pp. 591-92. Frederick Law Olmsted quotes a conversation which he had with a non-slaveholder. Upon asking the latter his opinion concerning the freeing of the slaves, the non-slaveholder replied: "I'd like it if we could get rid on 'em to yonst. I wouldn't like to hev 'em freed, if they was gwine to hang 'round . . . if they was free, no man couldn't live. . . . Now suppose they was free, you see they'd all think themselves just as good as we; of course they would, if they was free. Now, just suppose you had a family of children, how would you like to hev a niggar feelin' just as good as a white man? how'd you like to hev a niggar steppin' up to your darter? Of course you wouldn't; and that's the reason I wouldn't like to hev 'em free."—*Seaboard Slave States*, II, 218-19. Ulrich Bonnell Phillips quotes an extract from a plantation journal, written by an overseer, and points out that in addition to the economic interest of those connected with plantations, a million non-slaveholders as well "had a still stronger social prompting; the white man's ways must prevail; the negro must be kept innocuous."—"The Central Theme of Southern History," *American Historical Review*, XXXIV (October, 1928), 32.   [12] *Ibid*.

the fundamental issues involved in the Southern justification of slavery, the War Between the States, the opposition to radical Reconstruction policies, the political unit of the "Solid South," the present-day "Jim Crow" laws, and Southern resentment of outside interference in their domestic affairs.

The foundation of the social justification of slavery was the widespread belief that the Negro belonged to a different and inferior race. Governor McDuffie, in his message to the General Assembly of South Carolina in 1835, declared that the "intellectual inferiority and natural improvidence" of the Negro race were not the only evidences of inferiority, for their physical characteristics "marked" it upon their faces and skins.[13] He continued by stating that the Negroes were, "in all respects, physical, moral, and political, inferior to millions of the human race."[14] James Kirke Paulding asserted the following year that "there exist physical incongruities which cannot be permanently reconciled" between the white and black races.[15] Southern writers like Matthew Estes constantly maintained that "the African is naturally inferior to the Caucasian," and carefully listed the various physical and mental differences between the two races.[16] George Sawyer argued that not only did the history of the Negro race bear "strong testimony against them," but it furnished the "most undeniable proof of their mental inferiority."[17] This was explained in a letter to Calhoun from an American physician residing abroad, who asserted that "the *Negro* knows, acts and feels that God had put a mark of inferiority upon him."[18] Lack of mental alertness and forethought, a love of gaudy finery and "trifling amusements," a distaste for the routine of industry, and an inclination toward indolence, "as

---

[13] Governor McDuffie to South Carolina General Assembly in 1835, reprinted in Hart, *Source-Book of American History*, sec. 95, p. 245.

[14] *Ibid*.   [15] Beveridge, *op. cit.*, II, 35.

[16] Estes, *op. cit.*, pp. 49, 63-69.   [17] Sawyer, *op. cit.*, p. 192.

[18] Dr. J. B. Davis to John C. Calhoun, July 22, 1848, *Correspondence*, p. 1178; italics in *Correspondence*.

well as overpowering animal propensities," were all urged by the advocates of slavery as general characteristics of the African race.[19] One writer pointed out that the difference of color alone presented "an insuperable obstacle to emancipation and admission to the fraternity of social and political rights" on an equal basis with the whites.[20] A leading Southern magazine ridiculed the abolitionists for thinking that, because occasional Negroes exhibited some intellectual qualities, the entire race "might be elevated to the same standard" by merely declaring them free and insisting upon their equality with members of the white race.[21]

Without citing the numerous instances in which Southern writers stressed the inferiority of the Negro race, it should be pointed out that this argument was strongly emphasized. Thousands of Southerners, needing no further proof than their observations while in daily contact with the African, reached the conclusion that the Negro was an inferior being.[22] William Chambers, editor of *Chambers Journal*, after travelling extensively in America, asserted in 1855 that there was a "fixed notion" prevalent in the Slave States that the African was "by nature a subordinate race" and could not "be considered as equal to the white."[23] He declared that this view "lies at the root of American slavery."[24]

The general belief in the racial inferiority of the Negro was given a scientific foundation by the theories of a small group led by Dr. Samuel G. Morton, Dr. Josiah C. Nott, and George R. Gliddon. Previously, the inferiority and servility of the African had been attributed by the ministers

---

[19] "On Slavery," *DeBow's Review*, XVIII (April, 1855), 450.

[20] Southron (pseud.), "Thoughts on Slavery," *Southern Literary Messenger*, IV (December, 1838), 747.

[21] "Slavery at the South," *DeBow's Review*, VII (September, 1849), 211.

[22] "The Black and White Races of Men," *DeBow's Review*, XXX (April, 1861), 448.

[23] William Chambers, quoted in article "On Slavery," *DeBow's Review*, XVIII (April, 1855), 449.   [24] *Ibid.*

of the South to the direct curse of God upon the children of Canaan.[25] Without entirely discarding the scriptural doctrines, a more scientific group of Southerners explained the inferiority of the Negro on the basis of a fundamental difference in species. Instead of the "unity" theory, or the origin of the human race from a single pair, they maintained the "plurality" theory of several distinct types of mankind. According to the latter theory, the human family was composed of several distinct species, originating from different pairs and probably from widely separated points.

The scientific school of pro-slavery thought did not reach its climax until the 1850's. It is quite possible that it had been in the minds of Southern philosophers many years before. Thomas Jefferson, early in his contact with the Negroes, realized the possibility of their separate origin. However, no arguments maintaining this view were used by Southern writers until after the Garrisonian attack upon slavery in 1831. The abolitionist charge that slavery degraded the Negro was refuted in 1833 by Richard H. Colfax.[26] This writer, in a small pamphlet, contended that there were at least two distinct species of mankind and that the black race was the inferior species.[27]

Probably the earliest American scientist to support the "plurality" theory was Dr. Samuel George Morton of Philadelphia. Realizing the need of materials for the study of crania, he began in 1830 to collect skulls from widely separated localities. This resulted in a large museum of comparative craniology containing approximately 1,500 specimens, about 900 of which were human.[28] As a result of his research,

[25] See Chap. V on "Historical and Scriptural Justification."

[26] Richard H. Colfax, *Evidence Against the Views of the Abolitionists.*

[27] *Ibid.,* p. 8, cites Jefferson, Voltaire, Gibbon, Boyle and others as his authorities. This pamphlet consists of only thirty pages and therefore can hardly be compared with the later voluminous works of Nott and Gliddon.

[28] Appleton's *Cyclopaedia of American Biography,* IV, 432-33. This collection now belongs to the Philadelphia Academy of Natural Sciences.

aided by the specimens of Egyptian crania supplied by George R. Gliddon, an English archaeologist, Dr. Morton proved that the same diversities of racial types had existed for approximately four thousand years. Though he denied that climatic conditions produced a diversity of the races, Dr. Morton did not clearly contend in his publication of 1839 that the races were of separate origins.[29]

While Dr. Morton was carrying on his research in Philadelphia, Dr. Josiah Clarke Nott, a physician of Mobile, Alabama, was making a careful study of the fundamental differences between the white and black races.[30] Well prepared for work in ethnology, Dr. Nott gradually collected data from hundreds of Negroes before arriving at his later conclusions. As early as 1842, he gave expression to the theory that the Negro belonged to a different species from the white man. In two lectures delivered in Mobile in 1844, Dr. Nott focused the attention of Southern people upon the doctrine of diversity of origin and plurality of species. Nott stated that after twenty-five years of study of white and black races, their diseases, anatomy, and physiology, he had come to the conclusion that "the Almighty in his wisdom" had peopled the earth "from many distant centres, instead of one, and with races or species originally and radically different."[31]

The increased interest in the justification of slavery during the forties and early fifties caused Nott's theories to be examined by many other writers. In 1853 Dr. John H. Van

[29] See Samuel G. Morton, *Crania Americana*.

[30] Appleton's *Cyclopaedia of American Biography*, IV, 540. Dr. Nott, after graduating from South Carolina College and the medical department of the University of Pennsylvania, spent a year studying abroad. In 1836 he went to Mobile, where, in addition to his professional work, he established a Medical College which was later endowed and made a part of the State University by the Legislature of Alabama. During his professional career he had ample opportunity for studying the types of Negroes living in the Lower South. For a short time he was Professor of Anatomy at the University of Louisiana.

[31] Josiah C. Nott, *Two Lectures on the Connection Between the Biblical and Physical History of Man*, p. 5; these lectures were originally delivered in 1844.

Evrie upheld the same doctrine in a pamphlet[32] which he published later as a chapter in his *Negroes and Negro "Slavery"; the First, an Inferior Race—the Latter, its Normal Condition.* In 1854 Dr. Nott, in collaboration with George R. Gliddon,[33] published *Types of Mankind, or Ethnological Researches,*[34] which book gave the best scientific arguments for the "plurality" doctrine. Three years later the same writers published their *Indigenous Races of the Earth,*[35] which developed even more fully the original theories. Both works were contributed to by scientists like Morton, Agassiz, Maury, Pulszky, Meigs, and others.

Antagonism between this scientific school of pro-slavery writers and those engaged in a scriptural justification of the system was inevitable, and the conflict between science and religion which ensued can be compared with similar contests occurring approximately seventy-five years later over the theories of evolution. However, the members of the scientific school did not so much attempt to discredit the question of divine origin as they did to place a new interpretation upon creation through the application of scientific principles.[36]

[32] *Negroes and Negro Slavery . . . Introductory number: causes of popular delusion on the subject. . . .* (Baltimore, 1853). Later Van Evrie published *White Supremacy and Negro Subordination, or Negros a Subordinate Race* (New York, 1868).

[33] Gliddon was at that time a well-known authority upon Egyptian archaeology, having spent twenty-three years in that region. While visiting in the United States he lectured in Boston, Philadelphia, and New York upon Egyptian Antiquities. He had previously been of material aid to Dr. Morton in his study of Egyptian crania. See Appleton's *Cyclopaedia of American Biography,* II, 665.

[34] Josiah C. Nott and George R. Gliddon, *Types of Mankind, or Ethnological Researches, based upon the Ancient Monuments, Paintings, Sculpture, and Crania of Races, and upon the Natural, Geographical, Philological, and Biblical History.*

[35] Josiah C. Nott and George R. Gliddon, *Indigenous Races of the Earth, or New Chapters of Ethnological Inquiry.* Gliddon died in 1857, though Nott lived until 1873.

[36] Nott, *Two Lectures,* p. 5, on accepting divine influence. Dr. S. A. Cartwright, also a member of the scientific school, felt that the basis for their theories could be found in passages from Moses. See his *Essays, being Inductions from the Baconian Philosophy and Proving the Truth of the Bible and the Justice and Benevolence of the Decree Dooming Canaan to be a Servant of Servants,* p. 12.

Probably the most celebrated controversy was carried on in the *Charleston Medical Journal* between Rev. John Bachman of Charleston and Dr. Morton, who by 1850 had fully accepted the theory of the diverse origin of the human race.[37] As a naturalist, Bachman argued largely with analogies on hybridity drawn from human and other zoological examples, and became one of the leaders of the "unity" doctrine.[38] Thomas Smyth aided the latter cause somewhat by compiling many of the arguments in his treatise upon *The Unity of the Human Race Proved to be the Doctrine of Scripture, Reason, and Science*.[39] The *Southern Presbyterian Review* and other religious periodicals endorsed the "unity" doctrine.[40] On the other hand, the exponents of the "plurality" theory received strong support from such magazines as *DeBow's Review* and the *Southern Quarterly Review*.[41]

For the purposes of this chapter, it will not be necessary to do more than merely summarize the essential arguments for and against the "plurality" theory of the origin of mankind. It must be remembered, however, that these fundamental arguments were substantiated in voluminous works with scientific data and charts designating the variations in the crania and anatomical development of animal life in various parts of the globe, as well as biblical quotations.

The arguments of the scientific school of pro-slavery writers may be grouped under three main classes. First, it was maintained that instead of all races of mankind originat-

[37] Jenkins, *op. cit.*, p. 271. This controversy started over an article on "Hybridity" which Bachman published in the *Charleston Medical Journal*, V, 508. Dr. Morton replied and the controversy resulted.

[38] See John Bachman, *The Doctrine of the Unity of the Human Race, Examined on the Principles of Science.*   [39] Jenkins, *op. cit.*, p. 271.

[40] *Ibid.*, p. 263. The *Southern Presbyterian Review* was published at Columbia, S. C.

[41] See later citations of articles in each of these reviews. In article on the "Moral and Intellectual Diversity of Races," *DeBow's Review*, XXI (July, 1856), 63-70, a reviewer of Nott and Gliddon, *Types of Mankind,* disagrees with the authors' conclusions. Editor DeBow stated his disagreement with the reviewer's conclusion.

ing from one centre, there were "centres of creation," each developing its own peculiar species of the human family.[42] The basis of this assumption of the "plurality" of origins came from certain definite scientific principles of zoology and botany. It was pointed out that the surface of the earth was "naturally divided into several zoological provinces, each of which is a distinct centre of creation, possessing a peculiar fauna and flora,"[43] and that within these "climatical limits and geographical boundaries"[44] the original species of plant and animal life were developed and assigned to the appropriate province. It was contended that the human family offered no exception to this general principle but rather conformed to it. Therefore, the creation of mankind took place at several centres, developing different races, "each of which constituted a primitive element in the fauna of its peculiar province."[45] Much scientific data was brought together to form the foundation of this argument because it produced a basic explanation for many other contentions of the scientific group.[46]

The facts composing the second group of arguments supporting the diversity theory of human origin were drawn from anatomical studies, measurements, and observations.

[42] Nott and Gliddon, *Types of Mankind*, pp. lix, lxi, lxvi, cited by article "On the Unity of the Human Race," *Southern Quarterly Review*, X (October, 1854), 296-98.

[43] Nott and Gliddon, *Types of Mankind*, p. 465.

[44] "On the Unity of the Human Race," *Southern Quarterly Review*, X (October, 1854), 296-98; the "centres of creation" theory of Nott and Gliddon's work was largely the contribution of Dr. Louis Agassiz.

[45] Nott and Gliddon, *Types of Mankind*, p. 465; also *Indigenous Races of the Earth*, p. 457, quotes J. Blanchard, *Voyage au Pôle Sud, Covettes l'Astrolabe et la Zélée*, 1837-1840, as follows: "there exist different species of men; that these species, very proximate to each other, form a natural genus; and that these species were created in the very countries in which we find them at present. In résumé, the creation of mankind must have taken place upon an infinitude of points on the globe, and not upon a single point whence they have spread themselves, little by little, over the surface of the earth."

[46] See Nott and Gliddon, *Indigenous Races of the Earth*, chapter on "The Monogenists and the Polygenists," pp. 402-602, for a discussion of these theories.

Dr. Nott particularly had done a great deal of research along this line. It was agreed that the various races of men differed from each other "in physical structure to an extent which, in the case of other animals would induce naturalists to class them as radically distinct species."[47] Special emphasis was laid upon the differences in physical structure of the white and black races. It was pointed out that the color of the two races would alone show specific characteristics.[48] Dr. Van Evrie maintained that "color" was a "standard and exact admeasurement of the specific character" of the several human races.[49] According to his view, the Caucasian or white race was the "most superior" while the Negro, being black was the "most inferior," with the other colored races distributed between these two extremes.[50] Anatomical comparisons were made proving a vast difference in the physical structures of the Negro and the white man. One distinct characteristic was the additional layer of skin found in the black species.[51] In fact, it was asserted that the "whole anatomical structure, the feet, the hands, the limbs, the size and form of the head, the features, the hair, the color, the *tout ensemble* of the negro being" was so striking a contrast to the Caucasian that it unmistakably indicated Negro inferiority.[52] Particular attention was called to the covering of the head upon various types within the human family. It was pointed out that the hair of Negroes was wool, "eccentrically elliptical," while that of the Caucasian was "oval," and that of the American Indian "cylindrical."[53] Rather than the "straight lines of the figure, the expressive features," and

[47] "On the Unity of the Human Race," *Southern Quarterly Review*, X (October, 1854), 299. [48] *Ibid.*

[49] Van Evrie, *Negroes and Negro Slavery*, p. 90.

[50] *Ibid.*, pp. 88-91.

[51] "On the Unity of the Human Race," *Southern Quarterly Review*, X (October, 1854), 299.

[52] Van Evrie, *Negroes and Negro Slavery*, p. 95.

[53] "On the Unity of the Human Race," *Southern Quarterly Review*, Vol. X (October, 1854).

graceful carriage of the white man the Negro's peculiar anatomy, his "decided inclination to the quadruped posture," and small cerebrum definitely stamped the latter as a distinct species not far removed from the "ourang-outang."[54] These arguments inevitably led to the conclusion that the Negro was not only a distinct type but also an inferior race.

The third group of arguments upholding the "plurality" theory may be found in the study of history and archaeology. It should be mentioned in this connection that the use of materials from these sources was not confined to the scientific school, but that they were also used extensively by Dew, Hammond, Harper, Simms, and many other pro-slavery writers.[55] Nott and Gliddon made full use of Egyptian history and archaeology to show that from the earliest recorded history, no new type of race had appeared, while the intermixture of two or more types had not produced a "new and *Permanent* type."[56] It was asserted that for more than four thousand years the same types had existed around the Valley of the Nile, "consequently long prior to any alphabetic chronicles."[57] According to the monuments of the ancient Egyptians, the people of the earth were then divided into four distinct races.[58] The historian Herodotus in 450 B.C. wrote of the "black, woolly haired Africans" and described the other races as they appeared in modern times.[59] Therefore, it seemed quite probable that certain types of mankind had been "*Permanent* through all recorded time."[60] Each of these had evidently developed from a "distinct centre of

---

[54] Van Evrie, *Negroes and Negro Slavery*, pp. 92-97. See also his discussion of the "Features," "Brain," "Senses," and general summary, pp. 105-42.

[55] See essays by these writers in *Pro-Slavery Argument*, *passim*.

[56] Nott and Gliddon, *Types of Mankind*, p. 465.

[57] *Ibid.*, also Van Evrie, *Negroes and Negro Slavery*, pp. 65-66.

[58] Nott and Gliddon, *Types of Mankind*, p. 465. These conclusions were probably a result of Gliddon's twenty-three years of research in Egypt.

[59] "On the Unity of the Human Race," *Southern Quarterly Review*, X (October, 1854), 300.

[60] Nott and Gliddon, *Types of Mankind*, p. 465.

creation," for climatic conditions made but slight changes in racial characteristics and did not tend to form a new race.[61] Inasmuch as *"permanence* of type" was "accepted by science as the surest test of specific character," Nott and Gliddon concluded that there existed a *"Genus Homo,* embracing many primordial types or 'species.' "[62] Dr. Samuel Kneeland, Jr., after a careful study of the anatomy, general characteristics, and diseases of Negroes and mulattoes, had reached the same conclusion by 1855.[63]

The arguments in favor of the "unity" theory, the origin of the human race from a single pair, may also be classified under three groups. The basic contentions of this group of writers were largely drawn from scriptural passages. Rev. Bachman in his verbal controversy with Morton cited the Book of Genesis to prove that Eve "was the Mother of all living,"[64] thereby upholding the doctrines of the "unity" theory. It was pointed out that God "made of one blood all nations of men for to dwell on all the face of the earth."[65] The Scriptures also stated that "For as in Adam all die, even so in Christ shall all be made alive,"[66] and that the "first man Adam was made a living soul."[67] From these passages, Thomas Smyth reasoned that all races of mankind "interested in Christ" would necessarily "be of Adamic origin" and of the same "blood" and "stock." As a result of the command to "preach the gospel to every creature in the world" he argued that all races "must be of the same original Adamic

---

[61] "On the Unity of the Human Race," *Southern Quarterly Review,* X (October, 1854), 300, 303.

[62] Nott and Gliddon, *Types of Mankind,* p. 465.

[63] Dr. Samuel Kneeland, Jr., "The Hybrid Races," *DeBow's Review,* XIX (November, 1855), 537-39, states his conclusion that the *"genus Homo* consists of *several species."*

[64] Genesis, 3:20; "And Adam called his wife's name Eve; because she was mother of all living."

[65] Acts, 17:26; "And hath made of one blood all nations of men for to dwell on all the face of the earth, and hath determined the times before appointed, and the bounds of their habitation."

[66] I Corinthians 15:22.   [67] *Ibid.,* 15:45.

family."[68] These formed the general biblical argument for the "unity" theory advocates and received the support of the clergy and church groups as opposed to the doctrines of the scientific school.

An apparent, but rather weak argument was made for the theory of single species of the human race through a study of the mutual relationship of languages or philology. Despite the many great diversities in language among various nationalities, appearing from a superficial view, it was asserted that upon studying philology on a basis of "philosophical principles," the variations tended to disappear "and their racial unity to become more manifest."[69] It does not seem probable that this argument influenced many people to support the "unity" doctrine.

A third, and somewhat stronger, argument in favor of the unity of origin was based upon certain scientific rules of hybridity. According to the views of the exponents of the "unity" theory, all races of mankind belonged to the same species; otherwise they contended that the laws of hybridity must apply. Rev. John Bachman summarized this argument by stating that the "progeny of the horse and the ass is a mule or hybrid, incapable of continuing his kind," due to the fact that the parents of the mule were of different species. He then pointed out that "the offspring of a white man and a black woman is not so incapable; therefore Caucasians and Negroes belong to the same species."[70] Bachman was of the opinion that the production of fertile progeny through the amalgamation of various human races not only produced new varieties but also constituted "one of the most powerful and undeniable arguments in favor of the unity of the race."[71]

[68] "On the Unity of the Human Race," *Southern Quarterly Review*, X (October, 1854), 276.

[69] *Ibid.*, p. 282. Also see discussion of this argument on pp. 281-90.

[70] "On the Unity of the Human Race," *Southern Quarterly Review*, X (October, 1854), 290.   [71] Jenkins, *op. cit.*, p. 264.

The conflict of opinion between the "plurality" advocates and the exponents of the "unity" theory created considerable interest which is reflected in many articles and reviews in Southern literary periodicals during the fifties. Naturally, many of these took the form of refuting opposing arguments. In general, the advocates of the Adam and Eve origin took exception to the contentions of the scientific school as denying the Bible.[72] An example of the consternation produced by the publication of *Types of Mankind* may be found in a review of the work in the *Southern Literary Messenger*.[73] The reviewer, W. A. Cocke, placed Nott and Gliddon as the "most able defenders" of the faith supported by men like "Vicey, Borg de St. Vincent, Barton, Dr. Morton, Prof. Agassiz, Dr. J. C. Warren, Prof. Gibson, Dr. B. H. Coates, Des Moulin, Broc, Lord Kimes, Voltaire, and Thomas Paine."[74] He went on to state that the "diligent research of years" makes the book "an influential, as well as dangerous production."[75] Cocke felt that Nott's and Gliddon's views denied the biblical doctrines, because if there were "distinct species of Man, then the Bible is untrue"; acknowledgement that there were "other races than the descendants of Adam" freed the latter from "the penalty 'of man's first disobedience,' and the tragic scene of Calvary" became "but a mockery and delusion."[76]

---

[72] "Moral and Intellectual Diversity of Races," *DeBow's Review*, XXI (July, 1856), 63-70. This author (unknown) refused to agree with Nott and Gliddon's position in *Types of Mankind*, because it conflicted with the Bible. Also "Canaan Identified with the Ethiopian," *Southern Quarterly Review*, II O. S. (October, 1842), 328-83. The author of this article disagreed with the conclusions of Prof. Broc of Paris, who had recently been awarded a premium by the Royal Academy of Paris for his "anatomical and physiological researches touching the question of the common origin of man." Broc had concluded that the "Ethiopian race was a *distinct species* of mankind." P. 328. According to the author, this conclusion, if true, would refute the Bible.

[73] Wm. Archer Cocke, "Types of Mankind," *Southern Literary Messenger*, XX (November, 1854), 660-68.   [74] *Ibid.*, p. 661.

[75] *Ibid.*, p. 668.   [76] *Ibid.*, p. 661.

Despite the accusations, the advocates of the "plurality" theory expressed no desire to attack religion or the Bible.[77] It was even suggested that possible miracles performed by God upon Noah's children or at the Tower of Babel may have produced "the existing diversities of color and speech among men."[78] The statement of a "reverend" gentleman to the effect that "the doctrine of a single human race underlies the whole fabric of religious belief, and if it is rejected, Christianity will be lost to mankind!" was ridiculed by Dr. Van Evrie as "miserable folly."[79] He went on to state that "common sense" emphatically pointed to the fact that the black and white races were of distinctly different species. As an "undoubting believer" in the "doctrines of Christianity," he contended that the development of the several species was performed by the "act and will of the Almighty Creator."[80] This, however, was not entirely in accord with the views of Nott and Gliddon concerning the distinct centers of creation. Dr. Nott, in his early lectures, stated that "If the *unity* of the races, or species of men, be assumed, there are but three suppositions on which the *diversity* now seen in the white, black, and intermediate colors can be accounted for."[81] These were, first, the changing of one type into another through a direct act of God; second, gradual changes culminating from climatic and other physical conditions of environment; and third, "congenital or accidental varieties."[82] Lacking entirely any evidence on the first supposition, Nott set about refuting the second and third suppositions which were upheld by leaders of the "unity" theory.[83]

[77] "On the Unity of the Human Race," *Southern Quarterly Review*, X (October, 1854), 277.   [78] *Ibid.*

[79] Van Evrie, *Negroes and Negro Slavery*, p. 56.

[80] *Ibid.*, pp. 57-62.

[81] Nott, *Two Lectures*, p. 24.   [82] *Ibid.*

[83] *Ibid.* cites James C. Prichard, *Researches into the Physical History of Mankind*, as maintaining the second and third suppositions. Nott states of this work that it "is the grand reservoir in which everything is collected that can be said in

In refutation of the biblical arguments favoring the single species of mankind, the scientific group used other scriptural passages. If there were no other groups formed except Adam's family, where did Cain get his wife? they asked.[84] And "by whom was Cain afraid of being slain?"[85] Surely not by his own family. Therefore there must have been other types of the human race in the beginning, maintained Nott and Gliddon.[86] It was also pointed out that during the infancy of other sciences than ethnology fierce theological attacks had been made with the final result that the scientific principles were admitted to be in accord with the Scriptures.[87] This was done by way of explaining that the "plurality" theory was not the only scientific hypothesis that had been under fire from the clergy.

In the refutation of the arguments favoring the "unity" theory, one of the most important conflicts revolved around the question of hybridity. Bachman and others of the "unity" school using this argument had assumed a definition of species as those capable of successive reproduction.[88] On the other hand, Dr. Nott was concerned with a more permanent type. He defined species as meaning "a type, or organic form, that is permanent; or which has remained unchanged under opposite climatic influences for ages."[89] According to their definitions, Nott, Gliddon, and Morton distinguished the various degrees of hybridity. They maintained that the type of hybrid produced was determined by degree of proximity of the parent species. On the basis of this assumption, all hybrids

---

favor of the unity of the races." Nott refutes these arguments in *Two Lectures*, pp. 24-47.

[84] Nott and Gliddon, *Types of Mankind*, p. 553.

[85] "On the Unity of the Human Race," *Southern Quarterly Review*, X (October, 1854), 278.

[86] Nott and Gliddon, *Types of Mankind*, p. 553.

[87] "On the Unity of the Human Race," *Southern Quarterly Review*, X (October, 1854), 279-81.

[88] See discussion in Jenkins, *op. cit.*, p. 264.

[89] Nott and Gliddon, *Types of Mankind*, p. 375.

were classified under four distinct groups. First, the hybrid progeny of remotely related parent species, the offspring being incapable of reproduction; second, hybrids "incapable of reproducing *Inter se*," but capable of reproducing when united with the parent stock; third, "animals of unquestionable distinct species" that produced a "progeny prolific *inter se*," the dog and wolf being examples; and, finally, hybridity resulting from the union of "closely proximate species," like mankind, thereby producing a prolific progeny.[90] The scientific school of pro-slavery writers emphatically denied that the "*prolificacy* of distinct species, *inter se*," could be considered as absolute proof of "*common origin*."[91]

Though admitting that the black and white races were species of sufficient proximity to place their offspring in the fourth classification, Dr. Nott maintained that their affinity was not close enough to make amalgamation perfect. After many years of observation and study he contended that mulattoes partook of certain hybrid characteristics. Due to this fact they were the shortest lived of any human group, were of intermediate intelligence, had less hardihood and stamina than either parent race, and the mulatto women showed weakness for "a variety of chronic diseases." All these facts tended to indicate the inability of hybrids to survive or produce a permanent type.[92] As even greater proof of this, it was pointed out that mulattoes were far less prolific than either the blacks or the whites, or than the mulatto when crossed with one of the parent stocks.[93] These

[90] *Ibid.*, pp. 375-76. See Morton's classification discussion in "On the Unity of the Human Race," *Southern Quarterly Review*, X (October, 1854), 292.

[91] Nott and Gliddon, *Types of Mankind*, p. 465.

[92] "On the Unity of the Human Race," *Southern Quarterly Review*, X (October, 1854), 292-93.

[93] *Ibid.*, p. 293. Dr. Nott was well qualified to speak upon the prolificacy and mortality of Negroes and mulattoes, having collected material for many years. See his articles, "Life Insurance at the South," *DeBow's Review*, III (May, 1847), 358-76; "Statistics of Southern Slave Population," *DeBow's Review*, IV (November, 1847), 275-91.

explanations were used to refute the hybridity argument of the advocates of the "unity" doctrines and to build up the conclusion that the human family included several distinct species.[94]

It is difficult to determine the influence of the scientific school of thought upon Southern opinion. Because it developed somewhat later and was partially, at least, in conflict with the well-established biblical justification of slavery, it seems quite probable that its influence did not reach the masses. The necessity of a scientific knowledge for a complete understanding of the "plurality" theories of human origin also seems to bear out this conclusion. To those educated in science and medicine, the theories of Nott and Gliddon formed a logical argument which substantiated the previous conclusions resulting from personal observations. In other words, the exponents of the plural origin of mankind, led by Nott, rationalized with scientific principles the theory of Negro inferiority which had long been prevalent among the planters. Regardless of whether they considered the racial inferiority of the black a result of the curse of God upon Canaan or the inherent characteristic of a distinct species of mankind, the Southerners were practically unanimous in considering the Negro as inferior to the white race. The conflict between the two schools of thought resulted not so much from the relative position of the African in comparison to the Caucasian as from the original cause of his being assigned the inferior position.

Even without this unanimity of opinion concerning the inferiority of the Negro race, it is quite probable that racial consciousness and the difference in color of the two races would have brought about a social justification of slavery as a means of preserving white civilization. Amalgamation as a solution to the race problem was not acceptable to the South-

[94] Nott and Gliddon, *Types of Mankind*, p. 465.

erners.[95] It was pointed out that "two races so essentially different in character, intellect, habits," and physical structure could not "occupy the same territory as equals."[96] One race must dominate the other in order to maintain the racial integrity of each.[97] Under the usual circumstances of such a state of society with two diverse races dwelling together, it was thought that "the inferior caste must be in subjection to the higher."[98] But rather than this subordination of the inferior race being forced, Dr. Samuel Cartwright felt, in common with many other Southerners, that this was the normal condition.[99] From daily contact with the Negroes, the Southern people realized, he said, *"better than others that every attribute"* of the African *"character"* fitted them *"for dependence and servitude."*[100] In 1861, Dr. W. H. Holcombe of Virginia expressed a similar view by stating that "The negro is not a white man with a black skin, but of a different species, . . . the hopeless physical and mental inferior" of the white, and "organically constituted to be an agricultural laborer in tropical climates—a strong animal machine."[101]

From the assumption that the white race must maintain its supremacy over the inferior Negro race, it was but a step to the justification of slavery as a social necessity. As early as 1837 John C. Calhoun remarked that the maintenance of "the existing relations between the two races" inhabiting the Southern States was "indispensable to the peace and happiness of both."[102] Since the slaves were recognized as a distinct

[95] Thornton, *op. cit.*, pp. 146-48.
[96] "The Black Race in North America," *Southern Literary Messenger*, XXI (November, 1855), 676. [97] Thornton, *op. cit.*, p. 148.
[98] "The Black Race in North America," *Southern Literary Messenger*, XXI (November, 1855), 676.
[99] "On the Caucasians and Africans," *DeBow's Review*, XXV (July, 1858), 50.
[100] "Negro Freedom Impossible," *DeBow's Review*, XXX (May & June, 1861), 651, quotes sermon of Rev. Palmer of New Orleans; italics Cartwright's.
[101] Dr. William H. Holcombe, "Characteristics and Capabilities of the Negro Race," *Southern Literary Messenger*, XXXIII (1861), 401-10; also quoted by Beveridge, *op. cit.*, II, 35.
[102] John C. Calhoun, speech in Senate, Feb. 6, 1837, *Works*, II, 630.

race of mankind, separated by strongly marked moral and physical lines from the whites, there could consequently be no interchange of social rights and privileges between the whites and the blacks.[103] So far as intellectual development was concerned, the Southerners argued that the Negroes were not only unprepared for freedom but that they were incapable of any form of liberty in a democratic government.[104] The abolitionists of course disagreed on this point. In this connection, Beriah Green argued that the slaves could not become "better qualified" for liberty while "under the *influence of slavery.*"[105] He reasoned that the *"lower their character and condition, the louder, clearer, sterner, the just demand for immediate emancipation.*"[106]

On the other hand, Southern writers hurled at the abolitionists the question as to whether the barbarous Africans had been fitted for equality of political and social rights and privileges with the whites when first brought to American shores.[107] If they were prepared for the condition advocated by the abolitionists, why "did not the Puritans of New England allow them the sovereignty and equality?"[108] The advocates of slavery sarcastically stated that surely those who had but recently found an asylum in this country from the yoke of British oppressions would not have been deaf to the claims of justice and humanity in behalf of the African slave! On the other hand, the Southern writers pointed out that common sense as well as humanitarian principles had induced the New England Puritans to adopt a plan of domestic slavery for a race of barbarians that could not be absorbed by marriage and must therefore continue to exist as a separate and inferior race.[109]

So unprepared were the blacks for liberty, pro-slavery

[103] W. A. Smith, *op. cit.*, p. 177.   [104] *Ibid.*, p. 181.

[105] Beriah Green, *The Chattel Principle*, p. 18.

[106] *Ibid.*, pp. 18-19; italics Green's.   [107] W. A. Smith, *op. cit.*, p. 183.

[108] *Ibid.*, pp. 183-84.   [109] *Ibid.*, p. 184.

writers contended, that to confer a measure of self-government upon the slaves, either by direct or gradual emancipation, would be ruinous to them as well as injurious to the country as a whole. It was argued that if the Negro were given freedom, social and political equality would follow, resulting in the emancipated and enfranchised black becoming a "libertine in morals and an anarchist in politics."[110] Calhoun regarded such a condition of "social and political equality" of the two races as being an "impossible" one for the white race, to which the South would never submit.[111] Should emancipation come, it was quite probable that the Negroes would dominate local governments in the lower South, and would even place members of the inferior race in high positions in the national government. This would bring about a state of social and political chaos which could not be endured by white men and women.[112]

The failure of experiments in emancipation in Hayti, Jamaica, and Liberia was pointed out to prove the social necessity for slavery, just as they had been given as proof of the economic benefits of the institution. As a result of the exertions of the abolitionists, Hayti, "the brightest jewel in the French Crown," had been turned into a slaughterhouse.[113] A feud stirred up between the whites and mulattoes had extended to the blacks and ended in the open revolt of the slaves and the complete extermination of the whites from the island.[114] The atrocities of this terrible massacre could hardly be paralleled in all history. One historian described

---

[110] James Kirke Paulding, *Slavery in the United States,* pp. 89-90; quoted by Beveridge, *op. cit.,* II, 58. Also see letter of Charles O'Connor to a Committee of Merchants, New York, 1859, reprinted in Horace Greeley and J. F. Cleveland (comps.), *A Political Textbook for 1860.* Pp. 167-68.

[111] John C. Calhoun, Report on February 4, 1836, *Works,* V, 205-6.

[112] See discussion of this in Greeley and Cleveland, *op. cit.,* p. 168. Beveridge, *op. cit.,* II, 58, reaches similar conclusion.

[113] "Free Negroes in Hayti," *DeBow's Review,* XXVII (November, 1859), 528.

[114] *Ibid.,* p. 529. By 1804, 30,000 whites had been completely exterminated. Between 1791-1804, 150,000 persons perished in this bloody conflict of the races.

the procession of savage blacks marching "with spiked infants on their spears instead of colors."[115] Among the atrocities committed, it was asserted that the Africans "sawed asunder the male prisoners and violated the females on the dead bodies of their husbands."[116] Though liberty was proclaimed to the slaves on the island, it was pointed out that only anarchy was produced. With the outburst of unutterable brutality and frightful chaos, there arose another civil war, in which the "ambitious mulattoes," whose "insatiable desire for equality" had first started the conflagration, "perished miserably beneath the vengeance of the very slaves whom they had themselves roused from subjection and elevated into irresistible power."[117] After the extermination of the whites and mulattoes, the blacks became the arbiters of their own institutions and destiny, isolated and independent, yet they lapsed again into primitive barbarism.[118]

Another similar example cited by the Southern writers was the effect of the "glorious Act of British Emancipation" upon the largest and most valuable island of the British West Indies, the island of Jamaica.[119] Immediately upon the complete emancipation of the slaves in 1839, the prosperity and civilization of the island began to manifest signs of decay. Within a short time, "the negroes, who, in a state of slavery, were comfortable and prosperous beyond any peasantry in the world," and were rapidly reaching a higher plane of civilization, had been *by the act of emancipation irretrievably consigned to a state of barbarism.*"[120] The advocates of slavery scornfully remarked that this was indeed a poor return to the British people for the expense of emancipating the slaves. According to the theories of the abolitionists the free blacks should have stepped into a position of political

[115] Bledsoe, *op. cit.*, pp. 275-76.

[116] *Ibid.*, p. 276.   [117] *Ibid.*

[118] Fisher, "The North and the South," *DeBow's Review*, VII (October, 1849), 313-14; also Priest, *op. cit.*, pp. 352-53.

[119] Bledsoe, *op. cit.*, pp. 233, 243.   [120] *Ibid.*, p. 257; italics in Bledsoe.

and social equality and through the exercise of political sovereignty have established a prosperous Negro Republic. But they pointed out that the reverse was true and "Jamaica promises soon to become as pestiferous a sink of vice and corruption as the most libertine enthusiast can desire."[121]

The results of the attempts to colonize freed slaves in Liberia were also used to justify the contentions of the Southerners. There, under suitable conditions for development, only a few Africans showed any capacity for self-government.[122] It was asserted that "laziness, carelessness and improvidence" were the general characteristics of the colonists.[123] The pro-slavery writers argued that Liberia was but another example proving that the majority of the Negro race were either not sufficiently developed for self-government or were incapable of exercising political sovereignty, and that freedom would confer no benefit on them, but would rather inflict a deep injury upon both races and society.[124]

The lessons of Hayti, Jamaica, Liberia, and the bloody insurrection of Santo Domingo aroused the South to a fear of a horrible race war as the logical result of abolitionist measures. Calhoun asserted in 1836 that "the blind and criminal zeal of the abolitionists is directed" against the institutions of the South, which upon being destroyed would involve their "entire population in a deadly conflict, that must terminate either in the expulsion or extirpation" of the inferior race and engulf the country "in a sea of blood."[125] The social necessity of slavery was well expressed two years later by a writer in the *Southern Literary Messenger*. Condemning the plans of the abolitionists as the "wildest scheme that ever entered

[121] Paulding, *op. cit.*, pp. 57-58; Fitzhugh, *Sociology for the South*, p. 89; R. R. Madden, *A Twelve Months' Residence in the West Indies*, pp. 95-110; "Negro-Mania," *DeBow's Review*, XII (May, 1852), 521, cited by Beveridge, *op. cit.*, II, 36.   [122] W. A. Smith, *op. cit.*, p. 201.
[123] Edmund Ruffin, "Liberia and the Colonization Society," *DeBow's Review*, XXVII (October, 1859), 398.   [124] W. A. Smith, *op. cit.*, pp. 201-2.
[125] John C. Calhoun, "Report of President's Message," February 4, 1836, in *Works*, V, 205; see also Priest, *op. cit.*, p. 354.

the brain of visionary enthusiasts," this author asserted that if the Negroes were "to *remain among us*, the safety of the white man, and the happiness of the black, as the weaker party, require that the blacks should be retained in slavery."[126]

The turning of the Southern States into a second Hayti or Santo Domingo seemed quite probable to the Southern people if the more radical agitators were allowed to continue their campaign of propaganda. George Bourne, in speaking of the slaveholders, had prophesied that the "monsters" would be "caught and drowned in the Atlantic."[127] In another instance this same agitator compared the slaves to the Israelites in Egypt, and exhorted them to rise up and throw off the yoke of slavery. According to his idea, the Negroes would "constitute the scorpions with which the divine Liberator" would "chastise" the masters and overthrow the sinful and corrupt nation.[128] Southern leaders like Calhoun were not unaware of the terrible effects of a possible race conflict resulting from such abolitionist propaganda, spread by "ferocious zealots, blinded by fanaticism" who pursued their objective without regard for the "obligations of religion or morality."[129]

To prevent such disastrous occurrences, the maintenance of Southern institutions and civilization seemed absolutely essential. The patriarchal form of slavery in the South had to be continued in order to prevent a racial conflict. Not believing that the two races could live together in peaceful equality, the Southern people were quite sincere in their conviction that the Negroes should not be granted social and

[126] Southron (pseud.), "Political Religionism," *Southern Literary Messenger,* IV (September, 1838), 550-51.

[127] Bourne, *Slavery Illustrated in its Effects upon Women . . .,* p. 27.

[128] *Ibid.,* pp. 35-38; also see Hopkins, *op. cit.,* pp. 339-43, for quotations from abolitionist leaders like Emerson and Parker advocating violence.

[129] John C. Calhoun, speech on the circulation of incendiary papers in Senate, April 12, 1836, *Works,* II, 530-31.

political equality with the whites. It was declared that the free blacks could more effectually combine for insurrection if they were released from the vigilant superintendence of slavery, which served as a restraining influence.[130] Under conditions of equality, the unrestrained racial antagonisms and daily increasing hostility would inevitably result in the "war of the races" as predicted by Alexander Mackay, the English journalist, in 1846-1847.[131] A war between the Africans and Caucasians in the Southern States, and the horrors of Hayti and Santo Domingo would be reënacted and magnified a thousand times.[132] If the white population withdrew, leaving whole districts to the slaves, it was declared that the blacks would rapidly degenerate into primitive barbarism.[133] If the Negroes became predominant, it was asserted that then the whole "fabric of civilization and liberty, which consumed ages in its construction," would be completely demolished "by the relentless fury of ignorant barbarians." Instead of "free and enlightened States," the South would become "a New Africa."[134] In defending slavery, the Southerners declared they were defending their lives, their country, and even the slaves themselves, from the horrible consequences of emancipation.[135] Calhoun expressed this same sentiment only five years after the Garrisonian attack by asserting that the question "involves not only our liberty, but, what is greater (if to freemen any thing can be), existence itself." For two centuries the paternal form of slavery had regulated the social relationship between two distinct races occupying the Southern States. In doing so it had "entered into and modified" all Southern institutions, "civil and political," until no other

[130] *Pro-Slavery Argument*, pp. 89-90.   [131] Beveridge, *op. cit.*, II, 58.

[132] *Pro-Slavery Argument*, pp. 90, 147-49.

[133] Dr. Samuel A. Cartwright, "How to Save the Republic," *DeBow's Review*, XI (August, 1851), 189—"The White population of the Southern States have no other alternative but to keep them in slavery, or drive them out, wage a war of extermination against them, or go out themselves, and leave their fair land to be converted into a free negro pandemonium."

[134] *Pro-Slavery Argument*, p. 443.   [135] *Ibid.*, p. 90.

system could be substituted without disastrous results. On this basis Calhoun said, "We will not, cannot permit it to be destroyed."[136] The system of slavery was but one part of the whole scheme of Southern economic and social organization. Rather than the type of slavery described by the abolitionists, it was declared that the Negroes were "under a patriarchal form of government best calculated to improve their condition, add to their happiness, and develop their mental and moral faculties."[137]

When the Southern people thus viewed the possible horrors of emancipation, slavery became a social necessity. But when they viewed the great social benefits to both races accruing from the institution, slavery became more than a social necessity; it was a positive good. According to this view, slavery apparently distributed a great many blessings, bestowing them upon the black and white races alike. A "mysterious Providence" had seen fit to bring two distinct races from different sections of the earth and place "them together in nearly equal numbers in the Southern portion" of the United States, where the existing social relationship had "secured peace and happiness" for both.[138]

Southern leaders generally felt that the patriarchal system of slavery as practiced in their section was productive of great benefits to the Negroes.[139] As proof of their assertions, they pointed to Africa and contrasted the conditions of Southern slaves with that of the representatives of the Negro race in their native habitat. Of the fifty millions of inhabitants on

[136] John C. Calhoun, speech in Senate on March 9, 1836, *Works*, II, 488.

[137] Cartwright, "Negro Freedom Impossible," *DeBow's Review*, XXX (May & June, 1861), 652.

[138] John C. Calhoun, speech in Senate on Dec. 27, 1837, *Works*, III, 179. Calhoun adds: "under no other relation could they coexist together. To destroy it was to involve a whole region in slaughter, carnage, and desolation; and, come what will, we must defend and preserve it." Also see Estes, *op. cit.*, pp. 96-143.

[139] Walter L. Fleming, "Plantation Life in the South," *Journal of American History*, III (April-June, 1909), 233-46, states that Jefferson Davis and "most of his class" considered slavery as "a benefit to the negro."—p. 234.

that continent, it was estimated that forty millions bowed under the yoke of bondage. And such bondage—"the vilest slave that ever breathed the air of a Christian land could not begin to conceive the horrid iniquities of such a life"—they declared.[140] It was asserted that in the "boundless regions" of Africa slavery existed in its most horrible forms, the slaves being "three times more numerous than the freemen" and their condition "infinitely worse" than any other portion of the human race.[141] The pro-slavery writers pointed out that under the brutal and depraved system of African slavery men and women were used not only as beasts of burden but also as delicacies for the "palate of their pampered masters," while desirable portions of the bodies of young Negroes might be seen "hung on shambles and exposed for sale!"[142] From such a degraded and lawless existence the Southern Negro had been rescued and planted upon American soil, where, under the benign influence of the patriarchal system of the South, "his dispositions" had been "softened, his intellect sharpened, and his sensibilities roused into a new life, by society and Christianity!"[143] History, insisted the Southerners, could not point to any epoch, or to any place on the globe, where the condition of the Negro race, either physically or morally, could be compared with that of the slaves of the United States.[144] Southern leaders felt that through this system of slavery the superior civilization of the white man had been partially substituted for the immoral, barbarous, and savage characteristics of the black.[145] Sir Charles Lyell, who had reflected at length upon the evils of slavery during his visit to America, had expressed the conviction that Negroes

[140] Bledsoe, *op. cit.*, p. 294.
[141] *Pro-Slavery Argument*, pp. 295-96.
[142] Bledsoe, *op. cit.*, p. 293.   [143] *Ibid.*, p. 296.
[144] Nott, "Statistics of Southern Slave Population," *DeBow's Review*, IV (November, 1847), 279.
[145] Fleming, "Plantation Life in the South," *Journal of American History*, III (April-June, 1909), 234.

could be civilized only through slavery.[146] Professor Dew wrote that only slavery could "destroy those habits of indolence and sloth, and eradicate the character of improvidence and carelessness, which mark the independent savage."[147]

By being brought into contact with a civilized people, it was contended that the Negroes naturally imbibed new ideas, learned a rational religion, and were elevated in the scale of humanity. Many of them learned to read and write while all of them were taught some useful form of employment in agriculture, mechanics, or other trades, which, the advocates of slavery argued, increased their usefulness to mankind.[148] William Gilmore Simms, of South Carolina, in speaking of the Negro, boldly declared that "Providence has placed him in our hands, for his good, and has paid us from his labor for our guardianship."[149] It was felt that, under the guiding hand of Providence, the inferior black race had been made a "powerful instrument of progress and amelioration" where, through slavery, the Negroes had been used to reclaim from nature and make "tributary to the wants of man, those regions from which climate excludes the white labourer."[150] Rather than being degraded through slavery as charged by the abolitionists, it was declared that nowhere in the entire Christian world had so much been done to improve the physical and moral condition of three millions of blacks as had been accomplished by the Southern States through the institution of

[146] Nott, "Statistics of Southern Slave Population," *DeBow's Review*, IV (November, 1847), 279.

[147] *Pro-Slavery Argument*, pp. 328-29. The *Southern Literary Messenger*, Vol. I (January, 1835), quoted in *Pro-Slavery Argument*, p. 60, stated that slavery "has done more to elevate a degraded race in the scale of humanity; to tame the savage; to civilize the barbarous; to soften the ferocious; to enlighten the ignorant, and to spread the blessings of Christianity among the heathen, than all the missionaries that philanthropy and religion have ever sent forth."

[148] Nott, "Statistics of Southern Slave Population," *DeBow's Review*, IV (November, 1847), 279; also see Murray, *op. cit.*, pp. 356-67.

[149] *Pro-Slavery Argument*, p. 274.

[150] "The Negro Races," *Southern Literary Messenger*, XXXI (July, 1860), 8.

slavery.[151] Such a redemption for a continent of barbarians, asserted the pro-slavery writers, fully vindicated the "wisdom and benevolence of the providence of God" which had permitted their introduction and consequent subordination to domestic servitude as the "only means of accomplishing His humane design."[152] It was declared that "no calamity" could befall the Negro slaves "greater than the loss of that protection" which they enjoyed under the Southern "patriarchal system."[153] Considering the benefits of slavery it was asserted that "the coolest piece of important self-conceit . . . found on record" lay in the fact that Northern agitators who had never resided in the South, and lacked authentic knowledge of the character or condition of the African, assumed to understand the institution better than intelligent, pious, liberty-loving Southern people.[154]

Nor was it necessary to compare the condition of the slaves in the South with that of their African brothers in order to recognize the benefits of slavery, declared the pro-slavery writers. The intrinsic blessings of slavery could be easily perceived when contrasted with the evils of emancipation as represented by the free Negroes of the North.[155] The abolitionists were bitterly denounced for adding to their already long list of offenses the sin of hypocrisy. The "pious and polished New Englanders" affected great grief over the sufferings of imaginary black heroes and with "well-studied platform oratory" denounced as a damnable sin the reduction of humans to chattels. Though "fanatical on the subject of abolition," it was asserted that, instead of caring for the manumitted slaves around them, the Northerners shrank from

[151] Bledsoe, *op. cit.*, pp. 299-300. In speaking of the benefits of slavery upon the Negro, Calhoun stated that it had enabled him to attain "a degree of civilization never before attained by the black race in any age or country." John C. Calhoun, speech in Senate, Dec. 27, 1837, *et seq.*, *Works*, III, 179.

[152] W. A. Smith, *op. cit.*, p. 185.

[153] Cartwright, "Negro Freedom Impossible," *DeBow's Review*, XXX (May & June, 1861), 651.

[154] W. A. Smith, *op. cit.*, p. 188.   [155] Sawyer, *op. cit.*, pp. 227-32.

them "as if the touch were pollution."[156] Lacking the paternal system of slavery in the North, the freed blacks lapsed into degradation until they were considered a nuisance, a tax, and a burden to the white population as they filled the prisons, penitentiaries and almshouses.[157] Statistics were used to point out the fact that "crimes among the free blacks" were "three times as numerous as among the whites, and four and a half times more numerous than among the slaves."[158] It was admitted that even in the South the free Negroes were "a miserable set of vagabonds, drunken, vicious," and in far worse condition than those retained in slavery.[159] Southern writers declared that the abolitionists freed the slave and condemned him to a life of crime and misery, while the slaveholders bound the Negro and blessed him by providing a comfortable home, the necessities of life, and a slow but constant advancement toward a higher civilization.[160] Such were the benefits of slavery over emancipation. "The Southerner is the negro's friend, his only friend," declared Fitzhugh, "let no intermeddling abolitionist . . . dissolve this friendship."[161]

In general the social benefits accruing from slavery, as contrasted with the evil conditions caused by the free Negroes of the North, were similar and quite closely connected with the economic benefits which have previously been discussed.[162] The free Negroes of the North, being an inferior race and unprepared for liberty, lacking in ability and energy, were severely discriminated against by white competition.[163]

[156] "William Chambers on Slavery," *DeBow's Review,* XVIII (April, 1855), 451-52.

[157] *Pro-Slavery Argument,* pp. 433-35, quotes speech of Mr. Everett before the Colonization Society, as stating that "they [the free blacks] form, in Massachusetts, about one seventy-fifth part of the population; *one sixth of the convicts in our prisons are of this class.*" Italics Dew's.

[158] *Ibid.* Dew also compares the number of criminals among whites, blacks, and slaves in Virginia with the whites and free blacks in Massachusetts.

[159] Olmsted, *Seaboard Slave States,* I, 48.

[160] Beveridge, *op. cit.,* II, 51.   [161] *Ibid.*

[162] See Chap. VI, *supra.*   [163] Sawyer, *op. cit.,* pp. 228-30.

Unable to provide the necessities of life, they were victims of diseases arising from hunger, misery, and the severe winters, declared the Southern writers.[164] Actual statistics were used to show that their condition as freemen resulted in far higher mortality rates than among the slaves.[165] All of the evil conditions found among freemen, both white and black, in the industrialized East, were impressively portrayed by the Southern writers with painful truth. The petty competition, hatred, envy, malice, misery, and vice that marked the laboring classes in that section, where crowded conditions created difficulty in their obtaining a means of subsistence, were carefully enumerated.[166] Although the Southerners acknowledged that slavery was liable to abuse, they contended that for every instance of "cruelty, oppression, licentiousness, crime or suffering" in the South, an equivalent "evil or abuse" could be pointed out "in a five fold degree," in various "countries where Slavery does not exist."[167] On the other hand, statistics were used to prove that the inhabitants of the slaveholding states were the "most quiet and secure population in the world," for there were "fewer crimes and murders among them than in any other form in which society" could exist.[168]

Not only was slavery productive of much good to the African, but it was also beneficial to the white civilization, argued the Southern writers. It was asserted that a careful examination of the history of civilization, its rise and progress, gave proof to the theory that slavery was one of the fundamental principles of human society.[169] In considering the extensive part played by servitude in the history of mankind and the progress of civilization, the Southerners developed

---

[164] Nott, "Statistics of Southern Slave Population," *DeBow's Review*, IV (November, 1847), 275-91.   [165] *Ibid.*, p. 279. See Chap. IV, *supra*.

[166] *Pro-Slavery Argument*, pp. 21-22.   [167] *Ibid.*, p. 28.

[168] Dew, "Address on the Influence of the Republican System of Government upon Literature and the Development of Character," *Southern Literary Messenger*, II (March, 1836), 278.   [169] *Pro-Slavery Argument*, p. 1.

the conception that a blessing had practically been thrust upon them.[170] Southern leaders declared that the history of the "great republics of antiquity" taught that slavery was compatible "with freedom, stability and long duration of civil government, with denseness of population, great power, and the highest civilization."[171] It was pointed out that, according to ancient history, "personal servitude" had been the "lot of a large, perhaps the greatest portion of mankind."[172]

It was argued that a universal characteristic of the "uncultivated man" was his natural aversion to labor.[173] Even with the impelling motives of civilization, it was stated, this aversion could not be overcome in many individuals of the highest societies. The coercive effect of slavery alone was adequate to instill in the uncivilized man the habits of labor, without which "there can be no accumulation of property, no providence for the future, no tastes for comfort or elegancies, which are the characteristics and essentials of civilization."[174] It was maintained by Chancellor Harper that only when man was able to obtain "command of another's labor" did he begin "to accumulate and provide for the future," thereby laying the "foundations of civilization."[175] He declared that experience confirmed this theory, for since "the existence of man upon the earth" every society that had attained civilization had advanced through this process by the aid of domestic slavery.[176]

As proof of the socializing influence of the institution, the Southerners declared that the enduring achievements of human art and industry were monuments to the everlasting benefits of slavery.[177] "That magnificent shrine, the Temple of Solomon," the wonders of Egypt, the "venerable" pyr-

---

[170] *Ibid.*, p. 294; also Stringfellow, *op. cit.*, pp. 145-46.
[171] Harper, "Memoirs on Slavery," *DeBow's Review*, X (January, 1851), 49.
[172] *Pro-Slavery Argument*, p. 295.
[173] *Ibid.*, p. 3.   [174] *Ibid.*, p. 4.
[175] *Ibid.*   [176] *Ibid.*
[177] Harper, "Memoirs on Slavery," *DeBow's Review*, X (January, 1851), 57.

amids, which had endured from ancient times, the everlasting
works of Rome—all were pointed out as creations from the
labor of slaves.[178] It was asserted that the system had existed
in ancient Phoenicia, Carthage, Babylon, Assyria, Athens,
Sparta, and many other centers of early civilization. Nor were
the numbers few, for it was pointed out that in the whole
Grecian and Roman world the slaves outnumbered the freemen.[179]

In addition to the benefits of the system of domestic
servitude to the African and to the progress of civilization, it was asserted that its benevolent influences also rested
upon the slaveholders. Chancellor Harper declared that the
"tendency of Slavery is to elevate the character of the master."[180] Much earlier, in 1836, Professor Dew had written
that slavery was the only means of bringing civilization in
close contact with barbarism without "either dragging down
the civilized man to a level of the barbarian, or corrupting
and then exterminating the latter in the attempt to elevate
him."[181] The greatest benefit of the institution to the white
man was the acquisition of more leisure time.[182] By eliminating the necessity of physical labor for daily subsistence, the
system of slavery allowed the masters time for mental improvement and culture.[183] Chancellor Harper asserted that
"He who works during the day with his hands does not read
in the intervals of leisure for his amusement or the improvement of his mind."[184] Without boasting, Southern leaders
merely pointed to this benevolent grant of slavery, as the

[178] *Pro-Slavery Argument*, p. 295. Also see Harper, "Memoirs on Slavery,"
DeBow's Review, X (January, 1851), 57.

[179] *Pro-Slavery Argument*, pp. 294-96.

[180] *Ibid.*, p. 61.

[181] Dew, "Address on the Influence of the Republican System of Government
upon Literature and the Development of Character," *Southern Literary Messenger*,
II (March, 1836), 279.   [182] Estes, *op. cit.*, pp. 142-200.

[183] *Pro-Slavery Argument*, p. 115; also James H. Hammond's "Letters on
Slavery," *DeBow's Review*, VII (December, 1849), 490-91.

[184] William Harper, quoted by the *Republican Scrap Book*, p. 52.

secret of the success of Southern men in politics and other
fields where honor and power might be won by intellectual
superiority.[185] They declared that an historical view of the
political arena, where "the intellects of the free and slave
States" met "in full and fair competition," proved the results
of leisure time spent in a pursuit of knowledge and the increase of intellectual ability.[186] The fact that during sixty
years the presidential chair had been occupied forty-eight
years by slaveholders was referred to as proof of the superior
intellectual training which slaveowners were able to acquire.[187] It was also pointed out that in the conflicts of Congressional debates and in the diplomatic struggles of the
courts of Europe, Southerners had always shown themselves
the equal, and generally the superior, of the foremost intellects of the world.[188] The fact that Northern abolitionists
like Channing admitted the greater ability of Southern
leaders in political affairs was used by Southern literary organs as proof of the intellectual benefits of slavery.[189]

[185] *Pro-Slavery Argument*, pp. 115-16.   [186] *Ibid.*, p. 116.

[187] *Ibid.*, pp. 115-16; Dr. Samuel A. Cartwright, "Education, Labor, and
Wealth of the South," *DeBow's Review*, XXVII (September, 1859), 269. *DeBow's
Review*, VIII (January, 1850), summarizes the years in which Southern and
Northern men have occupied the principal national offices from 1790-1850. Also
quoted in Beveridge, *op. cit.*, II, 60 n.

President	North 12 years; South 48 years
Vice-President	" 40 " ; " 20 "
Chief Justice	" 11 " ; " 48 "
Secretary of State	" 20 " ; " 40 "
Secretary of Treasury	" 46 " ; " 14 "
Secretary of War	" 34 " ; " 25 "
Secretary of Navy	" 40 " ; " 19 "
Post Master General	" 35 " ; " 25 "
Attorney-General	" 20 " ; " 39 "
Speaker of House	" 23 " ; " 37 "

[188] George Fitzhugh, "Southern Thought," *DeBow's Review*, XXIII (October,
1857), 342.

[189] William Channing, *Duty of the Free States*, Pt. II, pp. 71-72, quoted in review: "Channing's Duty of the Free States," *Southern Quarterly Review*, II (July,
1842), 130-77. Channing stated that "The South has abler politicians, and almost
necessarily, because its most opulent class makes politics the business of life. . . .
At the North, politics occupy a second place in man's work. . . . We think more
of property than of political power; and this, indeed is the natural result of free
institutions."

The justification of slavery, first as a social necessity and later as a positive good, was enthusiastically developed to a defense of all existing human institutions. As a result of the Southern scriptural justification and the Constitutional guarantees upholding slavery, the abolitionists had been driven to the extreme point of denying both the authority of God and of the Federal Government. George Fitzhugh explained their position by stating that if slavery was "wrong in principle, wrong in the abstract, then all governmental institutions" were "wrong and should be abolished," and therefore the abolitionists assailed all human institutions "as modifications of slavery itself."[190] The fact that practically all of the leading abolitionists like Garrison, Parker, Foster, Phillips, Smith, Goodell, and others were also leaders and exponents of infidelity, socialism, free-love, anarchism, perfectionism, and no-government movements and united in what George Sawyer called an "amalgamated collocation," was strongly emphasized.[191] Because of the extreme radical alliances of the abolitionist leaders, it was charged that they were engaged in driving "assiduous wedges" for the purpose of "loosening the whole frame of society, and preparing for the glorious advent of Free Love and No-Government."[192] It was declared that all of the political, moral, and religious heresies of the North had grown out of the abolition theories. In assailing slavery, it was asserted that the abolitionists had soon learned that all types of government sponsored some form of slavery, and therefore the radical group had become anarchists and proposed to destroy all the institutions of human society.[193]

[190] Fitzhugh, "The Conservative Principle," *DeBow's Review*, XXII (April, 1857), 429.

[191] Sawyer, *op. cit.*, p. 384; also Fitzhugh, *Cannibals All!*, pp. 311-12, and Hopkins, *op. cit.*, pp. 333-40, shows views of Parker and Emerson.

[192] Fitzhugh, *Cannibals All!*, p. 312.

[193] Fitzhugh, "Southern Thought," *DeBow's Review*, XXIII (October, 1857), 343.

In justifying their social organization, the Southern philosophers declared that it was an established fact that servitude was the fundamental condition upon which civilization rested.[194]   In expounding his "mud-sill" theory of society, Senator Hammond of South Carolina stated that "all social systems" demanded a "class to do the menial duties, to perform the drudgery of life . . . a class requiring but a low order of intellect and but little skill."[195] According to his view, the "requisites" of this class were "vigor, docility," and "fidelity." Arguing that this class constituted the "very mud-sill of society and political government," Hammond declared that the South had fortunately "found a race adapted to that purpose," used them as such, and called them "slaves."[196] In discussing social systems, the Southerners classified all society as capitalist and laborers, the former owning the latter collectively through industry and government or individually in a state of domestic servitude such as existed in the South.[197] In this connection, George Fitzhugh declared that both the North and the South sponsored slavery and the slave trade, the former section enslaving the whites, the latter section merely enslaving an inferior race of blacks.[198] This Virginia sociologist severely attacked the so-called free labor system of the North as being far more cruel, exploiting, and exacting than the Negro slavery of the South.[199] Fitzhugh divided the free society of the North into four classes: the rich capitalists, who lived respectably and luxuriously without personal labor; the professional group and skilled artisans, who performed but little actual labor

[194] *Pro-Slavery Argument*, pp. 21, 27.

[195] J. H. Hammond, speech in United States Senate, March 4, 1858, quoted in E. Merritt, "James Henry Hammond," *Johns Hopkins University Studies*, XLI, 118; also see Speech of Watkin Leigh in Virginia Convention quoted in *Republican Scrap Book*, p. 51, and *Pro-Slavery Argument*, p. 27.

[196] *Ibid.*

[197] F. W. Pickens, of South Carolina, speech in Congress, January 21, 1837, quoted in *Republican Scrap Book*, p. 52.

[198] Fitzhugh, *Cannibals All!*, *passim*.   [199] *Ibid.*, pp. 25-32, *et passim*.

for high wages; the mass of poor laborers, who supported the other classes though bordering on starvation themselves; and, finally, the robbers, swindlers, and mendicants who, like gentlemen, lived without labor, existing upon the work of other people.[200] Under his comparisons the slave labor system of the South was much superior because it provided far greater comforts and benefits to the mass of laborers, even though the profits of the masters were less.[201] He declared that "Free society, asserts the right of a few to the earth—slavery maintains that it belongs, in different degrees, to all."[202]

Other Southern leaders also pointed out that slavery was the best form of servitude since laboring classes were taken care of without the eternal struggle for existence. It was declared that in free countries during eras of commercial disturbance, famines, depressions and other similar calamities the distress fell principally upon the laborers, while under the slave system it fell almost exclusively upon the slave-holders.[203] Even though the accumulation of individual wealth could not be as great in a slaveholding country as in one of free labor there would be consequently less inequality and less suffering. Chancellor Harper argued that slavery was the natural state of society and where it had been abolished the "order of nature" had been departed from and a "forced and artificial state" of social organization introduced.[204] John C. Calhoun voiced the same theory in 1837 when he declared that slavery formed the "most solid and durable foundation on which to rear free and stable political institutions."[205] Because of this he felt that the South would

[200] Ibid., p. 27. Calhoun expressed a similar view by stating that no "wealthy and civilized society" ever existed in which one portion did not "live on the labor of the other."—Works, II, 631.

[201] Fitzhugh, Cannibals All!, pp. 25-32, et passim.

[202] Ibid., p. 31.

[203] Pro-Slavery Argument, p. 26.   [204] Ibid., p. 28.

[205] John C. Calhoun, speech in Senate on the reception of abolition petitions, February 6, 1837, Works, II, 632; also quoted in Republican Scrap Book, p. 52.

be able to withstand social, economic, and political conflicts between capital and labor much better than the Northern section, providing the Southern States were "not disturbed" by outside "interference."[206] Concerning this "interference," Calhoun pointed out "that emancipation itself would not satisfy these fanatics." Without realizing that he was predicting the scenes of radical Reconstruction thirty years later, he asserted that after emancipation "the next step would be to raise the negroes to a social and political equality with the whites; and that being effected, we would soon find the present condition of the two races reversed. They and their northern allies would be the masters, and we the slaves."[207]

The Southern leaders realized the disastrous effects that would follow the overthrow of their social system through emancipation. They were intense in their conviction that slavery was a social necessity and a positive good. Regardless of whether the system of slavery was good or bad, it may be concluded that it was so interwoven into the political and social life of the South that it had become a part of the Southerners' civilization—to be justified as they would justify their right of life, liberty, and pursuit of happiness. The dominant trend in the Southerners' philosophy and their justification of slavery was the necessity of maintaining white supremacy and civilization.[208] From the time Negroes became numerous enough to create a problem of race control the tendency was to maintain slavery as the most satisfactory means of controlling labor and providing for racial adjustment and social order. When the attack of the abolitionists threatened the institution which was the foundation of their agrarian civilization it was not long until both slaveholders and non-slave-

---

[206] Calhoun, *Works,* II, 632.

[207] *Ibid.,* p. 633. Also see Priest, *op. cit.,* p. 354; for an almost identical statement from a Northern man, see Charles O'Connor's letter to a Committee of Merchants quoted in Greeley and Cleveland, *op. cit.,* p. 168.

[208] See article by Phillips, "The Central Theme of Southern History," *American Historical Review,* XXXIV (October, 1928), 31.

holders rallied to its support. Pride of caste was strong, for no men loved liberty more cordially than did the Southerners. Liberty to them was a privilege and a distinction belonging to all white men—the symbol of white supremacy.[209]

Therefore, without necessarily being expressed in every instance, this philosophy served to unite all classes of Southern people. This attitude was admirably expressed by the editor of one of the leading Southern literary organs when he wrote:

For us there has come to be but one sentiment now—as Southerners, as Americans, as Men, we deny the right of being called to account for our institutions, our policy, or our government. For these there is no explanation to be made, no apology; it is sufficient that we, the people of a State, we the people of half the States of this Union, in our sovereign capacity, in our sovereign right, in our sovereign independence of all other people or peoples upon the earth, of all mortal men, have decreed our institutions as they are, and so will *dare maintain them.*[210]

[209] Fitzhugh, "Southern Thought," *DeBow's Review,* XXIII (October, 1857), 349.

[210] J. D. B. DeBow, *DeBow's Review,* III (May, 1847), 349.

CHAPTER VIII

THE POLITICAL SIGNIFICANCE OF THE ABOLITIONIST ATTACK

IN VIEWING the slavery controversy many years after it occurred, the historian is inevitably concerned as to the motives behind certain movements and the political significance of the dissemination of abolitionist propaganda during the period 1831-1860. Why did the descendants of Yankee slave traders condemn the South for possessing the article of commerce upon which many New England fortunes were founded? Why did a large portion of the Southern people regard slavery as an evil prior to 1831, only to reverse their opinion of the system after that date? Cotton profits, as suggested by some historians, seem too simple an explanation for the sweeping justification of slavery made by pro-slavery writers. Nor does this one fact fully explain the attitude of the thousands of non-slaveholders who supported the system. Too often in American histories the Garrisonian group of radicals are portrayed as being guided by purely humanitarian motives and high moral principles. If economic motives can be assigned to the Southern defense, it seems even more likely that behind the abolition propaganda lay deeper and more fundamental motives than a mere desire to emancipate the blacks. Why were so many of the radical abolitionists more interested in agitating the slavery question than in uplifting the free Negroes of the North or overcoming the evils of industrialism among the laboring classes of their own race found in factory centers? Granting even that the leading agitators were sincere in their attack, this still fails to explain the sectional support given to the propaganda by thousands of Northern citizens who were evidently not interested in the Negro or his condition in the Southern States. Only through a combination of factors other than freedom for the slaves was public opinion of the North finally united to support a sectional presidential candidate running on a sectional platform in 1860. Did the abolition propaganda discredit the South and create an opening for a sectional party? Were the sectional controversies arising prior to 1860 based upon slavery? Or was the slavery issue only one of several conflicts founded upon a more fundamental difference between the North and the South? Such questions naturally aroused the interest of history students in surveying the sectional controversy centering around slavery.

In general, as has been seen, Southern opinion considered slavery as an evil until the radical abolitionist attack. Early protests against the importation of Negroes into the Southern colonies were unsuccessful. Planted upon American soil by English and Yankee slave traders, as a result of the inadequate labor supply, fertile lands, staple crops, and a salutary climate the blacks flourished, multiplied, and labored until they became an essential part of the Southern social and economic order. Yet from the time their numbers created the menace of a race problem, colonization, manumission, and emancipation societies flourished in the Slave States. Desiring to rid themselves of the evil of slavery and the even greater evil of the free Negro, the Southern people especially supported schemes of colonization. During the Revolutionary period Southern leaders like Washington, Jefferson, Madison, Randolph and others looked forward to the possibility of eliminating slavery. Even the agitation against slavery aroused by Northerners during the Missouri controversy failed to stamp out this sentiment among the Southern people. For a decade following that sectional struggle, antislavery leaders and emancipation societies continued to receive their greatest support from Slave States.

In 1831, the radical Garrisonian attack burst upon this emancipation sentiment of the South. Not content with attacking the institution of slavery, the "New Abolitionists" launched a personal attack upon the slaveholders. This attack was not confined to the slaveowners alone; every Southern institution was condemned because of its connection with the iniquities of the slave system. No term was too severe to be used in heaping vituperation upon the South. Fervid imaginations of zealous fanatics ran riot in describing Southern outrages attributed to slavery. Aided by English abolitionists and spurred on by monetary contributions, the American abolitionists flooded the country with incendiary propaganda in the form of tracts, newspapers, and pictures. Because the foundations of slavery lay deep, the unrestrained fanaticism of the abolitionists carried them to the point of denying the Bible which seemed to sanction slavery, attacking the American Church, burning the Constitution, flaunting the laws, advocating disunion, inciting the slaves to bloody race wars, and eventually carried the leaders off on tangents in the form of infidelism, anarchism, free-love, and communistic and utopian schemes of government.

The South, alarmed at the violence and incendiary character of the attack in 1831 and shocked by the rebellion of Nat Turner which followed, viewed with grave apprehension the future effect of such propaganda upon her civilization. Although they believed slavery to be an evil, the Southern people faced a real situation instead of an abstract theory. Knowing that the abolitionist charges were false and entirely exaggerated, they soon turned to a defense in the form of answering the charges. This defense demanded a careful study of the institution of slavery in all of its potentialities and this in turn led to a realization of many positive benefits of the system. From the Bible it was found that slavery was recognized in the Old Testament and sanctioned in the New.

Even more important was the curse placed upon the descendants of woolly-headed, black-skinned Ham. Economically, the Southerners insisted that slavery was of great benefit. Through the institution an improvident race was compelled to labor toward the upbuilding of civilization. By means of slavery, unhealthful swamps within semi-tropical latitudes were transformed into fertile plantations producing cotton, sugar cane, and rice which furnished food and clothing to millions and incidentally provided raw materials for the world's industries. What other human institution was productive of such great economic benefits? asked the defenders of slavery.

In addition to their economic justification, the Southerners argued that slavery was a social necessity. It provided a form of social organization under which two distinct and radically different races could peacefully dwell together for the welfare of both. They were quite intense in their belief that the Negro was inferior to the white race. Whether they attributed this fact to a direct act of God or to the separate creation and origin of a distinct species, their conclusion of Negro inferiority was common to all. The fundamental racial differences between white and black, aside from other considerations, would have served to unite Southern opinion in a determination to maintain white supremacy and white civilization. So interwoven was slavery in the social and economic life of the South that this justification of Southern institutions became vital to their very existence. Was slavery so essential per se or was it merely a part of an agrarian civilization? The answer to this question may be readily seen in the answer to another. Was the South agricultural because it possessed slaves, or did it own slaves because the system provided an adequate supply of agricultural laborers in a climatical area unfavorable to white labor? A study of the reasons why the New England colonies became commercial and industrial centers while the Southern colonies became agricultural easily answers both questions.

Thus a study of the slavery controversy finally narrows down to a study of sectionalism. The late Frederick Jackson Turner wrote that "Such a struggle as the slavery contest can only be understood by bearing in mind that it was not merely a contest of North against South, but that its form and its causes were fundamentally shaped by the dynamic factor of expanding sections, of a West to be won."[1] From this view, early sectional rivalries between the Eastern and Southern colonies were transferred after the Revolution into a gigantic contest for controlling the ever expanding West. A Southerner wrote in *DeBow's Review* in 1847:

A contest has been going on between the North and South not limited to slavery or no slavery—to abolition or no abolition, nor to the politics of either whigs or democrats as such, but a contest for the wealth and commerce of the great valley of the Mississippi—a contest tendered by our Northern brethren, whether the growing commerce of the great West shall be thrown upon New Orleans or given to the Atlantic cities.[2]

Leaders in both the North and the South realized the political and economic importance of the Western States upon sectional issues.

Very early in the history of the English colonies in America divergent sectional interests were created. Ethnical differences were augmented by climatic variations, topographical features, and other factors dominating the physical environment, which, combined with the colonial policies of the mother country, created distinct sectional interests. In brief, the Eastern colonies became centers of commerce and industry in the New World while the Southern group naturally turned to agriculture, based upon the plantation system and

---

[1] Frederick Jackson Turner, *The Significance of Sections in American History*, pp. 33-34.

[2] *Ibid.*, p. 32, quotes from *DeBow's Review*.

the production of great staples. The interests of the two sections were inevitably bound to conflict. Through a system of compromises these discordant elements were brought together under a union of federated states. The principles of government enunciated by leaders of the Federalist party like Hamilton, Washington, and Adams controlled the policy of the national government during the early years of the new republic. Thomas Jefferson was able to unite the discontented elements and draw great support from the new settlements west of the Alleghanies in order to effect the so-called revolution of 1800. There followed a quarter of a century in which the Federalist party was discredited and the New England section, feeling themselves to be a minority, feared possible sectional legislation that would prohibit great profits in commerce and industry. Fundamentally the sectional issues might be described as a conflict between the agrarianism of the South and the industrialism of the East. From this basic difference, many sectional conflicts flared up in the period prior to 1860. The tariff struggle, the question of internal improvements, the fight for a centralized bank, and above all the continuous controversy concerning westward expansion which affected the sectional balance of power merely reflected the divergent sectional interests. These were all major controversies but cannot be developed in a study of the slavery controversy. Basically, these sectional conflicts were more important than the slavery issue, but they lacked the opportunities for an emotional appeal which slavery so conveniently provided. The American people have always been susceptible to a well-organized system of propaganda, though one which takes the form of high principles, is garbed in morality, and develops a slogan of freedom strikes a more popular note with the mass of the citizens.

These divergent sectional interests made the demand for sectional control of the Federal Government. Soon after the

War of 1812, Northern leaders such as Rufus King and John Quincy Adams felt the need of either rejuvenating the old Federalist Party or organizing a new sectional party along geographical lines. The basic elements of sectionalism were back of the Missouri controversy. At that time Rufus King openly avowed that fundamentally the struggle was a sectional "contest for political power."[3] Even prior to this Northern leaders realized the possible benefits of using the slavery issue as a means of accomplishing certain political ends. By agitating the slavery question the new states of the Northwest Territory might be converted to the anti-slavery group and alienated from their natural ally, the agricultural South. Men were sent into the Western States for the purpose of agitating the slavery issue and becoming political leaders in that section. In this light the Missouri struggle was but a slight skirmish of the outposts preceding the major conflict.[4]

That the abolition agitation was used as a means of discrediting the South, especially in the Northwest, and aided in the later formation of a sectional party seems undeniable. As to the actual connection between leading abolitionists and certain politicians, it remains for their biographers to determine. Parke Godwin,[5] a Northern journalist and free-soil politician, stated the issue clearly in his *Political Essays* pub-

[3] See discussion in "The Black Race in North America," *Southern Literary Messenger*, XXI (November, 1855), 642; Turner, *Rise of the New West*, p. 173.

[4] Edmund Ruffin wrote in 1857 that "The present contest between the Northern and Southern States in regard to negro slavery, has been growing in violence for a long time. It was begun with the iniquitous aggression of attempting to exclude Missouri from the Union as a slaveholding State, and in the successful exaction of the Missouri Compromise, in relation to which, both the general enforcement and exceptional violation of it by the North, have been exercised and varied, the more to wrong the Southern States."—Article on "Consequences of the Abolition Agitation," *DeBow's Review*, XXII (June, 1857), 586. Thomas Cooper of South Carolina in 1826 "attributed the agitation against slavery to sectional interest and blind sentimentalism and philanthropy. . . ." Malone, *op. cit.*, p. 288.

[5] Parke Godwin was for many years associated with William Cullen Bryant on the *New York Evening Post*. Politically, he was at first a Free-Soil Democrat and later became a Republican. See biographical sketch in *Dictionary of American Biography*, VII, 351-52.

lished in 1856. The "real issue at the bottom" of the slavery controversy was, according to his view, "the struggle of two incompatible orders of civilization for the mastery of a common field."[6] He asserted that the contest between the "Northern and Southern civilizations" presented two aspects. It was a struggle, first, to determine which civilization should exert a dominant influence in the Federal Government; and second, to decide which civilization should exert a determining influence in the organization of the new territories.[7] Naturally the section succeeding in regard to the first point would be able to dictate the second. On the other hand, whichever section could influence the second point would in a short time be able to control the policies of the Federal Government. Godwin went on to announce that "Among the politicians of the South, it has become a desperate struggle for the retention of their ascendancy, and among those of the North, a desperate gamble for success."[8] Thus behind the agitation of slavery lay the threat of sectional legislation by control of the Federal Government.

It should be noted, however, that the leading anti-slavery agitators were not always in agreement as to the means of conducting the attack or the ends to be achieved. The violence of the extreme radicals led by Garrison aided the organization of the American Anti-Slavery Society, developed the incendiary propaganda, and reacted to create the necessity for the Southern defense and justification of slavery. This class of abolitionists openly advocated the scrapping of the Constitution and the dissolution of the Union. "No union with slaveholders" became a slogan under which this group disseminated revolutionary propaganda.[9] Another clan of abolitionists, no less violent in their attack upon the South, but using better judgment as to the method of gaining their

[6] Parke Godwin, *Political Essays,* pp. 283-85.
[7] *Ibid.,* p. 286.   [8] *Ibid.,* pp. 303-4.
[9] See *Anti-Slavery Bugle,* July 25, 1845.

ends, were interested in the political effects of the agitation.[10] This difference, together with the submergence of abolition-ism under a variety of other "isms" by the Garrisonian group, caused men like the Tappans, Jay, and others to break away from the old organization and form the American and Foreign Anti-Slavery Society in 1839-1840.[11] The latter or-ganization not only continued to spread propaganda discredit-ing the South but its leaders also aided in the formation of the Free-Soil Party and later the Republican Party.[12]

During the abolitionist attack, Southern leaders were fully aware of the political significance of the anti-slavery propaganda. Edmund Ruffin, an influential Virginia planter, wrote that the "fanaticism" of the abolitionists was "more truly, the unholy grasping for political power."[13] Still another Southern writer characterized them as being dom-inated by "selfish ambition."[14] Twenty years before the Re-publican Party nominated a candidate for president, Calhoun predicted that the abolition agitation would form the "basis of a powerful political party, that will seek advancement by diffusing, as widely as possible, hatred against the slavehold-ing States."[15] Southerners were also conscious of the fact that they represented a minority section.[16] "The slaveholding states are now and ever must be in a minority," wrote Duff Green in 1846, and he contended that the abolition agitation

[10] Lewis Tappan to L. A. Chamerovzow, October 29, 1854; Tappan, *A Side-Light on Anglo-American Relations*, p. 346.

[11] *Ibid.*; also letter of John Scoble to the committee of the British and Foreign Anti-Slavery Society, Feb. 14, 1853, quoted in *ibid.*, pp. 314-15.

[12] *Ibid.*, pp. 315-19, 346-50.

[13] Ruffin, "Consequences of the Abolition Agitation," *DeBow's Review*, XXII (June, 1857), 583.

[14] Publicola (pseud.), "Present Aspects of Abolitionism," *Southern Literary Messenger*, XIII (July, 1847), 430. See similar expressions in Priest, *op. cit.*, pp. 350-51; J. R. Jones, *op. cit.*, p. 6.

[15] Report of Select Committee on President's Message of Feb. 4, 1836, Cal-houn, *Works*, V, 206-7.

[16] Jesse Thomas Carpenter, *The South as a Conscious Minority, 1789-1861: A Study in Political Thought*, passim.

was for the purpose of creating "a sectional northern party" and placing the "Government in the hands of *northern* men."[17] Realizing their minority position and the disastrous effects upon the agricultural system that would inevitably result from the industrialists controlling the executive and legislative branches of the national government, Southern statesmen determined to maintain their equal representation in the Senate. "Our only safety is in *equality* of POWER," wrote Senator Hammond in 1850.[18] Already outnumbered in the House of Representatives, the South's only hope of preventing discriminatory sectional legislation lay in keeping the number of Free and Slave States and consequently the number of senators equal. This necessity for maintaining an equal balance of power must be borne in mind while considering the struggle over territories during the period before 1860.

Fundamentally this struggle for political power formed the background for the Missouri controversy, the Northern opposition to the annexation of Texas, the conflict concerning the disposition of the Mexican cession, and the war in Kansas. Slavery would have been unprofitable in a large portion of the acquired territories and probably would not have been an issue at all had it not been for the abolition agitation and the political struggle. For propaganda purposes the slavery issue was dragged into each of these conflicts by the abolitionists who built up an emotional appeal throughout the North to oppose the alleged aggressions of what they called the "slave-power." The general purpose of their efforts, of course, was the splitting of the two major parties into Northern and Southern wings just as had been done in the case of several Protestant churches. As the agitation increased it became

[17] Letter of Duff Green to Calhoun, Feb. 22, 1846, in Calhoun, *Correspondence*, pp. 1073-74; italics Green's.

[18] J. H. Hammond to Calhoun, Mar. 5, 1850, in *ibid.*, p. 1210; italics and capitalization Hammond's.

more and more difficult for the old parties to avoid the slavery issue and maintain unity within their ranks. The Whig Party contained a large number of anti-slavery supporters and Calhoun feared that the Wilmot Proviso would prove to be the "apple of discord" that would divide the Democratic Party.[19] So bitter did the struggle over the territories become that Hammond felt that the vast acquisition of Northern strength from additional free states would enable that section to "ride over" the South "rough shod." He wrote Calhoun in 1850 that "If we do not act now, we deliberately consign our children, not our posterity, but *our children* to the flames."[20] Nor was the bitter prospect confined to the South, for Henry Ward Beecher characterized the Sharp's rifle as a "truly moral agency" before his congregation and exhorted them to use it upon "the slaveholders of Kansas" as a more effective instrument "than a hundred Bibles."[21]

The widespread abolition propaganda, the increase of anti-slavery sentiment in the North which sponsored antagonism toward the South, and the work of the political abolitionists naturally resulted in effecting the politics of the period. The two major parties of this era, the Democrats and the Whigs, were of a strength so nearly equal that a relatively small block of voters in a pivotal state could wield the balance of power and occasionally swing a presidential election. For a number of years both the Democrats and the Whigs had regarded the growing number of abolitionists as a "band of agitators," interfering with an institution which was none of their concern. Both parties had expressed their "unstinted condemnation" of this "pestilent sect."[22] Despite

---

[19] Letter of Calhoun to Lewis S. Coryell, Nov. 7, 1846, in *ibid.*, p. 710.

[20] J. H. Hammond to Calhoun, March 5, 1850, in *ibid.*, pp. 1210-11; italics Hammond's.

[21] Henry Ward Beecher, at a public meeting held in his church to promote emigration to Kansas, quoted in M. W. Cluskey (editor), *The Political Textbook, or Encyclopedia*, p. 20.

[22] Herbert, *The Abolition Crusade*, p. 96.

the protests of the abolitionist press, questionnaires to candidates, and politico-abolitionist meetings, the old party organizations sought to avoid the slavery issue. The politically-minded anti-slavery leaders, dissatisfied with the stand of the major parties, sponsored a third-party movement and in 1840 organized the Liberty Party.[23] But a majority of the anti-slavery voters were Whigs, and the enthusiasm of the "Tippecanoe and Tyler Too" campaign did not allow many of them to desert their old allegiance and vote for a purely anti-slavery ticket. The Liberty Party candidates, James G. Birney and Thomas Earle, received only about seven thousand votes in the entire country.[24] Since the voting strength of the membership of the anti-slavery societies alone reached at least 70,000 in 1840, evidently only a small percentage allowed their abolition sentiments to alienate their political affiliations.[25]

But the radical political abolitionists, applying their "religious zeal" to the more practical affairs of politics, were bound sooner or later to make inroads upon the national parties. Naturally, some concrete result would be expected from the continuous denunciation of the Federal Government, the personal charges against all national leaders even remotely connected with slavery, and the vigorous ridicule of all Northerners who voted for anyone but an outright abolitionist. Stephen S. Foster, writing in 1843, bitterly assailed those in charge of the Federal Government by denouncing President John Tyler as "a veteran slave-breeder—a negro thief" who had "long supported his own family in princely luxury by desolating the domestic hearth-stones of his defenceless neighbors." With the usual abolitionist inability to see other than a high standard of morality in his own section,

[23] See discussion in Theodore Clarke Smith, *The Liberty and Free Soil Parties in the Northwest*, pp. 38-39. This rather old work gives a scholarly treatment of these parties and their relation to the anti-slavery movement.

[24] De Alva Stanwood Alexander, *A Political History of the State of New York*, II, 89.   [25] T. C. Smith, *op. cit.*, pp. 46-47.

he charged that President Tyler's crimes were so great that
if they had been "perpetrated" in the North, he would have
been confined in prison for "at least two centuries, or until
released by death from his ignominious confinement." The
same appellation of "negro-thief" was applied without dis-
crimination to most of the cabinet, to five members of the
Supreme Court, the vice-president, the commanding general
of the army, and the majority of the United States ministers
to foreign countries.[26] With an eye to the possible election
of Clay in 1844, Foster declared that the Northern people
"looked upon John Tyler as he robbed the frantic mother of
her babe, and forthwith made him President of the United
States! They have seen Henry Clay and John C. Calhoun
tear the tender and confiding wife from the fond embrace of
her husband, and sell her to a stranger," and yet "they are
now eager to confer on them the same splendid honors."[27]
The pamphlet enunciating these doctrines had wide distribution during the summer of 1844 and perhaps acted as campaign propaganda not so much for Mr. Birney as against any
candidate leaning toward slavery. Foster often expressed the
same views in numerous anti-slavery meetings, churches, and
other public gatherings.

With the sectional struggle for political power in the
background, the request of President Tyler that Congress
provide for the annexation of Texas by means of a joint resolution created a distinct issue for the presidential campaign
of 1844. Clay was the logical candidate for the Whigs. In the
Democratic Convention, after a deadlock created by a bloc
of Southern delegates who were unable to nominate Calhoun
but were of sufficient strength to defeat Van Buren, the
delegates finally turned unanimously to Governor Polk of

[26] Foster, *op. cit.*, pp. 23-24.

[27] *Ibid.*, p. 24. George Bourne had previously published similar material violently condemning the leading statesmen as "perjured men-stealers," "women-
scourgers and women-destroyers," etc.—*Slavery Illustrated in its Effect upon
Women . . .* , pp. 19, 22.

Tennessee, who became the first "dark horse" candidate in the history of the presidency.[28] At the beginning it seemed that the Whigs had an advantage in securing the abolitionist vote. Clay's avowed opposition to annexing Texas was considered as being satisfactory to the anti-slavery Whigs.[29] In the meantime, the political abolitionists had been enthusiastically building a national organization for the Liberty Party. At their New York convention early in 1841, James G. Birney and Thomas Morris were selected as the candidates for president and vice-president respectively for the campaign of 1844.[30] For three years this group spent much time in organizing all of the Northern States.

As the time of election drew near, the Democrats desired, particularly in New York, to strengthen the Liberty Party by characterizing Clay as a slaveholder. Since the Liberty Party was founded upon a cornerstone of hostility to slavery and slaveholders, it seemed likely that this strategy might attract a number of anti-slavery Whigs in the state to the abolitionist cause and have only negligible effects upon the Democratic ranks. The Whigs met this thrust with some success by arguing that not slaveholding but the annexation of Texas and the possible extension of the system of slavery was the real issue. They asserted that "a vote for Clay, who once advocated emancipation in Kentucky and is now strongly opposed to Texas, is a vote in behalf of freedom."[31] Clay, desiring the presidency and attempting to straddle the issue, shifted his position somewhat, in a letter to Stephen Miller of Alabama, by stating that he would like to see Texas added to the United States "upon just and fair terms" though he felt that "the subject of slavery ought not to affect the question one way or the other."[32] The effect of this letter upon

[28] Eugene Irving McCormac, *James K. Polk, A Political Biography*, pp. 236-47.
[29] Alexander, *op. cit.*, II, 83.
[30] T. C. Smith, *op. cit.*, pp. 52-54. [31] Alexander, *op. cit.*, II, 87.
[32] Letter of Henry Clay to Stephen Miller, Tuscaloosa, Ala., July 1, 1844, quoted in *ibid.*, pp. 87-88.

Northern anti-slavery Whigs was disastrous. Many, though they admired Clay, could not reconcile themselves to his position. The Whig chances of annexing the Liberty Party vote were lost because the political abolitionists immediately started a campaign of abusive censure against the Whig candidate. They denounced Clay with violent but irrelevant terms such as "gambler," "duelist," and "negro-thief." Such tactics, however, alienated those anti-slavery Whigs who were devotedly loyal to Clay and they rallied to his support.[33] On the other hand, in New York a large number of the Whig abolitionists decided to support Birney. So unfavorable was the effect of Clay's letter that Seward summed up its results in New York by stating that "It jeopards, perhaps loses, the State."[34]

The abolitionists ordinarily would have been glad to have dealt the annexation of Texas a severe blow by voting with the Whigs, but by the time of the election they were so aroused that they would not support any candidate that did not believe that slavery was the most important issue involved in the controversy.[35] The Whig Party made a vigorous fight against Birney by charging that the latter was allied with Polk in order to defeat Clay.[36] In doing so they probably lessened the Liberty Party vote from what it might have been. The Liberty Party, however, made a strong contest in order to keep the following it had built up during the three preceding years of campaigning.[37] As a result of the con-

[33] See discussion of these points in T. C. Smith, *op. cit.*, pp. 71-73.
[34] Alexander, *op. cit.*, II, 88.
[35] Edward Channing, *History of the United States*, V, 545.
[36] See discussion in T. C. Smith, *op. cit.*, pp. 76-80.
[37] *Ibid.*, pp. 77-79. One of their campaign songs, later reprinted in the *Anti-Slavery Bugle*, July 1, 1845, went as follows:

> "We will vote for *Birney*,
> We will vote for *Birney*,
> For *Birney* and for *Morris*,
> And for freedom through the Land."

It might be pointed out that the *Bugle* sided with the Garrisonian group and opposed the Liberty Party. Considerable controversy took place in 1845 between the

troversy Birney attracted enough votes away from the Whig electors in New York to give Polk the electoral vote of that state and elevate him to the presidency.[38] It may be concluded then that the work of the political abolitionists, in seeking to apply the prejudices of the ordinary anti-slavery sentimentalists more aggressively to practical politics, had not been in vain from 1839 to 1844, for "abolitionism" had become a factor in national politics.

During the three years following the election of 1844, the Liberty Party steadily declined.[39] A branch of the party inclined away from the narrowness of the one-issue idea and became transformed into a general radical reform element. This new radical party organized in 1845 as the Liberty League.[40] One of the new abolitionist doctrines that had been growing up was the theory that the Constitution of the United States was an anti-slavery document and consequently slavery was unconstitutional in all states.[41] This theory, worked out by Lysander Spooner and supported by William Goodell, created new possibilities for anti-slavery action.[42] These doctrines were adopted by the convention of the Liberty League in 1847 in a series of resolutions. At the same time the League nominated Gerrit Smith as candidate for president and Elihu Burritt for the vice-presidency. In addi-

---

Bugle and the *Ohio American,* a Liberty Party paper. See *Bugle,* June 20 and August 1, 1845.

[38] See Greeley and Cleveland, *op. cit.,* p. 219; gives popular vote in New York: Polk—237,588; Clay—232,482; Birney—15,812. If we add the Birney votes to those of Clay, based on the supposition that all the anti-slavery voters might have voted for Clay, he would have received 248,294 votes. The 36 electoral votes of New York were selected at large in 1844 and in this case would have been given to Clay; 36 votes subtracted from Polk's 170 and added to Clay's 105 would have resulted in Clay—141 votes; Polk—134 votes. See *House Journal,* 28th Cong., 2nd sess., p. 372. Also Herbert, *op. cit.,* pp. 94-96.

[39] T. C. Smith, *op. cit.,* p. 85.

[40] See letter of John Scoble to Committee of British and Foreign Anti-Slavery Society, Feb. 14, 1853, quoted in Tappan, *A Side-Light on Anglo-American Relations,* p. 317.   [41] T. C. Smith, *op. cit.,* pp. 98-99.

[42] Lysander Spooner, *The Unconstitutionality of Slavery;* William Goodell, *Views of American Constitutional Law, in its bearing upon American Slavery.*

tion to the Spooner-Goodell doctrines the League's platform advocated free trade, limitations upon ownership of land, free public lands, free suffrage, and other reformist proposals of the time.[43] This movement received but little support outside of New York State.[44]

Nearer the election of 1848, a diverse group of former Liberty men, a few New York Barnburners, "Conscience" Whigs, and "Free-Soil" Democrats assembled at Buffalo in a great Free-Soil Convention. After considerable arranging of back-room deals while fiery oratory kept the delegates enthusiastic, a platform was finally arranged to please various elements; this was headed by Martin Van Buren and Charles Francis Adams as the nominees for the presidency and vice-presidency respectively. This movement swept aside the possibility of a distinct Liberty Party and gained greater support in the Northwest than could have possibly been achieved by the Liberty League.[45]

As a result of the Free-Soil movement in 1848, the abolitionist vote was again the deciding factor in a presidential election and again New York was the pivotal state.[46] The nomination of Lewis Cass, who represented many Southern principles, by the Democrats, and the selection of Zachary Taylor, the Southern owner of four hundred slaves, as the Whig candidate placed the anti-slavery groups in both major parties in quite a dilemma. Van Buren's party was able to unite discontented elements from both of the old party organizations as well as nearly all varieties of abolition sentiment under the banner of "Free Soil, Free Speech, Free Labour, and Free Men."[47] In contrast to the 1844 election, this time it was the anti-slavery Democrats who bolted the party ticket in New York. Through the urging of such

---

[43] Letter of John Scoble in Tappan, *A Side-Light on Anglo-American Relations*, p. 317.

[44] T. C. Smith, *op. cit.*, pp. 101-2.   [45] See discussion in *ibid.*, pp. 138-54.

[46] Herbert, *op. cit.*, p. 99.   [47] Alexander, *op. cit.*, II, 132.

leaders as John Van Buren, son of the former president, many of the anti-slavery Democrats supported the Free-Soil candidates. This resulted in the splitting of the normal Democratic vote in New York and throwing the state electoral vote to Taylor, thereby insuring his election.[48] In this election the anti-slavery element determined the campaign issues in New York, New England, and in some sections of the West, and as one writer expressed it, opposition to slavery had become "respectable in politics."[49]

Insofar as local and congressional elections were concerned the methods of the Free-Soilers were quite different from those of the former Liberty Party. The latter group of political abolitionists relied entirely upon separate action and largely ignored the candidates of the old parties. In contrast, the Free-Soil Party was ready to form coalitions with either the Whigs or the Democrats in order to elect men advocating their principles or to secure aid from the major parties in placing Free-Soil candidates in office. Though numerically weak, the Free-Soilers were able through a system of coalitions to place a number of anti-slavery candidates in office.[50] The abolition cause was aided by the sending of such men as Chase, Giddings, Julian, and others to Congress. Though the coalition method was effective in this manner, it brought about the rapid disintegration of the Free-Soil Party, thereby failing in the endeavor to establish a permanent Northern party.[51]

[48] Herbert, *op. cit.*, pp. 99-100; Alexander, *op. cit.*, II, 143-44. The Free-Soil group almost divided the Democratic vote in New York in two: Van Buren—120,000; Cass—114,000; Taylor—218,000. As Taylor's electoral majority was only 36 over that of Cass, if the abolitionists had not split the Democratic vote in New York, Cass would have been elected President. See George P. Garrison, *Westward Extension, 1841-1850*, p. 283. The total national vote was as follows: Taylor—1,360,099; Cass—1,220,544; Van Buren—291,263.—T. C. Smith, *op. cit.*, p. 154.　　[49] Alexander, *op. cit.*, II, 142.

[50] T. C. Smith, *op. cit.*, p. 300. In addition to state officials, some of the men which the Free-Soil movement aided to elect to Congress were Chase, Campbell, Giddings, Newton, Root, Townshend, and Edward Wade from Ohio; Conger, Penniman, and Sprague from Michigan; Julian from Indiana; Durkee and Doty from Wisconsin.　　[51] *Ibid.*, p. 301.

Another phase of this general movement which should be mentioned is the era of the "Free Democracy." The Free-Soil Party declined steadily from 1848 to 1851. An attempt was made to revive the anti-slavery party in 1851 and from that date until 1854 the third party was officially known as the "Free Democracy." In contrast to the 1848 movement, this time the impetus for organization came from the Northwestern States. Meeting at Pittsburgh in 1852, the delegates representing this new movement were quite enthusiastic despite the recent disruption of the Free-Soil vote.[52] John P. Hale was the unanimous choice for presidential candidate while George W. Julian was selected as his running mate. The platform was quite similar to that of 1848 with the addition of condemnation of the Compromise of 1850 and the Fugitive Slave Law, a demand for recognition of Hayti, and other minor planks not connected with the slavery issue.[53] Though making an active campaign, the Free Democrats failed to exercise any direct result upon the election. Pierce, the Democratic candidate, was overwhelmingly elected over General Winfield Scott, the Whig nominee.[54] The Free Democrats polled only about 150,000 votes but their grouping proved the important fact that the political phase of the anti-slavery movement had been definitely established in the West.[55] In general, the Free Democrats, by following either a policy of complete separation or one of unrestrained coalition, were able to maintain a middle course more conducive to the preservation of a third party.

Specialized studies of the Liberty and Free-Soil movements in politics show that their results like the general abolition crusade were largely in the form of an educational conquest. By means of the politico-abolitionist press, cam-

[52] *Ibid.*, pp. 246-47, cites *National Era*, Aug. 19-26, 1852.
[53] T. C. Smith, *op. cit.*, pp. 247-48.
[54] *Idem, Parties and Slavery, 1850-1859*, pp. 36-37.
[55] *Idem, Liberty and Free Soil Parties*, p. 257.

paign speakers, house-to-house canvasses, and the dissemination of anti-slavery political propaganda the slavery issue was kept constantly before the voters. In this way, these third parties paved the way for the splitting of the major parties into sectional alignments. Their continuous offensive and the control at times of the balance of voters in a pivotal state forced the older parties to assume a defensive position. Through coalitions with the older parties the anti-slavery groups were able to place representatives in Congress who continued the agitation in the Federal Legislature and thereby influenced national politics. Even more important than these evidences of success were the scattered organizations, the political experience gained by their leaders, and the sectional distrust which had been engendered; all of these factors constituted important foundations for the establishment of the Republican Party in 1854. Though the aim of the Buffalo Free-Soil Convention to found a permanent Northern party was not realized in 1848, the efforts of this group led to success six years later and the fundamental issue of the earlier platform was practically identical with that of the Republican Party in the campaigns of 1856 and 1860.

Since it is not possible in this treatment of the slavery controversy to elaborate upon party history, suffice it to say that there was a direct connection between the abolition propaganda and the agitation of the slavery issue with the formation of a major sectional party. William Lloyd Garrison, speaking before the New England Anti-Slavery Convention in 1856, stated that in his opinion the organization of the Republican Party was the necessary result of their "moral agitation."[56] During the same year the *National Anti-Slavery Standard* pointed out that the movement which created the Republican Party sprang from the anti-slavery movement and "whatever strength and hope it has lies in the anti-slavery

[56] William Lloyd Garrison, speech of May 29, 1856, quoted in Cluskey, *op. cit.*, p. 19.

feeling of the northern minds."[57] At last the political possibilities of the anti-slavery agitation, foreseen forty years before by only a few, were reaching a climax. The propaganda to discredit the South which came to the surface in the Missouri controversy and burst with such violence in the thirties had almost done its work. The disruption of the Union through sectional struggle, though averted by compromises in 1820 and 1850, was about to be forced through the destruction of the political balance of power. A candidate in Massachusetts said of the Republican Party: "The object to be accomplished is this; that the free States shall take possession of the government by their united voters. . . . We have the power in number; our strength is in Union."[58]

The radicalism of Garrisonian concepts, carried over into political leadership characterized by men like Seward, Chase, Sumner, Stevens, tended toward the destruction of the Supreme Court and the nullifying of the guarantees of the Constitution. If the South lost its equality in the Senate, the leaders in that section believed that Southern institutions and civilization would be endangered to such an extent that they must either secede or become a minority exploited in a Union dominated by the industrial East. The signal which sounded the alarm of immediate danger was the election of 1860. Because of the division of the Democratic Party along sectional lines in 1860, resulting largely from thirty years of continuous agitation to discredit the South, a sectional president was elected on a platform which threatened the rights of the Southern people. The event predicted by Southern leaders like Cooper, Calhoun, Ruffin, Hammond, and others had occurred. The industrial East had alienated the West from the agrarian South and the previous compromises pre-

[57] *National Anti-Slavery Standard* (New York), June 21, 1856, quoted in *ibid.*, pp. 18-19.

[58] Simon Brown, candidate for Lieutenant-Governor in Mass., quoted in *ibid.*, p. 20.

serving the sectional balance were destroyed. The South could only hope to preserve her civilization separately.

The fundamental causes of the South's withdrawal from the Union were perhaps most clearly stated in the instructions of R. M. T. Hunter, Confederate Secretary of State, to James M. Mason, on September 23, 1861. Hunter declared that the South was not to be considered as "revolted provinces or rebellious subjects seeking to overthrow the lawful authority of a common sovereign." Tracing the historic background of the Constitution, he pointed out that the Union had been founded upon a document which granted the Federal Government certain powers "to be exercised for certain declared purposes, and restricted within well defined limits." Under such a Constitution, he asserted, "when a sectional and dominant majority persistently violated the covenant conditions of that compact," then the states whose "safety and well being depended" upon its guarantees were "justly absolved from all moral obligations to remain in such a Union." Recognizing the fact that the Union had been formed with two different social systems, Hunter declared that "when the Government of that Union instead of affording protection to their social system, itself threatened not merely to disturb the peace and security of its people, but also destroy their social system, the States thus menaced owed it to themselves and their posterity to withdraw immediately from a union whose very bonds prevented them from defending themselves against such dangers. Such were the causes which led the Confederate States to form a new Union to be composed of more homogeneous materials and interests." Speaking of the Southern people, he asserted that "experience had demonstrated to them that a union of two different and hostile social systems under a government in which one of them wielded nearly all the power was not only ill assorted but dangerous in the extreme to the weaker section whose scheme of society was thus unprotected." According to his view, eleven sovereign states, bound by the ties of a "common social system" and "identical interests," formed a new government "to preserve their old institutions, and preserve through their new organic law the very ends and purposes for which they believed the first was formed." Due to these factors, he maintained that "it was because a revolution was sought to be made in the spirit and ends of the organic law of their first union by a dominant and sectional majority operating through the machinery of a government which was in their hands and placed there for different purposes, that the Confederate States withdrew themselves from the jurisdiction of such a government and established another for themselves."[59] The attempt of the Confederate States to carry out this program is another story, in which the sectional controversies of the period from 1831 to 1860 were transferred to the Theater of War for another tragic act.

[59] R. M. T. Hunter to James M. Mason, September 23, 1861, *Official Records of the Union and Confederate Navies*, Series II, III, 257-58; also in Virginia Mason, *The Public Life and Diplomatic Correspondence of James M. Mason with Some Personal History*, pp. 248-49; also partially quoted in Frank L. Owsley, *op. cit.*, pp. 225-26.

SELECTED BIBLIOGRAPHY

I. PRIMARY SOURCES

A. GOVERNMENT DOCUMENTS

Annals of Congress, 1789-1824; published from 1825-1837 as the *Register of Debates in Congress;* the *Congressional Globe,* which overlaps the *Register,* covers the debates from the period, 1834-1874. All published in Washington, D. C.

Benton, Thomas Hart, *Abridgment of the Debates of Congress from 1789-1856,* 17 vols., New York, 1857-1861.

Documents Accompanying the President's message of December, 1824 (18th Cong., 2nd Sess., Sen. Doc. 1). Washington, 1824.

Message from President in relation to the abuse of the flag of the United States in subservience to the African slave trade, . . . (28th Cong., 1st Sess., Sen. Doc. 217). Washington, 1844.

Message from the President of the United States (Polk) communicating a Report from the Secretary of State, with the correspondence of Mr. Wise, late United States Minister to Brazil, in relation to the Slave Trade (30th Cong., 1st Sess., Sen. Ex. Doc. 28). Washington, 1848.

African Colonization Report of Mr. Kennedy, from the Committee on Commerce to whom was referred the memorial of the friends of African colonization, assembled in convention in the city of Washington, May, 1842. To which is appended, a collection of the most interesting papers on the subject of African colonization, and the commerce, etc., of western Africa, together with all the diplomatic correspondence between the United States and Great Britain, on the subject of the African Slave Trade (27th Cong., 3rd Sess., House Rep. 283). Washington, 1843.

Report of the Secretary of State (Webster) communicating the report of Rev. R. R. Gurley, who was recently sent by the Government to obtain information in respect to Liberia (31st Cong., 1st Sess., Sen. Ex. Doc. 75). Washington, 1850.

Slavery in the District of Columbia; report made by Hon. H. L. Pinckney, to the House of Representatives, May 18, 1836 (24th Cong., 1st Sess., House Rep. 691). Washington, 1836.

Report, made by Mr. Calhoun, with Senate Bill no. 122. The Select Committee to whom was referred that portion of the President's message which relates to the attempts to circulate, through the mail, inflammatory appeals, to excite the slaves to insurrection, submit the following report (24th Cong., 1st Sess., Sen. Doc. 118). Washington, 1836.

African Slave Trade (31st Cong., 2nd Sess., Sen. Ex. Doc. 27). Washington, 1851.

Message from the President of the United States, communicating information in regard to the slave and coolie trade (34th Cong., 1st Sess., House Ex. Doc. 105). Washington, 1856.

Message from the President of the United States, transmitting a report of the Attorney-General, relative to the introduction of slaves into the United States, contrary to existing laws. May 6, 1822 (17th Cong., 1st Sess., Sen. Doc. 93). Washington, 1828.

United States Departments

Department of Navy. Letter from the Secretary of Navy transmitting information in relation to the introduction of slaves into the United States, Jan. 7, 1820 (16th Cong., 1st Sess., Ex. Papers 36). Washington, 1820.

Department of Navy. *Official Records of the Union and Confederate Navies*, Series II, Vols. I-III, Washington, 1894-1927.

Department of Treasury. Letter from the Secretary of Treasury, transmitting information in relation to the illicit introduction of slaves into the United States; with a statement of the measures which have been taken to prevent the same (16th Cong., 1st Sess., Ex. Papers 42). Washington, 1820.

Extracts from documents in the Departments of State, of the Treasury, and of the Navy, in relation to the illicit introduction of slaves into the United States (15th Cong., 2nd Sess., House Doc. 100). Washington, 1819.

Alabama. Journal of the House of Representatives of, 17th sess.
Governor Gayle's message to the Alabama Legislature.
Mississippi. Dept. of archives and history.
    The Mississippi Territorial Archives, 1798-1803, Nashville,
    1905.

B. OFFICIAL REPORTS AND PUBLICATIONS OF THE ANTI-
SLAVERY, COLONIZATION, MANUMISSION, ETC., SOCIETIES

Alabama State Colonization Society
    Constitution of the Alabama State Colonization Society, and
    the officers for 1852, with an address, by the President to the
    people of the State.

American Anti-Slavery Society
    Annual Report . . . 1st-6th, 22-28; 1834-39, 1855-61. New
        York, 1834-61 (12 vols.). (Title varies slightly: 1834-
        37, Annual report of the American Anti-Slavery Society.
        1838-61, Annual report of the American Anti-Slavery
        Society by the executive committee.) Nos. 8-21 never
        published.
    The Declaration of Sentiments and Constitution of the Amer-
        ican Anti-Slavery Society. New York, 1837.
    American Slavery as it is: testimony of a thousand witnesses.
        Prepared by Theodore Weld. New York, 1839.
    Anti-Slavery Tracts
        New York, published by the American Anti-Slavery So-
        ciety. 1855-1856.
                            Contents:
    No.
        1. "The United States and the Constitution."
        2. "White Slavery in the United States."
        3. Frothingham, O. B. "Colonization."
        4. Higginson, T. W. "Does Slavery Christianize the
            Negroes?"
        5. Palfry, J. G. "The inter-state slave trade."
        6. Hildreth, R. "The 'ruin' of Jamaica."
        7. "Revolution is the only remedy for slavery."
        9. "Influence of slavery upon the white population."

10. Burleigh, C. C. "Slavery and the North."

11. Hodges, C. E. "Disunion our wisdom and our duty."

13. Stowe, Mrs. H. E. "The two altars."

14. Chapman, Mrs. M. "How can I help to abolish slavery?"

15. Cabot, S. C. "What have we, as individuals, to do with slavery?"

16. Hartford, Conn. Fourth Congregational Church. The unanimous remonstrance . . . on the subject of slavery.

17. Beecher, C. "The God of the Bible against Slavery."

18. "The fugitive slave law, and its victims."

19. Whipple, C. K. "Relations of anti-slavery to religion."

20. Higginson, T. W. "A ride through Kansas."

New Series

1. Child, Mrs. L. M. "Correspondence between Lydia Maria Child and Gov. Wise."

2. "The new 'reign of terror.' "

4. "The New 'Reign of Terror' in the Slaveholding States for 1859-60."

7. Brown, J. "Testimonies."

8. Phillips, W. "The Philosophy of the abolition movement."

10. Garrison, W. L. "The 'infidelity' of abolitionism."

11. Hossack, J. "Speech."

13. "No slave hunting in the old Bay State."

14. "A fresh catalogue of Southern outrages upon Northern citizens."

15. "The fugitive slave law and its victims."

16. Channing, W. E. "Tribute of William Ellery Channing to the American Abolitionists, for the vindication of Freedom of Speech."

Letter to Louis Kossuth, concerning freedom and slavery in the United States. In behalf of the American anti-slavery society. Boston, 1852.

A Letter "The District of Columbia" to the people of the United States by the Executive committee. n.d.

The Constitution of the American Anti-Slavery Society, with the Declarations of the National Anti-Slavery convention, at Philadelphia, Dec., 1833, and the address to the public. New York, 1838.

Platform of the American Anti-Slavery Society and its auxiliaries. New York, 1853. Later edition, New York, 1855.

American Colonization Society

Address of the Managers of the American Colonization Society to the People of the United States. (Adopted at meeting of June 19, 1832.) Washington, 1832.

Annual report of the American colonization society, with the minutes of the annual meeting and of the board of directors. 1st-91st, 93rd, 1818-1910. Washington, 1818-1910 (91 vols.).

Note: 1st-22nd and 26th reports, 1818-1838, 1853, bear the earlier name of the society: American society for colonizing the free people of color of the United States. General index to 1st-18th reports in the 18th report.

Colonization society. Memorial. Washington, 1828.

Condition of the American colored population, and of the colony at Liberia. Boston, 1833.

Emigrants from New Orleans. New York, 1835.

The memorial of the American Colonization Society. Washington, 1826.

A view of exertions lately made for the purpose of colonizing free people of color, in the United States, in Africa, or elsewhere. Washington, 1817.

Memorial of the Semi-Centennial Anniversary of the American Colonization Society—celebrated at Washington, Jan. 15, 1867 (with Documents concerning Liberia). Washington, 1867.

Report of Committee at an adjourned meeting of the friends of the American Colonization Society, in Worcester County. Held in Worcester, Dec. 18, 1830 (Proceedings, etc.). Worcester, 1831.

American and Foreign Anti-Slavery Society

Address of the inhabitants of New Mexico and California, on the omission by Congress to provide them with territorial governments, and on the social and political evils of slavery. New York, American and Foreign Anti-Slavery Society, 1849.

Address to the non-slaveholders of the South, on the social and political evils of slavery. New York, 1849 (1st ed., N. Y., 1843, signed by Lewis Tappan).

Address to the Anti-Slavery Christians of the United States signed by Arthur and Lewis Tappan, Chas. Francis Adams, John Pierpont, Wm. Tay, J. R. Gibbings, and 36 others. New York, 1852.

Annual Reports . . . with Addresses and Resolutions, 8-11, 13; 1848-51, 1853. New York, 1848-53.

American Convention of Abolition Societies.

"Reports of the American Convention of Abolition Societies on Negroes and on Slavery, their Appeals to Congress, and their Addresses to the Citizens of the United States," *Journal of Negro History,* VI (July, 1921), 310-74. Note: Above reference reprints the original reports.

American Convention for Promoting the Abolition of Slavery and Improving the Condition of the African Race

Address of the American convention for promoting the abolition of slavery and improving the condition of the African race, assembled at Philadelphia, in Jan., 1804, to the people of the United States. Signed: Mathew Franklin, Pres. Philadelphia, 1804.

Minutes . . . 1794-1837. Philadelphia, Etc., 1794-1839. 25 vols. (Library of Congress set incomplete, lacking 11th, 1806; 15th, 1817; 16th, 1819; 18th, 1823; and adjourned meeting of 1826.)

American Tract Society

The Tract Society and Slavery. Hartford, 1859.

American Union for the Relief and Improvement of the Colored Race

Exposition of the objects and plans of the American Union for the relief and improvement of the colored race (published by the Executive Committee). Boston, 1835.

Anti-Slavery Convention of American Women

An appeal of the women of the nominally free states, issued by an anti-slavery convention of American women. Boston, 1838.

Proceedings of the Anti-Slavery convention of American women, held in the city of New York, May 9th, 10th, 11th and 12th, 1837. New York, 1837.

Proceedings of the Anti-Slavery convention of American Women held in Philadelphia, May 15, 16, 17, 18, 1838. Philadelphia, 1838.

Proceedings of the third Anti-Slavery convention of American women held in Philadelphia, May 1st, 2nd, 3rd, 1839. Philadelphia, 1839.

An address from the Convention of American women, to the Society of Friends, on the subject of slavery. Philadelphia, 1840.

Anti-Slavery Society

Preamble and Constitution of the Anti-Slavery Society of Hanover College and Indiana Seminary. Hanover, Ind., 1836.

Association for the Religious Instruction of the Negroes, in Liberty County, Georgia

Eleventh Annual Report of the Association for the Religious Instruction of the Negroes in Liberty County, Georgia. Savannah, 1846.

Thirteenth annual report of the Association for the religious instruction of the negroes, in Liberty County, Georgia. Savannah, Ga., 1848.

Auxiliary Society of Frederick County, Virginia, for Colonizing the Free People of Colour in the United States

Annual report of the Auxiliary society of Frederick County, Va., for colonizing the free people of colour in the United States. Winchester, Va., 1820.

Boston Female Anti-Slavery Society

Report of the Boston Female Anti-Slavery Society; with a concise statement of Events, previous and subsequent to the Annual meeting of 1835. Boston, 1836.

British and Foreign Anti-Slavery Society (London)

American slavery. Address of the committee of the British and foreign anti-slavery society to the moderator. Office bearers and members of the Free Church of Scotland. London, 1846.

American slavery and British Christians, a tract containing reprints of the addresses to Christians of all denominations . . . issued by the committee of the British and foreign anti-slavery society in April, 1853 and 1854. London, 1854.

Proceedings of the General Anti-Slavery Convention called by the Committee of the British and Foreign Anti-Slavery Society, and held in London from June 13 to June 20, 1843. Edited by J. F. Johnson. London, 1843.

The crisis in the United States. London, 1862.

Christian Anti-Slavery Convention

The minutes of the Christian anti-slavery convention, Assembled April 17-20th, 1850. Cincinnati, 1850.

Cincinnati Colonization Society

Proceedings of the Cincinnati colonization society, at the annual meeting Jan. 14, 1833. Cincinnati, 1833.

Colonization Society of the State of Connecticut

An address to the public by the manager of the Colonization society of Connecticut. New Haven, 1828.

Sixth Annual report of the Managers of the Colonization society of the State of Connecticut, May, 1833. Hartford, 1833. Bulletin.

Colonization Society of Virginia (1849-1858)

Minutes of the society. Manuscript in the Collection of the Virginia Historical Society. Richmond.

Sixth annual report of the Colonization society of Virginia. Richmond, 1837.

Convention of Abolitionists, West Bloomfield, N. Y., 1847

An address from the American abolitionists to the friends of the slave in Great Britain. Newcastle-on-Tyne, 1847.

Convention of the Friends of Freedom in the Eastern and Middle States, Boston, 1845

Proceedings of the great convention of the friends of freedom in the eastern and middle states, held in Boston, Oct. 1-3, 1845. Lowell, 1845.

Free Soil Association of the District of Columbia

Address of the Free Soil Association of Columbia to the people of the United States; together with a memorial to Congress, 1060 inhabitants of the District of Columbia praying for the gradual abolition of Slavery. Washington, 1849.

Friends, Society of. Philadelphia Yearly meeting

A brief statement of the Rise and Progress of the Religious Society of Friends, Against Slavery and the Slave Trade. Philadelphia, 1843.

Friends, Society of. New England Yearly meeting

Address of the yearly meeting of Friends for New England, held in Rhode Island, in the sixth month, 1837, to its own members, and those of other Christian communities. New Bedford, 1837.

Address of the yearly meeting of the religious society of Friends, held in the city of New York, in the sixth month, 1852, to the professors of Christianity in the United States, on the subject of slavery. New York, 1852.

An appeal to the professors of Christianity, in the southern states and elsewhere, on the subject of slavery; by the representatives of the yearly meeting of Friends for New England. Providence, 1842.

Friends, Society of. New York Yearly meeting

An address of Friends of the yearly meeting of New York, to the citizens of the United States, especially to those of the southern states, upon the subject of slavery. New York, 1844.

Friends, Society of.

The appeal of the religious society of Friends in Pennsylvania, New Jersey, Delaware, etc., to their fellow-citizens of the United States on behalf of the coloured races. Philadelphia, 1858.

An exposition of the African slave trade from the year 1840, to 1850, inclusive. Prepared from official documents, and published by the representatives of the religious society of Friends, in Penn., N. J., and Del. Philadelphia, 1851.

Illinois Anti-Slavery Convention

Proceedings of the Illinois Anti-Slavery Convention, held Oct. 26-28, 1837, at Upper Alton, Ill. Alton, 1838.

Indiana State Anti-Slavery Society

Proceedings of the Indiana Convention, assembled to organize a State Anti-Slavery Society, held at Milton, Ind., Sept. 12, 1838. Cincinnati, 1838.

Kentucky Colonization Society

The proceedings of the colonization society of Kentucky, with the address of the Hon. Daniel Mayes, at the annual meeting, at Frankfort, Dec. 1, 1831. Frankfort, 1831.

Ladies' Association, Auxiliary to the American Colonization Society, Philadelphia

First annual report of the Ladies' Association, auxiliary to the American Colonization Society. Presented May 7, 1833. Philadelphia, 1833.

Manumission Society of North Carolina

An address to the People of North Carolina on the evils of Slavery. By the friends of Liberty & Equality. Greensborough, N. C., 1830.

Maryland. Board of Managers for Removing the Free People of Color

Colonization of the free colored population of Maryland, and of such slaves as may hereafter become free. Statement of facts for the use of those who have not yet reflected on this important subject (managers appointed by the state of Maryland). Baltimore, 1832.

Maryland Colonization Society

African colonization. Proceedings of a meeting of the friends of African colonization, held in the city of Baltimore, Oct. 17, 1827.

Maryland Society for Promoting the Abolition of Slavery

Constitution of the Maryland society for promoting the abolition of slavery, and the relief of free Negroes, and others, unlawfully held in bondage. Baltimore, 1789.

Maryland State Colonization Society

Address of the board of managers. Baltimore, 1833.

Communication from the board of managers to the president and members of the convention now assembled in Baltimore, in reference to the subject of colonization. Baltimore, 1841.

Massachusetts Anti-Slavery Society

An address to the abolitionists of Massachusetts, on the subject of political action. By the board of managers. Boston, 1838.

Annual Report . . . 1st-21st, 1833-1853. 21 vols., Boston, 1833-1853.

> Note: Title varies: 1833-35, Annual report of the Board of Managers of the New England Anti-Slavery Society; 1836-53, Annual report of the Board of Managers of the Massachusetts Anti-Slavery Society. The reports were presented in January and cover the years 1832-52 together with the reports of the annual meetings for 1833-53. Continued after 1853 by the American Anti-Slavery Society.

Proceedings of the Massachusetts Anti-Slavery Society at the annual meetings held in 1854, 1855, 1856; with the treasurer's reports and general agent's annual statements. Boston, 1856.

Massachusetts Colonization Society

Proceedings of the annual meeting of the Massachusetts colonization society, held Feb. 7, 1833. Boston, 1833.

A Statement of facts respecting the American Colonization Society and the colony at Liberia. Princeton, N. J., 1831.

Massachusetts State Disunion Convention, Worcester, 1857.
> Proceedings of the state disunion convention held at Worcester, Mass., Jan. 15, 1857. Boston, 1857.

New England Anti-Slavery Convention
> Proceedings of the New England Anti-Slavery Convention held in Boston on May 27-29, 1834. Boston, 1834.
> Proceedings of the New England Anti-Slavery Convention held in Boston, May 24-26, 1836. Boston, 1836.
> Proceedings of the fourth New England Anti-Slavery Convention held in Boston, May 30-31 and June 1-2, 1837.
> Second annual Report of the Board of Managers with an appendix (of 18 pages of W. L. Gaurson's report of his mission to England). Boston, 1834.

New England Emigrant Aid Company, Boston
> Two tracts for the times. The one entitled "Negro-Slavery, no evil," by B. F. Stringfellow of Missouri; the other, An answer to the inquiry "Is it expedient to introduce Slavery into Kansas?" by D. R. Goodloe, of N. C. Boston, 1855.

New Hampshire Anti-Slavery Convention
> Proceedings of the (first) convention, Nov. 1834. Includes an Address to the People of New Hampshire and a description by an eye witness of the Washington Slave market. Concord, 1834.

New Jersey Colonization Society
> Proceedings of the 1st-2nd annual meeting of the N. J. Colonization Society. Held at Princeton, July 11, 1825, and July 10, 1826. 2 vols. Princeton, 1825-26.

New Jersey Society for Promoting the Abolition of Slavery
> Address of the president of the New Jersey Society for promoting the abolition of slavery to the general meeting at Trenton, Sept. 26, 1804. Trenton, 1804.
> Constitution with extract of laws, 1786-88. Burlington, 1793.

New York City Anti-Slavery Society
> Address of the New York City Anti-Slavery Society to the people of the city of New York. New York, 1833.

New York State Anti-Slavery Society

Annual report presented to the New York Anti-Slavery Society by its Executive committee. First, May 12th, 1854. New York, 1854.

Proceedings of the first annual meeting of . . . convened at Utica, Oct. 19, 1836.

Proceedings of the New York Anti-Slavery Convention, held at Utica, Oct. 21 and the New York State Anti-Slavery Society, held at Perboro', Oct. 22, 1835. New York, 1835.

New York State Colonization Society

Address of the New York City Colonization Society to the public. New York, 1834.

Note: The colonization society of the city of New York, founded in 1831, was incorporated in 1855 as the New York State Colonization Society.

African Colonization. Proceedings of the New York State Colonization Society; together with an address to the public, from the managers thereof. Albany, 1831.

African Colonization. Proceedings, on the formation of the New York State Colonization Society; together with an address to the public, from the managers thereof. Albany, 1829.

Third annual report with proceedings of annual meeting, May, 1835. New York, 1835.

Seventh Annual report. New York, 1839.

Fourteenth Annual Report. New York, 1846.

Eighteenth Annual Report. New York, 1850.

Twenty-eighth Annual Report of the Board of Managers. New York, 1860.

Emigration to Liberia. One-thousand applicants for a passage to Liberia in 1848. An appeal in behalf of two-hundred slaves liberated by Captain Isaac Ross. A brief history of the Ross slaves. New York, 1848.

Ohio Anti-Slavery Society

Condition of the people of color in the State of Ohio. With interesting anecdotes. Boston, 1839.

Memorial of the Ohio Anti-Slavery Society to the General Assembly of the State of Ohio. Cincinnati, 1838.

Report on the condition of the people of color in the state of Ohio. From the proceedings of the Ohio Anti-Slavery Society held at Putnam, on the 22nd, 23rd, and 24th of April, 1835. Putnam, 1835.

Ohio State Colonization Society

A brief exposition of the views of the Society for the colonization of free persons of color, in Africa; published under the direction of the board of managers of the Ohio State Colonization Society. Addressed to the citizens of Ohio. Columbus, 1827.

Pennsylvania Colonization Society

Addresses delivered in the hall of the House of Representatives, Harrisburg, Pa. on April 6, 1852, by William V. Petit, esq., and Rev. John P. Durbin, D. D. Published by the order of the Pennsylvania Colonization Society. Philadelphia, 1852.

Report of the board of managers of the Pennsylvania Colonization Society. Philadelphia, 1830.

Reports of the board of managers of the Pennsylvania Colonization Society with an introduction and appendix. Philadelphia, 1831.

Pennsylvania Society for Promoting the Abolition of Slavery

An historical memoir of the Pennsylvania society, for promoting the abolition of slavery; the relief of free Negroes unlawfully held in bondage, and for improving the conditions of the African race. Compiled from the minutes of the society and other official documents, by Edward Needles, and published by the authority of the society. Philadelphia, 1848.

Memorial presented to the Congress of the United States of America by the different societies instituted for promoting the abolition of slavery, in the states of Rhode Island, Conn., New York, Penn., Md., and Virginia. Philadelphia, 1792.

The present state and condition of the free people of color, of the city of Philadelphia and adjoining districts, as exhibited by the reports of a committee of the Pennsylvania society for promoting the abolition of slavery etc., Jan. 5, 1838. Philadelphia, 1838.

A review of a pamphlet, entitled "An appeal to the public on behalf of a house of refuge for colored juvenile delinquents." Philadelphia, 1847.

To the people of color in the state of Pennsylvania. Philadelphia, 1838.

Pennsylvania State Anti-Slavery Society

Proceedings of the Pennsylvania Convention, assembled to organize a state anti-slavery society, at Harrisburg, on the 31st of Jan. and the 1st, 2nd and 3rd of Feb., 1837. Philadelphia, 1837.

Philadelphia. Anti-Slavery Convention

Proceedings of the anti-slavery convention, assembled at Philadelphia, Dec. 4-6, 1833. Philadelphia, 1833.

Southern and Western Liberty Convention

Principles and measures of true Democracy. The address of the Southern and Western Liberty Convention, held at Cincinnati, June 11, 12, 1845, to the people of the United States; also, the letter of Elihu Burritt to the convention. Cincinnati, 1845.

Western Methodist Anti-Slavery Convention

Proceedings of the Western Methodist Anti-Slavery Convention, held in Cincinnati, Oct. 20, 1841. Cincinnati, 1841.

C. CONTEMPORARY NEWSPAPERS, PERIODICALS, PAMPHLETS, AND PETITIONS

Abbey, R., "Cotton and the Cotton Plantings," *DeBow's Review*, III (January, 1847).

"Africa in America," *Southern Literary Messenger*, XXII (January, 1856).

African Observer, The

Edited by Enoch Lewis, Vol. I, April, 1827-March, 1828. Philadelphia, 1827-28.

African Repository, The
> Published by the American Colonization Society. Vols. I-LXVII (monthly, 1825-74; semi-monthly, Feb., 1839-Feb., 1842; quarterly, 1875-1892, except July, 1880-June, 1881, monthly). Washington, 1826-1892.

African Repository and Colonial Journal
> January-December, 1846. Washington, 1846.

American Anti-Slavery Almanac, The
> 1836-1839 numbered: Vol. I, nos. 1-4. 1836-1838 edited by Nathaniel Southard; 1843 compiled by L. M. Child. The Imprint varies: 1837, Boston, N. Southard & D. K. Hitchcock; 1838, Boston, I. Knapp; 1839, Published for the American Anti-Slavery Society, New York.

"American Slavery in 1857," *Southern Literary Messenger*, XXV (August, 1857).

Anti-Slavery Bugle
> Published weekly by the Ohio American Anti-Slavery Society at New Lisbon, Ohio; later published at Salem, Ohio. June 20, 1845-June 8, 1849.

Anti-Slavery Examiner, The
> Published by the American Anti-Slavery Society. New York, 1837-1845.

Anti-Slavery Record
> Published by the American Anti-Slavery Society. Vols. I-III; January, 1835-December, 1837. New York, 1835-1838.

Anti-Slavery Reporter
> Monthly magazine printed for the London Society for the mitigation and abolition of slavery in the British Dominions. Vol. I, June, 1825-1827, London, 1827. Vol. III, Feb.-Oct. 5, 1830, London, 1830.

Baptist Anti-Slavery Correspondent
> Edited by Cyrus P. Grosvenor, and published by the Executive Committee of the American Baptist Anti-Slavery Convention. Worcester, Mass., Vol. I, no. 1, Feb., 1841; no. 2, April, 1841.

"The Black and White Races of Men," *DeBow's Review*, XXX (April, 1861).

"The Black Race in North America," *Southern Literary Messenger*, XXI (November, 1855).

Blanchard, J., and Rice, N. L., *A Debate on Slavery held in the City of Cincinnati on the 1st., 2nd., 3rd., and 6th., days of October, 1845*, Cincinnati, 1846.

Campbell, John, "Negro-Mania," *DeBow's Review*, XII (May, 1852).

"Canaan Identified with the Ethiopian," *Southern Quarterly Review*, II O. S. (October, 1842).

Cartwright, Samuel A., "Education, Labor, and Wealth of the South," *DeBow's Review*, XXVII (September, 1859).

——, "How to Save the Republic," *DeBow's Review*, XI (August, 1851).

——, "Negro Freedom Impossible," *DeBow's Review*, XXX (May & June, 1861).

——, "On the Caucasians and Africans," *DeBow's Review*, XXV (July, 1858).

"Channing's Duty of the Free States," *Southern Quarterly Review*, II (July, 1842).

Charter Oak
Magazine published by the Connecticut Anti-Slavery Society. Vol. I, no. 1, March, 1838. Hartford, Conn., 1838.

Christian Statesman
Weekly organ of the American Colonization Society. Dedicated to "African Colonization and civilization, to literature and general intelligence." August 9, 1851-March 13, 1852. Washington, 1851-1852.

Cocke, William Archer, "Types of Mankind," *Southern Literary Messenger*, XX (November, 1854).

Colonizationist and Journal of Freedom, The
Magazine published by George W. Light, April, 1833-April, 1834. Boston, 1834.

Danson, I. T., "Connection between American Slavery and British Cotton Manufacture," *DeBow's Review*, XXII (March, 1857).

Deming, D. D., "The Power of Cotton," *DeBow's Review*, XXII (May, 1857).

Dew, Thomas R., "Address on the Influence of the Republican System of Government upon Literature and Development of Character," *Southern Literary Messenger*, II (March, 1836).

———, "Slavery in the Virginia Legislature, 1831-1832," *DeBow's Review*, XX (March, 1856).

"Domestic Slavery Considered as a Scriptural Institution," *Southern Literary Messenger*, XI (September, 1845).

Dunn, Jacob Piatt (editor), "Slavery Petitions and Papers," *Indiana Historical Society Publications*, Vol. II, no. 12, Indianapolis, 1894.

"Early Congressional Discussions on Slavery," *DeBow's Review*, XXIII (July, 1857).

Emancipator, The

> Seven numbers issued monthly, April to October, 1820. Published by Elihu Embree, Jonesborough, Tenn., 1820. A reprint of *The Emancipator*, "to which are added a biographical sketch of Elihu Embree, author and publisher of *The Emancipator*, and two hitherto unpublished antislavery memorials bearing the signature of Elihu Embree," was published by B. H. Murphy, Nashville, Tenn., 1932.

"A Few Thoughts on Slavery," *Southern Literary Messenger*, XX (April, 1854).

Fisher, Elwood, "The North and the South," *DeBow's Review*, VII (October, 1849).

Fitzhugh, George, "The Conservative Principle," *DeBow's Review*, XXII (April, 1857).

———, "Southern Thought," *DeBow's Review*, XXIII (October, 1857).

"Free Negroes in Hayti," *DeBow's Review*, XXVII (November, 1859).

Genius of Universal Emancipation, The

> A monthly periodical containing original essays, documents and facts relative to the subject of African Slavery. Edited by Benjamin Lundy. Founded at Greenville, Tenn., 1821, but was later moved to Baltimore. Greenville, Tenn., and Baltimore, Md., 1821-1836.

Hammond, James H., "Letters on Slavery," *DeBow's Review*, VII (December, 1849).

Harper, William, "Memoir on Slavery," *DeBow's Review*, X (January, 1851).

Holcombe, William H., "Characteristics and Capabilities of the Negro Race," *Southern Literary Messenger*, XXXIII (1861).

Human Rights
  Monthly publication of the American Anti-Slavery Society. December, 1837, deals with Lovejoy. New York, 1837.

Jackson, L. P. (collector), "Manumission Papers of Petersburg, Virginia," *Journal of Negro History*, XIII (October, 1928).

Johnson, J. H. (collector), "Anti-Slavery Petitions presented to the Virginia Legislature by various Counties," *Journal of Negro History*, XII (October, 1927).

Kettell, T. P., "The Future of the South," *DeBow's Review*, X (February, 1851).

Kneeland, Samuel, Jr., "The Hybrid Races," *DeBow's Review*, XIX (November, 1855).

Liberator, The, Boston, Jan. 1, 1831-Dec. 29, 1865. Edited by William Lloyd Garrison.

Liberty Bell, The, Boston, 1845. An abolition annual.

"Management of a Southern Plantation," *DeBow's Review*, XXII (January, 1857).

"Management of Negroes," *DeBow's Review*, XI (October, 1851).

"Management of Negroes upon Southern Estates," *DeBow's Review*, X (June, 1851).

"Moral and Intellectual Diversity of Races," *DeBow's Review*, XXI (July, 1856).

"The Negro," *DeBow's Review*, III (May, 1847).

"The Negro Races," *Southern Literary Messenger*, XXXI (July, 1860).

New York Colonization Journal
  August, 1851. Four-page journal containing interesting articles on Slave Trade, Liberia, Fugitive Slaves in Canada, etc. New York, 1851.

Niles Weekly Register . . ., Vols. I-LXXV; September 7, 1811-June 7, 1849. Baltimore, 1811-1849.

Norfolk Herald, 1831.

North Star, The
>Periodical edited by Frederick Douglass; subsequently changed name to "Frederick Douglass' Paper." Rochester, N. Y., 1847-1850.

Nott, Josiah C., "Life Insurance at the South," *DeBow's Review,* III (May, 1847).

————, "Statistics of Southern Slave Population," *DeBow's Review,* IV (November, 1847).

"On Slavery," *DeBow's Review,* XVIII (April, 1855).

"On the Unity of the Human Race," *Southern Quarterly Review,* X (October, 1854).

Owen, Thomas M., "An Alabama Protest against Abolitionism in 1835," *Gulf States Historical Magazine,* II (July, 1903).

Perkins, John, "Relation of Master and Slaves in Louisiana and the South," *DeBow's Review,* XV (September, 1853).

Publicola (pseud.), "The Present Aspects of Abolitionism," *Southern Literary Messenger,* XIII (July, 1847).

Quarterly Anti-Slavery Magazine
>Edited by Elizar Wright, Oct., 1835-Jan., 1837. Published by the American Anti-Slavery Society. New York, 1835-1837.

Quarterly Christian Spectator
>Magazine containing articles dealing with slavery, etc., Vol. VIII, 1836. New Haven, 1836.

Richmond Enquirer, August 30, 1831.

Richmond Whig, September 26, 1831.

Roane, A. S., "Reply to Abolition Objections to Slavery," *DeBow's Review,* XX (June, 1856).

Ruffin, Edmund, "Consequences of the Abolition Agitation," *DeBow's Review,* XXII (June, 1857).

————, "Liberia and the Colonization Society," *DeBow's Review,* XXVII (October, 1859).

"Slavery at the South," *DeBow's Review,* VII (November, 1849).

Smith, A. A., "A Southern Confederacy," *DeBow's Review*, XXVI (May, 1859).

Southron (pseud.), "Political Religionism," *Southern Literary Messenger*, IV (September, 1838).

————, "Thoughts on Slavery," *Southern Literary Messenger*, IV (December, 1838).

"A Summary View of America," *Blackwood's Magazine*, XVI (December, 1824). London.

Tarver, M. "Domestic Manufacturers in the South and West," *DeBow's Review*, III (March, 1847).

Tourist, The
A literary and anti-slavery journal. Printed under the superintendence of the Agency Anti-Slavery Society. Vol. I, nos. 1-44; Sept. 17, 1832-May 27, 1833. London, 1833.

Walker, David, *Walker's Appeal*, Boston, 1830.

Walker, Robert J., "Appeal for the Union," *DeBow's Review*, XXI (December, 1856).

Wesleyan Anti-Slavery Review, The
Printed in Boston. Vol. I, 1838, contains an appeal to the Methodist Episcopal Church by Rev. O. Scott. Boston, 1838.

"William Chambers on Slavery," *DeBow's Review*, XVIII (April, 1855).

D. Letters, Diaries, Autobiographies, Memoirs, Speeches and Writings

Adams, John Quincy, *The Diary of John Quincy Adams, 1794-1845*, Allan Nevins (editor), New York, 1928.

Calhoun, John C., *Correspondence of John C. Calhoun*, edited by J. Franklin Jameson, Washington, 1900.

————, *The Works of John C. Calhoun* (edited by Richard K. Crallé), 5 vols., New York, 1853-1855.

Child, Lydia Maria, *Correspondence between Lydia Maria Child, and Gov. Wise and Mrs. Mason of Virginia*, New York, 1860.

Colton, Calvin, *Life, Correspondence and Speeches of Henry Clay*, 6 vols., New York, 1857.

Davis, Jefferson, *Jefferson Davis, Constitutionalist, His Letters, Papers, and Speeches*, Dunbar Rowland (editor), 10 vols., Jackson, Miss., 1923.

Earle, Thomas, *The Life, Travels and Opinions of Benjamin Lundy, including his Journeys to Texas and Mexico; with a sketch of Contemporary events, and a notice of the Revolution in Hayti* (compiled under the direction and on behalf of his children), Philadelphia, 1847.

Garrison, William Lloyd, *Selections from the Writings and Speeches of*, Boston, 1852.

Grayson, William J., *The Hireling and the Slave, and Other Poems*, Charleston, 1856.

Jefferson, Thomas, *The Writings of Thomas Jefferson*, Paul Leicester Ford (editor), 10 vols., New York, 1892-1899.

———, *The Writings of Thomas Jefferson*, A. A. Lipscomb and A. E. Bergh (editors), 20 vols., Washington, 1917.

Kemble, Frances Anne, *Journal of a Residence on a Georgia Plantation, 1838-1839*, New York, 1863.

"Letters to Anti-Slavery Workers and Agencies," *Journal of Negro History*, X (July, 1925).

Lovejoy, Joseph C., and Owen, *Memoir of Rev. Elijah P. Lovejoy; who was murdered in defence of the Press at Alton, Ill., Nov. 7, 1837*, New York, 1837.

Mann, Horace, *Slavery: Letters and Speeches*, Boston, 1851.

Monaghan, Frank (collector), "Anti-Slavery Papers of John Hay," *Journal of Negro History*, XVII (October, 1932).

Nott, Josiah C., *Two Lectures on the Connection Between the Biblical and Physical History of Man*, New York, 1849.

Orme, William (editor), *The Practical Works of Reverend William Baxter*, London, 1830.

Phillips, Wendell, *Speeches, Lectures, Letters*, Boston, 1864.

Russell, William Howard, *My Diary, North and South*, Boston, 1863.

Smedes, Susan D., *A Southern Planter*, 4th ed., New York, 1890.

Sumner, Charles, *The Barbarism of Slavery*, New York, 1863.

Tappan, Lewis, "Correspondence of Lewis Tappan and others with the British and Foreign Anti-Slavery Society," *Journal of Negro History*, XII (April-July, 1927).

————, *A Side-Light on Anglo-American Relations, 1839-1858*, A. H. Abel and F. J. Klingberg (editors), Lancaster, Penn., 1927.

Webster, Daniel, *Works of Daniel Webster*, 6 vols., Boston, 1851.

Weld-Grimké Letters, edited by Barnes, Gilbert, and Dumond, Dwight L., 2 vols., New York, 1934.

Whitefield, George, *A Select Collection of Letters of Late Reverend George Whitefield . . .*, London, 1772.

Williams, James, *Letters on Slavery from the Old World*, Nashville, 1861.

E. Controversial Books and Collections Dealing with Slavery

Abbott, John Stevens Cabot, *South and North*, New York, 1860.

Adams, Nehemiah, *A Southside View of Slavery*, Boston, 1854.

Adger, John Bailey, *The Christian Doctrine of Human Rights and Slavery*, Columbia, 1848.

Armistead, Wilson (compiler), *Five Hundred Thousand Strokes for Freedom*, or *Leed's Anti-Slavery Tracts*, London, 1853.

Armstrong, George Dodd, *The Christian Doctrine of Slavery*, New York, 1857.

Bachman, John, *The Doctrine of the Unity of the Human Race, Examined on the Principles of Science*, Charleston, 1850.

Barnes, Albert, *An Inquiry into the Scriptural Views of Slavery*, Philadelphia, 1846.

————, *The Church and Slavery*, Philadelphia, 1857.

Birney, James G., *A Collection of Valuable Documents, being Birney's Vindication of Abolitionists—Protest of the American Anti-Slavery Society—to the People of the U. S., or, to Such Americans as Value their Rights, etc.*, Boston, 1836.

————, *The American Churches, the Bulwarks of American Slavery*, Boston, 1843.

————, *The Sinfulness of Slaveholding in all Circumstances, Tested by Reason and Scripture*, Detroit, 1846.

Bledsoe, Albert Taylor, *An Essay on Liberty and Slavery*, Philadelphia, 1856.

Bourne, George, *An Address to the Presbyterian Church, enforcing the duty of excluding all slaveholders from the "communion of saints,"* New York, 1833.

———, *The Book and Slavery Irreconcilable, with Animadversions upon Dr. Smith's Philosophy,* Philadelphia, 1816.

———, *A Condensed Anti-Slavery Bible Argument: by a citizen of Virginia,* New York, 1845.

———, *Slavery Illustrated in its Effects upon Women and Domestic Society,* Boston, 1837.

———, *Man-Stealing and Slavery Denounced by the Presbyterian and Methodist Churches,* Boston, 1834.

———, *Picture of Slavery in the United States of America,* Middletown, Conn., 1834.

———, *A Condensed Anti-Slavery Bible Argument,* New York, 1845.

Bremer, Fredrika, *Homes of the New World,* 2 vols., New York, 1853.

Brisbane, William Henry, *Slaveholding Examined in the Light of the Holy Bible,* Philadelphia, 1847.

Brown, Isaac V. A., *Slavery Irreconcilable with Christianity and Sound Reason, or An Anti-Slavery Bible Argument,* Trenton, 1858.

Cairnes, John Elliott, *The Slave Power: Its Character, Career, and Probable Designs! being an Attempt to explain the real issues in the American Conflict,* New York, 1862.

Campbell, John, *Negro Mania, an Examination of the Falsely Assumed Equality of the Races of Men,* Philadelphia, 1851.

Cartwright, S. A., *Essays, being Inductions from the Baconian Philosophy and Proving the Truth of the Bible and the Justice and Benevolence of the Decree Dooming Canaan to be a Servant of Servants,* Natchez, 1843.

Chambers, William, *American Slavery and Color,* London, 1857.

———, *Things as They Are in America,* London, 1854.

Channing, William Ellery, *Duty of the Free States,* Boston, 1842.

———, *Slavery,* Boston, 1835.

Cheever, George B., *God Against Slavery! and the Freedom and Duty of the Pulpit to Rebuke it, as a Sin against God,* Cincinnati, American Reform Tract and Book Soc. publication, n.d.

———, *The Guilt of Slavery and the Crime of Slaveholding Demonstrated from the Hebrew and Greek Scriptures*, New York, 1860.

———, *Responsibility of Church and Ministry respecting the Sin of Slavery*, Boston, 1858.

Chevalier, Michael, *Society, Manners and Politics in the United States*, translated from the 3rd Paris edition, Boston, 1839.

Child, Mrs. Lydia Maria, *Anti-Slavery Catechism*, Newburyport, Mass., 1836.

———, *An Appeal in Favor of that Class of Americans Called Africans*, Boston, 1833.

Christy, David, *Cotton is King*, Cincinnati, 1855.

Cluskey, M. W. (editor), *The Political Textbook, or Encyclopedia*, Philadelphia, 1860.

Cobb, Howell, *A Scriptural Examination of the Institution of Slavery in the United States, with its Objects and Purpose*, Georgia, 1856.

Cobb, Thomas R. R., *An Inquiry into the Law of Negro Slavery in the United States of America, to which is prefixed, An Historical Sketch of Slavery*, Philadelphia, 1858.

Cochin, Augustin, *The Results of Slavery*, translated by Mary L. Booth, Boston, 1863.

Coffin, Joshua, *An Account of Some of the Principal Slave Insurrections*, New York, 1860.

Colfax, Richard H., *Evidence Against the Views of the Abolitionists*, New York, 1833.

Cooper, Thomas, *On the Constitution of the United States and the Questions that have arisen under it*, Columbia, 1826.

Dalcho, Frederick, *Practical Considerations founded on the Scriptures relative to the Slave Population of South Carolina*, Charleston, 1823.

DeBow, James Dunwoody Brown, *Industrial Resources of the Southern and Western States*, 3 vols., New Orleans, 1852-1853.

Dew, Thomas R., *Review of the Debate in the Virginia Legislature of 1831 and 1832*, Richmond, 1832.

"Documents relating to Slavery," *Massachusetts Historical Society Proceedings*, XX (December, 1907), ser. 2.

Donnan, Elizabeth (editor), *Documents Illustrative of the Slave Trade to America*, 3 vols., Washington, 1930-1932.

Duffield, George, *A Sermon on American Slavery, its Nature and Duties of Christians in Relation to it*, Detroit, 1840.

Eliot, Chas., *The Bible and Slavery; in which the Arabic and Mosaic Discipline is considered in connection with the most Ancient Forms of Slavery; and the Pauline Code on Slavery as related to Roman Slavery and the Discipline of Apostolic Churches*, Cincinnati, 1857.

Elliott, E. N., *Cotton is King, and Pro-Slavery Arguments; comprising the writings of Hammond, Harper, Christy, Stringfellow, Hodge, Bledsoe, and Cartwright, on this important subject, with essays by the Editor on Slavery in the light of International Law*, Augusta, Ga., 1860.

Estes, Matthew, *A Defence of Negro Slavery as it Exists in the United States*, Montgomery, Ala., 1846.

Fitzhugh, George, *Cannibals All! or Slaves without Masters*, Richmond, Va., 1857.

———, *Slavery Justified: by a Southerner*, Fredericksburg, Va., 1850.

———, *Sociology for the South, or The Failure of Free Society*, Richmond, Va., 1854.

Fletcher, John, *Studies on Slavery, in Easy Lessons*, Natchez, 1852.

Foster, S. S., *The Brotherhood of Thieves; or A True Picture of the American Church and Clergy*, Boston, 1844.

Fowler, William Chauncey, *The Sectional Controversy*, New York, 1862.

Freeman, George Washington, *The Rights and Duties of Slaveholders*, Charleston, 1837.

Fuller, Richard, and Wayland, Francis, *Domestic Slavery considered as a Scriptural Institution*, 5th ed., New York, 1856.

Furman, Richard, *Exposition of the Views of the Baptists relative to the Colored Population of the United States in a Communication to the Governor of South Carolina*, Charleston, 1823.

Ganse, H. D., *Bible Slaveholding not Sinful*, New York, 1856.

Godwin, Parke, *Political Essays*, New York, 1856.

Godwyn, Morgan, *Trade Preferred Before Religion and Christ made to give place to Mammon,* London, 1865.

Goodell, William, *The American Slave Code in Theory and Practice,* New York, 1853.

———, *Views of American Constitutional Law in its bearing upon American Slavery,* Utica, N. Y., 1845.

Goodloe, Daniel Reaves, *The Southern Platform: or, Manual of Southern Sentiment on the Subject of Slavery,* Boston, 1858.

Greeley, Horace, and Cleveland, John F. (compilers), *A Political Textbook for 1860,* New York, 1860.

Green, Beriah, *The Chattel Principle,* New York, 1839.

Green, Duff, *Facts and Suggestions Relative to Finance and Currency,* Augusta, Ga., 1864.

Hall, Marshal, *The Two-Fold Slavery of the United States,* London, 1854.

Harper, William, *Memoir on Slavery,* Charleston, 1837.

Harrison, W. P. (compiler), *The Gospel Among the Slaves,* Nashville, 1893.

Hart, Albert Bushnell, *Source-Book of American History,* New York, 1925.

Hartzel, Jonas, *Bible Vindicated, A series of Essays on American Slavery,* Cincinnati, 1858.

Hatch, Reuben, *Bible Servitude reexamined, with special reference to Pro-Slavery Interpretation,* Cincinnati, 1862.

Hersey, John, *An Appeal to Christians on the Subject of Slavery* (3rd edition), Baltimore, 1853.

Hopkins, John Henry, *Scriptural, Ecclesiastical, and Historical View of Slavery, from the days of the Patriarch Abraham to the 19th century,* New York, 1864.

Hundley, Daniel Robinson, *Social Relations in Our Southern States,* New York, 1860.

Ingraham, Joseph Holt, *The Southwest: by a Yankee,* 2 vols., New York, 1835.

Jacobson, J. Mark, *The Development of American Political Thought, A Documentary History,* New York, 1932.

Janney, M., *A History of the Religious Society of Friends, from its Rise to the Year 1828,* Philadelphia, 1867.

Jay, William, *An Examination of the Mosaic Law of Servitude*, New York, 1854.

——, *An Inquiry into the Character and Tendency of the American Colonization and American Anti-Slavery Societies*, New York, 1835.

Jones, Charles C., *Religious Instruction of the Negroes in the United States*, Savannah, 1842.

Jones, John Richter, *Slavery Sanctioned by the Bible*, Philadelphia, 1861.

Kramer, J. Theophilus, *The Slave Auction*, Boston, 1859.

Livermore, George, *An Historical Research Respecting the Opinions of the Founders of the Republic on Negroes as Slaves, as Citizens, and as Soldiers*, Boston, 1862.

Lord, Nathan, *A Letter of Inquiry to Ministers of the Gospel of all Denominations on Slavery* (4th edition), Hanover, Mass., 1860.

——, *A Northern Presbyter's Second Letter to the ministers of the Gospel of all Denominations on Slavery*, Hanover, Mass., 1855.

Lyell, Sir Charles, *A Second Visit to the United States of North America*, New York and London, 1849.

McCaine, Alexander, *Slavery defended from Scripture against the Attacks of the Abolitionists*, Baltimore, 1842.

Mackay, Charles, *Life and Liberty in America*, New York, 1859.

McTyeire, Holland Nimmons, *Duties of Christian Masters* (edited by Thomas O. Summers), Nashville, 1859.

——, *Duties of Masters to Servants: three Premium Essays*, Charleston, S. C., 1851.

Madden, R. R., *A Twelve Months' Residence in the West Indies*, Philadelphia, 1835.

Martineau, Harriet, *Retrospect of Western Travel*, 2 vols., London, 1838.

——, *Society in America*, 2 vols., Paris, 1837.

Matlack, Lucius C., *The Anti-Slavery Struggle and Triumph in the Methodist Episcopal Church*, New York, 1881.

——, *The History of American Slavery and Methodism, from 1780 to 1849 . . .*, New York, 1849.

Mitchell, D. W., *Ten Years in the United States* . . ., London, 1862.

Morton, Samuel G., *Crania Americana*, Philadelphia, 1839.

Murray, Henry Anthony, *Lands of the Slave and the Free*, London, 1855.

The North and South, or Slavery and its Contrasts. A Tale of Real Life, Philadelphia, 1852.

Nott, Josiah C., and Gliddon, George R., *Types of Mankind: or, Ethnological Researches, based upon the Ancient Monuments, Paintings, Sculpture, and Crania of Races, and upon the Natural, Geographical, Philological, and Biblical History*, Philadelphia, 1854.

————, and ————, *Indigenous Races of the Earth; or, New Chapters of Ethnological Inquiry*, Philadelphia, 1857.

Noyes, John H., *History of American Socialism*, Philadelphia, 1870.

O'Connor, Charles, *Negro Slavery Not Unjust*, N. Y., 1859.

Olmsted, Frederick Law, *The Cotton Kingdom: A Traveler's Observations on Cotton and Slavery in the American Slave States*, 2 vols., New York, 1862.

————, *Journey and Explorations in the Cotton Kingdom*, London, 1861.

————, *A Journey in the Back Country*, New York, 1863.

————, *A Journey in the Seaboard Slave States*, 2 vols., New York, 1904.

————, *A Journey Through Texas*, New York, 1857.

Paulding, James K., *Slavery in the United States*, Philadelphia, 1836.

Phillips, Ulrich Bonnell (editor), *Plantation and Frontier Documents: 1649-1863, illustrative of the Industrial History in the colonial and ante-bellum South;* . . . Cleveland, 1909.

————, and Glunt, James David (editors), *Florida Plantation Records, from the papers of George Noble Jones, Missouri Historical Society Publications*, St. Louis, 1927.

Pillsbury, Parker, *The Church as it is, or the Forlorn Hope of Slavery*, Boston, 1847.

Pond, Enoch, *Slavery and the Bible*, Boston, n. d. American Tract Society publication.

Priest, Josiah, *Bible Defense of Slavery, or The Origin, History and Fortunes of the Negro Race.* Also added in same volume, *A Plan of National Colonization Adequate to the entire Removal of the Free Blacks*, by Rev. W. S. Brown, of Glasgow, Ky. Louisville, Ky., 1851.

Pro-Slavery Argument; . . . containing the several essays on the subject of, . . . By Chancellor Harper, Governor Hammond, Dr. Simms, and Professor Dew, Charleston, 1852.

Raphall, M. J., *Bible View of Slavery, A Discourse,* New York, 1861.

Republican Scrap Book . . ., Boston, 1856.

Romans, Bernard, *A Concise Natural History of East and West Florida*, Vol. I, New York, 1775.

Ross, Fred. A., *Position of the Southern Church in Relation to Slavery,* New York, 1857.

————, *Slavery Ordained by God*, Philadelphia, 1857.

Russell, Wm. Howard, *Pictures of Southern Life, Social, Political, and Military*, New York, 1861.

Sawyer, George S., *Southern Institutes: or, An Inquiry into the Origin and Early Prevalence of Slavery and the Slave Trade,* Philadelphia, 1858.

Schaff, Philip, *Slavery and the Bible, A Tract for the Times,* Chambersburg, Penn., 1861.

Seabrook, W. B., *An Essay on the Management of Slaves and especially their Religious Instruction,* Charleston, 1834.

Smith, William Andrew, *Lectures on the Philosophy and Practice of Slavery,* Nashville, 1856.

Spooner, Lysander, *The Unconstitutionality of Slavery,* Boston, 1860.

Stiles, Joseph C., *Modern Reform Examined: or, the Union of North and South on the Subject of Slavery,* Philadelphia, 1857.

————, *The National Controversy,* New York, 1861.

Stringfellow, Thornton, *Scriptural and Statistical View of Slavery,* 4th ed., Richmond, 1856.

Stroud, George McDowell, *A Sketch of the Laws Relating to Slavery in the Several States of the United States of America,* Philadelphia, 1856.

Thompson, Joseph Parish, *Teaching of the New Testament on Slavery*, New York, 1856.

――――, *A Fugitive Slave Law tried by the Old and New Testaments*, New York, 1850.

Thornton, T. C., *An Inquiry into the History of Slavery*, Washington, 1841.

Thornwell, J. H., *The Rights and Duties of Masters*, Charleston, 1850.

Van Evrie, J. H., *Negroes and negro "slavery": the first, an inferior race: the latter, its normal condition*, New York, 1861.

Wayland, Francis, *The Elements of Moral Science*, Boston, 1848.

II. SECONDARY SOURCES

A. GENERAL AND SPECIAL ACCOUNTS

Adams, C. F., *Trans-Atlantic Historical Solidarity*, Oxford, 1913.

Adams, Henry, *History of the United States*, 9 vols., New York, 1921.

Alexander, De Alva Stanwood, *A Political History of the State of New York*, 3 vols., New York, 1906.

Andrews, Charles M., *Colonial Self-Government, 1652-1689* (American Nation Series, Vol. V), New York, 1904.

Babcock, K. C., *The Rise of American Nationality, 1811-1819* (American Nation Series, Vol. XIII), New York, 1906.

Ballagh, J. C., *A History of Slavery in Virginia*, Baltimore, 1902.

Barnes, Gilbert Hobbs, *The Antislavery Impulse*, New York, 1933.

Brown, Everett Somerville, ed., *The Missouri Compromises and Presidential Politics, 1820-1825*, St. Louis, 1926.

Buckley, J. M., *History of Methodists in the United States*, New York, 1896 (American Church History Series, Vol. V).

Carpenter, Jesse Thomas, *The South as a Conscious Minority, 1789-1861: A Study in Political Thought*, New York, 1930.

Channing, Edward, *History of the United States*, 16 vols., New York, 1905-1925.

――――, *The Jeffersonian System, 1801-1811* (American Nation Series, Vol. XII), New York, 1906.

Chitwood, Oliver Perry, *A History of Colonial America*, New York, 1931.

Coulter, E. Merton, *A Short History of Georgia*, Chapel Hill, 1933.

Dodd, William E., *The Cotton Kingdom* (Chronicles of America Series, Vol. XXVII), New Haven, 1919.

Drewry, William S., *The Southampton Insurrection*, Washington, 1900.

Dumond, Dwight Lowell, *The Secession Movement, 1860-1861*, New York, 1931.

Flanders, Ralph Betts, *Plantation Slavery in Georgia*, Chapel Hill, 1933.

Flower, Frank A., *History of the Republican Party*, Springfield, Ill., 1884.

Fox, Early Lee, *American Colonization Society, 1817-1840*, Baltimore, 1919.

Garrison, George P., *Westward Extension, 1841-1850* (American Nation Series, Vol. XVII), New York, 1906.

Greene, E. B., *Provincial America, 1670-1740* (American Nation Series, Vol. VI), New York, 1904.

Hart, Albert Bushnell, *Slavery and Abolition, 1831-1841* (American Nation Series, Vol. XVI), New York, 1906.

Herbert, Hilary A., *The Abolition Crusade and its Consequences*, New York, 1912.

Herold, A. L., *James Kirke Paulding: Versatile American*, New York, 1926.

Hildreth, Richard, *History of the United States*, Vols. I-VI, New York, 1877-1880.

Jenkins, William S., *Pro-Slavery Thought in the Old South*, Chapel Hill, 1935.

Keifer, J. W., *Slavery and Four Years of War*, 2 vols., New York, 1900.

Klingberg, Frank J., *The Anti-Slavery Movement in England: A Study of English Humanitarianism*, New Haven, 1926.

Locke, Mary S., *Anti-Slavery in America from the introduction . . . to the prohibition . . . (1619-1808)*, Boston, 1901 (Radcliffe College Monographs, No. 11).

Lynch, William O., *Fifty Years of Party Warfare, 1789-1837*, Indianapolis, 1931.

McLaughlin, Andrew C., *The Confederation and the Constitution, 1783-1789* (American Nation Series, Vol. X), New York, 1904.

McMaster, John B., *History of the United States*, 8 vols., New York, 1884-1913.

McNeilly, James H., *Religion and Slavery*, Nashville, Tennessee, 1911.

Macy, Jesse, *The Anti-Slavery Crusade*, New Haven, 1919.

Merriam, C. E., *A History of American Political Theories*, New York, 1924.

Moore, Glover, "Missouri Compromise Controversy" (unpublished thesis, Vanderbilt University, Nashville, Tennessee, 1936).

Morison, S. E., *The Oxford History of the United States*, 2 vols., London, 1928.

Munford, Beverley B., *Virginia's Attitude Toward Slavery and Secession*, New York, 1909.

Muzzey, David S., and Krout, J. A., *American History for Colleges*, Boston, 1933.

Owsley, Frank L., *King Cotton Diplomacy*, Chicago, 1931.

Phillips, Ulrich Bonnell, *American Negro Slavery*, New York, 1918.

———, *Life and Labor in the Old South*, Boston, 1929.

Rhodes, James Ford, *History of the United States*, 9 vols., New York, 1928.

Schouler, James, *History of the United States of America under the Constitution 1783-1861*, 6 vols., Revised edition, New York, 1894-1899.

Smith, Theodore Clark, *Liberty and Free Soil Parties in the Northwest*, New York, 1902.

———, *Parties and Slavery, 1850-1859* (American Nation Series, Vol. XVIII), New York, 1906.

Sydnor, Charles Sackett, *Slavery in Mississippi*, New York, 1933.

Taylor, Rosser Howard, *Slaveholding in North Carolina: An Economic View* (The James Sprunt Historical Publications, Vol. XVII, nos. 1-2), Chapel Hill, 1926.

Turner, Frederick Jackson, *Rise of the New West, 1819-1829* (American Nation Series, Vol. XIV), New York, 1906.

——, *The Significance of Sections in American History*, New York, 1932.

Tyler, Lyon Gardiner, *England and America, 1580-1652* (American Nation Series, Vol. IV), New York, 1904.

Weeden, William B., *Economic and Social History of New England, 1620-1789*, 2 vols., Boston and New York, 1890.

Wertenbaker, Thomas Jefferson, *The First Americans, 1607-1690* (A History of American Life Series, Vol. II), New York, 1927.

Whitfield, Theodore M., *Slavery Agitation in Virginia, 1829-1832*, Baltimore, 1930.

B. BIOGRAPHY

Beveridge, Albert J., *Abraham Lincoln, 1809-1858*, 2 vols., Boston and New York, 1928.

Birney, William, *James G. Birney and His Times*, New York, 1890.

Bowen, Clarence W., *Arthur and Lewis Tappan*, New York, 1883.

Craven, Avery, *Edmund Ruffin, Southerner: A Study in Secession*, New York, 1932.

Curtis, George Tichnor, *Life of James Buchanan*, 2 vols., New York, 1883.

Dodd, William E., *Jefferson Davis*, Philadelphia, 1907.

Driver, Leota S., *Fanny Kemble*, Chapel Hill, 1933.

Frothingham, Octavius B., *Gerrit Smith—A Biography*, New York, 1879.

Garrison, Wendell Phillips, and Garrison, Frances Jackson, *William Lloyd Garrison*, 4 vols., New York, 1885-1889.

Hoss, Elijah Embree, *Elihu Embree, Abolitionist*, Nashville, 1897.

McCormac, Eugene Irving, *James K. Polk, A Political Biography*, Berkeley, 1922.

Malone, Dumas, *The Public Life of Thomas Cooper, 1783-1839*, New Haven, 1926.

Mason, Virginia, *The Public Life and Diplomatic Correspondence of James M. Mason with some Personal History*, Roanoke, Va., 1903.

Merritt, Elizabeth, *James Henry Hammond, 1807-1864*, Baltimore, 1923 (Johns Hopkins University Studies, Vol. XLI).

Tanner, Henry, *An Account of the Life, Trials, and Perils of Rev. Elijah P. Lovejoy, who was killed by a Pro-Slavery Mob at Alton Ill. on the night of Nov. 7, 1837*, Chicago, 1881.

Tappan, Lewis, *The Life of Arthur Tappan*, New York, 1870.

Tyerman, L., *The Life and Times of John Wesley*, 3 vols., New York, 1872.

White, Laura A., *Robert Barnwell Rhett: Father of Secession*, New York, 1931.

C. NEWSPAPERS, PERIODICALS, AND PAMPHLETS

Ballagh, J. C., "Anti-Slavery Sentiment in Virginia," *South Atlantic Quarterly*, I (April, 1902).

Fleming, Walter L., "Plantation Life in the South," *Journal of American History*, III (April-June, 1909).

Hawes, Ruth B., "Slavery in Mississippi," *Sewanee Review*, XXI (April, 1913).

Haywood, Harry, and Howard, Milton, *Lynching*. Published under the direction of the Labor Research Association, New York, 1932.

Hill, James D., "Some Economic Aspects of Slavery," *South Atlantic Quarterly*, XXVI (January, 1927).

McGrady, Edward J., "Address," *Southern Historical Society Papers*, XVI (January-December, 1888).

Martin, Asa Earl, "Anti-Slavery Societies in Tennessee," *Tennessee Historical Magazine*, I (1915).

Munford, B. B., "Vindication of the South," *Southern Historical Society Papers*, XXVII (January-December, 1899).

Parks, Edd Winfield, "Dreamer's Vision—Frances Wright at Nashoba, 1825-1830," *Tennessee Historical Magazine*, Ser. II, II (January, 1932).

Phillips, Ulrich B., "The Central Theme of Southern History," *American Historical Review*, XXXIV (October, 1928).

————, "Economic Cost of Slaveholding in the Cotton States," *Political Science Quarterly*, XX (1905).

Van Horn, John Douglas, "The Southern Attitude Toward Slavery," *The Sewanee Review*, XXIX (July, 1921).

Wannamaker, William H., "The German Element in the Settlement of the South," *South Atlantic Quarterly*, IX (April, 1910).

Weeks, Stephen B., "Anti-Slavery Sentiment in the South," *Publications of the Southern History Association*, II (April, 1898).

————, "The Slave Insurrection in Virginia," *Magazine of American History*, XXV (1891).

D. General Reference Works

Appleton's *Cyclopaedia of American Biography*, 7 vols., James Grant Wilson and John Fiske (editors), New York, 1887-1900.

A Classified Catalogue of the Collection of Anti-Slavery Propaganda in the Oberlin College Library, Oberlin, 1932.

Dictionary of American Biography . . ., edited by Allen Johnson, 20 vols., New York, 1928-1936.

National Cyclopaedia of American Biography, Vols. I-XIII, New York, 1893-1906.

INDEX

Miscegenation, charged by abolitionists, 83-99.

Mississippi Colonization Society, forms African colony, 19.

Mississippi, probable effects of emancipation on, 208.

Missouri, applies for admission as state, 39-40; struggle over, 41-48.

Missouri Compromise, proposed by Thomas of Illinois, 44-45; sectional contest during decade following, 102.

Missouri controversy, sectional contest for political power, 270, 273.

Monetary problems, not considered by abolitionists, 194.

Monroe, James, head of Colonization Society, 19; signs Missouri Compromise, 47.

Mormons, receive converts in North, 57.

Morris, Thomas, Liberty Party candidate for vice-president, 277.

Morton, Dr. Samuel G., gives scientific basis for inferiority of Negro, 228; supports "plurality" theory, 229, 232; views on hybridity, 240.

Mosaic Laws, sanction slavery, 178-184.

Moses, slavery sanctioned by, 178.

Mott, Lucretia, leader in anti-slavery convention, 57.

Murray, William V., opposes taxing slaves as property, 32.

NASHOBA Colony, socialistic experiment, 57.

National Anti-Slavery Standard, edited by Mrs. Child and husband, 84; points out origin of Republican Party, 283.

Navigation Act, encourage shipbuilding in New England, 6; effect on colonial trade, 11.

Negro churches, models of decorum, 154.

Negroes, inferiority of the race of, 227-244, 249, 267; theory of difference in species of, 229-43; differences in physical structure of, 234-35; slavery best form of government for, 250; conditions in Africa of, 251.

Negro slavery, causes for growth of, 11-13; views of Southerners on, 15, 16-17, 20, 23-25, 27-30, 33-35, 102-103, 111, 129, 165-66; economic aspects of, 16, 195-97, 215-18, 221;

discussed in South, 20, 107; decline of, checked, 22; involved with political interests, 26, 43-44, 47-48, 126, 281; sanctioned by the Bible, 46, 266; assailed by Garrison, 49-53; produced minority ruling group, 66-67; agitated in legislatures of North, 69; injurious effects on South, 107-108; Northern sentiment growing against, 71, 118; South begins defense of, 120-25; defense unites various elements in South, 127; social aspects of, 131, 159, 176, 224, 227-28, 247-50, 262-63; South reverses position on, 161, 165; scriptural justification for, 166; defense of, by churches and ministers, 166-71; compared with systems in other countries, 172; not sanctioned by Bible, 172-74; economic aspects not considered, 194; advantages of, 198-99, 201, 255-56, 258, 266; forced upon South, 225, 265; contrasted with conditions of Negroes in Africa, 251; less cruel than free labor system of North, 260-61; vital to existence of Southern institutions, 267; provided emotional appeal for American people, 269; used to alienate West from South, 270.

Negro slaves, fear of, 11-13, 17, 112; as solution to labor problem, 11-12, 201; sold by North to South, 14; supplant indentured servants, 16; better suited to Southern climate, 17; representation in Congress, 28; considered as property in Constitution, 29; taxes on, 32-33; marriages of, 71-73; reported inhuman treatment of, 74-80; equality claimed for, 82; effect of *Walker's Appeal* on, 104; value of, in Virginia, 109; South passes more stringent laws for control of, 111-12, 119-20, 123; special characteristics of, 128, 130, 132, 150-51, 158; punishments compared with Northern and English, 130-31; care of, by planter, 132-34, 136-37, 148, 150-51, 154, 156-57, 197; contrasted with free Negroes, 146-47, 201-205, 253-54; increase by same rate as whites, 149; some economic factors concerning, 197-98, 205-206, 211; unfit for freedom, 202, 244-45, 247.

"New Abolitionists." *See* Abolitionists, radical.

South Carolina, first cotton exported from, 21; delegates apologize for slavery, 27; protests against petitions, 29; representatives defend slavery, 31; dependent on slave labor, 31; desires restrictions on slavery, 34; synods of, denounce abolition societies, 170.

Southern churches, teach duties of masters and slaves, 153; begin movement to Christianize Negroes, 152-54; inter-denominational meeting held in Charleston, 154; hold masters responsible for slaves, 155; astounded by violence of abolitionists, 162; ministers use Scriptures to defend themselves, 162; called bulwarks of slavery, 191; separate from Northern churches, 171.

Southern colonies, most prosperous before Revolution, 195; demand for labor exceeds supply in, 196.

Southern leaders, success due to slavery, 257-58; equal to foremost intellects of world, 258. See also Pro-Slavery writers.

Southern Literary Messenger, reviews in, 238.

"Southern Outrages," Northern newspapers print atrocities under heading of, 75, 113.

Southern people, oppose continuance of slave trade, 13, 34-35; realize gravity of slavery issue, 25, 128, 211, 265; aroused to defend slavery, 59, 122-25, 266; abolition movement causes change of opinion of, 69, 111, 119-25, 164; not aroused by philosophical abolitionists, 61; charged with miscegenation, 83-99; slow to change views, 102; fear free Negroes, 103; stirred by rumors of insurrection, 111; oppose tactics of radical abolitionists, 112; gratified by Northern opposition to abolitionists, 117; investigate Scriptures on slavery, 163, 184; have controversy with North over slavery, 166; claim slavery justified in Scriptures, 176; realize benefits of their social system, 188; charge North with infidelity, 190; study economic aspects of slavery, 195, 205; opinions of slavery before 1860 formed by economic justification, 221; disclaim responsibility for origin of race problem, 224-25; all

classes agree on necessity of white supremacy, 226; fear race war, 247-49; feel slavery best for Negroes, 250; claim slavery best form of servitude, 261; realized disastrous effects of emancipation, 262; all classes united in defense of slavery, 263; realize political significance of abolition attack, 272; claim Southern rights threatened, 284.

Southern planters, part of Christy's "tripartite alliance," 218; proud of slaves' appearance, 136; invest profits in more land and slaves, 196. See also slaveholders.

Southern Presbyterian Review, endorses "unity" theory, 232.

Southern Quarterly Review, advocates "plurality" theory, 232.

Southern States, development of agriculture in, 4, 12, 268-69; racial and religious elements in, 4-5; geographic conditions in, 5-6, 10; social organization in, 9, 224; development of staple crops in, 9-10, 194, 214; large plantations of, 11-12; labor problem in, 12, 23, 198; sectional antagonism of New England toward, 26; basis for representation of slaves of, 28-29; representatives favor tax on slaves, 32; rivalry with North for control of West, 39-48, 268; depopulation by emigration, 40; control of national elections, 40; spread of slavery would mitigate evil in, 45; rise of minority consciousness in, 40-41, 44, 48, 272; controlled by large slaveholders, 66; alienated by anti-slavery sentiment, 68; condemned for non-recognition of slave marriages, 71-73; discredited by reports of inhuman treatment of slaves, 74-80; new philosophy of slavery developed in, 125; vice compared with other sections, 158-59; religious revival in, 155, 192-93; suffer from high protective tariff, 196; contain few paupers, 200; results of emancipation in, 201, 207; value of slaves in, 206; destruction will affect other sections as well, 207-208; monopoly on cotton justified "King Cotton" doctrine, 222; Negro problem underlies all fundamental issues in, 227; social relationship in, regulated by slavery, 249; conditions of Negroes con-